JAPAN'S NEW ECONOMY

WITHDRAWN

JAPAN'S NEW ECONOMY

Continuity and Change in the Twenty-First Century

Edited by
Magnus Blomström
Byron Gangnes
Sumner La Croix

OXFORD
UNIVERSITY PRESS

*This book has been printed digitally and produced in a standard specification
in order to ensure its continuing availability*

OXFORD
UNIVERSITY PRESS

Great Clarendon Street, Oxford OX2 6DP

Oxford University Press is a department of the University of Oxford.
It furthers the University's objective of excellence in research, scholarship,
and education by publishing worldwide in

Oxford New York

Auckland Bangkok Buenos Aires Cape Town Chennai
Dar es Salaam Delhi Hong Kong Istanbul Karachi Kolkata
Kuala Lumpur Madrid Melbourne Mexico City Mumbai Nairobi
São Paulo Shanghai Taipei Tokyo Toronto

Oxford is a registered trade mark of Oxford University Press
in the UK and in certain other countries

Published in the United States
by Oxford University Press Inc., New York

ISBN 0-19- 924173-2

CONTENTS

LIST OF CONTRIBUTORS

Shigeyuki Abe
Center for Southeast Asian Studies
Kyoto University
46 Shimoadachi Cho, Yoshida, Sakyoku
Kyoto 606-8501
JAPAN

F. Gerard Adams
Northeastern University
409 Hayden Hall
Boston MA 02115
USA

Magnus Blomström
European Institute of Japanese Studies
Stockholm School of Economics
Box 6501
SE-113 83 Stockholm
SWEDEN

Thomas F. Cargill
Department of Ecnonomics
University of Nevada Reno
Reno, NV 89557–0207
USA

Byron Gangnes
Department of Economics
University of Hawaii
Honolulu, HI 96822
USA

Steven Globerman
Western Washington University
College of Business and Economics
Bellingham, WA 98225
USA

Charles Yuji Horioka
Institute of Social and Economic
Research
Osaka University
6-1, Mihogaoka, Ibaraki
Osaka 567-0047
JAPAN

Takatoshi Ito
Institute of Economic Research
Hitotsubashi University
Kunitachi Tokyo 186
JAPAN

Ari Kokko
European Institute of Japanese Studies
Stockholm School of Economics
Box 6501
SE-113 83 Stockholm
SWEDEN

Denise Eby Konan
Department of Economics
University of Hawaii
Honolulu, HI 96822
USA

Sumner La Croix
Department of Economics
University of Hawaii
Honolulu, HI 96822
USA

Bruce Henry Lambert
European Institute of Japanese Studies
Stockholm School of Economics
Box 6501
SE-113 83 Stockholm
SWEDEN

Chung Lee
Department of Economics
University of Hawaii
Honolulu, HI 96822
USA

Robert E. Lipsey
National Bureau of Economic Research
365 Fifth Avenue, 5th Floor
New York, NY 10016
USA

James Mak
Department of Economics
University of Hawaii
Honolulu, HI 96822
USA

Andrew Mason
Department of Economics
University of Hawaii
Honolulu, HI 96822
USA

Michael Melvin
Department of Economics
Arizona State University
Tempe, AZ 85287
USA

Naohiro Ogawa
Population Research Institute
Nihon University
1-3-2 Misaki-cho, Chiyoda-ku
Tokyo 101-8360
JAPAN

Marcus Rebick
Nissan Institute of Japanese Studies
27 Winchester Road
Oxford, OX2 6NA
UNITED KINGDOM

Örjan Sjöberg
European Institute of Japanese Studies
Stockholm School of Economics
Box 6501
SE-113 83 Stockholm
SWEDEN

Fredrik Sjöholm
Department of Economics
National University of Singapore
10 Kent Ridge Crescent
SINGAPORE 119260

Marie Söderberg
European Institute of Japanese Studies
Stockholm School of Economics
Box 6501
SE-113 83 Stockholm
SWEDEN

David E. Weinstein
Department of Economics
Columbia University
New York, NY 10027

Edward N. Wolff
Department of Economics
New York University
269 Mercer Street, Room 700
New York, NY 10003
USA

Introduction

MAGNUS BLOMSTRÖM, BYRON GANGNES, AND SUMNER LA CROIX

1. Introduction

By the early 1990s, Japan had emerged as the main challenger to the United States for the position as the world's leading economy. The Japanese economy had outgrown the US for several decades, and the appreciation of the yen had pushed Japanese per capita income (calculated on an exchange-rate basis) almost 50 per cent above US levels in 1995. Japanese export industries generated massive export surpluses, despite the appreciated currency. The Japanese success was considered nothing less than a miracle.

The past decade has been less miraculous. The collapse of the stock market boom and real estate bubble around 1990 marked the beginning of a decade of stagnation. The overhang of bad debt paralyzed the financial sector, and the Japanese government initiated few reforms of the banking system until the end of the decade. Since 1992, annual real GDP has grown only 1 per cent on average.[1] Poor economic performance has persisted despite ambitious macroeconomic measures taken throughout the 1990s to restore growth.

The low growth rates of the 1990s are partly due to cyclical factors, and these have been made worse by ill-conceived and poorly executed macroeconomic and financial policies. But the chaos in macroeconomic policymaking has demonstrated the challenges facing the country's economic institutions in coping with a changing environment. Many of these institutions were designed in the 1950s to facilitate the rapid accumulation of resources in a converging, developing economy. By the end of the 1980s, Japan had become a wealthy country at the industrial cutting edge, with a rapidly aging population, and facing very different external conditions. The transition to new institutions compatible with Japan's mature economy is now underway, and the structure of the Japanese economy is changing, with the pace of change varying dramatically across different sectors of the economy.

The new Japan emerging from this institutional facelift has still not been fully revealed. Japan is clearly borrowing elements from the Anglo-American formula of deregulated product and financial markets, smaller government and lower taxes, free trade, and privatization, and yet no one expects the new Japanese economy to emerge looking exactly like the US and UK economies. There are several fundamental reasons for this. First, Japan's factor and resource endowments differ substantially from those in the United Kingdom and the United States and may require a somewhat different set of political and economic institutions for the endowments to be used efficiently.

---

[1] Through September 1999.

Second, institutional change is typically a path-dependent process (North, 1990), in which the future path of institutional change is conditioned by earlier institutional development. The special features and the interlocking nature of Japanese economic institutions certainly increase the likelihood that new institutions will retain a uniquely Japanese face.

The process of institutional change also depends on the ability of politicians, intellectuals, and managers to fashion an ideological consensus around distinct types of institutional change. The 1990s have, however, been a turbulent period for Japan politically, with new political parties forming and reforming, national governments enjoying less support and spending shorter terms in office, and major institutional reforms already in place, e.g. the voting system for the Diet, and waiting in the wings, e.g. the reorganization of government agencies and the financial "Big Bang." In this turbulent political environment, it remains an open question whether the Japanese public will favor institutional reforms that support future growth (Curtis, 1999). A rapidly aging population could become increasingly conservative and reject institutional change—or, sensing the crisis of current institutions, embrace economic and political change as more promising for their golden years.

Our specific objectives in this volume are twofold:

- To analyze the ongoing demographic, structural, and institutional changes currently transforming Japan's economy.
- To identify factors likely to induce structural and institutional change in Japan's economy over the next twenty-five years and to use economic theory, simulation modeling, econometric techniques, and cross-country comparisons to provide insights on the likely course of these changes.

Over the next twenty-five years, Japan will transform the way it produces, consumes, trades, and governs itself. By focusing on the forces underpinning such institutional and structural change, this volume's essays aim to provide a clearer understanding of these changes. We caution that while some of our authors may claim to have seen a glimpse of the future, the reader surely knows the limits to such prognostication. No one can tell precisely what Japan's future will bring. What we can do is to identify and analyze the direction and intensity of current trends, look for the presence of the usual suspects producing institutional change, and see what we can learn from Japan's historical responses to similar challenges. Our intent is clear: to provide a unique forward-looking perspective on the future path of Japan's economy and its relationship to the rest of the world.

2. The Japanese Economy: From Miracle to Stagnation

Japan was the first and archetypal Asian Miracle economy. Between 1950 and 1973, the Japanese economy doubled in size every seven years, rising rapidly to a place among the world's major economies. Japan's development success spawned a generation of imitators in Asia and would-be imitators in Latin America and the rest of the developing world. By the late 1980s, the period of rapid growth had all but ended, but by then, Japan had achieved one of the highest living standards in the world, Japanese multinationals had become common household names around the globe, and Japanese foreign investment was spurring growth in developed and developing countries alike.

While the perception in the West is of a Japan that "rose from the ashes" of the Second World War to global strength, the country's rapid industrialization began in the late nineteenth century (see, e.g. Howe, 1996). Following the Meiji Restoration in 1868, Japan made a fairly quick transition onto a path of modernization and development. During the 1870s modern institutional structures in banking, police, post and telegraph, armed forces, primary and secondary schooling, and the judiciary were borrowed from Western European countries and the United States and modified to fit Japanese circumstances. From this solid institutional base, real output in Japan grew between 1880 and 1940 by nearly 3.5 per cent per year (Ito, 1992). Over this sixty-year period, the economy gradually switched from being primarily a producer of agricultural products to a producer of light manufactures, e.g. textiles, light industrial goods, and services. Large, integrated businesses, known as *zaibatsu*, came to dominate manufacturing and finance.

Immediately after the Second World War, Japan's economy grew slowly as various political and economic reform measures were implemented, with varying degrees of success. With the start of the Korean War in June 1950, American purchases of raw materials and manufactured goods for the war effort sparked new Japanese economic growth that lasted far beyond the end of the Korean War. Between 1950 and the onset of the first oil crisis in 1973, the economy expanded at a 10 per cent annual rate. This was the era of rapid expansion in Japanese heavy industries—iron, steel, and chemicals—sectors which had benefited from wartime pressures to innovate and supply the Japanese military machine with products previously purchased overseas. This era also saw the emergence of new strength in automobiles and the infant consumer electronics industry. Japan became famous for its powerful Ministry of Finance (MOF) and Ministry of International Trade and Industry (MITI), which helped direct economic development through subsidies and other incentives.

By 1973, Japan's real GDP per capita in purchasing power parity terms stood at 59 per cent of the US level, compared with 17 per cent in 1950. (Heston *et al.*, 1995). It would be 79 per cent of the US level by 1990. In little more than two decades, Japan had closed much of its gap in output and living standards with the rest of the developed world.

There is by now a well-established view of the forces that propelled Japan to rapid growth. (See, for example, Flath, 2000; Ito, 1992; James, Naya, and Meier, 1989; Patrick and Rosovsky, 1976; and World Bank, 1993.) Japan was able to maintain a very high domestic savings rate (30–5 per cent of GDP in the 1960s) that supported high rates of investment in new plant and equipment. Savings were in turn supported by prudent macroeconomic policies that restrained inflation and promoted wealth accumulation. A strong financial system and capital controls on external inflows and outflows assured that saved resources would be channeled to productive domestic investment. Strong primary and secondary schooling provided Japan with a well-educated work force that could provide the human resources needed for growth.

The government's intervention in "picking winners" is more controversial. At the same time, its encouragement of export development forced Japanese manufacturing companies to develop world class efficiency, while protectionism in early years probably played a role in facilitating the growth of infant industries. Japan was also lucky enough to have access to the very open and large American market during this period, as well as the protection of the US security umbrella.

Japan's growth had tailed off by the early 1970s. In part, the external macro-economic environment had become less benign. After the end of the Bretton Woods monetary system in 1971–3, Japan had adopted an expansionary monetary stance to hold down the yen's appreciation. When the OPEC oil price shock hit in 1973, a large inflationary spurt occurred. Japan suffered a recession in 1974 and saw inflation of more than 30 per cent that year. Investment rates fell in the 1970s, and output growth slowed to the 5 per cent per year range in the late 1970s. This slowdown in economic growth was partly due to the lingering effects of the OPEC oil price shock, but more fundamentally it also reflected the rapidly diminishing returns to new investment as Japan converged with other developed market economies.

In the 1980s, mushrooming Japanese current account surpluses and the massive associated outflow of capital presented new economic and political challenges for the country. As the US economy surged in 1983–5 and the dollar soared in value, US imports from Japan rose dramatically, prompting protectionist pressures. Worse for Japan, imports were concentrated in a high-profile, unionized industry—automobiles—so that a policy response was inevitable. The US had already imposed voluntary export restraints on Japanese automobiles in 1981, and these were maintained, albeit at slightly higher levels, throughout the decade. In 1985, President Reagan for the first time imposed "Super 301" trade sanctions against Japan, giving the administration authority to retaliate against alleged Japanese barriers to imports.

Growing current account imbalances prompted G5 countries to agree in 1985 to coordinated action to reduce the value of the dollar on world markets. Whether as a result of the September 1985 Plaza Accord and subsequent central bank interventions or market forces that were already correcting the overvalued currency, the dollar fell from 238 yen to 154 yen by June 1986.[2]

In the post-1985 *endaka* period, Japan found itself squeezed between two conflicting problems. On the one hand, the dramatically rising yen was severely harming profitability and competitiveness of Japan's export producers; on the other hand, the trade deficit with the US was stubbornly slow to close, so that Japan continued to face international pressure to reduce its trade surplus. To halt further appreciation of the yen, Japanese monetary policy shifted toward a more expansionary stance. Between 1985 and 1987, the Bank of Japan discount rate was cut in half, from 5 per cent to

---

[2] For an interesting behind-the-scenes look at international financial politics during this period see Volcker and Gyohten, 1992.

2.5 per cent, and it remained at this level through 1989. At the same time, Japan embarked on a program of financial liberalization, partly in response to foreign pressure for more open competitive markets.

The combination of financial liberalization and monetary expansion is generally blamed for creating—or at least accommodating—asset price inflation in the second half of the 1980s (Ito, 1996). First stock and then land prices rose dramatically after 1985, more or less doubling in value over several years. The rapid rise in wealth, as well as measures to liberalize trade, stimulated consumption spending and helped to close a large portion of the trade surplus by the end of the decade. Financial liberalization had allowed major manufacturing firms to bypass banks in raising investment funds, and banks had consequently lost some of their best business. They responded by refocusing on real estate lending. The lower-quality, over-extended loan portfolios left Japanese financial and non-financial firms exposed to considerable risk. When monetary policy was tightened in 1989 and 1990, stock and land prices quickly shed most of their gains of the previous four years.

Japan's economy entered a growth recession in 1992. Output growth fell from the 4–5 per cent range in the 1980s to 1 per cent in 1992 and 0.3 per cent in 1993. In part the slump was homegrown, the result of monetary contraction and widening bad debt problems from the collapse of Japan's "bubble economy." But the external environment also turned very unfavorable. A global economic slowdown began in the second half of 1990 and was aggravated by Gulf War disruptions of commerce.

Japan's slowdown was not particularly notable, but its failure to recover as the 1990s wore on drew increasingly critical domestic and international attention. Growth was less than 1 per cent through 1994, and did not break 2 per cent until 1996. The Japanese government responded by implementing highly publicized fiscal measures to try to stimulate aggregate demand and spark a recovery. Five fiscal packages were enacted between 1992 and 1995, with a cumulative official size of 54 trillion yen (McKibbin, 1996). Measures were undertaken to support land prices and to assist troubled financial institutions. Monetary policy became increasingly expansionary. But economic growth remained stagnant. There was a brief pickup in 1995–6, but the economy soon faltered once again with a premature increase in the consumption tax. Stagnant growth turned to outright recession with the Asian financial crisis of 1997.

There is much room for debate about the causes of Japan's extended weakness; some consideration of this issue is taken up below. Clearly the fiscal stimulus provided by the government in early years was not as large as advertised, since a part of the stimulus packages was previously announced spending. The back-loading of some government spending may have driven up long-term interest rates and encouraged appreciation of the yen (McKibbin, 1996). In addition, the government reversed course on fiscal policy when the economy began to expand mid-decade, raising the consumption tax and undercutting growth. But microeconomic problems also plagued the economy. Many Japanese firms and banks entered the 1990s with a heavy debt burden left over from the bubble years. Many manufacturing firms had substantial excess capacity after the investment boom of the 1980s (Makin, 1996). Slow growth in the 1990s in part reflected the need to work down these excesses through negative investment and, finally, layoffs. The institutional resistance to these changes has prolonged complete recovery.

3. Risutora

Post-Second World War Japan has been characterized by a high level of governmental involvement and regulation in many industries. Japan's postwar development strategy was fundamentally grounded on a public–private partnership. The government sought to modernize the economic base by selecting promising industries and actively nurturing capacity by limiting competition, supporting research, development, and technology transfers, and encouraging the extension of credit to its favored targets. Industries with a potential to achieve economies of scale and scope were particularly favored and permitted to form horizontal and vertical cartels that cooperated on pricing, R&D, and production cutbacks during industry recessions. Japan has viewed American competition policy as encouraging waste—unregulated competition in oligopolistic industries that leads to excessive entry and unnecessarily high production costs, wasteful advertising expenditures, and duplication of R&D costs. The government also aimed to protect a variety of special interests supporting the governing party, the Liberal Democratic Party (LDP). Farmers, small retail shops, and service providers were protected against competition through a complex system of licensing, regulation, and quality control standards.

This close partnership between business interests and the Japanese government is in direct contrast to the Western, and particularly the American model, which is grounded in a tradition of strong antitrust policy, market competition, and private ownership. The American occupying authorities incorporated American antitrust laws and institutions into their package of reforms for the Japanese economy, but the effort to impose a vigorous antitrust policy floundered when priorities changed with the start of the Korean War in June 1950. The independent antitrust institutions imposed by the Americans were nominally retained, but effectively sidelined when the American occupation ended in April 1952, and various ministries assumed control over the nominally independent commissions.

The American occupying authorities were more successful in imposing other parts of their "revolution from above" on the Japanese economy, including wide-ranging land and tenancy reform programs, the breakup of *zaibatsu* holding companies and the removal of *zaibatsu* family members as controlling shareholders, and promotion of worker rights. In an ironic twist, the American occupying authorities were also partly responsible for the extensive regulatory powers that Japanese bureaucrats would exercise throughout the high-growth period. Beginning in April 1949, President Truman's "economic czar" for Japan, Joseph Dodge, used two large, centralized ministries, the Ministry of Finance (MOF) and the new Ministry of International Trade and Industry (MITI), to push through his program via a series of directives. Dower (1999) observes that that "for decades to come, the ministry [of Finance] continued to exercise exceptional prerogatives *vis-à-vis* other ministries and the Diet in controlling budgetary and monetary policy." (p. 544)

The 1950s saw the emergence of the mature form of numerous economic institutions commonly associated with Japanese business. Throughout the decade, companies formerly part of a *zaibatsu* group began to reaffiliate through interlocking stockholdings. The resulting horizontal *keiretsu* usually consisted of a main bank, industrial enterprises, and other financial firms; it was characterized by joint ventures among group firms, extensive intragroup purchasing, and loosely integrated group decision making.[3] Lifetime employment, bonus payments, seniority wages, and enterprise unions became institutionalized as employment practices of virtually all large corporations.

More controversial than the above business practices was Japanese industrial policy. Under the direction of MITI, some industries were targeted as ones in which Japan would have a future comparative advantage. MITI employed a wide array of methods to promote favored sectors, including subsidized credit, subsidies for cooperative R&D research, preferential access to foreign exchange, and multiple tax incentives. These explicit tools were complemented by "administrative guidance," an informal system of regulation administered by MOF and MITI bureaucrats. Based on the licensing function of these ministries, administrative guidance provided a flexible means of adjusting policy towards targeted industries. Some industries were targeted by MITI not for sunrise potential, but for sunset reorganization. In these industries, typically raw materials and labor-intensive manufactures, MITI organized "recession" and "rationalization" cartels to ease the adjustment burden of output cutbacks. Weinstein (1995) found that in the mid-1960s, over 1,000 government-sanctioned cartels were in place involving over 43 per cent of all manufacturing output.

The effectiveness of Japanese industrial policy has been much debated since the 1970s. Johnson (1982), Fallows (1994), Prestowicz (1988) and other political scientists have argued that MITI's industrial policy was the key to Japan's rapid postwar growth. Economists have been more guarded in their evaluation. Weinstein and Beeson (1996) found that industries receiving government assistance did not register particularly strong productivity gains. Others have argued that MITI's policies were not large enough to provide the stimulus ascribed to them.

The constant focus on the effectiveness of Japanese industrial policy has often obscured its ongoing transformation, a process that began in the late 1960s. The use of officially sanctioned cartels declined dramatically in the 1970s and 1980s; a program of (semi-) privatization of state-owned railroads, utilities, and Japan Tobacco was phased in during the 1980s; financial reform lifted controls on interest rates and many foreign exchange transactions in the late 1970s and 1980s; and import restrictions were removed or liberalized in numerous sectors.

Yet, as the downturn of the 1990s refused to go away, Japan slowly began deregulating a wide variety of industries in which regulation was still relatively intact,

---

[3] The text describes a horizontal *keiretsu*. Several other types of interfirm linkages were common. See Flath (2000) for a more complete exposition.

including transportation, communication, energy, and financial, insurance, and real estate industries. Pressure for deregulation came not only from within, but also from global competitive forces exercising an increasingly large influence on Japanese industries. The broad program of financial deregulation being phased in through 2003 (known as the "Big Bang") was partly motivated by domestic political considerations, but the overriding force behind its adoption was from the rapid decline of Tokyo in the 1990s as a world financial center. Other developed countries have pushed Japan to adopt arrays of proposed reforms, but they have had little success in getting Japan to follow through on their agendas. At the start of the twenty-first century, economic forces appear to be more important than political or ideological forces in spurring industrial reform.

Deregulation in Japan has followed a uniquely Japanese model, just as regulation assumed uniquely Japanese forms. It has provided firms with increased freedom to adjust prices and output and has prompted additional firms to enter various industries. It has, however, not meant the end of administrative guidance, although it has meant a dramatic change in the attitude of MOF and MITI regulators towards competition. While the heavy hand of the regulator has been lifted from the controls, the administrative apparatus still lurks in the background.

At the turn of the century, gloomy reports are still dominating the macroeconomic picture of Japan, yet extensive changes are occurring at the microeconomic level. The ongoing crisis is forcing the government to implement reforms, although the pace has slowed down during the administration of Prime Minister Obuchi. In the long run, these reforms will act to create new markets, attract foreign investment, and stimulate competition. Foreign acquisitions of Japanese firms grew more than sixfold in value during 1998, and are continuing to grow (though volume is still small). Compared with foreign rivals, many Japanese firms are either too small or too dependent on their home market to survive. By paring away jobs and unprofitable businesses, they are restructuring to regain competitiveness. This process—known as *risutora*—is rapidly changing those sectors of the Japanese economy that are open to competition.

Throughout its history, Japan has risen to various challenges by restructuring its society and economy. The changes during this century have been particularly dramatic. Japan has moved from agriculture and low-tech manufacturing to high-quality and high-tech sectors. Its present problems have already led to extensive reforms and will undoubtedly lead to more over the next decade. Many of the policies needed for a prosperous future are already in place, and the structural changes needed to get the growth machine working again are in progress. If Japan can finally find the right mix of macroeconomic policies to overcome the current deflationary bias, we may yet be surprised by the vigor with which the underlying economy responds.

4. Organization of the Book

The volume's fourteen essays were selected to cover important aspects of Japan's economy that are likely to undergo substantial change over the next twenty-five years.

Our introductory chapter takes stock of Japan's position at the end of the twentieth century and provides a brief sketch of the process of restructuring now underway. The remaining essays explore past trends and potential future developments in three broad areas: the macroeconomy, the organization of industry, and the global economic and political environment. Short introductions to each chapter follow.

4.1. A changing macroeconomic climate

Japan's growth success has been characterized both by high rates of accumulation of resources and rapid technological catching up. In recent decades, economic growth has outstripped absorption, so that current account surpluses and capital outflows have become the norm. Macroeconomic conditions supported this growth, including a young and growing population that generated a large pool of savings and workers, rapidly growing demand abroad that provided markets for Japanese exports, and stable macro policies that favored savings, an educated work force, and long-term business planning.

These macro conditions are changing. As Japan's economy approaches the technological frontier in many areas, as its citizenry ages and becomes wealthier, and as external conditions change, the macroeconomic environment is likely to evolve very differently than in the past. The likelihood of lower growth rates coupled with rapid aging will pose severe challenges for macroeconomic policymaking.

Fundamental changes in Japan's macroeconomy may already be evident in the poor performance of the past decade. It is not a simple matter to determine how much of the 1990s slump is attributable to structural causes, and how much may simply reflect a cyclical downturn. Some, like Krugman (1998) and Ito (1996), have attributed a large role to policy errors both in the onset of the crisis and its intractability. Japan's central bank allowed excessive monetary expansion during the bubble economy period of the late 1980s and then faltered, both in providing adequate fiscal stimulus and in dealing with the banking crisis in the 1990s. But others (Ito, 1996 and Weinstein, 1996) have also seen indications of fundamental emerging growth problems for Japan's economy.

David Weinstein views Japan's 1990s performance in historical perspective in Chapter 1. He asks whether domestic and foreign observers may be too pessimistic about Japan's performance during the 1990s because they have attributed too much of the crisis to structural rather than cyclical factors. He argues that there is a general tendency to give excessive weight to structural explanations for Japan's fortunes, going as far back as Japan's first modern crisis in the 1880s and as recently as Prestowitz's (1988) concern that the US and Japan were trading places. Looking at the historical record, Weinstein concludes there is nothing peculiar about the 1990s slowdown. He writes, ". . . with the exception of the immediate postwar experience, recessions and periods of relative stagnation have always been a feature of Japanese economic development."

Weinstein does not completely dismiss structural explanations for Japan's recent growth slowdown. But if an argument is to be made that Japan has a performance problem, it must be related to evidence of productivity problems in particular sectors. Here, he finds that while there has been significant convergence in Japanese manufacturing productivity in recent decades, nonmanufacturing sectors have actually fallen further behind their American counterparts. Why have nonmanufactures fared so poorly? Weinstein observes that the poorest performers in this group are also the industries that are most heavily regulated—agriculture, construction, transportation, and communications. To Weinstein, this represents Japan's primary structural problem. Other service sectors must be permitted to follow the road of financial services, where deregulation appears to have improved productivity performance.

It is by now widely appreciated that Japan is leading the developed world in the progression toward an aged society. Increased life expectancy and falling fertility rates have reduced population growth and shifted an increasing share of the population into older age categories. By 2010, overall population growth is likely to cease and the number of elderly will surpass those younger than 20. As Andrew Mason and Naohiro Ogawa forcefully argue in Chapter 2, these demographic changes will represent powerful forces of macro change in years to come, affecting the size of the labor force, rates of saving and capital formation, the burden on social infrastructure, and the ongoing evolution of family and social institutions.

The demographic transformation in Japan during the twentieth century was dramatic. According to Mason and Ogawa, at the end of the nineteenth century, life expectancy in Japan was forty years, and more than 50 per cent were under the age of 20. Population growth surged with a reduction in mortality rates early in the twentieth century, but tapered off by 1960 with declining fertility rates. Today, Japan has the highest life expectancy of any country, and the average woman has only 1.4 children. While there are uncertainties surrounding these forecasts—of future marriage and fertility behavior, mortality improvements, and immigration policy—it is virtually certain that Japan's population will begin to decline early in the twenty-first century.

Extrapolating from the demographic projections to their likely economic effects is a more difficult enterprise that raises some intriguing questions. The total labor force is likely to decline, but how much of this might be offset by higher female participation rates? By a reversal of the trend toward earlier retirements? Will government policies be altered to remove retirement incentives or to permit significant immigration? Mason and Ogawa consider each of these issues in turn.

An important macroeconomic effect of population aging is a potential decline in Japan's famously high savings rate. Empirical studies of Japanese savings have, however, reached widely differing conclusions. To place the issue on a firm conceptual footing, Mason and Ogawa view Japan's savings decision within a life-cycle framework that relates the demand for household wealth—and therefore the evolution of savings over time—to macro and demographic determinants. The model predicts first a rise in savings rates as the aging population builds assets for retirement, followed by a decline to a lower steady-state savings rate.

How far will the savings rate fall? Mason and Ogawa offer an estimate midway between the low or negative net savings rates implied by macro-based econometric models and the much higher savings rates typically found by studies that extrapolate results of household survey data. Both of these empirical approaches have flaws that suggest caution in interpreting some of the more extreme predictions. In particular, Mason and Ogawa are doubtful about forecasts of sharply negative net savings rates. They write, "[i]n the absence of more complete support, such drastic declines in savings strike us as alarmist."

The problem of forecasting savings rates clearly involves many of the same policy uncertainties that arise with projecting labor force participation rates. For example, will the modern social safety net permit reductions in private savings, or will the fiscal burden of rising social security outlays require cutbacks that force an increased reliance on private savings? There are also important links between demographic change, savings behavior, and the evolution of Japanese social arrangements. As Mason and Ogawa explain, there is evidence of a gradual breakdown of traditional family ties, with elders relying less on their children for support. This may raise savings needs, but also reduce the amount of money set aside for bequests.

Notwithstanding the many complexities that arise, Mason and Ogawa's conclusion for the Japanese macroeconomy are clear: Japan will likely grow much slower in the future than it has in the past. Its growth increasingly will need to be driven by productivity improvements and offshore production, rather than domestic factor accumulation.

The projected decline in savings rates has implications for Japan's overall balance of payments position. The past two decades have seen the emergence of large and persistent Japanese current account surpluses, as the country's excess of savings over investment has flowed abroad. Japan's export of financial capital has supported global investment and growth, but the accompanying trade balance deficit has created political tension in some countries such as the US. With the projected decline in savings rates, financial changes that may affect the willingness to invest abroad, and the continued strengthening of the yen, Japan's current account surplus could soon become a distant object in the rearview mirror.

In Chapter 3, F. Gerard Adams and Byron Gangnes evaluate prospects for Japan's current account balance. They begin by reviewing the macroeconomic causes of Japan's ongoing surpluses. In large part, surpluses in recent years can be attributed to the life-cycle considerations that have favored high savings, as described by Mason and Ogawa in Chapter 2. But the economy's rapid rate of growth through the 1980s may also have boosted savings, as did government net savings in the 1980s. And Japan's strong appetite for foreign assets has prevented yen appreciation that might otherwise have begun to close the trade gap.

What developments are likely to affect the current account in coming years? Clearly population aging will work to lower the surplus, to the extent that it reduces savings and redirects demand toward nontraded products and services. Investment may also fall off as a smaller work force reduces demands for capital, but Adams and Gangnes conclude that overall net savings are still likely to fall. Two other structural changes are likely to affect the current account: Japan's increasing reliance on imports from

Asia and financial liberalization associated with Japan's Big Bang. While the former should reduce the surplus, the effects of the latter are harder to predict.

To the extent that these forces push Japan toward a lower current account path, they will also create pressure for structural adjustment at the level of individual industries. A decline in the surplus means a decline in net exports and so a shift of production toward nontradable goods and services. These changes may in turn impose painful macroeconomic costs during the transition period. Adams and Gangnes explore the effects of such change using simulations of a large-scale macroeconometric model. In three simulations—import opening, aging, and financial liberalization—the authors illustrate likely effects on the macroeconomy and on particular sectors. Adams and Gangnes conclude that while a smaller surplus may be welcome to Japan's trade partners, there may be rough waters ahead for Japanese industry.

If the current account may ultimately be headed lower, prospects for Japan's fiscal balance are also for greater deficits. The same aging process that reduces net savings outflows will create significant fiscal challenges for Japan's government. Recently, the budget deficit has soared to nearly 10 per cent of GDP as the government has attempted to jump-start the moribund economy. Much of the recent deficit increases are, of course, cyclical, but in just a few years an aging population will place increased pressure on public pension systems and other social services at the same time that income and tax revenue growth slows. This scenario is not unique to Japan, but like the aging process overall, the urgency of the problem is greatest here.

Charles Horioka analyzes prospects for Japan's public pension system in Chapter 4. He describes the evolution of the existing system, its inherent problems, and some proposals for reform. To Horioka, the problems with the pension programs go well beyond solvency. He argues that in their current form the programs have an adverse impact on the inter- and intragenerational allocation of resources, on private labor supply decisions, and on tax compliance.

Patterned after programs in other developed economies, Japan's public pension programs are pay-as-you-go systems, with benefits for current retirees funded by taxes on current workers. As Horioka explains, the origins of such systems are easy to explain: they permit a mechanism for redistributing income from relatively prosperous current generations to less well-off older generations, and they delay a part of the financing burden to later years. Other aspects of Japan's system also appear to stem from political expediency, such as the exclusion of dependent spouses from taxation, introduced in the 1980s. Japan was late in setting up its public pension programs, with universal coverage only in 1961. Benefit levels were increased sharply in the early 1970s, with Japan's emergence as a rich, highly developed country.

While the structure of Japan's pay-as-you-go system is understandable, Horioka argues that it has undesirable economic effects. Projected lifetime benefits far exceed contributions for current retirees, with the reverse for the current working-age population. The rapid aging of Japan's population contributes to this problem as does unrealistically high levels of current benefits. Within age cohorts, the burden is also uneven, primarily because of the exemption of bonuses and lump-sum retirement payments from taxation, and because of the exemption of spouses with income below a threshold level. The tax exemption for spouses also discourages female labor supply, as does income testing of retirees' pension benefits and their ability to "double dip" retirements and unemployment benefits. And the pay-as-you-go system may reduce national savings.

What should be done to address these problems? Horioka argues for an immediate move to an actuarially fair system, where expected pension benefits are matched with pension contributions. The burden of the government's net contributions to the program should be spread out as evenly as possible over current and future generations. Intragenerational inequities should be redressed by ending tax exemptions for nonworking spouses, bonus income, and lump–sum retirement income as well as limiting benefit deductions for high–income retirees. Extending the mandatory retirement age would also help address incentive problems and the likely future labor shortages.

Unfortunately, recent government reform proposals do not measure up very well to this yardstick. The Ministry of Health and Welfare/Liberal Democratic Party proposal includes a number of changes to reduce growth in future pension outlays. Although some elements reduce intragenerational inequities, as a whole the program would make intergenerational burdens even more pronounced. Horioka prefers a competing proposal offered by two Japanese economists, Tatsuo Hatta and Noriyoshi Oguchi, but acknowledges that there are severe political obstacles to any plan that would reduce current benefits or raise current taxes dramatically.

Japan has long been known for its perennially low rates of unemployment. While measurement differences may somewhat exaggerate Japan's labor market performance, there is little doubt that Japanese labor market institutions generate an unusually high level of employment stability and low rates of job turnover. The system of lifetime employment commitments may have been a useful tool during the period of rapid economic development, as it facilitated a reliable supply of labor to industry and reduced worker uncertainty. At the same time, the low unemployment rate reduced the need for the social safety net programs that represent a major drain on public finances in other industrialized countries.

The long 1990s slump has led to a significant rise in the unemployment rate, and has raised concerns that traditional employment practices may be stifling firm productivity. In Chapter 5, Marcus Rebick looks for evidence that the prolonged slowdown is inducing changes in labor market practices. Pressures for change have come from the yen's appreciation in recent years and the stagnant economy that has left many firms with a surplus of labor. Because of Japan's steeply rising wage profiles, population aging has increased the wage bill, adding additional cost pressures to firms. There are plenty of media reports that fundamental labor market change is occurring, but, according to Rebick, the evidence is much less clear.

Rebick examines several institutions that have played major roles in Japanese labor markets since the Second World War. These include lengthy employment tenure, a focus on acquisition of general job skills rather than specialization, limited mainstream opportunities for women employees, and seniority-based compensation schemes. Using statistical evidence as well as qualitative reports, Rebick explores whether one can find hard evidence of significant change in labor market practices. His results are mixed. In some ways, Japan's labor markets do appear to be changing. Japanese firms are making somewhat greater use of temporary labor than in the past, and there are reports of increased specialization among workers. The wage profile has flattened overall, and there is also an apparent move toward tying compensation more closely to performance rather than seniority. Wage dispersion has increased for particular age groups.

None of these changes seem likely to sweep away the traditional system of lifetime employment. Rebick calculates that, if anything, Japanese tenure has actually increased in recent years! For prime-age male employees at major firms, it is far from clear whether there have been fundamental changes in the terms of employment or career advancement. Neither is there much evidence of improvement in employment opportunities for females. Women continue to gravitate away from the core job tracks and to have long periods of part-time employment. Rebick argues that these fundamental aspects of the Japanese labor system appear likely to persist for the foreseeable future.

Even the limited changes that are occurring may have important macroeconomic implications. One area is organized labor. With continued flattening of wage profiles and growing emphasis on individual performance, labor unions may hold less appeal for workers. New union memberships have declined markedly in recent years. Another area that we have already touched on is the overall labor market performance, measured by the unemployment rate. Unemployment has risen considerably, but most of the increases have been borne by older men and women of child-bearing years. In Rebick's view, it is unlikely that unemployment rates will go much higher for core male employees, but it is possible that the more marginal groups will increasingly be used as a safety valve for troubled companies.

4.2. The regulatory regime and industrial restructuring in Japan

The events of the past decade have forced Japan to steadily adjust its institutions and attitudes. Deregulation has been a particular focus. Thomas Cargill launches the discussion of deregulation in Chapter 6, with his analysis of Japan's ongoing financial deregulation and its banking crisis. He shows how the bubble economy and its collapse forced Japan to change both institutions and attitudes underpinning its financial system.

Cargill begins by discussing the type of financial regime that emerged after the Second World War and analyzes the critical role that it played in Japan's reindustrialization process and emergence as the second largest economy in the world by the 1980s. Elements of this system were already in place before the war. By the first part of the century, Japan's financial sector had developed a distinctive structure that depended heavily on indirect finance. Large banks forged long-term relationships with major nonfinancial enterprises, often with implicit government approval. The government itself acted as financial intermediary by funneling postal savings deposits to favored projects. The central bank had little autonomy, acting largely as an arm of the Ministry of Finance. In the postwar period, this bank-finance model continued to support Japan's dynamic growth by funneling vast flows of household savings to Japan's dynamic export-oriented firms.

The emergence of new economic, technological, and political forces in the 1970s and 1980s, increasingly rendered the old regime obsolete and in a sense, made the old regime "an accident waiting to happen." As early as the mid-1970s, Japan had become aware of emerging financial difficulties and had begun to undertake modest reforms. The Bank of Japan gained more de facto independence and engineered a successful resolution to the inflationary pressures of the two oil shocks. The Japanese government accomplished limited reform of financial markets, including interest rate deregulation, increased latitude for bank asset diversification, and greater integration with global capital markets. Still, fundamental aspects of Japan's traditional bank-finance model remained.

The asset inflation of the 1980s and the resulting financial distress laid bare the inadequacy of the old system for the new Japanese economy. Cargill shows that the government's response to the collapse of asset prices and bank balance sheets continued to be rooted in the old regime of mutual support and nontransparency despite market forces rendering this approach counterproductive. Only when a new set of economic and political forces emerged in late 1997 and early 1998, were authorities in Japan finally convinced that a new regime needed to be implemented. Basic components of the new regime included establishment of the Financial Reconstruction Committee in the Prime Minister's Office to manage the resolution of failed institutions, manage the financial crisis in general, audit and inspect financial institutions, and oversee the operations of the Financial Supervisory Commission. Nationalization of the Long Term Credit Bank and the Nippon Credit Bank, an injection of public funds into banks meeting stringent qualifying criteria, and the consolidation of several agencies created to deal with the banking crisis indicated a renewed purpose and resolve on the part of the authorities.

Cargill concludes by focusing on the short-term prospects of resolving the financial distress and the need for continued restructuring of financial firms in the private sector and regulatory institutions. In the short run, he argues that the critical need is for the Bank of Japan to reverse the deflationary process that has characterized Japan throughout the 1990s. Institutional reforms that direct the Bank of Japan to prevent deflation and inflation could help to improve the long-term policy environment. Cargill warns that longer-run problems, such as the potentially large liabilities of the government-run postal savings system, the declining role of banks, and changes in the age distribution of the population must also be addressed if Japan is to develop a more efficient financial infrastructure over the next decade.

In Chapter 7, Takatoshi Ito and Michael Melvin examine the Big Bang program of financial deregulation and present econometric analysis of the early impact of the reforms in the foreign exchange market. The term "Big Bang," borrowed from Great Britain's 1970s program of financial deregulation, is itself a misnomer, as the program is comprised of various reforms in the banking, securities, and insurance sectors, scheduled to be phased in over a four-year period, from 1998 to 2001. The Big Bang began on April 1, 1998 with two measures that effectively "burned the bridges" on implementing future reforms. Controls on foreign exchange transactions were effectively eliminated, and Japanese investors were given the green light to open and maintain accounts with financial institutions in foreign countries. These measures were intended to secure the implementation of the remainder of the Big Bang package, as they effectively open most Japanese financial markets to international competition. If Big Bang reform measures strengthening the competitive position of Japanese businesses are not implemented, then businesses and individuals in Japan could conduct their transactions with more competitive financial firms operating from London, New York, or Singapore.

Major Big Bang reforms include: (1) removing restrictions on banks' marketing of mutual funds to their customers; (2) removing restrictions on financial holding companies, thereby allowing banks, securities firms and insurance companies to be controlled and coordinated within a single company; and (3) ending the segmentation of the insurance industry into three categories—life insurance, non-life insurance, and "other" insurance—and ending many restrictions on the pricing of insurance products.

Ito and Melvin focus their empirical analysis on the effects of the 1 April, 1998 deregulation of the foreign exchange market, which ended the monopoly of Japanese banks in foreign exchange trading. This regulatory change should have allowed more Japanese firms and households to diversify their asset portfolios at a lower cost. Since interest rates were lower in Japan than in Europe or the United States, the deregulation could be expected to induce a shift from yen to dollars and a consequent yen depreciation. Movements in the yen–dollar exchange rate are consistent with this hypothesis as the yen depreciated in the period leading up to April 1 and in the week following the deregulation. However, the evidence is far from conclusive, as plenty of bad news on the Japanese economy was revealed during this period, and this news could also have depressed the yen value.

Ito and Melvin bolster their empirical analysis by conducting econometric analysis of the bid-ask spreads for Japanese and foreign banks in the foreign exchange market. Holding other factors affecting the spread constant, they find that the spreads of Japanese banks, which were higher than the spreads of foreign banks before April 1, converged to the spreads of foreign banks after April 1. Other econometric tests indicate that the deregulation of the foreign exchange market also served to reduce the volatility of exchange rates, holding other factors constant. Their analysis provides important early evidence that the "burning bridges" phase of the Big Bang was completed effectively, increasing the probability that the entire package of financial reforms will ultimately be carried out.

In his essay in Chapter 1, David Weinstein highlighted two contrasting trends in the productivity performances of Japanese businesses. Productivity in Japan's manufacturing industries had converged with or even exceeded productivity in US manufacturing industries, while productivity in Japan's highly regulated industries—agriculture, construction, transportation, communication, and energy—had lagged way behind their US counterparts. Weinstein's findings raise numerous questions concerning the source of these divergent trends. Are they the consequence of continued regulation of service industries in Japan coupled with their deregulation in the United States? Can Japan close the gap by deregulating its service industries along the lines of the US model? Will Japan have the political will to follow through with deregulation if it produces losers as well as winners?

In Chapter 8, Edward Wolff begins to examine the divergent trends in productivity between Japan and other OECD countries by investigating whether they are linked to changes in Japan's industrial structure. He finds that Japan experienced larger changes in its pattern of specialization and industrial composition than two other high-income countries, Germany and the United States. This rapid change in industrial structure raises the important question of whether Japan's newly developed industries may have randomly turned out to be the industries in which productivity growth was relatively low in the late 1980s and 1990s. If this were to be the case, then it would raise new hopes for increased productivity growth over the next decade, as rapid industrial change could leave Japan specialized in new industries with higher productivity growth.

Wolff concludes, however, that Japan's rapid transition to new industries did not retard its economic growth. Using counterfactual methods of analysis, he demonstrates that Japan's productivity growth rates between 1970 and 1995 would not have changed substantially if it had developed the same mix of industries as Germany or the United States. Instead, Japan's slowdown in economic growth was primarily due to declines in the rate of technological progress in almost all industries. In other words, Japan's poor performance stemmed from poor productivity results across its many industries rather than from particularly poor performances in just a few industries. Wolff suggests that this pattern of poor productivity growth is particularly worrisome, as Japan spends a higher percentage of its GDP on research and development activities than the other G-7 countries. How then is Japan to get out of its slump if it is already spending significant resources on improving productivity? While deregulation of industries with low productivity growth may seem a reasonable answer, Wolff rightly cautions that we do not know whether industry regulation is the root cause of the productivity slump in Japan. In fact, economists have generally had a difficult time explaining the reasons underlying long swings in productivity growth, in particular the slowdown in US productivity growth since 1973.

An interesting example of how things are changing at the microlevel in today's Japan is the case of the *sogo shosha*, discussed in Chapter 9 by Örjan Sjöberg and Marie Söderberg. Centrally positioned within Japan's postwar system of trade and manufacturing, these general trading companies have seen their position eroded over the past few decades as the composition of trade and the manner in which it is conducted has changed. In earlier years, the *sogo shosha* were virtually exclusive suppliers of critical trading skills and were much better informed about conditions in foreign markets than most Japanese firms. The long export boom from 1950 to 1989 diffused many of these skills to a vast number of firms involved in international trade, which, as they grew larger, began to have the option of internalizing these operations. As a result, fellow *keiretsu* member companies increasingly made do without the services of "the master merchants of Asia."

Sensing that there was no future in their traditional role, the general trading companies opted for a change of direction during the 1990s. They designed strategies that would decisively move the *sogo shosha* away from raw material imports and the exporting of manufactured goods. Instead, foreign direct investment, the provision of infrastructure, and various types of business services other than trade were to be the foci. This change in direction also entailed a more pronounced focus on Asia in general and Southeast Asia in particular as well as increased efforts to forge new alliances with foreign companies. New industries, such as space, media, and entertainment, were also mentioned as promising directions for expansion or redirection.

Although these strategies, as formulated by individual *sogo shosha* and their national association alike, have proven less profitable than expected, the shift of emphasis is indicative of the changes underfoot. The Japanese business conglomerate is no longer a world unto itself; increasingly it has had to adapt to the ways of the rest of the world. The cozy relationship between politicians, top civil servants, and business leaders is being broken up, and the information provided by the *soga shosha*, once the eyes and ears of all three groups in foreign countries, has become less valuable to these parties. This change has been accompanied by shrinking price margins on services provided to manufacturing companies within the *keiretsu*, as the services rendered are no longer the exclusive preserve of the *sogo shosha*.

The fact that their attempts during the 1990s to reinvent themselves have had only mixed success—despite efforts to streamline operations, earnings and profits have plummeted—has made further soul searching a favorite activity among the master traders. Trade is becoming less attractive, general trade even less so, and the need to move into an entrepreneurial role is emphasized. According to Sjöberg and Söderberg, this in turn presupposes a restructuring, not only of operations, but also of management. Strategic management and operating functions need to be separated in order to increase flexibility and transparency. Management standards and practices must be realigned to conform to international standards. Speed of decision making and the importance of risk management must be emphasized.

It remains to be seen whether the above measures will prove sufficient to maintain the standing of the trading companies. The s*ogo shosha* have proved resilient in the past and may eventually adapt well to their changed circumstances. Even so, Sjöberg and Söderberg suggest, chances are that Japan's general trading companies will have to contend with a reduced role. If so, it is a sign of the times in an era of increasing liberalization and deregulation throughout Japan.

In Chapter 10, Sumner La Croix and James Mak survey the course of regulation and deregulation in four major industries—airlines, electricity, telecommunications, and retailing—and analyze the economic, political, and social factors that paved the way for the continuing regulatory reforms of the 1980s and 1990s. They argue that the origins of industry regulation can be found in the control economy of the Second World War. The American occupying authorities used the command-and-control apparatus of the Ministry of Finance and the newly created Ministry of International Trade and Industry to implement their economic directives, particularly those associated with the Dodge Line. With the restoration of Japanese sovereignty in April 1952, the regulatory system quickly came to be supported by a nexus of interest groups and supporting ideologies. Administered by a corps of elite bureaucrats, Japan's regulatory measures have often been far broader and more detailed than those called for by the enabling statutes, typically taking the form of administrative guidance (*gyosei shido*). Regulation alleviated business and government concerns about "excessive competition" by carefully limiting (or prohibiting) entry into the regulated industry and restricting price competition. In many industries, e.g. rail, telephone, and airlines, industry regulation was coupled with extensive public ownership of major firms.

The post-Second World War regulatory system was able to achieve its initial objectives of fostering rapid economic growth without major tears in the social fabric. In agriculture and retailing, small firms were protected against competition from large firms. By providing a measure of "ex post equity" to the losers from economic development, most industry regulation acted to temper the process of creative destruction and slow economic growth in particular industries. The effect on overall growth was, however, surely more ambiguous. By reducing the social conflicts arising from rapid growth, protective industry regulations may have helped to maintain the stability of the overall economic system during a period of rapid transition from labor-intensive to capital-intensive industries.

In their case studies of four industries, La Croix and Mak find that there has been ongoing privatization and deregulation in each industry since the early 1980s, with the pace quickening significantly in the 1990s in response to the post-bubble Japanese slump. Despite recent deregulation measures, Japan's transportation, public utility, and communication industries are still moderately to highly regulated. Most regulation continues to be informal, administered by national government ministries. Entry and price regulations have been somewhat relaxed in most industries, but are still binding constraints. In Japan "liberalized entry" typically means more competitors, not free entry. Licenses to enter are still granted on an "as needed" basis. Simple oligopoly models predict that additional competitors will reduce industry prices somewhat, but perhaps not as low as in other countries with a similar number of firms, because of the higher barriers to entry. These barriers reduce competitive pressure normally provided by potential entrants. In sum, regulatory reform has increased competition in Japan, but the basic parameters of regulation have not changed in most industries, with the exception of retailing and finance.

La Croix and Mak argue that deregulation in Japan in the 1980s and 1990s was primarily driven by competitive pressures stemming from increased globalization, and that this channel will continue to be the primary source of deregulation in Japan after 2000. Ideological suspicion of the adverse distributional effects of the free market, close ties between government ministries and regulated firms, and administrative reluctance to shed regulatory powers slowed the pace of regulatory reform over the last two decades. In the absence of more fundamental political reforms, La Croix and

Mak expect that this slower pace of reform—more European than American in style—will likely continue.

4.3. Foreign direct investment and regional integration

This part of the book covers the rapidly changing international aspects of the Japanese economy. Chapter 11, by Magnus Blomström, Denise Konan and Robert Lipsey, examines how inward and outward foreign direct investment (FDI) have influenced the restructuring of the Japanese economy and can be expected to continue to do so in the future. Outward investment is a way of maximizing the rents on the accumulated knowledge and skill of a country's firms, or preserving them as long as possible when the country itself has lost its comparative advantage in their industries, and the industries, or parts of them, must relocate. Inward investment may bring new firm-specific skills and new industries to countries that lack them, or preserve the rents on workers' skills in sectors where domestic firms have lost their firm-specific advantages.

Blomström, Konan, and Lipsey find that outward investment has helped Japanese firms to sustain foreign market shares and contributed to the restructuring of the Japanese economy away from older industries. By shifting from exporting to affiliate production, there has been a geographical reallocation of the activities of Japanese firms, particularly those of multinational manufacturing firms. They find, however, that Japanese outward FDI is still not very large relative to the Japanese economy, despite the rapid growth since the mid-1980s, and that there is still scope for significant increase when compared with the levels of most other OECD countries. The outsourcing and relocation of production are particularly expected to affect labor-intensive manufacturing operations, not least because of demographic factors. On the domestic scene, this will facilitate the necessary restructuring of the Japanese economy towards more advanced activities with higher value added.

Inward FDI will presumably have an even stronger impact on the restructuring of the Japanese economy, according to Blomström, Konan, and Lipsey. Although the stock of inward foreign direct investment is still very small, there are important changes under way. Deregulation has opened up much of the industrial and service sectors to foreign multinationals. In combination with the economic crisis, this has begun to weaken the cross-shareholding relationships within the *keiretsu* groups, and has facilitated mergers and acquisitions between Japanese and foreign firms. The consequences of increasing foreign participation in the Japanese economy are likely to be highly beneficial. The level of competition and the inflow of foreign technology will increase, with higher productivity growth as a major result.

In Chapter 12, Steven Globerman and Ari Kokko discuss some future developments in the economic relationship between North America and Japan, and try to assess the implications of these developments for the Japanese economy and Japan's economic policies. Their exercise is based on an overview of recent trade and investment flows between the two regions, as well as a brief assessment of how these linkages are likely to change over the next 10–20 years.

Regarding trade relations between the two regions, Globerman and Kokko argue that the US is likely to remain Japan's preeminent trading partner and a major contributor to Japan's trade surplus for the foreseeable future. However, Japan is becoming a relatively less important trade partner for the US, and this trend is also likely to continue. At the same time, they project that Japan is likely to become an absolutely and relatively more important destination for US FDI, and that this increase in FDI has the potential to transform US–Japanese economic relations in more substantial ways than bilateral trade negotiations have done in the past. The sectors that have particularly great potential in this context include financial services, health care, tourism, and consulting. Domestic demand for the outputs of these sectors will grow in Japan, partly for demographic reasons and partly because of the relatively high income elasticities characterizing those outputs. US companies also enjoy well-recognized firm-level advantages in a number of these sectors. Indirect economic integration between Japan and the US might also proceed through technical cooperation in areas such as defense, health, and environmental protection, where companies and nonprofit institutions in both countries are carrying out research and development activities.

Although future developments in these areas offer potential economic gains, they also contain seeds of conflict. It seems likely that relations with North America will influence the direction of Japanese economic policy primarily through US threats to the bilateral trade relationship rather than through perceived gains to closer economic integration. In the trade area, Globerman and Kokko foresee continued US pressure on Japan to reduce various nontariff barriers to trade and to continue to reform competition policy. This type of pressure is not new to Japan, but US threats of retaliation may become more credible as Japan's relative importance as a trading partner for the US diminishes. Slow progress in resolving outstanding trade disputes may provoke the United States to focus its policy attention elsewhere, including a renewed commitment to implementing a Free Trade Area of the Americas Agreement, deeper economic integration with the EU, and perhaps also closer economic relations with China. The consequences for Japan might be an increasingly isolated position among the developed countries in formulating trade and investment policies, as well as heightened risks of serious disruptions of its trade flows with North America.

One consequence of the tougher American negotiation stand is a potential for much higher economic costs to Japan associated with its maintaining formal and informal barriers to protect domestic producers. At the same time, the continued severe recession in Japan and the boom in the US are promoting increased US FDI in Japan. Increased FDI flows offer the potential for mutual economic gains. It would not only contribute to making the Japanese economy more dynamic, but it could also diffuse frictions that characterize trade relations between the United States and Japan. However, in most industries, foreign investors have been kept out by the same barriers that impede the entry of new domestic firms. What is needed to facilitate FDI in these sectors is not only more active investment and competition policy, to keep markets contestable, but also changes in some of the structural characteristics of

Japanese industry, such as cross-shareholding, discriminatory treatment of minority shareholders, rigid labor markets, and so forth.

Increased technological cooperation between the United States and Japan offers the prospect of mutual gains in the form of increased innovation in "public goods" activities, such as defense and environmental protection. It might also diffuse US–Japanese tensions surrounding US policy concerns that it has undertaken a disproportionately large share of basic R&D carried out by developed countries, while Japan has disproportionately exploited the technological spillovers of US-funded basic research for commercial purposes. Bilateral cooperation might involve the Japanese government assuming a heavier funding responsibility for basic research having "public goods" qualities, possibly in collaboration with US academic and government research organizations.

In summary, the paper by Globerman and Kokko points to a number of areas where the bilateral relationship between Japan and North America is likely to result in pressure for reform of the Japanese economy. In some cases, this pressure will likely succeed in bringing about significant changes in the Japanese economy. In particular, US calls for an opening up of the Japanese service sector to increased foreign ownership will coincide with increases in Japanese domestic demand for many services, as a result of demographic and economic factors. It is also possible that a substantially increased presence of US-owned companies in Japan will contribute to further Japanese trade and investment liberalization, as well as to further domestic deregulation, as the perception spreads among Japanese interest groups that the rents generated by domestic protection are increasingly being shared by foreign producers.

A couple of decades ago, Ezra Vogel's book *Japan as Number One* illustrated the common view that the US and Japan were the main players in the race for the top position in the world economy. Recently, however, international statistics on trade and market size have established a ranking with *Japan as Number Three*. The emergence of the European Single Market in the early 1990s has made the European Union (EU) the world's largest exporter, the second largest importer, and the world's second largest market. The establishment of the European Monetary Union (EMU) in 1999 and the introduction of the European common currency, the euro, have strengthened the Single Market and have also led to increased coordination of national economic policies within the EU. This development has been somewhat of a surprise for both Japan and the EU—in many respects, the relations between Japan and Europe form the weak link in the Japan–US–Europe triad. The central question in Chapter 13, written by Ari Kokko, Bruce Henry Lambert, and Fredrik Sjöholm, is whether European integration will motivate a change in Japanese behavior towards Europe.

Kokko, Lambert, and Sjöholm discuss how European integration has influenced and will continue to influence relations between Japan and Europe. The first part of the chapter describes Japanese past trade and foreign direct investment relations with Europe. The second part discusses how the Single Market Program, the EMU, and the plans for an Eastern enlargement of the EU may affect Japanese trade and foreign direct investment.

At the macrolevel, it is clear that the establishment of the Single Market and the EMU have made Europe more similar to the US as a potential destination for Japanese exports and as a location for Japanese FDI. This implies significant increases in the trade and investment contacts between Japan and Europe. Comparing Europe with the US, Kokko, Lambert, and Sjöholm suggest that the largest potential for increased Japanese exports and direct investments should be found in the automobile and electronics industries: in both these industries, Japanese firms hold significantly smaller market shares in Europe than in the US.

However, developments at the microlevel are likely to temper these conclusions. Various kinds of trade and investment barriers have restricted Japanese sales and investments in some European markets in recent years, and are likely to limit the Japanese responses to European integration in the future as well. Moreover, the industrial policies of various EU governments, e.g. in the form of investment subsidies to foreign as well as domestic investors, may affect the location as well as the volume of inward investment. It is also difficult to predict how the closer contacts between Japan and the EU in political issues, economic policy, and other areas of common interest will affect the extent of trade and investment contacts. Yet, in the longer run, it is very likely that Europe will receive more attention from Japan. How much depends on how European integration progresses. In particular, it will be important to follow the development of the EMU, as well as the plans for the Eastern enlargement of the Union.

In the final chapter (Chapter 14), Shigeyuki Abe and Chung Lee discuss the implications for Japan of continued rapid economic development in China. They assume that China will continue with its market-oriented reforms and, thus, maintain high rates of economic growth, albeit lower than the roughly 10 per cent growth rates of the 1980s and 1990s. Abe and Lee then argue that the economic relationship between China and Japan has closely replicated the historical relationship that Japan had with the West while it was catching up, as well as a similar relationship between Japan and other newly industrializing economies in Asia. This "flying geese" pattern of development portrays the development of a technologically lagging country as a progression through successive stages of increasing technological sophistication. Thus, a developing country first imports simple labor-intensive products, next undertakes their domestic production, and then finally exports them to the economies lagging even further behind in technology. It repeats this process as it moves up the product ladder to more sophisticated, capital-intensive products until it finally catches up with the industrially advanced countries of the world. Abe and Lee caution that China's process of catch-up may be slower than Japan's due to the millions of unskilled, uneducated agricultural workers still to be absorbed by the labor-intensive manufacturing sector.

How will China's expanding economy affect Japan? First, it may help to revitalize the Japanese economy by expanding the market for Japan's sophisticated capital equipment and technologies. Second, the growing technological capability of China and its abundant supply of cheap labor will make China an attractive host country for Japanese overseas direct investment. Third, as Japan's net private savings rate declines, a by-product of its rapidly aging population, and China's net private savings rate increases, China may begin to supply Japan with capital.

More importantly, the Japan-led flying-geese pattern of development of the second half of the twentieth century may be replaced by a new multipolar East Asia, with Japan and China as its major players. Many politicians and academics in Japan are, however, wary of China's rise and now view China as being overbearing toward the region and, worse, as having hegemonic ambitions. Whether or not the large potential gains from trade, investment, and technology exchange between the two countries are realized will depend very much on how the region's two major powers relate to each other politically. Lee and Abe argue that development in China will induce structural change in Japan and that close coordination of the two countries' economic policies will be needed to ensure a harmonious relationship. At the same time, the two countries must learn to coexist as great powers in the Asian region, an arrangement that is without precedent. The challenge is to see whether both objectives can be achieved simultaneously.

5. Conclusion

Change is a tradition in Japan. More than once in the twentieth century, Japan has been forced to restructure its economy and institutions to meet new challenges. Today, that process of restructuring is underway again, but not always in ways that are transparent. Creeping, incremental change in many areas leaves the danger that Japanese and foreign observers will not recognize Japan's new economy until long after it's up and running. This volume strives to identify key developments that over the next decade may have a decisive impact on Japan's economy. The historical record cautions us from engaging in simple projections of growth or decline within today's public and private institutions. Rather, the contributors have tried to pin down ongoing or potential institutional, demographic, and structural forces that will drive change in coming years.

While any such list is speculative, it is instructive to note the wide compass of changes that are already afoot in Japan. Some of these are widely acknowledged, both in Japan and abroad; others may have a stealthlike quality to them, their true import hidden from view to all but the most savvy of futurologists. The overall message, however, is that it would be a mistake to take Japan's present predicament, bad as it is, for a good guide to the future. A Japan increasingly geared to the requirements and pressures of globalization is waiting in the wings.

While it is not particularly realistic to expect a return to the rates of growth and speed of structural change experienced during the golden years of postwar ascendancy, Japan still has the capacity to excel in many areas. It may not be the undeniable leader in many industrial fields, and the 1990s has served to widen rather than narrow the per capita income gap (computed with purchasing power parities) with the United States. But this does not imply that Japan has fallen behind once and for all. Just as in the past the overall economy has proven surprisingly resilient. In the face of devastating shocks, Japanese industry has shown a remarkable ability to reinvent itself. And there is little to suggest that this particular talent has been lost. As a business climate is slowly created allowing entrepreneurial energies to be released, it does not take a great leap of faith to see in Japan an economy that possesses a good platform for future growth and renewed competitiveness.

To be sure, one also sees a Japan with its fair share of problems, ranging from still-stifling rigidities in labor and retail markets to mounting demographic pressures in the form of rapidly increasing dependency ratios. And while issues of institutional adjustment are being addressed—sometimes reluctantly, sometimes less so—the question remains whether the pace of institutional change can keep up with Japan's rapidly changing economic environment. Even here, it is worth noting how economic changes, such as the ongoing demographic shifts, are refocusing public debate and prompting changes in private and public policies. A case in point is the keen interest shown in the experiences with social security and pension reform undertaken in the other industrialized economies. Another is the equally intense focus on the pros and cons of the educational system, itself under intense pressure to adapt to changing circumstances and expectations.

What will the new Japanese economy look like? It will be founded on the new demands of a much older population that will want new products and services from the private and public sectors. It will be a more balanced economy, less dependent on traditional export industries for growth. It will be a less regulated economy in many spheres, if not the wide open marketplace that the West might favor. And government will continue to play a visible but not always transparent role in promoting egalitarian as well as competitive aims.

Whatever the face of Japan's new economy, the outside world neglects new Japanese products, industries, and institutional innovations at its own peril. To other industrial economies, Japan remains a formidable competitor and a source of ceaseless product and process developments. It should also be seen as a source of new policy experiments that may help others in similar straits find workable solutions. Just as Japan's development juggernaut became an important object of study in the postwar period, Japan's new economy deserves serious attention at the dawn of the new millennium.

REFERENCES

Curtis, G. L. (1999), *The Logic of Japanese Politics: Leaders, Institutions and the Limits of Change* (New York: Columbia University Press).
Dower, J. (1999), *Embracing Defeat: Japan in the Wake of World War II* (New York: New Press).
Fallows, J. (1994), *Looking at the Sun* (New York: Pantheon).
Flath, D. (2000), *The Japanese Economy* (Oxford: Oxford University Press).
Heston, A., R. Summers, D. Nuxoll, and B. Aten (1995), *The Penn World Tables*, Version 5.6.
Howe, C. (1996), *The Origins of Japanese Trade Supremacy* (Chicago: Chicago University Press).
Ito, T. (1992), *The Japanese Economy* (Cambridge, Mass.: MIT Press).

Ito, T. (1996), "Japan and the East Asian Economies: A 'Miracle' in Transition," *Brookings Papers on Economic Activity*, 2: 205–60.

James, W., S. Naya, and G. Meier (1989), *Asian Development: Economic Success and Policy Lessons* (Madison: University of Wisconsin Press).

Johnson, C. (1982), *MITI and the Japanese Miracle* (Stanford: Stanford University Press).

Krugman, P. (1998), "It's Baaack: Japan's Slump and the Return of the Liquidity Trap," *Brookings Papers on Economic Activity*, 2: 137–87.

Makin, J. (1996), "Japan's Disastrous Keynesian Experiment," *AEI Economic Outlook*, December.

McKibbin, W. (1996), "The Macroeconomic Experience of Japan Since 1990: An Empirical Investigation," mimeo, Research School of Pacific and Asian Studies, Australian National University, November.

North, D. C. (1990), *Institutions, Institutional Change, and Economic Performance* (New York: Cambridge University Press).

Patrick, H. T. and H. Rosovsky (1976), *Asia's New Giant: How the Japanese Economy Works* (Washington: Brookings Institution).

Prestowitz, C. V. (1988), *Trading Places: How America Allowed Japan to take the Lead* (Tokyo: Charles E. Tuttle Co.).

Voloker, P. and T. Gyohten (1992), "Bringing Down Superdollar," ch. 8 in *Changing Fortunes: The World's Money and the Threat to American Leadership* (New York: Random House).

Weinstein, D. (1995), "Administrative Guidance and Cartels in Japan, 1957–1988," *Journal of the Japanese and International Economies*, 9: 200–23.

——(1996), "Comments on T. Ito's 'Japan and the East Asian Economies: A "Miracle" in Transition'," *Brookings Papers on Economic Activity* 2: 261–7.

——and R. Beason (1996), "Growth, Economies of Scale, and Targeting in Japan, 1955–1990," *Review of Economics and Statistics* 78: 286–95.

World Bank (1993), *The East Asian Miracle: Economic Growth and Public Policy* (New York: Oxford University Press).

Part I

MACROECONOMIC CHANGES IN JAPAN

1 Historical, Structural, and Macroeconomic Perspectives on the Japanese Economic Crisis

DAVID E. WEINSTEIN

1. Introduction

Paul Krugman once noted that it is not remarkable that people tend to favor structural interpretations for economic problems. Losing one's job or seeing one's wealth fall by a factor of two or three is often a tragedy for workers and their families. It is an anathema that this might be the result of some bureaucrat accidentally miscalculating the money supply in one's own country or, even worse, in some other country. How can such pain be caused by something so trivial as misreading information about monetary aggregates? Yet, these are exactly the explanations that economic theory suggests are critical in understanding business cycles. Hence, it is not surprising that in all countries there is a tendency to give business cycles a structural interpretation.

Consider, for example, the first Japanese macroeconomic crisis for which detailed data exist. Between 1876 and 1880, Japan began the process of developing a modern banking sector. As in the 1980s, the liberalization of finance had unintended monetary consequences. Namely, the money supply grew due to the very rapid increase in circulation of private bank notes. Hence, while government paper money grew by about 4 per cent per year over this time period, the total money supply, comprised of government and national bank notes, grew at an annual rate of 11 per cent (Rosovsky, 1966: 128). This rapid expansion in the money supply was coupled with a dramatic fall in taxes which were based in part on the nominal value of land. Government tax revenue as a share of net domestic product fell by almost a factor of two. This combined fiscal and monetary stimulus led to substantial overheating of the Japanese economy. Between 1878 and 1880, Ohkawa (1958) estimated that Japanese per capita real income grew at the astonishing annual rate of 18 per cent (p. 340).

In 1881, the Japanese Minister of Finance, Matsukata Masayoshi, cut the money supply dramatically. This had the predictable effect of causing a dramatic contraction in the economy. Japanese taxes as a share of NDP also rose sharply, largely eliminating the benefits to taxpayers that had accrued in the earlier period. As a result of this, Japanese real per capita income growth went sharply negative, averaging around minus 7 per cent for the first two years of Matsukata's term. This, coupled with a

I want to thank, without implicating, Robert Lawrence, Gary Saxonhouse, and an anonymous referee for extremely helpful comments on this draft. I also want to thank Dale Jorgenson and Masahiro Kuroda for graciously providing data, and Pao-Li Chang and Carolyn Evans for excellent research assistance.

worldwide slump in the early 1880s, meant that income did not return to its 1880 level until 1885.

As one might expect from such a contraction, there was considerable hardship for both financial and nonfinancial firms. As Rosovsky notes, the number of joint stock companies fell by over half. Moreover, the impact on the financial sector was also severe. Eight per cent of Japan's banks had failed by 1884. While deposits in Japanese banks rose by 35 per cent between 1881 and 1885, lending fell by 18 per cent over the same time period. Japan was experiencing a credit crunch.

It is interesting to note how Western observers reacted to the crisis at the time. Allen (1946: 41) provides two quotes from the leading English language newspaper in Japan at the time, the *Japan Gazette*,

Wealthy we do not think Japan will ever become: the advantages conferred by nature, with the exception of climate forbid it. (1881)

The national banking system of Japan is but another example of the futility of trying to transfer Western growth to an Oriental habitat. In this part of the world principles, established and recognized in the West, appear to tend fatally towards weediness and corruption. (1882)

Many authors have used quotes such as these as evidence of the shortsightedness of foreigners observing the Japanese system. Certainly it is fair to say that very few people predicted the eventual rise of Japan over the next century. However, one should also bear in mind how difficult it is to predict the future. How many of us could accurately predict which country is likely to have the world's highest per capita income in one hundred years?

For the purposes of this paper, however, what is most striking about these quotes is not how badly observers in the 1880s predicted the 1980s, but rather how badly they understood what was happening in the 1880s. It was absolutely obvious that the crisis in the 1880s was macroeconomic, not structural, but the interpretations seem oddly preoccupied with structural features of the Japanese economy. Certainly, the failure of many banks was due to the fact that they were mismanaged, but given that the Japanese price level fell by 25 per cent between 1881 and 1884, there is little doubt that many banks ran into difficulty because they simply failed to predict inflation accurately.

Indeed, by trying to explain macroeconomic shocks with structural explanations, not only did contemporary analysts miss the true explanation of what was happening, they also misunderstood the important structural changes that were taking place. The really big story in the 1870s and 1880s was the very successful creation of the banking system, stock market, educational system, and governmental structure that were to be the foundation of future Japanese economic growth. With perhaps the exception of the banking system, these institutions were only tangentially related to the short-term macroeconomic performance of Japan. Somehow, however, it was hard for contemporary observers to separate Japan's impressive attempts to adopt foreign knowledge and institutions from their contemporaneous growth rates.

Of course the major question we are faced with today is to what extent the current Japanese recession reflects structural factors and to what extent is it simply a macroeconomic phenomenon. We are certainly not immune from conflating the two explanations. It now seems fairly clear that an overvalued dollar and an over-expansionary monetary policy contributed to very rapid Japanese growth in the 1980s. However, when the yen was trading at 250 to the dollar, the success of Japan was often attributed to industrial policy, just-in-time delivery, permanent employment, and a host of cultural characteristics. Today, America's resurgence is popularly attributed to restructuring. However, it is also obvious that the yen's movement from an average level of 239 to the dollar in 1985 to 94 in 1995 probably has something to do with the difficulties that US producers faced at the beginning of the period relative to now.

What is quite surprising, in retrospect, is how hard it was for people to see how important the macroeconomic phenomena were even in the 1980s. It was not uncommon to observe contemporary observers writing statements that now seem strangely at odds with the present. Authors such as Clyde Prestowitz in *Trading Places* (1988) claimed that "Few, if any, American companies can compete with the Japanese in areas the latter deem important." Because of this, Prestowitz argued the US and Japan would "trade places." In some sense, Prestowitz was right. In the 1980s, the US was a troubled economy while Japan was seen as the model to emulate. Today, the reverse is true. Japan and the US have traded places, although not in the way Prestowitz imagined.

One of the major problems with trying to explain economic performance with structural explanations is that structural features of an economy change very slowly. Structural features of economies may be very important in understanding long-run phenomena, but they are probably less important in understanding short-run patterns. If one wants to explain short-run growth patterns by focusing on structural features, one must be prepared to rapidly adjust what one considers to be strengths and weaknesses. Fortunately, we seem to have a tremendous capacity for "doublethink." As Eugene Dattel (1993) has pointed out, the very same features that were seen as tremendous Japanese assets are now seen as liabilities. For example, in 1987 *Business Week* wrote:

As American Business has ample reason to know, when the Japanese home in on a new market, they aim at the bull's eye. In three short years, guided by strategic planning that subordinates quick profits to long-term market growth, four major Japanese firms, Nomura, Daiwa, Nikko, and Yamaichi, are well on their way to becoming major players in US financial markets. [Sept. 7: 122]

Of course, Yamaichi is now bankrupt and the other three firms are struggling for their survival. Within three short years *The Economist* would conclude, "Japanese financial institutions border on the primitive" (December 8, 1990: 3). If *The Economist* is right, one must question how these primitive institutions convinced the world they were guided by "strategic planning."

Or consider views of Japan's bureaucracy. In 1995, Chalmers Johnson, long a proponent of the ability of the Japanese bureaucracy to guide the economy successfully, wrote:

The US must either begin to compete with Japan or go the way of the USSR. . . . Even if they must ignore or fire some academic economists, Americans can no longer ignore the view that 'countries that try to promote higher value, higher-tech industries will eventually have more of them than countries that don't.'

Three years later the *Wall Street Journal* opined in an editorial, "Japanese officialdom seems especially clueless" (April 16, 1998). Were Japanese bureaucrats ever prescient or clueless or do these gyrations in opinion reflect the difficulty of attributing macroeconomic shocks to structural features? The point is not that the first set of observers was wrong and the second set right. Rather, economies change much more rapidly than their institutions, so one should be cautious about attributing any short-run phenomenon, be it good or bad, to structural features.

With perfect hindsight, it appears clear that a major problem with our interpretation of the 1980s was that there was some confusion between macroeconomics and structural interpretations of the Japanese economy. A relevant question is whether at least some of our current pessimism about Japan isn't also conflating the two factors.

Consider the current crisis. Between 1989 and 1997, real per capita GDP grew at an annual rate of only 1.4 per cent. This crisis has been widely characterized as the worst postwar economic crisis that Japan has faced. This is somewhat misleading. Japan started the postwar period in 1946 with a per capita GDP level that was approximately the same as thirty years earlier. As Ito (1996) and others have shown, the first twenty or so years of Japanese postwar development represented a period of catching up to the trends established in the prewar period. Since Japan spent much of this time period returning to the prewar growth path, it is not surprising that its growth rate was relatively fast until it returned to its path in 1963.

What is more puzzling is why Japan's real per capita GDP grew at an average rate of 8.5 per cent between 1963 and 1973. One important factor to bear in mind is that Japan's good performance was not unique. Over the same time period, real per capita US GDP expanded at an average rate of 2.9 per cent. This period marks a time of remarkable expansion for the US economy. Between 1938 and 1960, real per capita GDP grew at an average rate of 3.4 per cent (Maddison (1982)) as opposed to only 1.9 per cent between 1900 and 1938.

This trend acceleration in the US is relevant because a major determinate of Japanese growth is technological catch-up. The prewar Japanese growth rates of 2.9 per cent were sufficient to generate convergence with a much slower growing US. If Japanese growth rates had just returned to the level of GDP predicted by its prewar trend and then continued at that growth rate, the US and Japan would have diverged between 1938 and 1973. Because per capita GDP level was only 37 per cent of that in the US in 1963, Japan would have had to have grown at a 6.4 per cent per capita rate just to converge to 50 per cent of the US level by 1973.

Other authors have looked at this more formally. Baumol, Blackman, and Wolff (1989) plot annual GDP per work-hour growth rates and initial GDP per work-hour for sixteen industrialized countries between 1950 and 1979. Convergence theory suggests that there should be a negative relationship between these variables. Their analysis suggests there is. The Japanese point lies almost exactly on the fitted line; there is simply nothing distinctive about Japanese growth rates relative to the rest of the OECD over this period. While there are interesting questions surrounding why Japan did better than many African, South Asian, and Latin American economies, Japan's long-run performance relative to the OECD is not a puzzle. More to the point, given the forces of convergence at work, it is not surprising that Japan did not experience any prolonged recession in the first thirty years of the postwar period.

Japan's short-run recent experience is more complex, however. Japan's first major postwar recession followed the first oil shock, when the Japanese real GDP growth rate suddenly fell from 8 per cent in 1973 to −1 per cent in 1974. The recovery was slow and painful; between 1973 and 1978, the Japanese real per capita GDP growth averaged only 2.1 per cent. This is not much faster than the 1.9 per cent rate recorded between 1989 and 1994. Certainly considering that Japan was relatively a much poorer country in 1973 than in 1989, and hence should have grown much faster, the performance over these two time periods is actually quite comparable.

It is often argued that part of the reason for the poor performance in this period was that the Bank of Japan (BOJ) conflated structural and macroeconomic problems.[1] Following the first oil shock, the BOJ decided to target its policy at eliminating the inflationary aspects of the oil shock rather than treating the rise in energy prices as a negative supply shock. The growth rate of $M_2 + CD$'s fell from an average of over 20 per cent per year for the three years before 1973 to 11.9 per cent per year in 1974. The tighter monetary policy had the desired effect of reducing inflation but at the cost of a major recession.

While the Japanese economy performed comparably in the first five years following the first oil shock and the first five years following the bursting of the bubble, the performance over the next five years was quite different. The early 1980s mark a period in which the dollar became substantially overvalued relative to the yen. Because the BOJ learned from its mistake after the first oil shock, when the second one hit, the BOJ did not raise rates. By contrast, a tight money policy in the US caused interest rates to rise substantially, leading to a dramatic appreciation of the dollar against the yen in the early 1980s.

As the dollar fluctuated between 210 to 249 yen, Japanese exports surged (see Figure 1.1). Between 1978 and 1981, the volume of Japanese exports rose by 30 per cent and import volumes remained virtually unchanged. By 1985, the volume of Japanese exports had risen by 69 per cent while imports had only risen by 16 per cent. This dramatic rise in exports helped speed Japan's recovery and generated tremendous frictions with Japan's trading partners.

The macroeconomic picture following the recent bubble stands in sharp contrast to what we have seen in the early 1980s. The tight money policy pursued by the BOJ, even in the face of the East Asian crisis, has contributed to a tremendous appreciation. The strong yen explains why export volumes rose by 16 per cent between

---

[1] I am indebted to an anonymous referee for suggesting I pursue this line of argumentation.

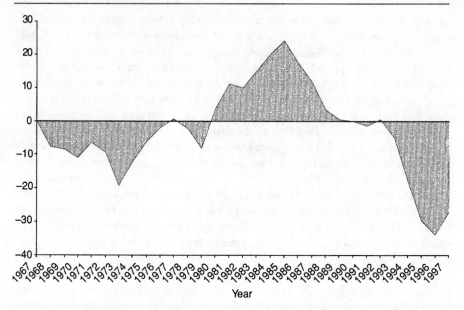

FIGURE 1.1. *Export volume less import volume (exports and imports in 1990 set to 100)*
Sources: IMF (various years), *International Financial Statistics Yearbook* (Washington: IMF).

1993 and 1997, but import volumes rose by 36 per cent. While monetary policy helped Japan export its way out of the first crisis, this has not happened in the current crisis.

The notion that the cause of Japan's current ills are fundamentally macroeconomic is bolstered by the fact that the Japanese economy does seem to respond to standard macroeconomic stimuli. For example, in 1996 a temporary tax cut caused the Japanese real per capita GDP to grow at 3.6 per cent. This was faster than any other country in the G7 and led the government to raise taxes in the belief that the worst was behind them. It is an open question whether this would have been the right decision had the East Asian crisis not struck in 1997. However, given the good fortune of having the dollar overvalued in the 1980s and the misfortune of having the current Asian crisis strike just as Japan was getting back on its feet, one should not underestimate the role played by bad luck.

Today's long-term economic crisis is not without precedent. The historical record suggests that there have been numerous occasions in which Japan stagnated for relatively long time periods. The prewar period produced many such slumps punctuated by remarkable periods of growth. According to the Long Term Economic Statistics (Ohkawa, 1974), Japan's real per capita income growth rate averaged 2.1 per cent between 1885 and 1940. This is comparable to the 2.7 per cent real per capita GDP growth rate that the Japanese economy recorded between 1973 and 1996. What is perhaps most surprising is that despite the slightly more rapid overall prewar growth rate, the earlier period was punctuated by many recessionary or slow growth periods.

For example, before the Second World War there were two long periods (1895–1914, 1919–32) in which per capita income growth rates averaged under 0.6 per cent. By this standard, the recent recession would not even count. In other words, with the exception of the immediate postwar experience, recessions and periods of relative stagnation have always been a feature of Japanese economic development. These slow growth periods account for about one-third of the prewar economic period.

2. Structural Impediments to Growth

Our previous emphasis on macroeconomic phenomena does not mean that structural features are unimportant. One can identify a number of ways in which structural characteristics have affected the current situation in Japan. First, few people would deny that the mountain of bad debt held by Japanese financial institutions constitutes a severe structural problem. The insolvency of the financial sector may spill over into other sectors as well. Indeed, Peek and Rosengren (1997) present persuasive evidence that Japan is experiencing a credit crunch arising from the unwillingness of Japanese banks to lend money. Obviously the resolution of this banking crisis is something that is of paramount importance for Japanese economic prosperity.

While the insolvency of the financial sector may be seen as a structural problem, banking crises that arise from severe asset deflations are not unique to the Japanese economic system. In the 1930s and 1980s, the US also had banking crises that had real economic effects. Other countries whose land and stock prices have risen and fallen dramatically have also experienced similar crises. Given that Japanese stock prices fell by a factor of three from their peak and urban land prices fell by as much as 70 per cent, it is not surprising that Japanese financial institutions found themselves saddled with large amounts of bad debt. I therefore would like to consider the banking crisis, per se, part of the macroeconomic explanation.

Posen (1998) has forcefully argued that beyond the banking crisis, it is safe for policymakers to ignore structural issues as a means of pulling Japan out of the recession. Posen cites an OECD (1998) study that found that structural reform would not raise Japanese GDP by more than 5.6 per cent. This number is quite small compared to potential macroeconomic gains from pulling out of the current recession.

One of the problems with this argument is that the gains from structural reform are likely to be much larger than those suggested by the OECD. Moreover, structural reform may be a necessary complement to the macroeconomic policy. There are several reasons why one might believe that structural reform is more important than the OECD suggests. First, the substantial deregulation that has already occurred in the 1990s was not counted toward the potential gains; only future reforms were considered. This works to push down the impact. Second, financial market, insurance, and construction deregulation was not allowed to have any impact in the calculation of Japan's number even though these are precisely the areas that are often seen as most important in the reform effort. Third, the OECD *assumed* that the impact of deregulation on productivity was 6 per cent or less in four of the five sectors that they examined. As I shall argue shortly, this number seems far too small.

More importantly, in reviewing the causes of the bubble, it seems hard to argue that one can divorce Japan's current dilemma from its structural problems. While it probably was the case that the BOJ pursued an overly expansionary monetary policy during the late 1980s, it is important to ask why. The first thing to recognize is that this was not a simple policy mistake but was deeply linked to the Japanese government's recalcitrance about structural reform.

As Miller and Milhaupt (1997) have documented, deregulation of the foreign bond market coupled with widespread interest rate regulation in other sectors caused Japan's heavily regulated financial system to pump large amounts of money into real estate investment. Similarly, the liberalization of the domestic bond market in the 1980s fundamentally changed the relationships between monetary policy and monetary aggregates. Had Japan not opened its markets to international capital flows and had Japan's regulatory system not forced certain investors to hold real estate, it is unlikely that the BOJ would have misjudged money supply growth. Indeed, the linkages to BOJ policy were sufficiently murky that even economists interested in the reasons behind the asset inflation at the time did not see BOJ policy as central. For example, French and Poterba (1990) wrote a paper entitled, "Are Japanese Stock Prices Too High?" that sought to explore the reasons for the rise in Japanese stock prices. Interestingly, they made no mention of BOJ policy. Even after the crash, when the paper appeared a year later (French and Poterba, 1991) with the new title, "Were Japanese Stock Prices Too High?" monetary policy was still not seen as the culprit.[2]

While this does not prove that monetary policy was unimportant, it certainly was not obvious to extremely insightful economists that this was the principle explanation of what was happening in Japan. Indeed, the argument that what happened in Japan was purely driven by macroeconomic policy is not as airtight as some would suggest. In order to believe that the BOJ caused the bubble to burst by raising interest rates in 1989, one must also believe that the central bank could control long-run interest rates. This is often seen as beyond the purview of central banks. Indeed, when Ueda (1990) tested whether stock prices were being driven by interest rates, he rejected the hypothesis. Hence, it is not unreasonable to question whether there were other factors involved.

There is good reason to believe structural reform is intimately linked with the current crisis. Financial liberalization probably helped cause the money supply to expand faster than the BOJ had expected. While raising interest rates may have slowed the economy, it is not at all clear that BOJ policy was the sole cause for the tremendous asset inflation and deflation. Macroeconomic policy mattered a lot but so did other policy. Much of Japan's problem during the 1980s and 1990s arose from the fundamental inconsistency of having returns demanded by the market differ from those being set by the government. Fundamentally, it was incompatible for Japan to allow firms to move capital freely in and out of the country while maintaining a system whereby some institutions were paying above market returns and others were paying

---

[2] I am indebted to Anil Kashyap for making this point about French and Poterba's paper.

below market returns. Structural reform in Japanese finance seems to be a necessary condition for stable Japanese economic development.

Of course, structural reform in Japan is occurring in many sectors beyond finance. The 1990s probably will be seen as a watershed period in Japanese development similar to the immediate postwar period. The character of Japanese finance, insurance, telecommunications, transportation, and retailing are undergoing dramatic changes. As Saxonhouse (1988) has argued, one of the hallmarks of Japanese development has been rapid structural change in industries: Japan's ability to reinvent itself. The rapid rise and fall of industries has placed considerable pressure on foreign countries that held seemingly insurmountable leads. The real question for the future is whether the Japanese are going to be able to do in finance, telecommunications, insurance, and other nontradables what they did in cars, electronics, steel, and semiconductors.

Japan's accomplishments in manufacturing are even more surprising given the widespread pessimism about Japan following the Second World War. Japan started this period with much of the country in ruins, and it was very hard for contemporary scholars to see how Japan could adjust to a nonmilitarized, noncolonial future. For example, as late as 1950, the eminent scholar Edwin O. Reischauer saw many reasons for pessimism, writing,

It is unlikely that Japan can recover economically without the restoration of trade with Northern Korea, Manchuria, and China proper. And yet it is not difficult to visualize the continuation of the present situation in which trade with these regions is all but nonexistent. . . . Even if Japan should be able to restore normal trade with the rest of the world, it is still not certain that she can reestablish a viable economy. . . . Add to this situation the heavy cost of rebuilding her cities and reconstructing her damaged and disrupted industries and the resulting picture is one of almost unrelieved gloom. (pp. 298–9)

Despite these problems, Japan was able to make the necessary structural adjustments and grew at 8 per cent per year over the next decade. The fact that Japan's future success has never been obvious to contemporary observers should temper our characterizations of Japanese firms as "primitive." On the one hand, it is hard to see Japan catching up to the US in finance. On the other hand, it was hard to see Japan catching up the US in automobiles too.

While it is impossible to predict the future, we can make some headway into understanding what is at stake in Japanese structural reforms. To do this we shall focus on two issues. The first is whether there is evidence of large-scale inefficiency in some or all of the Japanese economy. The second is whether there is evidence that Japanese government policy may have insulated firms from competition and therefore nurtured inefficient industries. If all the stories about relative Japanese inefficiencies are correct, then these should have a counterpart in terms of productivity.

Fortunately Jorgenson and Kuroda (1990) have painstakingly put together a data set that matches productivity levels in Japan and the US for twenty-eight sectors comprising all elements of each economy. Jorgenson and Kuroda used 1970 purchasing price parities to calibrate industry total factor productivity (TFP) and then calculated TFP growth rates that account for capital, energy, materials, labor, and labor quality growth. These data are the most carefully constructed series for international comparisons.

An unfortunate feature of the Jorgenson and Kuroda data is that the series only go until 1985. This makes it impossible to use these series for understanding more recent trends. Therefore, I have updated these series by using TFP indices generated by the OECD. The OECD's International Sectoral Database contains compatible information on TFP in manufacturing and nonmanufacturing sectors for ten OECD countries.

The data quality of the OECD numbers is lower than that of the Jorgenson and Kuroda numbers for several reasons. First, rather than basing the TFP numbers on output, they are based on value added. Second, the only inputs that are used in the calculation are aggregate labor and capital. This means that the TFP numbers are going to be an amalgam of productivity due to TFP and improvement in the quality of inputs. However, because most of the increase in educational attainment in Japan and US occurred prior to 1985, these problems are probably not severe in the more recent data.

Jorgenson and Kuroda have already noted that there is only limited evidence in favor of productivity convergence. In this section we begin by repeating the Jorgenson and Kuroda exercise by aggregating the TFP indices. The results from this exercise are plotted in Figure 1.2. Not surprisingly, data reveal a very similar pattern as that reported in Jorgenson and Kuroda. Overall there is no evidence of convergence in aggregate productivity between Japan and the US. Figure 1.2 also

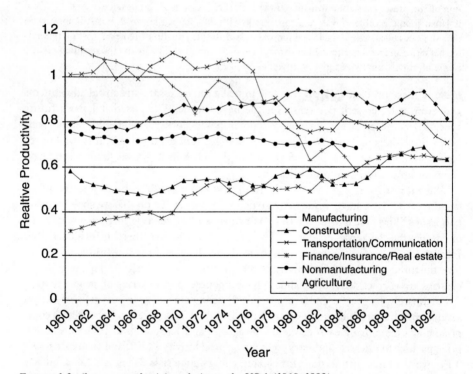

FIGURE 1.2. *Japanese productivity relative to the USA (1960–1993)*

presents evidence on relative productivity in manufacturing and nonmanufacturing sectors. When we examine these series an interesting pattern emerges. Between 1960 and 1980 Japanese TFP in manufacturing rose from being only 79 per cent of the US level to 94 per cent and persisted at this level for over a decade.[3]

Lawrence and Weinstein (1999) have investigated some of the determinants of this technological catch-up between Japan and the US more formally. The data reveal that manufacturing industries in Japan that were farther behind tended to catch up more quickly after controlling for a number of industry characteristics. In other words, there is evidence of convergence *in manufacturing*. Moreover, we find no evidence that sectors that exported more intensively grew faster. On the contrary, we find that higher levels of import intensity are associated with more rapid technological convergence. In other words, those advocating "export-led growth" have it exactly backwards. It is imports that matter.

Lawrence and Weinstein (1999) argue that the principle mechanism through which imports have historically raised productivity in Japan is by inducing higher levels of competition. Japanese firms may not like to compete with foreigners in their domestic market, but the evidence suggests that the competition makes them better firms. In other words, the main message from the Lawrence and Weinstein work is that liberalization to foreign competition is an important conduit for growth in manufactures. Since one can easily think of similar channels operating in nonmanufacturing sectors, it is reasonable to conjecture that the absence of significant foreign competition in Japanese nonmanufacturing sectors may have important productivity consequences. Likewise efforts to liberalize these sectors today may raise future productivity.

If the data tell us overall productivity did not converge but manufacturing productivity did, then the reason for the lack of convergence must be divergence in the nonmanufacturing sectors. This is exactly what we see in Figure 1.2. Between 1960 and 1985, the relative gap in productivity in nonmanufacturing sectors actually increased by 11 per cent. The cause of this was stagnation of productivity growth in the Japanese services sector. Between 1960 and 1985, aggregate TFP in manufacturing rose by 29 per cent and in Japan as a whole by 11 per cent. By contrast in nonmanufacturing sectors, it only rose by only 3 per cent. This is quite different from the US experience in which productivity growth in manufacturing and nonmanufacturing rose by 18 and 15 per cent, respectively.

This failure to obtain convergence evenly across Japanese sectors helps explain an important phenomenon regarding the price level in Japan and is clear evidence of the well-known Balassa–Samuelson effect. Purchasing power parity between Japan and

---

[3] It is interesting to note that the relative catch-up in manufacturing persisted until 1991 when there was dramatic divergence. Between 1991 and 1993 Japanese productivity in manufacturing fell from 93 per cent of the US level to 81 per cent. This very recent divergence arises in part because of the procyclicality of measured productivity. With the US coming out of a recession, measured productivity rose in the US by 7 per cent over this time period while productivity in Japan fell by a similar margin. To some extent this probably reflects the fact that employment and capital stock numbers move relatively slowly compared with output and prices. This tends to cause productivity to rise during booms and fall during busts, and makes it relatively easy to conflate structural and macroeconomic problems. Permanent employment makes Japanese firms seem less productive during recessions when output is low and employment high and more productive during booms when the reverse is true. Furthermore, it is also possible that some of this decline reflects real economic costs for manufacturers as a result of the banking crisis in Japan.

the US has long been seen as out of line with the exchange rate.[4] The TFP evidence suggests a reason. The exchange rate is determined in part by equilibrating the prices of tradables across countries. The convergence in TFP in manufacturing meant that tradables prices tended to be quite similar in Japan and the US. However, the lower productivity in Japanese nonmanufacturing sectors meant that the prices of nontradables in Japan were significantly higher than in other countries. While this is not the only explanation for why prices in Japan have tended to be so high, the magnitudes suggested by this analysis are impressive. If the exchange rate were set at a rate in 1985 that equilibrated the prices of Japanese and US goods, then this implies that the prices of nontradables in Japan should have been 35 per cent higher than non-tradables in the US.[5] This certainly helped contribute to the notion that something was quite different about the structure of the Japanese economy.

A second important result from these data underscores the importance of measurement in doing international TFP comparisons. The Jorgenson and Kuroda study represents the most careful international comparison of TFP levels in the literature. In fact, the data requirements were so stringent that no other countries have ever been compared in as careful a manner. This raises the question of whether careful measurement matters. At least for Japan and the US, the answer appears to be "Yes." Bernard and Jones (1996) and Ito (1996) use OECD data to examine productivity growth rates in Japan and the US and come up with substantially different results. Both of these papers find fairly rapid productivity growth rates in nontraded goods sectors, and Bernard and Jones find fairly rapid convergence between Japan and the US in both manufactured and nonmanufactured goods. The most likely explanation for their results is that by not accounting for improving Japanese labor productivity, they overstated the rate of growth of Japanese productivity.

If we take the Jorgenson and Kuroda numbers as accurate, we still have an important unanswered question: why has productivity growth been so slow in nonmanufacturing sectors. Certainly these sectors are measured with the most error. Measuring the output of a bank or a consultant is notoriously difficult, and it is possible that our results are in part due to this difficulty. However, it still is puzzling why in the US productivity grew at approximately the same rate in both manufacturing and nonmanufacturing, but in Japan, manufacturing did so much better than nonmanufacturing. While we cannot rule out measurement error, we would like to also consider some alternative hypotheses.

One possible explanation for these different trends is the level of government involvement in these sectors. Government intervention in sectors can adversely affect productivity growth in a country through two important channels. First, if government interventions prop up inefficient industries, that will tend to hold back growth by funneling too many of a country's resources into inefficient activities. Second, if government policies are misguided, they may actually retard efficient investments or innovations within industries.

---

[4] See Marston (1987) for a more detailed discussion and analysis of this point.
[5] I am considering agriculture to be a nontradable good. Given the high level of protection in Japan during this time period, this assumption is not groundless.

Beason and Weinstein (1996) examined targeting by the Ministry of International Trade and Industry and found that Japanese targeting tended to focus on slow-growth industries. That paper also examined the role of industrial policy in Japanese TFP growth and found little impact. A related question is whether the targeting of sectors led to faster convergence between Japan and the US. Using the Beason and Weinstein data I calculated correlations between the level of targeting as given by the importance of JDB loans, subsidies, tariffs, and taxes to each industry. These indexes were then correlated with the growth rate of relative TFP over the period 1960 to 1985. For every policy measure except net subsidies, there was a negative correlation between the degree of assistance and the amount of convergence. This indicates that sectors that converged the most were those that tended to have little assistance.

The one policy that is positively correlated with convergence is net subsidies. However, upon closer inspection it appears that this result is driven by two outliers. Processed foods and petroleum and coal had extremely negative net subsidy rates and extremely poor performance. Indeed the magnitude of their negative net subsidy rates was between four and six times higher than that of any other industry in the sample. When we drop these industries from the sample, the correlation for the remaining industries is −0.44. This indicates that while there may be some evidence that extremely high tax rates may be associated with poor performance, there appears to be, in general, either no relationship or a negative relationship between targeting and convergence in manufacturing. In other words, both channels of government impact seem important. Industrial policy in Japan appears to have increased the size of slow-growth sectors and impeded their technological convergence.

It is much more difficult to establish a linkage between government policy in nonmanufacturing sectors, because industrial policy in these sectors is often non-transparent and quite complex. Rather than try to approach this formally, we take a more casual approach, remembering that correlation is not necessarily an indicator of causation.

If we look at nonmanufacturing sectors there are a few sectors that stand out (see Figure 1.2). First, three sectors exhibit either no evidence of convergence or actually diverge: agriculture, construction, and transportation and communication. In agriculture, productivity not only fell relative to the US but also in absolute terms within Japan. Despite (or perhaps because of) tremendous protection, subsidies, and other policies, Japanese agriculture started out approximately even with US agriculture in 1960 but fell to one half the US level by 1985 (see Figure 1.3). This was due to a 47 per cent rise in the productivity of US agriculture coupled with a 26 per cent decline in Japanese productivity. In construction, which is another very heavily regulated industry, Japanese productivity fell by 24 per cent over this time period.

Transportation and communication are others examples of industries with radically different regulatory histories in Japan and the US (see Figure 1.4). In the US, deregulation of airlines, trucking, telephone, and television was accompanied by extremely rapid growth rates in productivity. Productivity growth in transportation and telecommunications in the US was more than double that in any other services

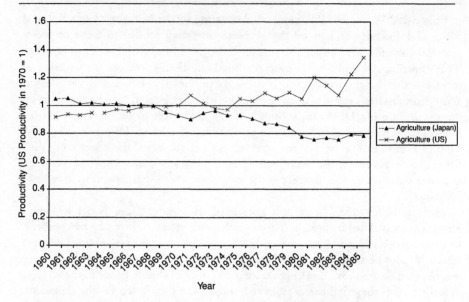

FIGURE 1.3. *Productivity growth in agriculture in Japan and the USA*

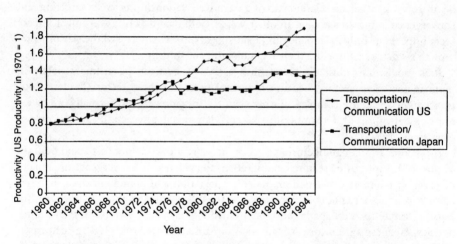

FIGURE 1.4. *Productivity growth in transportation and communication in Japan and the USA*

sector, averaging a whopping 3.4 per cent per year between 1960 and 1993. In Japan, deregulation has proceeded far more slowly. Productivity growth over the same time period was less than half that in the US. It is not hard to understand why regulation of airline and trucking pricing and routes and the slow liberalization of telecommunications may have held back productivity growth in Japan, but whatever the cause, the failure of Japan in this realm is staggering. In 1960, regulation restrained competition in this industry in both Japan and the US, and Japanese productivity in this sector was within 1 per cent of the US level. By 1993, the tremendous growth of productivity in the US in this sector caused the Japanese level of productivity to fall to only 71 per cent of the US level.

These data suggest that there are very serious structural problems in Japan. Very heavily regulated and protected sectors seem to perform significantly worse than in the US. Moreover, we do not see evidence of convergence in these sectors. Japan is behind, and the gap is widening.

Other sectors exhibit more complex patterns. Of particular interest is what has been happening in Japanese financial services and real estate. Interestingly, this is a sector that had been converging at one of the fastest rates of any sectors in the Japanese economy. However, what is interesting about this sector is that its path of convergence has been very uneven. In 1960, Japanese finance was the most undeveloped sector in the Japanese economy in terms of its productivity relative to the US. The Jorgenson and Kuroda data reveal that Japanese financial institutions were less than one-third as productive as US institutions.

This may account for some of the early rapid productivity growth in financial services and real estate. Between 1960 and 1973, productivity in Japanese finance rose by 4.9 per cent per year. By contrast, productivity in nonmanufacturing industries as a whole rose only by 0.7 per cent per year over this same time period. Hence, even by Japanese standards the productivity gains in finance were quite impressive. However, between 1973 and 1982, productivity growth in financial services stagnated. In fact, there was literally no growth in productivity over the entire decade. If we look at other Japanese sectors over the same time period, we find that there was a slight decline in productivity for nonmanufacturing industries as a whole over this time period and a slight increase in manufacturing sectors. If we use the US as the reference point a very similar pattern emerges. Between 1960 and 1973, the productivity level of Japanese financial services grew from being less than one-third that of the US to just over one-half. Over the next decade its level relative to that of the US hardly rose at all. What might explain this pattern?

An obvious candidate is regulation. Over the course of the 1960s and early 1970s, the Ministry of Finance and the Bank of Japan became increasingly involved in Japanese financial markets. In 1962, Japanese tax law was changed to favor trust banks and insurance companies over mutual funds, thereby helping solidify the *keiretsu* system (see Weinstein (1997) for a more complete treatment). In addition, government regulations over portfolio management, as well as large-scale interventions in the Japanese stock market, helped to favor the dominance of banks and insurance companies over smaller financial institutions. Between 1960 and 1973, the share of equity owned by financial institutions rose from 23.1 per cent to 33.9 per cent, as trust banks and insurance companies solidified their holdings of other corporations. Over the next twenty years, the share of financial institution holdings would only rise by another 5.5 percentage points and most of that rise occurred before 1980. In other words, the financial dominance of financial institutions was far more clear in 1973 than in 1960.

The rise of corporate groups in Japan was paralleled by a rise in regulation. One crude measure of the growth of regulation in this industry is the sheer number of pages of the MOF's banking law. Seiichi Katayama and I have compiled an index of how many pages of banking regulations the MOF had on its books. Between 1960 and 1973, MOF banking regulations almost doubled from 656 pages to 1,297 pages. Over the next nineteen years, the number of pages of banking regulation only increased by 89 pages. To the extent this is a measure of the degree of financial regulation, 1973 marks the finalization of the rules governing Japanese regulation of financial services.

The low rate of TFP growth in finance continued until Japan began serious liberalization of its financial markets in the subsequent decade. The watershed event was the revision of the Foreign Exchange Control Law in 1980. Weinstein and Yafeh (1998) argue that the most important factor driving the transformation of the Japanese system was the dramatic liberalization of the Japanese bond market in 1982. Interestingly, many of these policy changes correspond to break points in the TFP data.

Regardless of whether one believes that regulation was the cause of this slow-down in productivity growth in Japanese financial services, the point remains that for approximately one decade prior to the beginning of Japanese financial market liberalization, productivity in Japanese finance was stagnant. What is equally striking is what has happened to productivity in Japanese finance over the period between 1982 and 1994. Despite all of the financial disasters in the Japanese finance, insurance, and real estate sectors, productivity growth over this period has averaged 0.9 per cent per year. This is faster than comparable rates in the US and faster than productivity growth in Japanese manufacturing. In 1993, Japanese finance was almost two-thirds as productive as finance in the US as opposed to being only half as productive in 1980.

Hence, there appears to be some concrete evidence that structural reform is occurring in Japanese finance and that this sector is beginning to converge with the US. Despite the popular notion that Japanese finance is "primitive," there is evidence that over the last two decades Japanese finance has become more efficient. Indeed, if these trends persist, Japan will converge with the US in finance in twenty years.

3. The Future

The productivity evidence indicates that the productivity gap significantly affects Japanese standards of living. This information can be used to obtain estimates of how important structural reform is to Japanese standards of living. While we do not have good productivity data for all industries up to 1993, we do have data for industries accounting for approximately three-quarters of Japanese GDP. Using GDP weights, our estimate for the average TFP level of Japan in 1993 is 75 per cent of that of the US.

In terms of understanding the importance of structural change, we need to address the counterfactual of what would happen in Japan if structural change does not occur. A dire prediction is that Japan would fall behind other countries, and we may actually observe divergence. A more reasonable assumption is that if Japan does nothing its productivity will tend to track that of the US, but convergence will not occur. Let's assume that Japanese productivity growth in the absence of any structural reforms will equal the rate of US productivity growth between 1983 and 1993. This would put predicted Japanese productivity growth at about 1 per cent per year.

Now we can consider how important structural reform is likely to be. Assuming that the US represents best practice in all industries, then if Japan were to eliminate all of its structural problems, its GDP would rise by 33 per cent. Obviously, this is going to take some time to achieve. Many of the reform proposals now being undertaken in Japan are going to take years to phase in and progress is undoubtedly going to be slow. Suppose that it takes twenty years for Japan to fully liberalize its economy to the level of the US. In this case, the convergence of Japanese productivity to US levels would raise Japanese growth rates by 1.5 per cent per year more than they would ordinarily be. Given that reasonable estimates for US long-run per capita growth rates tend to be in the 2–2.5 per cent range, structural change in Japan may result in Japan outgrowing the US by a substantial margin for many years to come. Clearly, a lot is at stake.

4. Conclusion

We have analyzed the Japanese economic crisis from a macroeconomic and structural perspective. Japan's macroeconomic situation, while poor in recent terms, is certainly not unprecedented. Historically, Japanese economic development has been quite bumpy and the recent postwar experience is exceptional in part due to the devastation caused by the Second World War and the exceptional performance of the US economy between 1938 and 1973. There are many reasons to believe that much of the poor performance of Japan during the 1990s is due to a series of macroeconomic shocks that have buffeted the economy, rather than simply a sudden collapse of the Japanese system.

However, the evidence also indicates that large structural problems exist in Japanese nontraded goods sectors, and these contribute to Japan's woes. Total factor productivity in these sectors is considerably below that of the US. Unlike in manufacturing many of these sectors do not appear to be approaching US levels of productivity. This exerts a substantial drag on the Japanese economy. Japanese finance, after having undergone a period of relative stagnation in the 1970s appears to be restructuring quite rapidly and enjoying impressive productivity gains. If other sectors perform similarly, Japanese productivity growth may be higher than US growth by 1.5 per cent for the next twenty years. This underscores the importance of structural reform in Japan.

REFERENCES

Allen, G. C. (1946), *A Short History of Modern Japan: 1867–1937* (London: Allen & Unwin).

Baumol, William J., Sue Anne Batey Blackman, and Edward N. Wolff (1989), *Productivity and American Leadership: The Long View* (Cambridge, Mass.: MIT Press).

Beason, Richard and David Weinstein (1996), "Growth, Economies of Scale, and Targeting in Japan (1955–1990)," *Review of Economics and Statistics*, 78.

Bernard, A. and C. Jones (1996), "Comparing Apples to Oranges: Productivity Convergence and Measurement Across Industries and Countries," *American Economic Review*, 86: 1216–37.

Dattel, Eugene (1993), *The Sun that Never Rose: The Inside Story of Japan's Failed Attempt at Global Financial Dominance* (Chicago: Probus Publishing Company).

French, Kenneth and James Poterba (1990), "Are Japanese Stock Prices Too High?" NBER Working Paper, no. 3290.

———(1991), "Were Japanese Stock Prices Too High?" *Journal of Financial Economics*, 29: 337–63.

Ito, Takatoshi (1996), "Japan and Asian Economies: A 'Miracle' in Transition," *Brookings Papers on Economic Activity*, 2: 205–72.

Johnson, Chalmers (1995), *Japan: Who Governs? The Rise of the Developmental State* (New York: W. W. Norton).

Jorgenson, Dale W. and Masahiro Kuroda (1990), "Productivity and International Competitiveness in Japan and the United States, 1960–1985," in Hulton, Charles R. (ed.), *Productivity Growth in Japan and the United States* (Chicago: University of Chicago Press).

Lawrence, Robert Z. and David E. Weinstein (1999), "The Role of Trade in East Asian Producitivity Growth: The Case of Japan," in Stiglitz, Joseph (ed.), *Rethinking the East Asia Miracle* (World Bank).

Maddison, Angus (1982), *Phases of Capitalist Development* (Oxford: Oxford University Press).

Marston, Richard (1987), "Real Exchange Rates and Productivity Growth in the United States and Japan," in Arndt, Sven and David Richardson (eds.), *Real-Financial Linkages among Open Economies* (Cambridge, Mass.: MIT Press), 71–96.

Miller, Geoffrey and Curtis Milhaupt (1997), "Cooperation, Conflict, and Convergence in Japanese Finance: Evidence from the 'Jusen' Problem," New York University (mimeo).

OECD (1998), *The OECD Report on Regulatory Reform*, ii: *Thematic Studies* (Paris: The Organisation for Economic Cooperation and Development).

Ohkawa, Kazushi (1958), *Nihon Keizai Tokeishu: Meiji, Taisho, Showa* (statistics reported in Nihon Tokei Kenkyusho) (Tokyo: Ozawa Insatsu Kabushiki Kaishya).

———(ed.) (1974), *Choki Keizai Tokei* (Long-Term Economic Statistics), i. *Kokumin Shotoku* (National Income) (Tokyo: Toyo Keizai Shimposha).

Peek, Joe and Eric S. Rosengren (1997), "The International Transmission of Financial Shocks: The Case of Japan," *American Economic Review*, 87: 495–505.

Posen, Adam (1998), *Restoring Japan's Economic Growth* (Washington: Institute for International Economics).

Prestowitz, Clyde V. (1988), *Trading Places: How America Allowed Japan to Take the Lead* (Tokyo: Charles E. Tuttle Co).

Reischauer, Edwin O. (1950), *The United States and Japan* (Cambridge, Mass.: Harvard University Press).

Rosovsky, Henry (1966), "Japan's Transition to Modern Economic Growth," in Rosovsky, H. (ed.), *Industrialization in Two Systems: Essays in Honor of Alexander Gerschenkron* (New York: Wiley), 91–139.

Saxonhouse, Gary (1988), "Comparative Advantage, Structural Adaptation, and Japanese Performance," in Inoguchi, Takashi and Daniel Okimoto (eds.), *The Political Economy of Japan*, ii. *The International Context* (Stanford: Stanford University Press), 225–48.

Ueda, Kazuo (1990), "Are Japanese Stock Prices Too High?", *Journal of the Japanese and International Economies*, 4: 351–70.

Weinstein, David E. (1997), "FDI and *Keiretsu*: Rethinking US and Japanese Policy," in Feenstra, R. (ed.), *Effects of U.S. Trade Protection and Promotion Policies* (Chicago: University of Chicago Press).

——and Yishay Yafeh (1998), "On the Costs of a Bank-Centered Financial System: Evidence from the Changing Main Bank Relations in Japan," *Journal of Finance*, 635–72.

2 Population, Labor Force, Saving, and Japan's Future

ANDREW MASON AND NAOHIRO OGAWA

1. Introduction

Japan is in the midst of a rapid and fundamental demographic transition that will continue well into the twenty-first century. Three important changes will dominate the future landscape. Population growth will slow and turn negative early in the next century. Rapid aging of the population will continue until Japan becomes one of the oldest, perhaps the oldest, population in the world. Family structure and relations will evolve in the face of economic and demographic pressure.

There is uncertainty about the future. Marriage and childbearing patterns may change in unexpected directions. Gains in life expectancy are difficult to anticipate. Labor shortages may eventually lead to an easing of restrictions on immigration. But barring some unforeseen event, the major demographic changes already underway will shape Japan's economy for decades to come.

Two important aspects of Japan's economy will be most directly influenced by demography: the labor force and capital accumulation. The twentieth century has been marked by a sustained expansion of the work force. Between 1920 and 1994, the labor force increased from 26 million to 66 million. The growth was largely a product of demographic changes—a tripling of the population of working age and declining birth rates that facilitated rising participation by women. During the coming century, demographic factors will lead to a declining work force. The working age population will be dropping, probably reinforced by declining participation among the elderly. Increases in the number of foreign workers and female labor force participation may lead to a somewhat slower decline in the work force but will surely not reverse the decline.

How changing demography will influence saving and capital accumulation is a much more controversial and difficult issue. The view advanced here is that Japan's high saving rate is a transitory phenomenon related to increases in life-expectancy and changes in age structure that have characterized demographic transition. As the transition ends, saving rates will drop to lower levels that are similar to those found in other industrialized economies. Some scholars have suggested that saving rates will approach zero or turn negative, but we find the evidence in support of such a pessimistic view to be unconvincing.

Labor force and saving trends taken together suggest that Japan's economy will grow more slowly in the future than it did during much of the post-Second World War era. Economic growth will depend increasingly on productivity increases and much less on factor accumulation. Although saving rates will decline, Japan will continue to be rich in terms of its material wealth and poor in terms of the size of its work force as compared with other countries. Thus, success will depend on a well-functioning global economy that facilitates trade and international capital flows.

2. Population in the Twenty-first Century

Japan's demographic transition shares features of those experienced in many other countries in the world. Before the transition began, mortality conditions were very poor. Survival of the population and the family required that women bear many children. Births and deaths were roughly in balance, and population growth was very modest in comparison with the modern era. Japan was in the early stages of the transition at the beginning of the twentieth century. In 1895, life expectancy was under 40 years. Women probably averaged about five births or more over their reproductive span. The population was growing moderately in excess of 1 per cent per year. The population had a relatively young age structure. About 50 per cent were under the age of 20 and 5 per cent over the age of 65 (Table 2.1).

Mortality rates declined slowly during the first half of the twentieth century, leading to increasing population growth that peaked around mid-century. Japan's population growth rates did not approach the high levels that typified many developing countries. Population growth was moderated by the decline in birth rates that began around 1930. After a short-lived postwar baby boom, childbearing dropped precipitously. By 1960, women were averaging two births each, a level sufficiently low to eventually yield zero population growth.

Since 1960, demographic conditions have continued to change. Mortality conditions have improved quite rapidly. In 1960, Japan had the lowest life expectancy among any of the OECD countries. In recent years, Japan has recorded the longest life expectancy of any country in the world. Rates of childbearing have dropped further, to a total fertility rate (TFR) of 1.4 births per woman. (Note: The total fertility rate is the expected number of births per woman if all women were subject to current age-specific fertility rates over their reproductive span.) Population growth has slowed but not yet ceased altogether.

Population growth continues in Japan because of *population momentum*. Population momentum is due to an age structure that temporarily favors population growth in two ways. First, a large portion of the population is concentrated in the childbearing years leading to a temporarily elevated birth rate. Second, a large portion of the population is concentrated in ages at which mortality rates are low, leading to a temporarily depressed death rate. Over time, changes in age structure lead to a decline in birth rates and a rise in death rates. Current expectations are that population growth will cease before 2010.

Forecasting demographic trends always involves uncertainty, but Japan's population will almost certainly begin to decline early in the twenty-first century.

TABLE 2.1. *Demographic variables, Japan, 1900–2025*

Year	Population		Total fertility rate	Life expectancy at birth	
	Total (1,000s)	Growth rate		Male	Female
1900	43,847	1.07	na	44.0	44.8
1925	59,737	1.31	4.87	42.1	43.2
1950	83,200	2.85	3.66	59.6	63.0
1975	111,940	1.53	1.94	71.7	76.9
1995	125,570	0.28	1.42	76.4	82.9
2005	128,520	−0.02	1.54	78.2	84.6
2025	121,700	−0.46	1.70	79.2	85.9

Note: Growth rates are for the quinquennia preceding the indicated year.

Sources: Statistics Bureau of Japan (1987), *Historical Statistics of Japan*, vol. 1 (Tokyo: Japan Statistical Association). Projections: Nihon University Population Projections, Nihon University Population Research Institute, personal communication.

Projections of the extent of the decline vary, but those employed here anticipate that the total population will drop from 129 million in 2007 to 122 million in 2025. A rise in the TFR from current low levels would slow the decline in population. But even if the TFR immediately recovered to replacement level, Japan's population would decline because its age structure is no longer conducive to population growth.

Changes in age structure have had an important impact on Japan's economy and are expected to play a crucial role in the future. The broad outline of those changes is charted in Figure 2.1. Three age groups are shown: young dependents (aged 0–19), old dependents (aged 65 and older), and the working-age population (aged 20–64). Two important changes are evident. The first is that Japan is experiencing a dramatic swing in the proportion of the population of working age. Before the 1950s fewer than half of the population was of working age. But between 1955 and 1970, the working population increased from 51 per cent to 60 per cent. Essentially the productive potential of the population increased by almost 20 per cent because of the increased concentration of the population in the working ages. The change, however, is a temporary one. Japan is now beginning to experience a gradual shift out of the working ages. By the middle of the twenty-first century about half of the population will once again be concentrated in the 20–64 age group.

Second, the nature of dependent population is also undergoing a dramatic change. Prior to the transition in age structure, about 9 out of every 10 members of the dependent population were children. Only 1 in 10 was elderly. By 2010, however, the number of elderly will pass the number under the age of 20. By 2045, 60 per cent of the dependent population is projected to be 65 and older.

Assessments of Japan's changing demography inevitably focus on population growth and age structure. However, closely related issues of social organization may prove even more important in the coming decades. Two issues stand out as

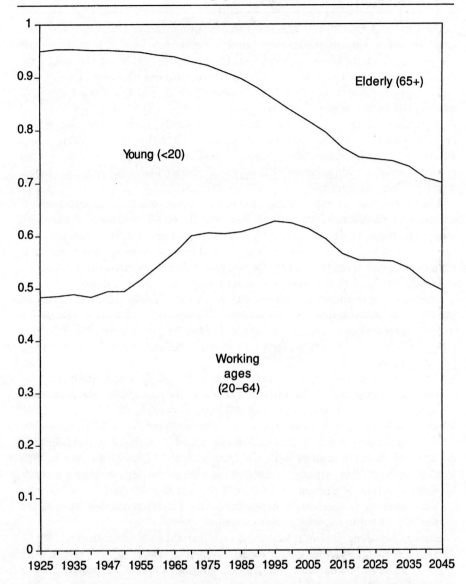

FIGURE 2.1. *Working-age proportion of population, Japan*

Sources: Statistics Bureau of Japan (1987), *Historical Statistics of Japan*, vol. 1 (Tokyo: Japan Statistical Association). Projections: Nihon University Population Projections, Nihon University Population Research Institute, personal communication.

important: first, changes in gender specialization and the economic roles of women; second, the place of the extended family in the lives of the elderly.

Changes in childbearing inevitably have implications for the roles of women. In traditional settings, women necessarily devoted a large portion of their adult lives to bearing and rearing children. But when women live longer and bear only two children, or fewer, specialization along gender lines begins to disappear. Economic changes reinforce the demographic forces. Changes in the nature of economic production, for example, lead to increases in the returns to brains relative to brawn. These changes lead to a rise in education among women, both absolutely and relative to men, and to a rise in female labor force participation.

A second important issue is the evolution of the family and its institutional role in an aging society. Confucian traditions in Japan heavily influence family obligations. Filial piety, the obligation of son to father, remains an important principle that guides many family relationships including living arrangements, line of authority, and inheritance and *inter vivos* transfers.

The development of modern institutions, e.g. public pension programs, financial institutions, and insurance, undermine the role of the family by providing alternative support mechanisms for the elderly. Demographic changes exert their own pressure. Because the elderly are living so much longer and because prime age adults have few siblings, the personal and financial responsibilities have greatly increased for children, especially daughters-in-law, who provide support to their elderly parents.

Data on living arrangements suggest that the extended family continues to play an important role but one that is slowly eroding. The percentage of elderly males living with children declined from 72 per cent in 1970 to 54 per cent in 1990. The percentage of elderly women living with their children declined from 70 per cent to 52 per cent during the same period.

Other data show that the system of support for the elderly is undergoing a fundamental change in its nature. Ministry of Labor data for Japan report the proportion of elderly dependent "primarily on their children's income" in 1980, 1983, and 1988. Thirteen to fourteen per cent of working men in each year depended on their children for the primary source of income. Among retired men, the proportion depending on children as the primary source of income declined from 37 per cent in 1980 to 23 per cent in 1988. Among working women, the percentage dependent on children declined from 37 per cent in 1980 to 28 per cent in 1988. And for women who were not working, the percentage depending on their children dropped from 52 per cent to 24 per cent in only eight years (Miyajima, 1994).

Surveys of young Japanese adults indicate that they are increasingly likely to discount the family as an important support system on which they can rely in their old age. Remarkable documentation about shifting attitudes is provided by a survey of ever-married women under the age of 50 conducted by the Mainichi Newspaper. Since 1950, women have periodically been asked: "Are you planning to depend on your children in your older age (including adopted children, if any)?" In 1950, 65 per cent replied that they expected to depend on their children, 16 per cent responded that they had never thought about the issue, and 20 per cent reported that they did not expect to depend on their children. By 1996, only 13 per cent responded that they expected to rely on their children, 27 per cent had never thought about it, and 60 per cent did not expect to depend on their children (Ogawa and Retherford, 1993*a*, 1997).

Beginning in 1963, the questions about filial care for elderly parents were added to the survey conducted by the Mainichi Newspapers. The question asked was: "What is your opinion about children caring for their elderly parents?" The principal response categories were "good custom," "natural duty," "unavoidable," and "not a good custom." The first two response categories can be considered to be supportive of the values and norms of filial piety. The proportion of respondents who chose the first two categories was fairly stable around 75–80 per cent between 1963 and 1986. In 1988, however, it fell dramatically to approximately 50 per cent, and has been continuously falling since then (Retherford, Ogawa, and Sakamoto, 1996).

3. Sources of Uncertainty

Japan's exact future course is uncertain and will be considerably influenced by three major sources of demographic change: (a) marriage and childbearing; (b) trends in life expectancy; and (c) immigration. Each of these demographic issues is discussed briefly below.

3.1. Marriage and childbearing

It is convenient to classify Japan's fertility decline since 1950 into three periods: (1) 1950–7, a period of rapid decline at the end of which total fertility reached the replacement level of about two children; (2) 1957–73, during which fertility did not change much; and (3) 1973–97, a period of resumed fertility decline, when total fertility fell to 1.39. By the early 1990s fertility was so low that the post-1973 decline was being referred to by some as Japan's second demographic transition.

Reduced marital fertility was the main source of Japan's fertility reduction during the 1950s. The decline of marital fertility was facilitated by a wide prevalence of abortions and an increased use of contraception (Hodge and Ogawa, 1991). Since the early 1970s, however, the delay of marriage has been playing a principal role in accounting for the decline of fertility (Ogawa and Retherford, 1993*b*). Over the period 1975–95, the singulate mean age at marriage (or SMAM, calculated from age-specific proportions single) increased from 27.6 to 30.7 for men, and from 24.5 to 27.7 for women, making Japan one of the latest-marrying populations in the world. During the same period, the proportion never marrying, as measured by the lifetime celibacy rate (calculated as the average of the proportions single at 45–9 and 50–4), rose especially for men. It was only 2 per cent in 1975, but increased to 9 per cent in 1995. For women, it grew only marginally from 4 to 5 per cent during the corresponding period. Over the same time period, the proportion of women who will never marry, calculated from age-specific first marriage probabilities pertaining to a particular calendar year, increased from 5 to 15 per cent for women and from 6 to 22 per cent for men— a far cry from the universal marriage society of earlier years (Retherford, Ogawa, and Matsukura, 1998).

The considerably greater rise since 1975 in lifetime celibacy for men than for women suggests a marriage squeeze on men with respect to availability of potential spouses. However, the squeeze was relatively brief and had disappeared by the mid-1980s, thus contributing only marginally to the increases in SMAM and the lifetime celibacy rate. If the marriage squeeze is not the major factor, what does explain the dramatic rise in these marriage-related indicators?

Two socioeconomic variables known to influence age at marriage and the proportion never marrying are urbanization and educational attainment. From 1975 to 1995, the proportion of those residing in urban areas increased only to a slight extent from 76 to 78 per cent. In contrast, the enrollment ratio for tertiary education recorded a remarkable increase, particularly for women. In 1975, 32 per cent of women of eligible age were enrolled in junior college or university, compared with 43 per cent for men. By 1995, these figures had risen to 43 per cent for men and 48 per cent for women, so that the enrollment ratio for women surpassed the ratio for men (Ministry of Education, 1998). Some of the recent empirical studies (Ermisch and Ogawa, 1994; Ogawa and Retherford, 1993b; Retherford, Ogawa, and Matsukura, 1998) have demonstrated, by using both macro- and microlevel data, that women's rising educational attainment is one of the main determinants driving recent marriage trends, and that urbanization is a relatively minor factor.

Female employment is another socioeconomic factor that exerts a strong influence on marriage. Rising educational levels of women, coupled with expanding job opportunities particularly in the service sector in the 1980s and 1990s, have been the main engine driving the expansion of female paid employment. Rising educational levels have led to higher wages, which have been shown to have a strong positive effect on the probability of a single Japanese woman working full-time. The effect of rising educational levels on women's full-time work is amplified in Japan, as in other industrialized nations, by the economic returns to tertiary education which are higher for women than for men (Clark and Ogawa, 1992a; Ogawa and Clark, 1995). The ratio of women's to men's hourly wage (including bonuses) for full-time work for those below age 30 increased from 70 per cent in 1970 to 86 per cent in 1995. The considerable rise in the ratio for younger persons occurred because of increasing gender equality not only in educational attainment, but also in job tenure as women married later and worked longer before resigning (if they did resign) to marry and start families.

Apart from these socioeconomic forces, the phenomenon of single adults continuing to live with their parents, which is quite common in contemporary Japan, is known as "parasite single," because these grown children tend not to contribute much to household expenses (Retherford, Ogawa, and Matsukura, 1998). Among single women age 22 and over, excluding students, the proportion living with parents was fairly steady during the 1990s at 95 per cent in 1990 and 94 per cent in 1998.

Working as a single person while living with parents and not contributing much to household expenses means that most single persons in Japan can afford a carefree and spendthrift single lifestyle. This lifestyle is closely associated with the so-called "new single concept," which refers to the enjoyment of single life without the pressure of getting married. Surveys conducted in 1988 and 1993 indicate that the proportion of single women favoring the new single concept was 78 per cent in 1988 and 76 per cent in 1993. Among single men, this proportion was 59 per cent in 1988 and 62 per cent in 1993. A multivariate analysis using these survey data shows that single women residing in urban areas, working as paid employees, and with high educational attainment are in favor of this concept (Retherford, Ogawa, and Sakamoto, 1996).

These value shifts have occurred together with a secular rise in the incidence of love matches in place of arranged marriages and a dramatic increase in the prevalence of premarital sex in the 1990s. Particularly, the latter is closely related to a more positive attitude toward cohabitation. Microlevel data gathered in the 1998 round of the national survey conducted by the Mainichi Newspapers show that the proportion of single women who were cohabiting was only 4 per cent at age 25–9 and 5 per cent at 30–4. However, more than 75 per cent of single women were supportive of cohabitation. A logit analysis has indicated that the only variable with a statistically significant effect was previous experience of sexual intercourse. This result seems to imply that the incidence of cohabitation may rise conspicuously in the years ahead in Japan.

The delayed timing of marriage has also contributed to reducing the completed family size. Up to the mid-1980s, a new home economics approach had provided a useful base for accounting for changes in marital fertility in Japan (Ogawa and Mason, 1986). In the recent past, however, the new home economics models have failed to keep track of marital fertility change. Several models incorporating the timing of marriage explain Japan's marital fertility trends much more efficiently.

A series of the national surveys conducted by the Mainichi Newspapers in the 1990s show that approximately 25 per cent of married women of reproductive age stated that they could not have as many children as they wished to have. In hopes of boosting marital fertility, the Japanese government implemented a childcare leave for working mothers in 1992 and the "Angel Plan" in 1993. To evaluate the impact of these government programs on actual fertility behavior is still premature.

3.2. Mortality

In postwar Japan, remarkable mortality improvements were achieved. In 1947, life expectancy at birth was 50 years for men and 54 years for women, but in 1997, it was 77 and 84 years, respectively. At present, the Japanese have the longest life expectancy in the world.

Japan has entered the fourth stage of the epidemiological transition, the stage in which the onset of degenerative disease is delayed. At present, three degenerative diseases, i.e. cancer, heart disease, and cerebrovascular disease, are the major sources of mortality. Unlike most developed countries where heart disease is the number-one killer, cancer has been the leading cause of death since 1981 in Japan. It is also worth noting that after adjusting for age compositional differences, Japan still has one of the highest death rates from cerebrovascular disease among the industrialized nations. It has been often hypothesized that this partially accounts for Japan's high incidence of bedridden cases (Ogawa, 1993; Ogawa and Retherford, 1997).

If the risk of dying from the three principal killers could be totally eliminated as a result of medical technological progress, life expectancy at birth would exceed 85 years for males and 90 years for females. One of the mortality studies has estimated that in the year 2010, Japanese life expectancy at birth will be 79 years for males and 86 years for females (Longevity Study Group, 1989). The same study has also suggested the possibility that it will be 80 years for males and 87 years for females in the year 2025.

The feasibility of these estimated levels of life expectancy depends upon a host of factors. These factors include the future government policy direction of health care programs, dietary changes, housing conditions, and smoking habits. Among these factors, government policy changes seem to have immediate and profound effects on the quality of life in old age. Since the early 1980s, the government has been making a series of efforts to curb the escalating costs of health care services under the social insurance system. For instance, to facilitate a shift of some responsibilities for providing care to elderly persons back to families, the government in 1990 launched a ten-year project called the Golden Plan to improve social services for the elderly and their families. It should be noted, however, that in view of recent sudden normative shifts of filial piety among adult children, as has been discussed earlier in this paper, the effectiveness of the Golden Plan is open to question.

3.3. Immigration

At present, the Japanese government still prohibits business firms from importing labor except for overseas second-generation Japanese (mostly from Brazil) and non-Japanese with highly specialized skills such as language teachers and professional athletes. In 1990, the proportion of foreign nationals in the Japanese labor force was estimated at 0.4 per cent, but since the early 1990s, it has been stable around 0.9 per cent. The amendment of the Immigration Law in 1990 contributed to this modest increase.

The amendments included the expansion of "highly specialized" categories from eighteen to twenty-eight. The expanded ten categories include medical doctors and dentists who have been educated in Japan. The 1990 amendments also stipulate that employers who employ "not highly specialized" foreign workers are penalized. One important feature of the 1990 revision is that it refers to training. It explicitly states several requirements on the part of employers. Training should be nonprofit, and firms should have accommodation facilities for the trainees. More importantly, there is a limit imposed upon the quota: it should not be more than 5 per cent of the total number of employees working for each firm.

Despite these amendments, the number of undocumented and illegal labor migrants from developing countries, particularly in Asia, has nevertheless been substantial. In

1996, it is estimated that there were 283,000 illegal foreign workers in Japan, which amounted to 45 per cent of all foreign workers in the Japanese labor market.

4. Labor Force Issues

As a result of the demographic shifts and accompanying socioeconomic changes, the annual rate of labor force growth has been slowly falling from 1.3 per cent in the 1960s to 0.9 per cent in the 1990s. In addition, the average annual hours of work have been gradually decreasing from 2,239 hours in 1970 to 1,891 hours in 1997. Hence, the effective supply of labor has been growing at a much slower pace in recent years. The total labor force is projected to start decreasing after the year 2001 (Ogawa and Matsukura, 1995).

4.1. Women's labor force participation

In a pattern that is consistent with similar trends in most industrialized countries, Japan's male labor force participation rate fell almost continuously, from 84.8 per cent in 1960 to 77.7 per cent in 1997. However, changes in female labor force participation in Japan differ considerably from those observed in many of the other developed nations. The overall level of female participation in Japan has not exhibited a consistent increase in recent decades similar to that observed in other industrialized nations. In 1960, the female labor force participation rate was 55 per cent; in 1997, it was actually lower, at 50 per cent. In the interim, it followed a U-shaped pattern, falling through the mid-1970s before rising again. The absence of any sustained upward trend in the level of female labor force participation in Japan during the recent few decades is primarily due to a decline in the proportion of women engaged in self-employed and family enterprises that have offset the increase in the proportion of women who are paid employees. It is worth noting, however, that the increase in the proportion of Japanese women in paid employment has been the most rapid in the recorded experience of developed economies (Shimada and Higuchi, 1985). In addition, the fact that a sizable proportion of Japanese women are still employed in the traditional sectors of the economy is a feature largely unique to Japan among the more developed countries (Ogawa and Clark, 1995).

The absence of any substantial trend in the level of female labor force participation is also attributable, in part, to the product of offsetting trends across various age groups of the population, and in part, to the sensitivity of female labor force participation to short-run economic fluctuations such as the oil crisis of the early 1970s. Due to the improved educational levels of women the proportion of university graduates obtaining jobs upon graduation has been increasing over the last few decades. The implementation of the Equal Employment Opportunity Law in 1986 seems to have partly contributed to such upward trends. Moreover, both the shortening of the reproductive span and the modernized lifestyle have given rise to a substantial increase in the labor force participation among middle-aged women.

Another facet of women's employment in Japan is the distinction between full-time and part-time work. Before marriage, most women working for pay do so full time. Among married women working for pay, slightly more than half of them worked part-time in 1998 (Retherford, Ogawa, and Matsukura, 1998). Certain peculiarities of Japan's tax code and social security system have contributed to the wide prevalence of married women's part-time employment. At present, approximately 70 per cent of married women in part-time jobs earn less than 1.03 million yen (US$9,000) per year. Couples in which the wife earns more than this amount pay income tax at a higher rate, and the wife loses her status as a dependent in her husband's salary calculation. Because of these adverse consequences of full-time work, many married women who might otherwise work full-time choose to work part-time.

If these tax rules are removed, the supply of women's labor force may increase to a considerable degree in the years to come. However, it is worth remarking that an increase in full-time paid employment among Japanese women may induce a further decrease in marital fertility (Ogawa and Ermisch, 1996) and a considerable rise in the divorce rate (Ogawa and Ermisch, 1994). In particular, in parallel with the expansion of full-time paid employment, Japan's divorce rate has been rising over the last few decades. Between 1960 and 1995, the total divorce rate computed for women below age 50 increased from 81 to 203 (Retherford, Ogawa, and Matsukura, 1998). Obviously, the rising rate of divorce is another factor making marriage less attractive to Japanese women.

4.2. Aging of the labor force and policy responses

The labor force participation rates for the youngest and oldest age groups for both sexes have been declining. The decline in the labor force participation rates among the young is attributable primarily to a large increase in enrollment in higher education. The continuous decrease in labor force participation among older people is due to the provision of improved old-age pension benefits and the retrenchment of the agricultural sector (Martin and Ogawa, 1988). Despite this declining trend, the labor force participation rate of Japanese older people still remains at a much higher level than the participation rates of older people in other industrialized nations.

The aging of the Japanese population has reduced the number of young workers entering the labor force each year and increased the number of older workers attaining their firms' traditional retirement age. These changes are requiring significant alterations in the compensation and personnel policies of many firms. The aging of the Japanese population is also placing considerable stress on the government as it attempts to finance retirement and health care systems for elderly people (Ogawa, 1993; Clark and Ogawa, 1996).

In response to the increased social security costs, the government has recently raised the age of eligibility for social security benefits to 65 (effective in the year 2013), and has been attempting to encourage firms to raise the age of mandatory retirement. Firms have been reluctant to increase their retirement age across the board because of the higher costs associated with older workers. This dichotomy of public interest in higher retirement ages and private employers' interests in not increasing labor costs is clearly seen in Japan (Clark and Ogawa, 1996).

Japan's mandatory retirement policies represent an extreme when compared with the practices of other industrialized nations. The proportion of firms with mandatory retirement rules has been increasing, not declining. Approximately 95 per cent of all firms employing more than 30 workers had such provisions in 1997, up from only 67 per cent in 1974. In 1995, the average retirement age for workers in large firms was 60.0 years, which is markedly low both in comparison with other highly developed countries, and in view of the remarkably high life expectancy in Japan.

One of the principal obstacles to raising the mandatory retirement age is related to the practice of the seniority wage system. Another deterrent is related to the provision of lump-sum severance benefits that are a function of the duration of an employee's service and final earnings. The importance of this lump-sum severance pay program has recently been substantially reduced as these plans have been incorporated into pension benefits provided by employers (Clark and Ogawa, 1996).

In response to the aging of the work force, many businesses, particularly large firms, have been gradually modifying the seniority-based wage system by introducing ability-oriented elements (Clark and Ogawa, 1992a). As a result of policy changes by firms, and a variety of demographic and economic shifts in the Japanese labor market, the age–earnings profile of Japanese workers has been changing. An empirical study (Clark and Ogawa, 1992b) comparing the tenure-earnings profile of male workers in 1971 and 1986 found that the lifetime earnings profile had "flattened" over time in response to increases in the age of mandatory retirement. Moreover, there is some evidence that the age–earnings profile for both men and women has been influenced by the changing age distribution of the labor force (Martin and Ogawa, 1988; Mason et al. 1994).

Many Japanese firms allow selected workers to remain with the firm after mandatory retirement. This practice is referred to as reemployment or employment prolongation. Reemployment plans require that workers first sever their employment relationship with the firm before being rehired whereas employment prolongation allows selected workers to continue working after mandatory retirement. These programs provide management with greater flexibility than do uniform increases in the retirement age because they are most often applied only to selected, upper-level employees (Clark and Ogawa, 1996). By 1997, 70 per cent of all companies with thirty or more employees had adopted one of these personnel retirement policies. A substantial proportion of older workers who are employed under these policies have lower work status and fewer job responsibilities, and they receive considerably reduced wages upon reaching the mandatory retirement age. These changes are more pronounced under reemployment programs than under the employment-prolonging programs, and among larger firms than among smaller ones.

Besides these changes in employment and wage practices among business firms, the government has been implementing a series of policy measures to encourage enterprises to employ a greater number of older workers up to age 65, so that the discrepancy between the pensionable age (65-years-old) and the mandatory retirement age (60-years-old) will be eliminated.

5. Saving and Wealth

The future of the Japanese economy will be greatly influenced by trends in saving, but empirical studies on saving rates reach widely varying conclusions about the future. Some studies conclude that saving rates will turn substantially negative within a few decades. Others forecast a rise in saving rates. Others range between the two extremes. In the face of such disarray, a close examination of the fundamentals is essential to establishing a baseline from which to consider the future of saving in Japan.

The connections between population growth, saving, and output per worker are captured by the simple neoclassical growth model. In the simple version of the neoclassical model, Solow (1957) shows that economic growth occurs as a consequence of capital deepening, i.e. a rise in capital per worker, k. Changes in capital per worker are governed, in turn, by two features of the economy, the rate of population growth, n (the labor force growth rate, to be more precise), and the net saving ratio, s. More formally, the change in the capital–labor ratio per unit of time, $\dot{k}$, is given by:

$$\dot{k} = sy - nk$$

The first term on the right hand side, sy, is the amount of output per worker available for increasing the capital stock. The second term, nk, is the amount required per worker to "equip" new workers at the prevailing capital intensity. More rapid economic growth occurs either because of an increase in the saving rate or because of a decrease in the population growth rate. Japan's rapid economic growth during the second half of the twentieth century was, in part, a consequence of both of these changes occurring simultaneously.

In the long run, given constant saving and population growth rates, the economy converges to a steady-state equilibrium in which $sy = nk$. No capital deepening occurs and, in the simple model, economic growth ceases. The important role of technological innovation is easily accommodated within the neoclassical framework. Assuming that technological change is labor augmenting, Solow showed that steady-state equilibrium is reached when $sy = (n + g)k$ where g is the rate of technological progress. Once steady-state equilibrium is established, output and capital both grow at $n + g$ and output per worker and output per capita grow at rate g. The steady-state equilibrium capital–output ratio is given by:

$$K/Y = s/(n+g)$$

Solow did not explain why the saving rate rises or falls or why it might persist at some equilibrium value. However, Tobin (1967) used the lifecycle model to show that under certain conditions, the demand for wealth, K/Y, will converge to a constant value. The result is a neoclassical equilibrium in which K/Y, s, and n are constant and output per worker grows at the rate of technological progress, g. However, the equilibrium demand for wealth and the associated saving rate are endogenous and will vary from one equilibrium to the next depending on the rate of income growth, interest rates (r), demographic factors, e.g. age-structure, birth rates, and life expectancy, tastes, e.g. attitudes towards risk and time preference, and other factors. The neoclassical *cum* lifecycle model can be summarized by two equations:

$$K/Y = f(g, r, \text{demography, tastes, other factors})$$
$$s = (n + g)K/Y$$

The interaction between demographic factors and the demand for wealth (K/Y) is illustrated by Figure 2.2 (Lee, Mason, and Miller, forthcoming *a*). According to the lifecycle model, adults accumulate wealth (or debt) in order to smooth consumption over their lifetimes. Figure 2.2 shows adults entering the work force and accumulating wealth. They continue to do so until they retire. Under some circumstances they may continue to accumulate wealth during the early years of their retirement living off interest income. At some point they begin to draw down their wealth supporting themselves from interest income and by "consuming" their principal. Tobin uses "pure" lifecycle models in which households leave no bequests, but Figure 2.2 is drawn to accommodate the possibility that households leave bequests. They may do so because of uncertainty about the timing of death, or as a buffer against uncertain income streams or consumption needs, or because of feelings of altruism towards their heirs, or as a means of extracting attention or personal care from their children. Irrespective of the motivation, wealth profiles typically increase with age. The extent to

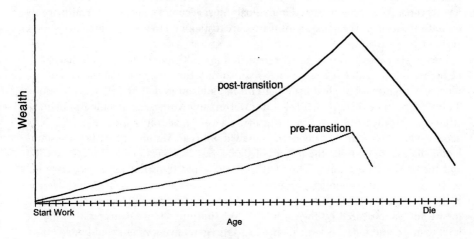

FIGURE 2.2. *Stylized wealth profiles*

which wealth declines among the elderly is an empirical issue about which there is considerable debate (Hurd, 1997; Hayashi, 1997).

Figure 2.2 is drawn to illustrate the impact of changes in mortality. The retirement motive for wealth accumulation is a relatively weak force in a high mortality population because the duration of retirement is so short. At the beginning of the twentieth century in Japan, a typical male could expect to live only 1 year after age 64 for every 10 years lived between the ages of 20 and 64. The typical female could expect to live 1.5 years. Under these conditions, a modest level of wealth was sufficient to finance retirement needs. Given the mortality conditions of present-day Japan, males can expect to live 3.2 years after age 64 and females 4.2 years after age 64 for every 10 years lived between the ages of 20 and 64. (See Figure 2.6 below). The wealth required to finance the longer retirement is correspondingly greater.

An upward shift in the profile associated with longer life expectancy produces an increase in the aggregate demand for wealth. So, too, does an increased concentration of the population at older ages. In a recent study Lee, Mason, and Miller (forthcoming *a*) examine the impact of changes in childbearing, life expectancy, and age structure on the demand for wealth. They find a wealth–income ratio of only 0.55 in a steady-state economy with a TFR of 3.95 and a life expectancy at birth of 43.5. This compares with a wealth–income ratio of 3.76 in a steady-state economy with a TFR of 1.72 and a life expectancy at birth of 75.9. The combined effect of the demographic factors over the transition is a more than sixfold rise in the demand for wealth.

Demographic factors will produce such a large increase in the demand for capital only if families meet retirement needs by accumulating material wealth. They may, however, rely on transfer wealth, i.e. wealth obtained through either family-based or public intergenerational transfer systems. In traditional Japan, transfer wealth was probably much more important than material wealth. The elderly lived with and relied on their children. As economic development has proceeded, family support systems have eroded. As this has occurred individuals must accumulate personal wealth or rely on state-sponsored transfer systems if they are to maintain living standards in the later years of their lives.

Steady-state results imply that the demand for wealth and saving rates in Japan will be higher in the middle of the twenty-first century than they were at the end of the nineteenth century, but shed little light on the interim period of 150 years or more. Two recent studies (Higgins, 1994; Lee, Mason, and Miller, forthcoming *a*) demonstrate that steady-state analyses can provide a very misleading picture, particularly about saving rates, during demographic transition. Lee, Mason, and Miller use simulation analysis to examine the impact of demographic transitions on lifecycle saving and the demand for wealth. They find that the rapid transitions that have typified several East Asian economies produce large swings in aggregate saving rates. Hence, if the lifecycle/neoclassical model captures important features of Japan, the demand for wealth, as measured by the ratio of wealth/output, should converge to a higher level than we find today. A large increase in aggregate saving rates should be followed by a large decline. However, the saving rate at the end of the transition will be higher than at the beginning.

5.1. Evidence for Japan

Key features of the Japanese economy are captured by the lifecycle/neoclassical model, not in equilibrium but in the midst of transition. The age–wealth profile shifted upward and aggregate saving rates increased substantially during the post-Second World War era. The increased demand for wealth led to greater capital-intensity of the economy which combined with productivity increases fueled rapid growth in output per worker.

The shift in the age–wealth profile is illustrated by Figure 2.3, based on data from the National Family Income and Expenditure Surveys for 1974 and 1994. Note that these profiles include financial wealth only. They do not include the value of a family business, the household's principal residence, nor other real property, nor the value of anticipated pension benefits, whether funded or not. Because the value of property is not included, we have also excluded home mortgages from the measure of net financial wealth. Despite these and other flaws, the profiles suggest a strong dependence of wealth on age. Moreover, the upward shift in the wealth profile from 1974 to 1994 is consistent with the rise in life expectancy that has occurred during the post-Second World War era.

Estimates of the aggregate demand for wealth are also broadly consistent with the lifecycle/neoclassical perspective. A variety of estimates of wealth are available, but a relatively broad measure is provided in Table 2.2. Two measures of net worth are shown. One includes the value of land; the second does not. For the relatively short time period covered, 1980–92, the ratio of net worth to national income increased from 4.1 to 5.5; net worth excluding land increased from 1.9 to 2.4. The upward trend in the demand for wealth reversed recently, reflecting the large decline in the real price

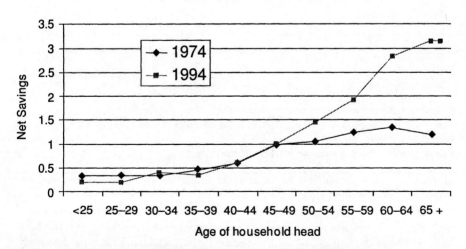

FIGURE 2.3. *Wealth profiles, Japan*

Sources: Japan Statistics Bureau (1975), *1974 Family Savings Survey* (Tokyo: Statistics Bureau), 32 (table 7); (1995), *1994 Family Savings Survey* (Tokyo: Statistics Bureau), 93 (table 7).

TABLE 2.2. *Household sector balance sheet, Japan*

	1980	1985	1990	1992
Net worth	856	1,237	2,393	2,180
National income	209	278	367	393
Ratio	4.09	4.45	6.53	5.54
Net worth excluding land	392	543	897	946
Ratio	1.87	1.95	2.45	2.41

Note: All values in trillions of yen; national income is at market prices.

Sources: Yamauchia, Naoto (1997), "The Effects of Aging on National Saving and Asset Accumulation in Japan," in Hurd and Yashiro (eds.), *The Economic Effects of Aging in Japan and the United States* (Chicago: University of Chicago Press), 131–51, (table 6.1); National income: Japan Statistics Bureau (1996).

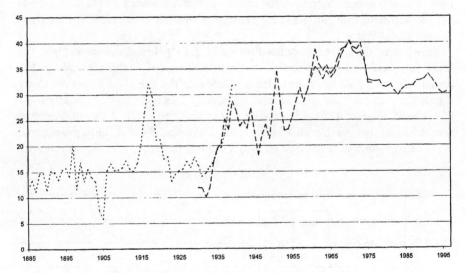

FIGURE 2.4. *Gross national saving rate, Japan 1885–1995*

Note: Measure of saving in earliest series does not include the value of change in inventories. Most recent series is gross domestic saving rate.

Sources: Japan Statistical Association (1987); World Bank (1999).

of property. This should not be taken as an indication that Japan necessarily has reached an equilibrium demand for wealth.

Net saving rates averaged around 5 per cent of GNP at the beginning of the twentieth century. A modest upward trend is apparent starting from that point, but high rates of saving did not occur until the early 1960s. Net saving rates have recently declined but are still well above the level that persisted a century ago (Figure 2.4).

The trend in saving rates is broadly consistent with the conceptual approach outlined above. Japan has experienced a rapid demographic transition. It has been accompanied by a substantial increase in the demand for wealth and net saving rates that are well above any long-run equilibrium level. Net saving rates have declined in recent years but probably remain above their long-run equilibrium level. If, for example, Japan's labor force growth rate drops to 0 and technological progress to 2 per cent a year, probably high-end equilibrium values, a net saving rate of 15 per cent of national income is consistent with a wealth–income ratio of 7.5. This is well above the current ratio of wealth (excluding land) to income shown in Table 2.2 and well above the simulated equilibrium values from Lee, Mason, and Miller (1997). Thus, further decline in the net saving rate and a rise in wealth–income ratio appears likely.

Many studies have investigated directly the issue of whether or not high saving rates are likely to persist in Japan. Most studies take one of two alternative approaches. One approach is based on the analysis of aggregate saving data for Japan, OECD countries, or a larger group of countries of the world. By and large, these studies typically conclude that population aging will lead to a substantial decline in saving rates.

Yashiro and Oishi (1997) provides a recent example of this approach. They estimate saving rate equations similar to one first employed by Leff (1969). For their baseline simulation, gross national saving as a per cent of GNP is regressed on the ratio of the old population to the working age population, the ratio of the young population to the working age population, and the rate of growth of per capita GNP. They use annual data for Japan for the period 1958–92 and estimate the saving relation using ordinary least squares methods. In their simulation, saving rates are depressed by the increased old-age dependency ratio and by the slowdown in the rate of growth of per capita income. They present four simulations with gross saving rates that vary from 5.8 per cent of GNP to 9.1 per cent of GNP by 2020–5. Given depreciation that averages 15 per cent of GNP, the average for the early 1990s in Japan, net saving as a percentage of net national product would range from –11.2 to –7.4 per cent of net national product. These forecasts imply that Japan will be entering a new period of disequilibrium during which the demand for wealth will decline rather substantially.

The finding that net national saving rates will decline to low or negative levels as economies and populations mature is a very robust one so long as the analysis is based on aggregate saving data. A number of such studies are summarized in Table 2.3. As can be seen, nearly all conclude that saving rates will drop substantially in the coming decades. There is, however, a wide range in just how substantial the decline is likely to be. Horioka (1991) for example forecasts a drop of the net private saving rate to –10 per cent. A more optimistic assessment is provided by Masson and Tryon (1990) who anticipate a decline to 7 per cent. Several recent studies based on international aggregate data reinforce the conclusion that saving rates will drop substantially. Williamson and Higgins (1997), for example, forecast a decline in Japan's gross national saving to 16.3 per cent of GNP in 2025. Analysis by Kelley and Schmidt (1996) also supports the conclusion that saving rates will drop precipitously as population aging continues and economic growth slows.

The second approach is based on household survey data rather than aggregate data. Typically, a household saving function is estimated which includes demographic

TABLE 2.3. *Summary of projections of Japanese saving*

Study	Data	2025 Forecast	Forecast percentage change		1995	2000	2005	2010	2015
			Medium term	Long term					
Gross national saving rate									
Yashiro and Oishi (1997)	Japanese aggregate data	9.1	−46.6	−61.4	31	23.6	23.6	12.6	12.6
Williamson and Higgins (1997)	International aggregate data	16.3	−32.9	−45.6	34.6	29.95	25.3	20.1	
Hayashi (1988)	Japanese aggregate data	5.7	−13.9	−62.6		15.1		13	
Net private saving rate									
Horioka (1989)	OECD, Japan aggregate data	−5.1	−86.6	−138.1	17.8	13.4	8	1.8	−5.3
Horioka (1991)	Japanese aggregate data	−10.6	−156.7	−258.2	10.9	6.7	1.9	3.8	−10.4
Masson and Tryon (1990)	G7 and Smaller Industrial Country Bloc	6.8	−23.8	−53.7	13.4	14.7	12.7	11.2	9.2
Household saving rate									
Mason et al. (1994)	NFIES	21.7	6.3	13.6	19.1	19.1	18.6	20.3	21.1
Ogawa, Fukui, and Mason (1997)	NFIES	14.5	−5.2	−5.2	15.1	15.3	15	14.5	14.3

Notes: Medium term is for 2000–10; long-term for 2000–25; forecast values interpolated if values for 2000 or 2025 were not available. Mason *et al.* (1994) is forecast of household saving/disposable income; Ogawa, Fukui, and Mason (1997) is forecast of household saving/national income.

determinants, e.g. the age and sex of the household head, the number of household members in each age group, etc. The simplest version constructs a saving profile that varies with the age of the household head. Projected household income by age of head is combined with the age–saving profile to construct a forecast of the aggregate household saving rate.

Mason *et al.* (1994) provide a recent example of a saving forecast based on micro data. The forecast of saving employs a saving equation based on analysis of the National Family Income and Expenditure Survey by Ando (1985) in which consumption as a fraction of labor income depends on the age of the household head and the number of household members in specified age categories. Forecast household saving as a fraction of disposable income is relatively constant between 1995 and 2005 and then rises by 2 percentage points by 2025! Other micro-based studies forecast saving rates will continue at a relatively high level or decline much more modestly than found by macro-based studies.

A cursory examination of the age–saving profile for Japan shows why micro-based forecasts do not anticipate any substantial decline in the household saving rate. The elderly appear to save at rates as high as many working age adults so that redistributions of income across age categories would not appear to have any important bearing on household saving rates. (Figure 2.5)

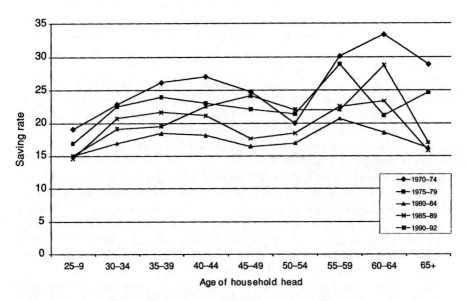

FIGURE 2.5. *Age profile and household saving, Japan*

Sources: Yamauchia, N. (1997), "The Effects of Aging on National Saving and Asset Accumulation in Japan," in Hurd and Yashiro (eds.), *The Economic Effects of Aging in Japan and the United States* (Chicago: University of Chicago Press), 131–51 (table 6.1).

How can such extraordinarily different forecasts of Japanese saving be reconciled? The studies use different measures of saving—typically, gross national saving rates by aggregate studies and household saving rates by micro-based studies. However, the differences in forecasts are so great that they cannot be reconciled plausibly by the differences in measurement.

In some respects, the forecasts based on aggregate data are doubtless flawed. Many of the causal factors are endogenous and identification problems have proved to be vexing. The saving–demography models have tended to be very parsimonious increasing the possibility that the strong relationship to demographic factors is spurious. Questions can be raised about the adequacy with which aggregate models have captured the complex dynamics that underlie the saving relationship. In the face of these and other difficulties, the divergence from micro-based estimates is cause for alarm.

Forecasts based on micro-data also face daunting problems. The idea behind the approach is that the behavior of one age group can be used to predict future behavior of a younger age group. However, this approach will fail if there are substantial cohort effects or time effects that are not factored into the analysis. First, the cohort effects. Those who are currently young in Japan may follow a different path than those who are currently old because their lifetime experiences are so different. Members of young cohorts married later, spent more time in school, have fewer siblings and are raising fewer children than members of old cohorts. They can expect to live longer. Their lifetime income will be greater but they may experience slower earnings growth. They may expect more old-age support from the state but less support from their children. Each of these factors has a potentially important bearing on saving. Some studies have considered the implications of some of these changes in limited ways, but most have not.

Trends in saving may also be influenced by changes in variables that cut across all age groups and cohorts. Interest rates provide an obvious example. Analysis of a single survey provides no direct information about how changes in interest rates influence saving behavior. If long-term interest rates decline as the capital intensity of the economy increases, saving rates will change in ways that cannot be captured through analysis of a single household survey.

Given these reservations and the limitations of existing studies of saving, what can we say about the likely course of saving in the future? A simple, alternative baseline scenario is produced by assuming that the 1994 wealth profile shown in Figure 2.3 persists over the coming decades and the demand for wealth only increases in response to changes in age structure. This possibility is easily explored using household projections for Japan (Mason *et al.*, 1996) in combination with the 1994 wealth profile adjusted proportionately to correspond to the total wealth (excluding land) reported in Table 2.2 for 1990. Further changes in Japan's age structure using this approach produce a rise in the demand for wealth of 22 per cent between 1990 and 2025. The ratio of wealth (excluding land) to income would rise from 2.45 to 2.99 between 1990 and 2025. A 2 per cent long-term equilibrium rate of growth yields an equilibrium net saving rate of 6 per cent.

This value is well below many micro-based forecasts of Japanese saving and substantially higher than many macro-based forecasts. There are several reasons why the actual outcome in Japan may differ substantially from this simple baseline approach. First, increased life expectancy may continue to lead to an upward shift in the demand for wealth and elevated saving rates. Figure 2.6 charts the trend in years lived after 65 to years lived between the ages of 20 and 64. Years lived after age 65 are much greater for young cohorts than old cohorts. Hence, the wealth profile should shift upward as longer-lived cohorts age. Moreover, life expectancy continues to rise especially for women reinforcing the rise in the demand for wealth.

Second, changes in intergenerational family relationships may have an important impact. Young cohorts have fewer children and expect to rely less on their children for old age support. The decline in family-based transfer wealth will lead to an increase in the demand for material wealth if the elderly are to maintain their living standards. However, if modernization or development undermine the mutual obligation between generations that exist in Japan, the elderly may fund greater consumption during their retirement years by reducing bequests. If this occurs, the net impact on the demand for wealth is very uncertain.

Similar issues arise with respect to public policy toward social security or public pension programs. Reforms may reduce net public transfer wealth. As a consequence, households may increase their material wealth and saving rates as hypothesized by Feldstein and Horioka, 1980. Alternatively, they may increase their reliance on their

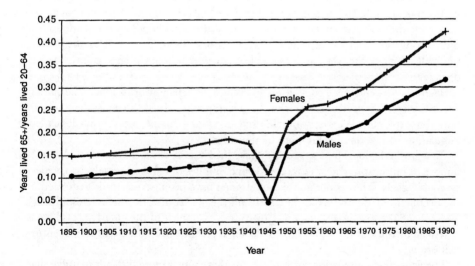

FIGURE 2.6. *Years lived after age 65, Japan*

Sources: Zenji, N. and K. Kobayashi (1985), "Cohort Life Tables Based on Annual Life Tables for Japanese Nationals Covering the Years 1891–1982," NUPRI Research Paper Series no. 23 (March); *Japan Statistical Yearbook 1998* (Tokyo: Statistics Bureau); *Jinko Mondai Kenkyū* (Journal of Population Problems), Ministry of Health and Welfare, no. 181 (Jan. 1987) and no. 201 (Jan. 1992).

children (or reduce their bequests), as hypothesized by Barro (1974), leaving the demand for wealth and saving unaffected. (See Lee (2000) for a more extensive discussion of these issues.)

The bottom line. The idea that saving rates will decline and economic growth will slow as Japan reaches the end of its demographic transition is a plausible one. How quickly this will happen is difficult to judge because it will surely depend not only on changing demographics but the institutional response to those changes. The responses include both reform to public pension programs and changes in generational relationships and the role of the extended family. Despite forecasts of negative net saving rates by a number of researchers in Japan, a strong case that this may come to pass has yet to be made. It is entirely unclear why the demand for wealth would begin to decline in the future.

6. Conclusions

The demographic changes that face Japan are qualitatively similar to those faced by other industrialized countries. As the end of the demographic transition approaches, Japan's population will cease growing and experience a period of decline. How much depopulation Japan will experience is uncertain and will depend on whether rates of childbearing recover and whether immigration policy will accommodate larger inflows from Japan's neighbors.

The age structure of Japan's population is also undergoing a major transformation. At the moment, Japan's population is heavily concentrated in the working ages, but this is a temporary phenomenon. Slowly, but steadily, the population will shift out of the working ages over the next half century. At that point, about half of the population will belong to the working ages and half the population will belong to the dependent ages.

Such a large dependent population was typical of Japan prior to 1950. The coming decline, then, is a return to normalcy. However, prior to 1950 the dependent population consisted almost entirely of children. Now and in the future, the dependent population will be dominated more by the elderly.

Changes in demographic aggregates have their family-level counterparts that have important implications for the ways in which families organize themselves to achieve economic goals. The economic roles of women have been permanently redefined by the decline in infant and child mortality and the consequent decline in childbearing. The role of the extended family as a provider of support to the elderly is also being redefined by the new demographic and economic realities that the twenty-first century will bring.

The economic implications of these changes are much more difficult to judge than are the demographic trends. Demographics frame the choices but the outcomes depend on the policies that are adopted and the responses of individuals to new circumstances. In two areas, changing demographic conditions will have a profound and fundamental impact.

The first is in the labor force area. The indigenous working age population of Japan is no longer growing and is beginning to decline. The changes are potentially enormous. The number of workers is projected to decline by 8 per cent by the year 2025. In contrast, the number of workers increased by 47 per cent between 1960 and 1995. Once economic growth resumes, labor "shortages" will emerge in the coming decades. Supply-side responses may affect the size of the work force. Female labor force participation may increase, average hours worked may rise, participation among the elderly may increase, and the number of migrant workers may rise. Note, however, that increases in the average hours worked or increased participation among the elderly would reverse current trends towards a short workweek and earlier retirement. Of these responses, only an increase in the number of migrant workers has the potential to offset the impact of demographic forces, but the changes in immigration policy required would be an enormous departure from current practice.

Realistically, the Japanese economy will surely face a reduced supply of labor and rising real wages for the foreseeable future. The impact on standards of living will depend on the success with which Japan "employs" foreign workers by shifting production abroad and successfully specializes in capital- and skill-intensive domestic production.

Aside from the decline of the growth of the labor force, standards of living in Japan will also be influenced by the decline in the *proportion* of the population of working age. A declining share of the population will be relying on earnings to support living standards and an increasing share will be depending on transfers and property income.

Efforts to forecast the course of saving and wealth in the future have produced diverse outcomes. There are difficult conceptual and technical issues that have not been entirely resolved, and there are considerable uncertainties about how Japan will respond to the challenges of an aging society. One possibility is that current and future generations of workers will accumulate the necessary material wealth to be self-reliant in their own retirement. If they do so, wealth may grow more rapidly than income for some time. But the demand for wealth for retirement is unlikely to sustain saving rates at current levels for long. As the age structure stabilizes, saving rates would decline to modest levels.

An alternative possibility is that current and future generations of workers will rely on transfers, either private or public, to maintain standards of living during their retirement years. Under these circumstances saving rates will drop more rapidly and to lower levels than would otherwise be the case.

Are negative saving rates likely? The evidence seems far from persuasive. Extrapolating aggregate trends may lead one to that result, but the behavioral underpinnings have not been carefully explained nor is such an outcome supported by empirical research at the microlevel. In the absence of more complete support, such drastic declines in saving strike us as alarmist.

As difficult as it might be to describe the future of the Japanese economy with much precision, it does seem clear that changes in the labor force and in capital accumulation favor a slowdown in economic growth to levels that are characteristic of the mature economies of the West. It is quite doubtful that high rates of economic growth can be sustained because demographic underpinnings will not support factor-driven economic growth. The success of the Japanese economy will increasingly depend on hard-won productivity gains, responses to a declining supply of labor, and its ability to maintain high rates of return to capital.

REFERENCES

Ando, Albert (1985), *The Savings of Japanese Households: A Micro Study Based on Data from the National Survey of Family Income and Expenditure 1974 and 1979* (Tokyo: Economic Planning Agency).

Barro, Robert J. (1974), "Are Government Bonds Net Worth," *Journal of Political Economy*, 82/6: 1095–117.

Clark, Robert L. and Naohiro Ogawa (1992a), "Employment Tenure and Earnings Profiles in Japan and the United States: Comments," *American Economic Review*, 82/1: 336–45.

——— (1992b), "The Effects of Mandatory Retirement on Earnings Profiles in Japan," *Industrial and Labor Relations Review*, 45/2: 258–66.

——— (1996), "Human Resource Policies and Older Workers in Japan," *The Gerontologist*, 36/5: 627–36.

Ermisch, John F. and Naohiro Ogawa (1994), "Age at Motherhood in Japan," *Journal of Population Economics*, 7/4: 393–420.

Feldstein, Martin and Charles Yuji Horioka (1980), "Domestic Savings and International Capital Flows," *Economic Journal*, 90: 314–429.

Hayashi, Fumio (1997), *Understanding Saving: Evidence from the United States and Japan* (Cambridge, Mass.: MIT Press).

——— Takatoshi Ito, and Joel Slemrod (1988), "Housing Finance Imperfections, Taxation, and Private Saving: A Comparative Simulation Analysis of the United States and Japan," *Journal of the Japanese and International Economies*, 2/3: 215–38.

Higgins, Matthew D. (1994), "The Demographic Determinants of Savings, Investment and International Capital Flows," Ph.D. dissertation, Harvard University.

Hodge, Robert W. and Naohiro Ogawa (1991), *Fertility Change in Contemporary Japan* (Chicago: University of Chicago Press).

Horioka, Charles Yuji (1989), "Why is Japan's Private Saving Rate So High?" in Sato, Ryuzo and Takashi Negishi (eds.), *Developments in Japanese Economics* (Tokyo: Harcourt Brace Javanovich/Academy Press), 145–78.

——— (1991), "The Determinants of Japan's Saving Rate: The Impact of the Age Structure of the Population and Other Factors," *Economic Studies Quarterly*, 42/3 (Sept.), 237–53.

——— (1993), "Is Japan's Household Saving Rate Really High?" ISER Discussion Paper No. 308, Institute of Social and Economic Research, Osaka University (Sept.).

Hurd, Michael D. (1997), "The Economics of Individual Aging," in Rosenzweig, Mark R. and Oded Stark (eds.), *Handbook of Population and Family Economics*, vol. 1B (Amsterdam: Elsevier), 892–966.

Japan Statistical Association (1987), *Historical Statistics of Japan*, iii (Tokyo: Japan Statistical Association).

Japan Statistics Bureau, Management and Coordination Agency (various years), *Japan Statistical Yearbook* (Tokyo: Japan Statistics Bureau).

Kelley, Allen C. and R. M. Schmidt (1996), "Saving, Dependency and Development," *Journal of Population Economics*, 9/4: 365–86.

Lee, Ronald D. (2000), "Intergenerational Transfers and the Economic Life Cycle: A Cross-cultural Perspective," in Mason, Andrew and Georges Tapinos (eds.), *Sharing the Wealth: Demographic Change and Economic Transfers between Generations* (Oxford: Oxford University Press), 17–56.

——Andrew Mason, and Timothy Miller (forthcoming *a*), "Saving, Wealth, and the Demographic Transition in East Asia," in Mason, Andrew (ed.) *Population Growth and Economic Development in East Asia* (Palo Alto: Stanford University Press).

——(forthcoming *b*), "Saving, Wealth, and Population," in Birdsall, Nancy, Allen C. Kelley, and Steven W. Sinding (eds.), *Population Does Matter: Demography, Poverty, and Economic Growth* (Oxford: Oxford University Press).

Leff, Nathaniel H. (1969), "Dependency Rates and Savings Rates," *American Economic Review*, 59 (Dec.), 886–95.

Longevity Study Group (1989), "Estimates on Life Tables up to 2025," *Life Span*, 9/1: 1–45 (in Japanese).

Martin, Linda G. and Naohiro Ogawa (1988), "The Effect of Cohort Size on Relative Wages in Japan," in Lee, Ronald, Brian Arthur, and Gerry Rodgers (eds.), *Economics of Changing Age Distributions in Developed Countries* (Oxford: Oxford University Press), 59–75.

Mason, Andrew, Yoke-Yun Teh, Naohiro Ogawa, and Takehiro Fukui (1994), "The Intergenerational Distribution of Resources and Income in Japan," in Ermisch, J. F. and Naohiro Ogawa (eds.), *The Family, the Market and the State in Aging Societies* (Oxford: Oxford University Press), 158–97.

——Rachel Racelis, Katsutoshi Nagashima, Naohiro Ogawa, and Takehiro Fukui (1996), *The Japan Homes Model: Household Projections, 1990–2025* (Tokyo: Japan Statistical Association, Nihon University Population Research Institute, and Program on Population, East–West Center).

Masson, P., T. Bayoumi, and H. Samiei (1995), "International Evidence on the Determinants of Private Saving," International Monetary Fund, Working Paper WP/95/51.

——and Ralph Tryon (1990), "Macroeconomic Effects of Projected Population Aging in Industrial Countries," International Monetary Fund, Working Paper WP/90/5.

Ministry of Education (1998), *Statistical Bulletin of Education* (Tokyo: Daiichi Hoki Shuppan).

Miyajima, Hiroshi (1994), "The Family Structure in Contemporary Japan," *Japanese Economic Studies*, 21/6 (Winter), 25–54.

Ogawa, Naohiro (1993), "Impact of Changes in Population and Household Structure upon the Allocation of Medical Resources in Japan," *Japan and the World Economy*, 5/2: 137–56.

——and Robert L. Clark (1995), "Earnings Patterns of Japanese Women: 1976–1988," *Economic Development and Cultural Change*, 43/2: 293–313.

——and John F. Ermisch (1994), "Women's Career Development and Divorce Risk in Japan," *Labour*, 8/2: 193–219.

————(1996), "Family Structure, Home Time Demands, and the Employment Patterns of Japanese Married Women," *Journal of Labor Economics*, 14/4: 677–702.

——and Andrew Mason (1986), "An Economic Analysis of Recent Fertility in Japan: An Application of the Butz-Ward Model," *Journal of Population Studies*, 9: 5–14.

——and Rikiya Matsukura (1995), "Population Change, Women's Role and Status, and Development in Japan," in ESCAP (ed.), *Population Change, Women's Role and Status, and Development* (Bangkok: Economic and Social Commission for Asia and the Pacific).

——and Robert D. Retherford (1993*a*), "Care of the Elderly in Japan: Changing Norms and Expectations," *Journal of Marriage and the Family*, 55/3: 585–97.

————(1993*b*), "The Resumption of Fertility Decline in Japan: 1973–92," *Population and Development Review*, 19/4: 703–41.

Ogawa, Naohiro and Robert D. Retherford (1997), "Shifting Costs of Caring for the Elderly Back to Families in Japan," *Population and Development Review*, 23/1: 59–94.

——Takehiro Fukui, and Andrew Mason (1997), "Saving in Japan," Conference on Population and the Asian Economic Miracle, East–West Center, Honolulu, Jan. 7–10.

Retherford, Robert D., Naohiro Ogawa, and Rikiya Matsukura (1998), "Late Marriage and Less Marriage in Japan," mimeo (Honolulu: East–West Center).

————and Satomi Sakamoto (1996), "Values and Fertility Change in Japan," *Population Studies*, 50/1: 5–25.

Shimada, Haruo and Yoshio Higuchi (1985), "An Analysis of Trends in Female Labor Force Participation in Japan," *Journal of Labor Economics*, 3/2: 355–74.

Solow, Robert M. (1956), "A Contribution to the Theory of Economic Growth," *Quarterly Journal of Economics*, 70/1: 65–94.

Tobin, James (1967), "Life Cycle Saving and Balanced Economic Growth," in Fellner, William (ed.), *Ten Economic Studies in the Tradition of Irving Fisher* (New York: Wiley Press), 231–56.

Williamson, Jeffrey and Matthew Higgins (1997), "The Accumulation and Demography Connection in East Asia," Conference on Population and the Asian Economic Miracle, Honolulu, East–West Center, Jan. 7–10.

Yashiro, Naohiro and Akiko Sato Oishi (1997), "Population Aging and the Savings–Investment Balance in Japan," in Hurd, Michael D. and Naohiro Yashiro (eds.), *The Economic Effects of Aging in the United States and Japan* (Chicago: The University of Chicago Press), 59–83.

3 Will Japan's Current Account Turn to Deficit?

F. GERARD ADAMS AND BYRON GANGNES

1. Introduction

Japan's current account has been in surplus for many years. From a Japanese perspective, the surplus has provided market outlets for Japanese manufactures and high-tech products and has been the basis for capital flows into foreign investment. From the perspective of other industrial countries, the surplus has represented a source of cheap foreign savings, but has also created political pressure through job losses in import-competing sectors. The Japanese surplus has been attributed to the structure of the Japanese economy: its high savings rate, its promotion of exports of manufactures, and, until recently, its reluctance to accept imports.

While the relative size of Japan's surplus has fluctuated since the early 1980s, it has remained in surplus territory, with the broadest measure of trade balance, the current account, ranging from 1 per cent to more than 4 per cent of GDP (Figure 3.1). The surplus receded in the late 1980s, following the dollar collapse mid-decade and an investment boom in Japan. But it picked up again with the end of the bubble economy, and the subsequent economic recovery in the US (See the discussion in Adams and Gangnes, 1996.) Following the yen's appreciation from 1993 to 1995 and some moderate recovery of the Japanese economy in the mid-1990s, the surplus once more fell back toward near balance measured in yen, though the politically sensitive dollar merchandise trade surplus remained in the US$80 billion range. The surplus has risen again recently, as robust US growth has continued and Japan's economy has faltered. While the Asian crisis has hit Japanese exports to the East Asian region, the surplus is likely to widen further as a result of the deep Japanese downturn that began in 1998.

The threat of an ever-widening Japanese surplus might be a matter of economic and political concern but for several developments likely to bring about an eventual narrowing of the trade gap. In the medium term, economic recovery in Japan will eliminate a large cyclical component of the surplus. Over the longer term, structural change in Japan's economy—population aging, the globalization of production, and financial market reforms—will alter the underlying determinants of the surplus.

The future path of Japan's current account balance has implications for Japan's economy domestically, for international political economy and for global capital markets. For the domestic economy, a reduction in the current account surplus would negatively impact aggregate demand. The effects would likely differ across sectors. Changes in trade balances and the industrial mix would require potentially painful adjustments in industrial and labor markets. These effects of trade adjustment could generate political resistance in Japan not unlike what we observed in the US in the 1980s.

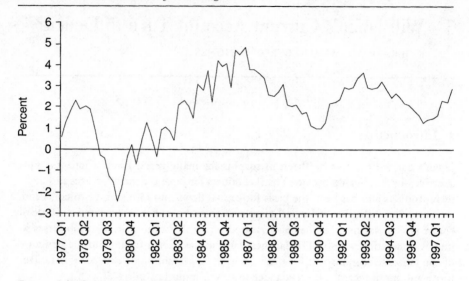

FIGURE 3.1. *Current account / GDP*
Sources: IMF, *International Financial Statistics*, data CD, and various issues.

From an international perspective, however, reduction of the Japanese trade surplus would ease political pressures. Arguments that the large surplus has enabled Japan to export its potential unemployment have served as a basis for imposing restrictions on Japanese exports in many markets. A decline in Japan's surplus trade balance would be welcomed by Japan's trading partners. On the other hand, Japan has recycled its trade surpluses as capital outflows to both the developed and developing world. A reduction in Japanese capital outflows would change the global savings–investment balance, probably raising world interest rates.

This paper looks at the prospects for Japanese current account balance adjustment in coming years. In Section 2, we describe the macroeconomic forces driving the trade surplus. We distinguish between the long-run structural surplus and short-run cyclical movements. In Section 3, we describe fundamental changes in Japan likely to influence the path of the trade balance in the first decades of the twenty-first century. Section 4 uses simulation analysis to study aspects of these changes and to assess their potential impact on the Japanese economy. We make concluding comments in Section 5.

2. The Macroeconomics of Japan's Current Account

We can learn something about the origin of the Japanese surplus and its future prospects by examining the surplus in the light of a simple conceptual model of the balance of payments. This model, incorporating both real and financial influences on the payments position, is useful for understanding medium-term current account adjustment and the determination of the long-run equilibrium path.[1]

The forces operating on the current account can be viewed from two perspectives, the trade perspective and the capital flow perspective. Abstracting from unilateral transfers, the current account equals the goods and services trade balance (NX) which reflects demand in the domestic economy (Y), foreign demand (Y_f), relative prices and the exchange rate ($P/P_f * XR$) acting on exports and imports:

$$NX = f(Y, Y_f, P/P_f * XR). \tag{1}$$

The long-term evolution of trade flows is driven by growth in incomes and changes in relative competitiveness, as well as any change in the propensity to import at home and abroad. Business cycle fluctuations in income and misalignments of the real exchange rate can exert strong influences on net exports in the medium run. In the Japanese case, import propensities have not been high, nor have trade flows been particularly sensitive to relative price or exchange rate movements. In part this reflects the strength of Japanese brands in export markets and, until recently, the difficulties of foreign producers in selling imported products in the Japanese market. Japanese firms have also tended to resist "passing through" to customers the effect of exchange rate appreciation, further limiting current account adjustment. (Marston, 1990; Knetter, 1993.)

From the capital flow perspective, the surplus on NX represents the supply of foreign exchange, which must equal net demand for foreign exchange, comprising capital outflows (CF) and changes in official reserves (dR):

$$NX = CF + dR. \tag{2}$$

Capital outflows (CF) represent net additions to holdings of foreign assets. The demand for these assets depends on the available flow of saving (the overall rate of asset accumulation) in the domestic economy (S) and the relative rates of return at home and abroad adjusted for the exchange rate and expectations about future exchange rate change (i, i_f, XR, dXR^e):

$$CF = f(S, i, i_f, XR, dXR^e) \tag{3}$$

Other factors that affect the desired asset mix may also affect net capital flows.[2] Strong demand for foreign assets can produce a capital outflow from the home country and therefore contribute to a current account surplus. This appears to be an important part of the story of the yen's relative weakness between 1995 and 1998. Japanese investors have displayed a continuing desire to accumulate foreign assets, driving down the value of the home currency and helping to generate a rising net export surplus.

---

[1] For recent discussions see McKibbin and Sachs (1991); McKibbin (1996); and Krugman (1998).

[2] This is essentially a portfolio balance story *à la* Kouri (1976) and Obstfeld (1981). We note that portfolio decisions involve stocks of assets rather than current saving, but changes in desired stocks imply flow savings adjustments. Expectations about the exchange rate are likely to reflect the relationship between current rates and long-term rates, perhaps PPP rates, as well as foreign exchange reserve positions.

The current account then depends on the interplay of international trade and competitiveness with underlying determinants of saving and asset allocation. The balance of payments relationships (1) through (3) are part of the broader macroeconomic system that includes domestic and foreign goods markets, financial relationships, and factor markets. In the absence of exchange rate intervention, equilibrium for the complete economic system entails the simultaneous determination of the remaining endogenous variables, including income, interest rates, exchange rates, and prices.

There are important differences in the macroeconomic adjustment process between the short run and the long run. In the short run, changes in the trade conditions, or in demand for foreign assets will impact the exchange rate and net exports. For example, an exogenously caused change in net exports will alter GDP and induce additional changes in savings and import demand. The current account both affects and is affected by business cycle conditions. In the long run, saving depends on intertemporal preferences for consumption relative to expected lifetime resources, as in the lifecycle model (Modigliani, 1966). Changes in international relative prices and interest rates will cause the excess of domestic saving over domestic investment at full employment to flow into international capital markets.[3] In this way, long-term trends in net savings imply a corresponding pattern for the current account balance (Razin, 1995; Obstfeld and Rogoff, 1996).

Intertemporal choice by Japanese residents may explain much of the persistent surpluses.[4] As is noted in Mason and Ogawa (Chapter 2 this volume), Japanese demographic characteristics and institutions have favored high private savings in the postwar period. Since the 1950s, the age composition of Japanese society has shifted dramatically toward the prime income-earning age groups and savings rates have risen. Current high savings rates, only a little below their 1980s peaks, may then reflect in part high levels of lifecycle savings by the postwar generation now in its peak earning years. Econometric models based on lifecycle consumption theory frequently find a significant negative savings effect from both youth and old age dependency ratios.[5] Further aging of the economy of course has implications for the future course of Japanese savings, an issue we will take up in Section 3. (For a wideranging discussion of factors behind Japan's high savings rate, also see Horioka, 1990.)

[3] Of, course the identity $(S - I) = CF = NX$ must always hold. But it is not possible simply to assume that S and I determine CF and NX unless one assumes an economy at full employment income. S is endogenously related to income. Given international competitiveness and demands for foreign assets, a decline in I could reduce Y and S leaving NX and CF unaffected. In the real world, adjustment is, however, also likely to involve relative prices, returns on investment, and the exchange rate.

[4] The importance of intertemporal behavior in Japan's current account experience is demonstrated by several historical episodes. Consistent with consumption-smoothing behavior, Japan's current account swung into deficit during the Russo-Japanese war 1904–5 and also at the time of the Tokyo earthquake in 1923. During the First World War boom, a period of high world interest rates, Japan switched from net international debtor to net creditor. (See Obstfeld and Rogoff, 1996.) We are indebted to an anonymous referee for this point.

[5] For a summary, see Heller and Symansky (1997). But not all studies support these conclusions; for example, see Bosworth (1993), and Adams and Prazmowski (1996). Higgins (1998), on the basis of a pooled cross-country analysis concludes that the shift in Japanese age distribution between the 1950s and the 1980s can account for a nearly 6 percentage point rise in the savings rate over this period.

The very fact that the Japanese economy was growing rapidly in the postwar period may explain high rates of savings. For most countries, the literature finds a tight link between rates of economic growth and rates of savings. (See, for example, Bosworth, 1993: 72; and Adams and Prazmowski, 1996.) In part, this may reflect the fact that rapidly growing populations have demographics that favor increased savings. But it may also reflect workers' desire to accumulate retirement wealth sufficient to support the higher living standards expected in the future, or simply an adjustment lag as households adapt to increased consumption opportunities. In any event, the implication is that slower growth in the future would mean lower saving.

Government saving or dissaving also has implications for Japan's balance of payments.[6] A number of writers have observed a link between government budget balances in the US and Japan and the emergence of large current account imbalances in the 1980s. (See, for example, Krugman and Obstfeld, 1997: 313, and Bergsten and Noland, 1993.) However, recent experience suggests a weaker link between government and national savings. There has already been a massive reversal of public sector saving in Japan, from surpluses in the 1980s and early 1990s to deficits running some 10 per cent of GDP at present. And further deficit financing is intended to boost the lagging Japanese economy. Still the current account surplus remains wide. Expectations of future tax liabilities may be encouraging higher private sector savings. No matter what one thinks of the doctrinaire Ricardian equivalence proposition, the Japanese government's on-again, off-again imposition of temporary tax cuts would make even the most spendthrift Japanese consumer cautious about spending all of the tax reductions.

Aside from these long-run considerations, cyclical factors have bolstered the Japanese surplus. Economic stagnation during the 1990s has limited the demand for all goods, including imports, raising the current account surplus above the level that would prevail at full employment. The yen's recent weakness may push the surplus up further, although this will be mitigated by weaker demand by Asian developing economies for Japanese exports.

An indication of the role of cyclical factors in the Japanese current account surplus can be obtained using a counterfactual simulation of recent Japanese macroeconomic experience. We have simulated a path for the Japanese economy during the period 1992–8, using the Japanese Long-term Model, described in greater detail in Section 4, below. The simulation imposes a flat path for the yen/dollar exchange rate at 128, its value in 1991, eliminating the appreciation/depreciation cycle over the period. Parallel adjustments were made against other currencies. Japanese private consumption was adjusted to maintain approximately a 3 per cent annual growth rate of real Gross National Expenditure (GNE), a much more rapid rate of growth than the 0.9 per cent actually experienced. The cyclically adjusted current account path is graphed alongside the actual path in Figure 3.2. Weak Japanese growth in the early 90s and a steadily appreciating currency contributed US$30 billion to US$40 billion to the

---

[6] We do not take into account here corporate savings, including allowances for capital consumption, though from a macroeconomic perspective these should also be considered. They may well be linked to the profitability and investment patterns of Japanese corporations.

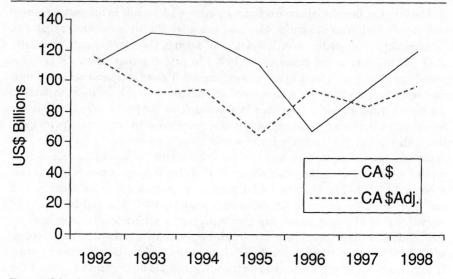

FIGURE 3.2. *Actual and cyclically adjusted Japanese current account*
Sources: IMF, *International Financial Statistics*, data CD, and authors' calculations.

current account balance in that period. This difference jumps in 1995 with the sharp transitory move to 85 yen/dollar. In 1996 the current account path was below its potential path because of the onetime growth surge associated with changes in Japanese consumption taxes. In 1998, about US$23 billion dollars (1 per cent of GNE) separates projected actual and cyclically adjusted paths.

Monetary and fiscal stabilization policy are critical considerations in influencing the business cycle path of the Japanese economy. The Japanese experience of the 1990s provides ample evidence of the importance of Keynesian views about the role of fiscal and monetary policy during recession (Krugman, 1998). Monetary policy has been driven to its limit, with extremely low interest rates—which at the same time make unlikely further monetary policy stimulus and reduce returns to assets in Japan, encouraging asset flows abroad.[7] Fiscal policy on the other hand, provided substantial stimulus in the mid-1990s, only to be turned off in 1997 by tax increases in a vain effort to balance the budget, with the anticipated negative effect on demand. Below we take a look at the role for policy in Japanese recovery by simulating the effects of fiscal stimulus to move the economy toward a full-employment growth path.

The discussion in this section leads us to draw the following conclusions about Japan's recent current account experience:

• The balance of payments surplus has reflected the continued competitiveness of Japanese manufactures in the world market and, perhaps, the difficulties encountered by competitors to introduce their products into Japan.

[7] Krugman (1998) returns to the traditional idea of the liquidity trap, and offers the controversial recommendation that Japan escape the trap by generating inflationary expectations.

- The persistence of the surplus reflects the large Japanese demand for foreign assets, a large volume of savings seeking opportunities for higher returns abroad. This strong foreign asset demand stems in part from lifecycle motives for high savings, and perhaps also the attractiveness of foreign investment opportunities.
- As a consequence, the equilibrium exchange rate has not adjusted to eliminate the current account surplus.
- The continued positive balance provides demand for products of the Japanese economy. On one hand, the surplus is the result of a depressed economy, on the other, the Japanese cyclical situation would be considerably worse but for the surplus.

3. The Future of Japan's Current Account Surplus

Many of the underpinnings of Japan's high rate of saving and current account surplus are likely to undergo substantial change over the next 10–25 years. Demographics that have favored rapid wealth accumulation will gradually be replaced by an aging population's need to draw down net savings. The structure of Japanese production and consumption is moving toward greater specialization on high-tech products and services and to increased reliance on imports of low- and medium-tech manufactures, perhaps raising Japan's overall import propensities. Deregulation of financial markets will eliminate many barriers to the free flow of international capital, with potential implications for the capital account. While there are considerable uncertainties, these changes are likely to produce a smaller, rather than larger, trade surplus.

3.1. The aging economy

The changes about which we know the most are the demographic ones. As has been discussed at length in Mason and Ogawa (Chapter 2 this volume), the aging process will accelerate in coming years, so that by 2025, 32 per cent of Japan's population will be over the age of 65, and the youth dependency ratio will fall to 19 per cent (United Nations, 1995).[8] While the process of change will be gradual, with only small changes perceptible during the next decade, these changes may ultimately have profound impacts.

3.1.1. A smaller labor force
A gradual decrease in the labor force is already under way as new entrants fail to replace those who leave it through death or retirement. In the short run, entries into the labor force are largely known, given the age distribution of the youth population. There remains uncertainty with respect to the length of time young people remain as students, the labor force participation of women, and immigration. Forecasting exits

---

[8] There has been considerable research on aging in Japan and other developed economics. See, for example, Hurd and Yashiro (1997), and Ermisch and Ogawa (1994).

from the labor force is more problematic because increased demand for labor and changes in retirement and pension policies may lengthen working life. On the other hand, the proportion of the elderly who work in Japan is unusually high, and recent trends have been toward earlier retirement.

The implications of a declining labor force translate into a tighter labor market, assuming there is no corresponding change on the demand side. In the short run, assuming a business cycle recovery, slower labor force growth means tighter labor market conditions and wage-cost pressures that may limit expansion and reduce Japan's international competitiveness. In the long run, the economy may adjust with rising wages relative to the return to capital. Slower labor force growth almost certainly means slower aggregate economic growth in Japan, although not a reduction in per capita growth.

3.1.2. Changes in aggregate saving and investment

A number of studies have projected the effect of aging on Japan's savings and investment. Because of differences in methodology and underlying assumptions, the studies give conflicting results (see Mason and Ogawa, Chapter 2 this volume; and Yashiro and Oishi, 1997). On the saving side, there are great difficulties in forecasting saving propensities in a world where more people are getting into the "high saving ages" before retirement, at the same time that more of them are retiring and living longer, a period of *dissaving*. There may also be changes in intergenerational family relationships or in public pension systems that affect retirement savings. The studies differ in their focus on private or national savings, and, in the case of the latter, their assumptions about fiscal policy. The consensus points to a likely reduction in the Japanese saving rate as the population ages.[9] This transformation is not unique to Japan, but its pace and extent are unusual. On this basis alone, one would expect the current account to narrow in coming years.

It is the balance of savings and investment that will determine the long-run evolution of Japan's current account. An older population and a declining labor force will favor less capital formation, because of lower demands for capital to equip new entrants to the work force. Also, fewer people will reach the age for family formation, reducing the demand for residential investment. On the other hand, increasing consumption propensities that accompany population aging may fuel a rise in investment spending, at least within the medium-term horizon of traditional macroeconomic forecasting. The net response of investment depends importantly on assumptions about how labor productivity will change with a declining labor force and the degree of international capital mobility, which affects the evolution of investment returns. (Yashiro and Oishi, 1997.)

---

[9] In addition to the discussion by Mason and Ogawa (Chapter 2 this volume) see, for example, Masson and Tryon (1990), and Higgins and Williamson (1996). Heller (1989) applies projections of demographic change to several published savings models and finds a reduction in private savings of 3 per cent to 12 per cent of GDP by 2010. Masson and Tryon (1990) predict a 3 per cent of GDP drop in national savings by 2010, similar to that of Wescott (1995). Higgins (1998) predicts a 6 per cent drop in savings by 2010 and greater than 9 per cent drop by 2025. Horioka (1993) estimates a greater than 15 per cent reduction in the private savings rate between 1990 and 2010, with private savings rates turning negative by some measures.

The consensus appears to favor a reduction in Japanese investment, but at a slower rate of decline than savings. Assuming a return to prosperity, the external balance will show smaller surpluses in coming decades.[10]

3.1.3. Change in the composition of expenditures

Changes in the composition of expenditures as the population ages may affect the industrial structure and trade, quite apart from changes in aggregate demand or the overall savings–investment balance. An older population spends its income on a higher proportion of personal and professional services (for example medical services, nursing-home care, and perhaps tourism and leisure activities) and a lower fraction of durable goods, which have presumably been accumulated at earlier stages of the life-cycle. This shift toward services almost certainly means a shift toward domestically produced goods and away from tradable goods, requiring significant structural adjustment of production to meet the new demands. In the case of Japan, an economy where labor is relatively scarce, a shift toward labor-intensive demand will aggravate labor market pressures. In addition, an aging society will make differing demands on government, requiring larger outlays for medical services and pensions, with reduced spending on education. (See Masson and Tryon, 1990; and Heller *et al.*, 1986.) These changes may ultimately have adverse impacts on aggregate growth as well as their sectoral effects.

3.2. Japan's changing relationship with Asia

The Japanese economy is closely tied to other East Asian economies, both as a supplier of capital and goods and services and as a purchaser. As East Asia has advanced up the "development ladder," this interaction has tended to expand and to change (Adams and Shachmurove, 1997). The ability of the developing Asian economies to produce high-quality consumer products at low cost has given them a competitive advantage in many product lines, beginning some years ago with processed foods and apparel and proceeding more recently to consumer electronics, automobiles, and other more sophisticated products. Japan has supplied parts and capital goods to the burgeoning industries of East Asia.

As an importer of East Asian products, Japan has lagged behind the United States and Western Europe, who have drawn increasing shares of their mass production

---

[10] Masson and Tryon (1990) predict a 1.8 per cent reduction in the investment-to-GDP ratio between 1995 and 2025, much smaller than a 4.3 per cent expected drop in savings. Noguchi (1990) sees much smaller declines in investment so that the current account rises in the 2000–10 period, before gradually declining after 2010. An Economic Planning Agency (1991) study sees relatively flat investment, but declining savings, so that current account balance turns to deficit soon after 2000. Yashiro and Oishi (1997) present scenarios with alternative assumptions regarding technological change and endogenous labor force participation, with the real current account declining to a deficit of −0.6 per cent to −2.8 per cent of GDP in the first decade of the twenty-first century. On the basis of an historical pooled cross-section model tying savings and investment to demographic change, Higgins (1998) predicts that investment will actually fall faster than savings, so that Japan's capital exports will increase by 2 per cent to 3 per cent of GDP over the next 25 years. Auerbach *et al.* (1989) predict a 2 per cent of GDP drop in the current account by 2010 and a shift to a 1.5 per cent negative current account by 2030.

consumer products from East Asia. In fact, Japanese consumption overall has been disproportionately served by domestic production, illustrated by the low Japanese import propensities compared with other developed economies (see Figure 3.3). Some evidence that this has begun to change can be seen in the upward trend in import propensities in the past decade and in the shift of imports from Asia to manufactured goods and high-tech capital goods. Japan is turning increasingly toward East Asia as a purchaser as well as a supplier.

Table 3.1 provides a rough breakdown of trade categories by resource intensity. Note that the labor- and land-intensive products may be best suited for countries at early stages of development. In turn, the high-tech category is clearly most appropriate for countries like Japan that lack land, labor, and other resources, but have physical and human capital. The composition of trade flows from and into Japan by principal sector in 1980 and in 1992 is then compared to comparable flows for Europe and the United States in Table 3.2. This table provides an indication of trends that may be anticipated to continue in the next decade.

Japanese imports and exports have changed in composition over the 1980 to 1992 time period. Imports in 1992 have a substantially higher content of mass-produced and high-tech products (the 5 and 6 categories) than in 1980. A similar change, of smaller dimension, is apparent in Japanese exports, which are predominantly in the high-tech category in 1992. Japan still lags far behind the United States and Europe

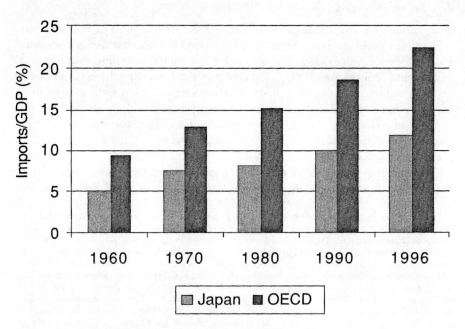

FIGURE 3.3. *Japan's import intensity compared with OECD total*
Source: OECD (1997), *National Accounts Statistics.*

TABLE 3.1. *Breakdown of trade by resource intensity*

Category	SITC	Resource intensity
1. Raw food	00–99	Land
2. Processed agricultural products	11–29, 41–43	Land, labor
3. Fuels	32–35	Natural resources
4. Industrial materials	51–59, 67–69	Natural resources, capital, labor
5. Mass-produced manufactures	61–66, 81–85	Labor, capital
6. High-tech goods	91–97, 81–89, 71–79	Capital, human capital

Source: Adams and Shachmurove (1997).

TABLE 3.2. *Sectoral breakdown of trade (per cent of total trade flow by trade category)*

	1	2	3	4	5	6	1	2	3	4	5	6
	1980						1992					
To Japan	9.9	18.2	50.1	8.4	4.4	9.0	14.4	13.6	23.0	12.9	12.7	23.3
To US	6.8	6.0	32.9	11.5	10.6	32.3	4.5	4.5	10.4	10.4	16.0	54.2
To Europe	9.0	5.1	8.1	22.5	15.4	39.8	8.9	4.5	3.1	20.2	15.6	47.6
	1980						1992					
From Japan	1.1	1.3	0.4	21.6	8.3	67.4	0.5	0.8	0.5	11.9	5.6	80.7
From US	6.8	6.0	32.9	11.5	10.6	32.3	4.5	4.0	10.5	10.5	16.1	54.4
From Europe	8.9	5.1	8.1	22.4	15.8	39.7	8.1	4.1	2.8	27.1	14.3	43.5

Source: Adams and Shachmurove (1997).

in its imports of high-tech goods, though it is catching up in imports of industrial materials and mass-production manufactures. In 1992, industrial materials and mass-production manufactures accounted for 25.6 per cent, 26.4 per cent, and 35.8 per cent of imports in Japan, the United States, and Europe, respectively; high-tech products account for 23.3 per cent, 54.2 per cent, and 43.5 per cent in the three regions.

It is likely that imports of industrial materials and mass-production manufactures will continue to increase over the next decade. This prediction reflects two parallel developments. First, Japanese producers are expected to continue to expand production of parts and intermediate materials in East Asia for shipment to their assembly operations in Japan. This shift from domestic industries toward foreign suppliers reflects shifting comparative advantage conditions in recent years, as Japan's production costs have risen relative to Asian developing economies. The current crisis in East Asia may accelerate this process by increasing the price competitiveness of offshore plants.[11] Second, Japanese inward foreign investment, which has been nearly negligible so far, is likely to increase (see Blomström, Konan, and Lipsey, Chapter 11 this volume). If patterns observed in other countries hold, foreign firms in Japan will rely heavily on intrafirm trade with the parent firm and its overseas subsidiaries. This will further raise Japanese imports of materials and manufactured products.

These changes will affect the total volume of imports as well as their composition. The sectoral, regional, and employment impacts are likely to be more severe than the effects on aggregate GDP and related measures of economic performance.[12] Industries like steel, auto parts, apparel, and small electronics are likely to be hurt. The workers displaced may not easily find alternative employment. Since these industries are concentrated geographically as well as sectorally, the burden of adjusting to these changes may be heavy in some localities.

3.3. Institutional change in financial markets and institutions

Important changes in Japan's financial markets and financial institutions are under way. The details of these changes and their implications are discussed by Ito and Melvin (Chapter 7 this volume).[13] At least in principle, the evolution in financial markets has the potential to affect Japan's external balance by changing domestic savings behavior and incentives for international capital flows. Because of the scope of ongoing changes and the complexity of likely economic responses to those changes, it is difficult to draw firm conclusions regarding their macroeconomic and balance of payments effect.

In 1996, the Japanese government announced the beginning of a comprehensive program of financial market reform, dubbed, as in the United Kingdom, "the Big Bang." The aim: to transform a highly restrictive, costly, and rule-bound financial system that had fallen behind technologically and operationally. The objective: to create in Tokyo a market that would be open, global, and competitive, to match markets operating in East Asia and, perhaps optimistically, in New York and London. The proposed steps remove regulatory barriers between various types of financial institutions and allow development of new financial products like derivatives which increase financial transparency. There are also proposals to remove restrictions on foreign exchange and on portfolio holdings, both domestic and foreign. Legally, all the requisite measures should be in place by 2001, but it is likely to take many years before they are fully operational. Moreover, they are coming at a time when the Japanese financial system is in great difficulty; that may complicate their implementation. (Taniuchi, 1997.)

Despite the likely delays, some measures are already in force, and some international financial companies have already drawn on them to expand their operations into the Japanese market. Viewing Japanese financial markets from a dynamic perspective,

---

[11] An important exception is China, which has not yet devalued its currency.
[12] Impacts on industrial structure in Japan are also discussed in Blomström, Konan, and Lipsey (Chapter 11 this volume).
[13] See also, Ministry of Finance (1997). An excellent evaluation is Dekle (1998).

over a span of many years, the Big Bang measures are likely to greatly intensify competition. The resulting shakeout can be expected to accelerate the pace of financial innovation, to improve economies of scale, and to reduce costs. Foreign financial institutions, whose expertise and experience far exceeds that of Japanese firms, are likely to be important beneficiaries (Dekle, 1998: 243).

Of particular importance to our discussion are the liberalization in the assets that may be held by pension funds, insurance companies and banks, and the amendment of the foreign exchange law to allow unrestricted holdings of foreign assets. The range of assets available to Japanese security holders will expand considerably, and it is highly likely that they will want to increase their holdings of foreign securities and accounts.

It is difficult, however, to pin down the macroeconomic impacts and balance of payments impacts. There are likely to be financial flows both in and out. Initially, Japanese financial markets will represent a target of opportunity for foreign financial enterprises, drawing a substantial capital investment into the market for a period of time. On the other hand, there is reason to expect net financial outflows. Security yields in Japan have been low by world standards and could go lower as competition and market efficiency increase. Diversification into high-return securities, many of them foreign, is likely to increase, and that will mean significant incentives for financial outflows at least until an equilibrium in asset holdings has been attained. On balance, this will mean outflows of capital, on top of the already large acquisition of foreign assets that is ongoing.

Will these changes increase aggregate saving? In view of the high personal savings rate that already prevails and because other considerations are likely to be more important, it is not likely that much higher saving rates will occur. More probably there will be diversion of funds from traditional domestic uses to mutual funds investing in equities at home and abroad. Ultimately some increase in Japanese interest rates—convergence to higher rates prevailing abroad—is likely, perhaps accompanied in the interim by a downward realignment of the yen.

While the impacts may not be large in terms of the macroeconomy, they may be very significant for sectoral development, for example for the financial sector and for development of capital-intensive, high-tech sectors. The financial sector is likely to expand greatly, with more active underwriting and trading, on the model of the effect of the Big Bang in London, though we have no illusions that Tokyo will rival London for many years to come. For sectors that require capital, interest rates may be higher, more in line with world standards, but there may be greater availability of funds for venture capital type enterprises. Greater financial market efficiency may raise productivity in important sectors of the economy.

4. How Japan Will Change: The Implications of Adjustment

The results of the previous section make clear that predicting the path of Japan's current account and its implications is far from simple. In the absence of other developments, the aging of Japan's population will lead to a decline in savings, which will likely exceed any fall in investment, and therefore reduce the surplus. But other developments may intervene, particularly the financial opening which may cause savings to flow abroad, presumably out of a smaller total. While the latter development may affect the value of the yen and the pace of trade adjustment, the consensus view clearly favors an eventual movement to a lower current account path. In this section we use simulation analysis to consider the implications for the Japanese economy of forces acting on the current account.[14]

The process of adjustment to a lower current account balance would involve changes at the macroeconomic level but also in the structure of the domestic economy. A surplus country moving toward balance experiences an increase in spending relative to income, and a shift of production from tradable to nontradable goods. The industry composition of output changes in response to changing total spending and relative prices, so that the leading industries for the surplus period may not be leading industries for a later period. These adjustments in economic structure need not be problematic with sufficiently flexible labor markets; resources would merely flow out of tradable and into nontradable goods. In reality, there are likely to be significant short-run economic dislocations associated with these adjustments.

4.1. Simulating the adjustment process

The simulation model employed in this analysis is the Japan Long-Term Model (JLM), an econometric model of the Japanese economy, developed by Shuntaro Shishido (Adams and Shishido, 1988; Adams, Gangnes and Shishido, 1993). The JLM model is a macroeconomic forecasting model with industrially disaggregated production, employment, and trade sectors. Such a model represents the economy on the computer in terms of, literally, thousands of interrelated behavioral, technical, and accounting relationships. It can be used to forecast and to evaluate macroeconomic adjustment. It also provides information on how the gains and burdens of adjustment are distributed among the various sectors of the economy. In other words, it provides a consistent picture of potential developments at the macro level and of their implications at the industry micro level. In many previous applications the JLM has been integrated into a world model system, Project LINK. But in the interest of clarity, for the present analysis the JLM is solved as a "stand alone" model with explicit assumptions about developments in the rest of the world.

A detailed exposition of the JLM model is beyond the scope of this paper. Here, we describe the model in general terms, with an emphasis on trade flows and adjustment (see the references above for more complete presentations). Structurally, the

---

[14] An issue beyond the scope of the present analysis is the effect of smaller Japanese current account balance on the global savings–investment balance. Japan has been the single largest provider of net capital to the global economy in recent years, and an end to this supply may raise world interest rates and retard global investment and growth. Whether or not a global savings shortage emerges depends on changes in savings supply from other countries. On this, the evidence is not yet clearly set. See Wescott (1995) and Higgins (1998) for optimistic appraisals and Heller and Symansky (1997) for a more sober assessment.

macro core of the JLM model combines Keynesian-type expenditure relationships and a Leontief interindustry system with important supply-side constraints. In the short-run, equilibrium is largely demand-determined. Demand, including net exports, determines production levels in each industry and the employment needed to produce this output. Labor market conditions determine wage growth, which together with excess demand conditions drives price inflation. Income growth feeds back to affect final demand, while wage and price changes influence final demand, production costs, and employment growth.

Over the longer term, the dynamics of the model are driven by capital accumulation and population growth. A demographic model determines the evolution of population and the labor force. Investment, determined in part by endogenous technical progress, generates capital accumulation and resulting changes in productive capacity. The monetary and fiscal sectors of the economy are fully modeled. With regard to the balance of payments, exports and imports are modeled at the industry level as functions of income and international competitiveness. As we have noted, net trade quantities directly affect demand for industry output. Import prices affect industry input costs. Aggregation of trade prices and quantities produces aggregate values for the trade balance and also affects other key macroeconomic variables.

Trade adjustment in the model comes about through changes in absorption and relative prices acting on the import and export equations. The sources of such change range from direct movements in income under a fiscal expansion to relative price changes associated with exchange rate realignment or changes in domestic inflation. Income and price elasticities influence the extent of adjustment, as do the multiplier properties of the model and the nature of interindustry linkages. Japanese export price equations incorporate varying degrees of pricing-to-market behavior when exchange rates change, limiting the extent of actual relative price movement. Changes in national price levels also create real money balance and wealth effects that further effect absorption and trade balance adjustment.

We evaluate the impact of policy changes and developments using forecast simulations of the JLM model. The simulation analysis is conducted by first establishing a baseline forecast for the period 1999–2005, assuming no significant changes in policy or the economic environment. The model is then re-solved with one or more changes in exogenous assumptions. Simulation results can then be compared to the baseline forecast path.

There are important limitations to the model and to this analysis. In this model, as in many macro systems, the current account is determined by trade response. There is no explicit modeling of the capital account or of its impact on the exchange rate. In other words, the model does not contain the asset demand/portfolio balance features of capital flow determination that we have noted above. The effects of capital flows on exchange rates must be handled through appropriate assumptions, and corresponding exchange rate adjustments must be made. The fiscal and monetary policy posture also requires judgmental adjustment. There are, moreover, no automatic mechanisms to enforce current account sustainability, absent appropriate assumptions by the modeler. To achieve a realistic picture of real world developments, great care must be taken to assure that structural changes that are handled by the model are matched by appropriate judgmental adjustments of nonmodeled variables.

4.2. Baseline forecast path

We begin by establishing a baseline simulation path for the Japanese economy for the period through 2005. This forecast path is determined by solving the model forward given recent history and reasonable assumptions about various exogenous influences, including demographic change and the external trade environment. The medium-term horizon reported here permits discussion of medium-run macroeconomic adjustments and allows us to anticipate fundamental changes that may not be fully felt for some time.

Macroeconomic policy assumptions have an important impact on the baseline. In fact, we found that in the absence of significant ongoing macro stimulus the forecast path for the economy would be very anemic. This is not surprising considering the economy's extraordinary recent weakness. However, we do not consider this a realistic scenario. As the string of 1990s fiscal packages makes clear, the government is likely to provide additional fiscal and perhaps monetary expansion as needed to buoy the economy. Following the spirit of recent proposals, we assume a package of personal tax cuts and government investment spending beginning in 1999. These policies amount to a net fiscal stimulus of 6 trillion yen in 1999 and about 10 trillion yen each year thereafter, or roughly 2 per cent of GNE per year. They are sufficient to restore 2.1 per cent growth in 2000, and to pull the unemployment rate down to the 3.8 per cent range by 2001. This is still weak performance by historical standards; the unemployment rate remains above 3 per cent until the final year of the forecast horizon. The government deficit increases by a cumulative 12 per cent of GNE over the period.

A summary of the baseline forecast is given in Table 3.3. The forecast path for the current account shows continued widening of the surplus, both in dollar terms and

TABLE 3.3. *Baseline forecast with fiscal stimulus*

	1998	1999	2000	2001	2002	2003	2004	2005
Real GNE (Growth rate, %)	−2.7	−0.2	2.1	2.5	2.5	2.9	3.1	2.8
Consumer prices (Growth rate)	0.6	0.2	0.9	1.6	1.1	1.0	1.5	2.2
Population (Growth rate)	0.3	0.3	0.3	0.3	0.2	0.3	0.3	0.1
Employment (Growth rate)	−0.8	−0.4	0.4	0.7	0.7	0.8	1.0	1.1
Unemployment rate (%)	4.1	4.6	4.3	3.8	3.9	3.7	3.3	3.0
Real exports (Growth rate)	−2.3	2.0	3.9	3.9	4.0	3.8	3.8	4.0
Real imports (Growth rate)	−8.0	1.4	2.0	2.4	2.7	3.6	4.6	5.1
CA/GNE ratio (%)	3.0	3.2	3.2	3.4	3.4	3.4	3.5	3.5
Current account ($ bn.)	119.2	134.6	143.3	155.8	165.3	176	190.6	200
Yen/dollar exchange rate	130.1	120.0	118.2	116.4	114.7	113.0	111.3	109.6

Note: 1998 figures are approximately historical data; 1999–2005 are forecasts.

as a share of GNE. This stems from relatively weak import demand compared with the assumed growth in real exports. Notice that this import weakness occurs despite an assumed gradual appreciation of the yen against the dollar during the period. This then sets the stage for a consideration of alternative scenarios that may involve adjustment to a smaller current account surplus.

4.3. Current account adjustment scenarios

We consider in turn scenarios to explore macroeconomic and current account implications of three potential developments discussed above: an increasing reliance on imported manufactures, particularly from Asia, the aging of Japan's population, and the effects of increased financial liberalization. In each case, an attempt is made to create a realistic scenario that can provide meaningful qualitative information about how adjustment might proceed, both at the macro level and at the level of individual sectors. By their nature such scenarios are speculative and involve somewhat arbitrary assumptions, and so should not be taken as giving specific forecasts of the actual Japanese adjustment path. In each case, the scenario takes the baseline forecast as a starting point and then assumes one or more changes in important driving influences. The model is re-solved and the results can be compared to the baseline path.

4.3.1. Increased imports of manufactured goods and materials

To capture aspects of the expected increase in Japanese reliance on Asian countries for manufactured goods production, we simulate an increase in Japanese manufacturing imports. Compared to the baseline forecast, we assume a higher rate of growth of Japanese imports of high-tech equipment, and to a lesser extent also industrial materials and mass-produced "low-tech" manufactures. These changes move Japanese import patterns closer to those prevailing in the US and Europe, as described in Section 3.2, above. In fact, the more rapid import growth in these sectors is sufficient to raise Japan's high-tech import share by 5 percentage points and other manufactures by 2 to 3 percentage points. Overall, the import adjustment amounts to about 7 per cent of aggregate imports by the end of the forecast period. Net increases for individual industries vary because of endogenous response to changing income and price conditions.

As shown in Table 3.4, the rise in imports reduces the current account-to-GNE ratio to 2.5 per cent, compared with its rise to 3.5 per cent in the baseline. The dollar current account falls below US$140 billion, a reduction of more than US$60 billion from the original baseline. To the extent that increased imports compete with domestic production, economic activity in Japan will suffer, at least during the short run. We see this in the simulation as a reduction of the GNE growth rate by 0.5 per cent to 0.7 per cent per year. Consumer prices rise a bit less rapidly as a result.

The potential adjustment challenge from increased reliance on imports can also be seen in the industry-level effects of Table 3.5. Here we show changes in real gross output for the same broad groups of industries identified in Section 3.2. The figures given are differences in output levels compared with baseline forecast levels. Notice

TABLE 3.4. *Increased imports of manufactured goods*

	2000	2001	2002	2003	2004	2005
Real GNE (Growth rate, %)	1.6	1.9	1.8	2.2	2.4	2.0
Cumulative difference from baseline	*−0.5*	*−1.1*	*−1.8*	*−2.4*	*−3.0*	*−3.8*
Consumer prices (Growth rate)	0.9	1.6	0.9	0.8	1.2	1.7
Real exports (Growth rate)	3.9	3.9	4.0	4.0	3.9	4.2
Real imports (Growth rate)	3.1	3.4	3.8	4.7	5.7	6.4
CA/GNE ratio (%)	3.1	3.0	2.9	2.8	2.7	2.5
Difference from baseline	*−0.2*	*−0.3*	*−0.5*	*−0.6*	*−0.8*	*−1.0*
Current account ($ bn.)	135.7	139.7	139.9	140.2	142.9	136.2
Difference from baseline	*−7.6*	*−16.2*	*−25.3*	*−35.8*	*−47.7*	*−63.7*

TABLE 3.5. *Increased imports of manufactured goods: resulting changes in real gross industry output (% difference from baseline)*

	2000	2001	2002	2003	2004	2005
Raw food and agricultural products	−0.2	−0.5	−0.8	−1.1	−1.5	−2.0
Processed foods and agricultural products	−0.1	−0.3	−0.4	−0.6	−0.8	−1.0
Fuels and products	−0.1	−0.4	−0.8	−1.3	−1.8	−2.5
Industrial materials	−0.4	−1.2	−1.9	−2.5	−3.1	−3.8
Mass-produced manufactures	−1.2	−2.6	−4.0	−5.3	−6.6	−8.2
High-tech goods	−0.8	−1.9	−2.8	−3.7	−4.5	−5.5
Services	−0.4	−1.0	−1.6	−2.1	−2.7	−3.4

that output declines relative to the initial baseline in all sectors of the economy, because of the recessionary impact of increased imports. But output contraction is centered in the manufactured goods sectors themselves, particularly in mass-produced goods, where significant percentage increases are assumed on a large initial import base. Nonmanufactured goods sectors and services fall relatively less. This implies substantial negative employment effects in manufacturing, and therefore the potential for severe labor market dislocation in regions that are heavily dependent on manufacturing industries.

4.3.2. Population decline and aging

In this simulation we evaluate the likely effects of changing Japanese demographics. The demographic issue becomes important over a longer time horizon than we are working with here. Nevertheless, we can gain insight into how these changes will influence the economy by simulating a decline in the population and a corresponding reduction in the savings rate. Population is assumed to decline at an annual rate of

TABLE 3.6. *Japanese population decline and reduction in savings rate*

	1999	2000	2001	2002	2003	2004	2005
Real GNE (Growth rate, %)	−0.3	3.2	3.8	3.6	3.9	4.2	2.8
Cumulative difference from baseline	*0.0*	*1.1*	*2.3*	*3.4*	*4.4*	*5.5*	*5.5*
Consumer prices (Growth rate)	0.4	1.4	3.0	2.6	2.2	2.8	4.1
Population (Growth rate)	−0.2	−0.2	−0.2	−0.3	−0.2	−0.2	−0.3
Employment (Growth rate)	−0.4	0.4	0.8	0.8	1.0	1.1	1.1
Unemployment rate (%)	4.2	3.5	2.7	2.8	2.9	2.5	2.1
Real exports (Growth rate)	1.9	3.7	3.4	3.3	3.3	3.3	3.4
Real imports (Growth rate)	1.5	3.1	4.0	4.1	4.8	6.2	5.9
CA/GNE ratio (%)	3.1	3.0	2.9	2.7	2.5	2.3	2.1
Difference from baseline	*0.0*	*−0.2*	*−0.5*	*−0.7*	*−1.0*	*−1.2*	*−1.4*
Current account ($ bn.)	134.4	137.2	141.2	140.7	140.5	141.9	140.5
Difference from baseline	*−0.2*	*−6.1*	*−14.6*	*−24.6*	*−35.6*	*−48.7*	*−59.4*
HH savings rate (difference from baseline, %)	*0.0*	*−0.2*	*−0.5*	*−1.1*	*−1.9*	*−2.6*	*−3.0*

0.2 per cent to 0.3 per cent per year over the forecast horizon. Consistent with an aging population, the ratio of savings to GNE falls by about 3 percentage points.[15]

The macroeconomic effect of these demographic changes is summarized in Table 3.6. The shift from savings to increased consumption provides a substantial demand-side stimulus to the economy. The extraordinarily high rate of saving that lies behind the sluggishness of the Japanese economy and its foreign surplus is reduced as older people draw on assets to meet consumption needs. Real gross national expenditure grows roughly 1 per cent faster than in the baseline forecast, and the unemployment rate falls to 2.1 per cent by the end of the simulation period. Growth is actually held back by supply-side constraints, lower labor force growth and increasingly severe labor market tightness. The combination of rising labor demand and falling population drives wages up by a cumulative 20 per cent after seven years (not shown). Consumer prices accelerate as well. Higher product prices in turn reduce Japanese international competitiveness that, along with stronger domestic demand, stimulates imports and restrains exports. The current account falls by 1.4 per cent of GNE over the simulation period, or US$60 billion compared with the baseline.

Clearly rapid population aging has the potential to substantially alter Japan's savings–investment balance and therefore its current account. The implied industrial restructuring that accompanies this current account turnaround would be greater than this simulation suggests, once one allows for the changing expenditure patterns that

---

[15] The assumed decline in savings propensity (and rise in consumption propensity) is consistent with previous estimates of the effects of aging on savings behavior. Masson and Tryon (1990) report that the effect of a 1 per cent rise in the elderly dependency ratio is to reduce the private savings rate by 0.5 per cent to 1.6 per cent in a group of well-known studies. The elderly dependency ratio is projected to fall by 3 percentage points between 2000 and 2005, so that a 3 per cent fall in the savings rate is near the middle of the range of estimates.

will result as an aging population shifts increasingly toward services and away from durable goods.

4.3.3. Financial liberalization

As we indicated above, it is difficult to anticipate the effects of Japanese financial market liberalization on the direction of financial flows and adjustments in exchange rates and other macroeconomic variables. Some aspects of ongoing and planned liberalization may facilitate capital outflows; others may permit domestic financial institutions to provide saving vehicles that are more competitive with those in the West, keeping more of Japan's saved resources at home. In the medium run, the former is perhaps the more likely scenario. Here we simulate the effect of capital outflows that might follow a complete liberalization of Japanese outward financial flows (see Table 3.7). The outflows are assumed to drive Japanese interest rates up to levels prevailing in the US, an increase in the bank lending rate of 250 basis points.

The yen can be expected to depreciate in response to increased capital outflows. We assume that the long-run exchange value of the yen falls by 5 per cent against the dollar. Because the closing of the interest rate gap takes several years, the yen overshoots moderately in the short run.

The impact effect of these changes on aggregate economic activity is approximately neutral. Investment begins to decline, but the yen's depreciation significantly stimulates export sales. The current account surplus increases in the short term. Once the interest rate increase is fully in effect, the investment contraction becomes very severe; business fixed investment falls 20 per cent below baseline levels after four years, reducing the level of real gross national expenditure 6 per cent below the baseline.

TABLE 3.7. *Japanese capital outflows*

	2000	2001	2002	2003	2004	2005
Real GNE (Growth rate, %)	1.5	2.8	−0.7	1.3	2.1	2.4
Cumulative difference from baseline	*−0.6*	*−0.3*	*−3.4*	*−4.9*	*−5.8*	*−6.1*
Bank lending rate (%)	3.1	4.0	5.1	5.1	5.1	5.1
Difference from baseline (ppts.)	*0.75*	*1.50*	*2.50*	*2.50*	*2.50*	*2.50*
Business investment (difference from baseline, %)	*−3.6*	*−8.1*	*−15.0*	*−19.8*	*−21.5*	*−21.6*
Real exports (Growth rate)	6.1	7.8	−0.3	3.5	3.2	3.6
Difference from baseline (%)	*2.2*	*6.0*	*1.7*	*1.4*	*0.8*	*0.4*
Real imports (Growth rate)	2.1	2.1	1.6	2.6	4.6	4.6
Difference from baseline (%)	*0.1*	*−0.3*	*−1.3*	*−2.2*	*−2.3*	*−2.7*
CA/GNE ratio (%)	3.0	3.9	3.5	3.6	3.6	3.7
Current account ($ bn.)	123.2	174.0	162.7	172.5	181.0	196.3
Yen/dollar exchange rate	126.0	123.1	120.5	118.7	116.9	115.1
Difference from baseline (%)	*6.6*	*5.7*	*5.0*	*5.0*	*5.0*	*5.0*

The export boom is eventually crowded out as higher interest rates raise prices throughout the Japanese economy and eliminate the competitive gains from depreciation. Falling income reduces import demand nearly 3 per cent over the course of the forecast, offsetting partly the yen's valuation effects that tend to raise the dollar cost of given import volumes. Overall, the simulation illustrates well the potential complexity of current account forecasting, with the trade balance moving first up, then down, and finishing not substantially different from its baseline level of US$200 billion dollars in 2005.

5. Conclusions

In this paper, we have examined the sources of Japan's continuing trade surpluses and the forces that will act on the surplus in coming years. Aspects of Japan's recent history may explain the country's tendency toward trade surplus. These include a population concentrated in the middle-age years, Japan's high rate of economic growth, cycles of government tax and expenditure policies, and institutional factors that favor exports over imports and capital outflows. Currently, Japan's surplus is augmented somewhat by the economy's unprecedented weakness. Slow growth and a yen appreciation cycle in the 1990s can account for perhaps a third of Japan's current surplus.

In the twenty-first century, anticipated change in these forces can be expected to reduce Japan's trade surplus. An aging economy will generate less need for savings and, consequently, relatively more consumption, probably for a mix of products with more services and fewer manufactures. The consensus in the literature favors a reduction in Japanese net savings, although the bulk of these effects may not be felt for many years. Changes in Japan's relationship with Asian economies and the substantial changes in domestic financial markets will also affect aggregate trade and capital flows, as well as the composition of such flows.

The current account surplus has represented a source of aggregate demand for Japanese produced goods. A reduction of the surplus would negatively impact demand and output in the medium term. At the same time, Japanese consumers are expected to buy more and save less as they age into the retirement years, perhaps offsetting part of any aggregate demand shortfall. It will be important for Japan to maintain an appropriate macro policy stance to sustain full employment during the period of adjustment to a lower current account balance.

While fiscal and monetary policy can offset adverse macroeconomic effects of current account adjustment, these aggregate economic impacts represent only a part of the story. Adjustment to a smaller (or even negative) trade balance has potentially profound implications for the structure of Japanese industry and employment. Shifts at the sectoral level—between domestic tradable and nontradable goods, between manufactured goods and services—are likely to be an economically costly and socially painful feature of the anticipated readjustment of the Japanese economy.

Just as Japan's emerging surpluses were observed with keen interest (and not a little fear) by other countries during the 1980s, their eventual reduction will be of great potential importance to the global economy. A reduction in the large surplus could bring welcome relief from protectionist political pressure in the US and Europe. However, similar voices of protest may emerge in Japan as the social consequences of industrial restructuring become apparent.

REFERENCES

Adams, F. G. and B. Gangnes (1996), "Japan's Persistent Trade Surplus: Policies for Adjustment," *Japan and the World Economy*, 8: 309–33.
——and P. Prazmowski (1996), "Why Are Saving Rates in East Asia So High? Reviving the Life Cycle Hypothesis," Department of Economics Discussion Paper, University of Pennsylvania.
——and S. Shishido (1988), *Structure of Trade and Industry in the U.S.–Japan Economy*, NIRA Research Output, NRS-85-1 (Tokyo: NIRA), Feb.
——and Y. Shachmurove (1997), "Trade and Development Patterns in the East Asian Economies," *Asian Economic Journal*, 11/4 (Dec.), 345–60.
——B. Gangnes, and S. Shishido (1993), *Economic Activity, Trade and Industry in the U.S.–Japan-world Economy: A Macro Model Study of Economic Interactions* (Westport, Conn.: Praeger Publishers).
Auerbach, Alan, L. Kotlikoff, R. P. Hagemann, and G. Nicoletti (1989), "The Economic Dyanamics of an Aging Population: The Case of Four OECD Countries," *OECD Economic Studies*, 12 (Spring).
Bergsten, C. Fred and Marcus Noland (1993), "The Macroeconomic Context, Chapter 2", in *Reconcilable Differences? The United States–Japan Economic Conflict* (Washington: Institute for International Economics).
Bosworth, Barry (1993), *Savings and Investment in a Global Economy* (Washington: The Brookings Institution).
Dekle, Robert (1998), "The Japanese 'Big Bang' Financial Reform and Market Implications," *Journal of Asian Economics*, 9/2: 237–49.
Economic Planning Agency (1991), *2010 Nen no Sangyo Keizai* (Simulation of the industry and economy in 2010) (Tokyo: Government Printing Office) (cited in Yashiro and Oishi, 1997).
Ermisch, John and Naohiro Ogawa (eds.) (1994), *The Family, the Market, and the State in Aging Societies* (Oxford: Clarendon Press).
Heller, Peter (1989), "Aging, Savings, and Pensions in the Group of Seven Countries: 1980–2025," *Journal of Public Policy*, 9/2: 127–53.
——and Steve Symansky (1997), "Implications for Savings of Aging in the Asian 'Tigers'," International Monetary Fund Working Paper No. Wp/97/136 (Oct.).
——Richard Hemming, and Peter W. Kohnert, with a staff team from the Fiscal Affairs Department (1986), "Aging and Social Expenditure in the Major Industrial Countries, 1980–2025," IMF Occasional Paper 47 (Sept.).
Higgins, Matthew (1998), "Demography, National Savings, and Intergenerational Capital Flows," *International Economic Review*, 39/2 (May).

——and Jeffrey G. Williamson (1996), "Asian Demography and Foreign Capital Dependence," NBER Working Paper No. 5560 (May).

Horioka, Charles (1990), "Why is Japan's Household Saving Rate so High?" *Journal of the Japanese and International Economics*, (March).

——(1993), "Future Trends in Japan's Saving Rate and the Implications Thereof for Japan's External Imbalance," ch. 18 in Klein, L. R. (ed.), *A Quest for a More Stable Economic System: Restructuring at a Time of Cyclical Adjustment* (Boston: Kluwer Academic Press).

Hurd, Michael D. and Naohiro Yashiro (1997), *Effects of Aging in the United States and Japan* (Chicago: University of Chicago Press).

International Monetary Fund, *International Financial Statistics* (various issues and Data CD).

Knetter, M. M. (1993), "International Comparisons of Pricing-to-Market Behavior," *American Economic Review*, 83: 473–86.

Kouri, P. (1976), "The Exchange Rate and the Balance of Payments in the Short Run and the Long Run: A Monetary Approach," *Scandinavian Journal of Economics*, 78: 280–306.

Krugman, P. (1998), "It's Baaack: Japan's Slump and the Return of the Liquidity Trap," *Brookings Papers on Economic Activity*, 2: 137–87.

——and M. Obstfeld (1997), *International Economics: Theory and Policy*, 4th edn. (Reading, Mass: Addison-Wesley).

Maddison, Angus (1992), "A Long-Run Perspective of Savings," *Scandinavian Journal of Economcis*, 94/2: 181–96.

Marston, Richard C. (1990), "Pricing to Market in Japanese Manufactures," *Journal of International Economics*, 29/3–4 (Nov.), 217–36.

Masson, Paul R. and Ralph W. Tryon (1990), "Macroeconomic Effects of Projected Population Aging in Industrial Countries," *IMF Staff Papers*, 37/3 (Sept.), 453–85.

McKibbin, Warwick J. (1996), "The Macroeconomic Experience of Japan Since 1990: An Empirical Investigation," mimeo, Research School of Pacific and Asian Studies, Australian National University, Nov.

——and Jeffrey D. Sachs (1991), *Global Linkages: Macroeconomic Interdependence and Cooperation in the World Economy* (Washington: The Brookings Institution).

Ministry of Finance, Japan (1997), "About the Financial System Reform," MOF web site, http://www.mof.gov.jp, July 13.

Modigliani, Franco (1966), "The Life Cycle Hypothesis of Saving, the Demand for Wealth and the Supply of Capital," *Social Research*, 33/2.

Noguchi, Yukio (1990), "The Age Structure of the Population and Saving/Investment: An Analysis Based on Cross-Country Comparison," Ministry of Finance, *Financial Review*, 17 (cited in Yashiro and Oishi, 1997).

Obstfeld, M. (1981), "Macroeconomic Policy, Exchange-Rate Dynamics, and Optimal Asset Accumulation," *Journal of Political Economy*, 89/6: 1142–61.

——and K. Rogoff (1996), *Foundations of International Macroeconomics* (Cambridge, Mass.: MIT Press).

Razin, A. (1995), "The Dynamic Optimizing Approach to the Current Account: Theory and Evidence," in Kenen, P. B. (ed.), *Understanding Interdependence: The Macroeconomic of the Open Economy* (Princeton: Princeton University Press).

Taniuchi, M. (1997), "Recent Developments in Japan's Financial Sector: Bad Loans and Financial Deregulation," *Journal of Asian Economics*, 8/2: 225–44.

United Nations (1995), *World Population Prospects 1950–2050: The 1994 Revision*, Department of Economic and Social Information and Policy Analysis, Population Division (New York: UN).

Wescott, Robert F. (1995), "Prospects for World Savings," in Ichimura, S. and F. G. Adams (eds.), *The East Asian Development Pattern: Forecasts to the Year 2010*, International Center for the Study of East Asian Development, Japan.

Yashiro, Naohiro and Akiko Sato Oishi (1997), "Population Aging and the Savings Investment Balance," in Hurd, M. D. and N. Yashiro (eds.), *Effects of Aging in the United States and Japan* (Chicago: Chicago University Press).

4 Japan's Public Pension System in the Twenty-first Century

CHARLES YUJI HORIOKA

1. Introduction

Japan's public pension system is essentially a pay-as-you-go system that is fraught with problems. It has an adverse impact on the inter- and intragenerational allocation of resources, on the labor supply of the aged and of women, and on national saving, and it implicitly condones the widespread evasion of pension contributions. Moreover, many of these problems can be expected to become even more serious as the aging of the population proceeds at an accelerating pace. The United States, Germany, and many other developed countries not only have pay-as-you-go public pension systems that are very similar to Japan's but also face very similar demographic trends. Thus, the Japanese experience with, and the Japanese debate about, pension reform are of great potential value to policymakers in these countries, especially since the problems with Japan's public pension system are in many ways more serious and the aging of the population is proceeding much faster than in other countries.

In this chapter, I discuss the current structure of Japan's public pension system (Section 2); the history of that system (Section 3); the *raison d'être* of a public pension system (Section 4); some of the defects with the current system (Section 5); the origins of those defects (Section 6); possible ways of alleviating those defects (Section 7); future prospects for Japan's public pension system in the face of rapid population aging (Section 8); and two proposals for reforming Japan's public pension system (Section 9).

2. The Current Structure of Japan's Public Pension System

In this section, I briefly describe the current structure of Japan's public pension system.[1] (See Kōsei Tōkei Kyōkai (1996); and Takayama (1996) for more details.) Japan's public pension system is currently a two-tiered system consisting of a universal pension—the National Pension (Kokumin Nenkin) or Basic Pension (Kiso

The author is grateful to Yoshibumi Asō, Yoshio Higuchi, Fumio Ohtake, Noriyuki Takayama, Midori Wakabayashi, participants of the Conferences on "Japan's Economy in the Twenty-first Century: The Response to Crisis," held at the Stockholm School of Economics, Stockholm, Sweden, on June 14–16, 1998, and in Honolulu, on January 7–8, 1999, the editors of this volume, and especially, to Tatsuo Hatta, for their helpful comments and discussions.

[1] I focus primarily on old-age pensions even though disability, survivors', and welfare pensions are also available.

Nenkin), and five second-tier pension programs for salaried workers—the Employees' Pension (Kōsei Nenkin) and four types of Mutual Aid Pensions (Kyōsai Nenkin). Those other than salaried workers (the self-employed, farmers, those not working, and students) belong only to the National Pension system. They pay a flat-rate monthly contribution between the ages of 20 and 59 and begin receiving a flat-rate monthly pension, the Basic Pension, starting at age 65.[2] Beginning with the fiscal year ending March 31, 1999, the monthly contribution rate has been 13,300 yen, and the basic pension has been about 67,000 yen for those contributing for the maximum period.[3] Spouses of salaried workers are exempt from paying monthly contributions if their annual income is below a certain level (currently 1,300,000 yen), as are certain other groups such as the handicapped and the low-income.

Salaried workers belong to both the National Pension system and to one of the five second-tier pension systems. Most private-sector workers belong to the Employees' Pension system, while national government employees, local government employees, employees of private schools, and employees of agricultural, forestry, and fishery organizations belong to one of the four Mutual Aid Pension systems. Workers belonging to these systems pay pension contributions equal to a certain percentage (17.35 per cent since October 1996 in the case of the Employees' Pension) of their monthly salary until age 59, with the burden being shared equally by employer and employee. They receive a two-tiered benefit—the basic pension plus an earnings-related component (30 per cent of average monthly real earnings for those contributing for the maximum period in the case of the Employees' Pension)—starting at age 60. This is five years earlier than in the case of those other than salaried workers.[4] According to Takayama (1996), the total benefits of a typical salaried worker with a nonworking spouse amount to about 68 per cent (80 per cent) of the average pretax (after-tax) monthly earnings of males who are currently working in the case of the Employees' Pension. Once lump sum bonuses are taken into account, however, the benefits picture changes somewhat. Salaried workers in Japan receive large bonuses two to three times a year, and these bonuses amount to four to five times one's monthly salary in the case of employees of large corporations. Public pension benefits replace only about 51 per cent (60 per cent) of pretax (after-tax) annual earnings *inclusive of bonuses* in the case of the Employees' Pension.

Japan's public pension system is essentially a pay-as-you-go system, with the benefits of current retirees being financed primarily by the contributions of current workers. Subsidies from the general accounts of the central government finance one-third of the base pension as well as administrative expenses, but the government does not subsidize the earnings-related component of benefits. Finally, with respect

---

[2] Those aged 60 to 69 and Japanese nationals living abroad are also eligible to enroll in the National Pension System on a voluntary basis. Those other than salaried workers ordinarily do not receive any earnings-related benefits, but since 1991 they can pay additional contributions and receive additional benefits under the National Pension Fund (Kokumin Nenkin Kikin) system.

[3] The yen–dollar exchange rate was about 110 yen/dollar as of late February 2000.

[4] Since 1966, large corporations can partially contract out of the earnings-related component of benefits by setting up a private fund called an Employees' Pension Fund (Kōsei Nenkin Kikin), but to do so, they must pay benefits that are at least 30 per cent higher than in the case of the Employees' Pension.

to the tax treatment of public pensions, employer and employee contributions are fully tax-deductible. Benefits are, in principle, taxable, but there is a generous deduction for public pension benefits, thereby leaving benefits largely untaxed.

3. The History of Japan's Public Pension System

In this section, I briefly discuss the history of Japan's public pension system. (For more details, see Niwata (1983) and Kōsei Tōkei Kyōkai (1996).) Japan's public pension system has a long history, but universal coverage was not achieved until 1961 and benefits were relatively modest until 1973. Noncontributory pension (onkyū) systems for retired army and navy servicemen and government officials were established in 1875 and 1884, respectively, and laws institutionalizing these pension systems were enacted in 1890. Moreover, noncontributory pension systems for schoolteachers and policemen were established during the middle to late Meiji period (1868–1912), and a contributory pension system for blue-collar government workers not covered by existing noncontributory pension systems was established in 1920. However, a comprehensive Mutual Aid Pension (Kyōsai Nenkin) system for national government employees was not established until 1949, and similar mutual aid pension systems for employees of private schools, employees of public enterprises, employees of agricultural, forestry and fishery organizations, and local government employees were not established until 1953, 1956, 1958, and 1962, respectively.[5]

The first public pension system for private sector workers (a pension system for seamen) was not established until 1939, and a comprehensive pension system for private-sector workers—the Employees' Pension (Rōdōsha Nenkin) system—was not established until 1941. Moreover, Japan's existing public pension system for private-sector workers broke down due to the chaos and hyperinflation of the early postwar period and had to be overhauled, a process that was not completed until the establishment of the new Employees' Pension (Kōsei Nenkin) system in 1954. Workers at companies with fewer than five employees, the self-employed, and farmers were not covered until 1961, when the National Pension (Kokumin Nenkin) system was established.

Thus, universal coverage was finally achieved in 1961, and continuity of coverage for those switching from one public pension system to another was achieved at the same time, but benefits remained relatively modest despite upward adjustments in 1965–6, 1969, and 1971–2. It was not until 1973 that benefit levels were increased enough to make the replacement rate comparable to what it is in the major developed countries (roughly 60 per cent), and it was not until the same year that automatic cost of living adjustments were introduced for the first time. Since then, benefits have been adjusted not only for consumer price inflation but also for increases in real wages.

---

[5] The Mutual Aid Pension systems for employees of formerly public enterprises (Japan Railways, Japan Tobacco, and Nippon Telephone and Telegraph) were absorbed by the Employees' Pension system in April 1997.

Additional improvements in the benefit levels and other provisions of public pensions were made during the remainder of the 1970s and in the early 1980s but by 1980, it had become clear that the imbalance between benefits and contributions and the rapid aging of the population would necessitate a fundamental reform of the system, and a number of important changes were made as part of the major pension reform package that passed the Diet in 1985 and took effect in April 1986. For example, this reform package provided for a gradual reduction in benefit levels over a twenty-year period, an increase in the contribution rate, and a partial unification of the various public pension systems into the current two-tiered system.

However, even this reform proved to be insufficient, and in 1989 and 1994, additional reforms were implemented. Space limitations preclude me from discussing the provisions of these reforms in detail, but two important features of the 1994 reforms should be noted. First, it was decided that the age at which salaried workers can begin receiving the basic pension would be gradually raised from the current 60 to 65 over the 2001–13 period.[6] Second, whereas the earnings-related component of the benefits of former salaried workers was formerly adjusted by the rate of increase in the pretax wages of current workers, it was decided that, starting in October 1994, the criterion would be the rate of increase in *after-tax* wages. Since the combined rate of income taxes and pension contributions is projected to increase steadily over time, the new adjustment method implies a slower rate of growth of benefits than under the old method.

4. The *Raison d'être* of a Public Pension System

My goal in the remainder of this paper is to evaluate, and identify defects in, Japan's public pension system and to propose ways of reforming that system, but before doing so, it is necessary to be clear about the *raison d'être* of a public pension system.

The public pension system has been used for at least three policy objectives: (1) old age security; (2) income redistribution; and (3) macroeconomic stabilization. I consider each of these in turn.

Old age security. One oft-stated goal of a pension system (be it public or private) is to provide old age security, by which I mean the guarantee of an adequate income during retirement, regardless of how long one lives, or to put it differently, to eliminate longevity risk (the risk of an uncertain lifetime). In my opinion, this should be the one and only goal of a public pension system. It is difficult, if not impossible, to simultaneously achieve two or more policy goals using the same policy instrument, and thus, each policy instrument should be assigned to the one policy target to which it is best suited. And the policy target to which the public pension system is best suited is old age security.

---

[6] Note, however, that they will be able to continue receiving the earnings-related component of benefits starting at age 60.

Income redistribution. There are some who argue that the public pension system should also be used to redistribute resources from the rich to the poor (from rich cohorts to poor cohorts and/or from rich individuals to poor individuals within the same cohort), but I am against doing so for at least two reasons. First, the public pension system is best suited to achieving the target of old age security and should be assigned exclusively to that target. A progressive income tax, a negative income tax, and/or transfer programs such as welfare are, in my opinion, the policy instruments best suited to achieving redistributional goals and should therefore be assigned to that target. Second, as discussed in more detail later, Japan's current public pension system redistributes resources from younger cohorts to older cohorts on a massive scale, and one rationale that is given for this is that younger cohorts have much higher lifetime incomes, on average, than older cohorts. However, not everyone in younger cohort groups is wealthy, and not everyone in older cohort groups is poor. Thus, intercohort income redistributions will entail substantial redistributions in the wrong direction (from poor individuals to wealthy individuals). To prevent such perverse results, income redistribution should be done at the individual level rather than at the cohort level and should be achieved via the tax and transfer systems rather than via the public pension system.

Macroeconomic stability. The Japanese government decided to temporarily suspend scheduled increases in the pension contribution rate as part of the 1999 pension reforms because the Japanese economy was in the midst of the worst recession of the postwar period. However, I am against using the public pension system as an instrument of stabilization policy because fiscal and monetary policies are far better suited to that purpose and because doing so will compromise the government's ability to meet the primary purpose of the public pension system (Hatta and Oguchi, 1999: 26–8). Indeed, Hatta and Oguchi (p. 163) show that suspending the scheduled increases in the pension contribution rate will further aggravate the already substantial intergenerational inequity of the public pension system.

Thus, I believe that the goal of the public pension system should be to provide old age security to everyone and that redistributional and stabilization goals should be left to other policy instruments. This implies that the public pension system must provide lifetime annuities that are actuarially fair (i.e. for which expected lifetime benefits precisely equal expected lifetime contributions) to all cohorts and to all individuals within each cohort and that it must not cause any systematic redistributions of income among and/or within cohorts. Moreover, it is also desirable that the public pension system be neutral and that it not distort people's behavior (saving behavior, labor supply behavior, etc.).

I turn next to the question of whether the provision of old age security can be left to the market (the private sector) or whether government intervention is warranted. What would happen if the government abolished the public pension system and got out of the business of providing old age security? Individuals who wanted to have old age security would purchase lifetime annuities from private insurance companies and individuals who did not want old age security would do nothing. This might seem fine, at first glance, but at least two problems would arise (Hatta and Oguchi, 1999: 10–17).

The first problem is that of "moral hazard." Assuming there is a safety net such as welfare, many (low-income) individuals would choose not to purchase any lifetime annuities and would rely instead on welfare to finance their living expenses after retirement. They would reason as follows: "Why should I purchase a lifetime annuity and pay monthly premiums throughout my working years when I can pay nothing and get almost as much during my retirement years in the form of welfare benefits?" In effect, taxpayers would have to pay for the old age security of such individuals, and individuals who purchased lifetime annuities would have to bear a double burden: they would have to pay not only for their own old age security but also for that of those who collect welfare during their retirement years. This is clearly not equitable.

The second problem is that of "adverse selection" caused by asymmetry of information. Insurance companies would ideally like to charge healthy individuals with longer life expectancies higher premiums for lifetime annuities because they can expect to have to pay such individuals benefits for a longer period of time. If insurance companies have less than full information about the health status of insurees, they cannot base premiums on health status and would have to charge all insurees the same premium. But if they did so, healthy individuals with longer life expectancies would be more likely to enroll because they could expect to get back more in the form of benefits than they would have to pay in premiums. By contrast, frail individuals with shorter life expectancies would be less likely to enroll because they would have to pay more in premiums than they could expect to get back in the form of benefits. And if such adverse selection occurred, premiums would have to be jacked up above what they would be if participation were made compulsory, and frail individuals would effectively be shut out of the market.

The best way to eliminate these two problems simultaneously is to make participation in the pension program compulsory, and making the system government-run is one way of doing so. Note, however, that it is not the only way—the government need only issue a decree making participation in the pension system compulsory; there is no need for the pension system itself to be government-run.

To summarize, the sole objective of a public pension system should be to provide old age security to everyone by providing them with actuarially fair lifetime annuities. The public pension system should not cause systematic redistributions of income among and/or within cohorts, should not be used for stabilization purposes, and should not distort people's behavior (e.g. saving behavior, labor supply behavior, etc.).

5. Defects in Japan's Current Public Pension System

In this section, I compare Japan's current public pension system to the ideal system described in the previous section and identify some defects in the current system.[7]

---

[7] Space limitations preclude me from discussing the Mutual Aid Pension systems, but they are very similar in structure to the Employees' Pension system.

Japan's public pension system suffers from the following five defects: (1) the adverse impact on intergenerational equity; (2) the adverse impact on intragenerational equity; (3) the adverse impact on the labor supply of the aged and of women; (4) the adverse impact on national saving; and (5) the widespread evasion of contributions to the National Pension system.

5.1. The adverse impact on intergenerational equity

As Hatta and Oguchi (1997, 1999) have shown using a generational accounting framework in the spirit of Kotlikoff (1992), lifetime benefits under the Employees' Pension system greatly exceed lifetime contributions in the case of cohorts who were born before 1962, with the gap increasing with age, while lifetime benefits fall far short of lifetime contributions in the case of cohorts who were born after 1962, with the gap being larger the younger the cohort. (Takayama *et al.* (1990a), Asō (1995), and Tajika, Kaneko, and Hayashi (1996) do similar calculations and obtain similar findings.) Thus, the Employees' Pension system is redistributing resources from younger cohorts to older cohorts on a massive scale.

There are at least two reasons for this. First, benefits were made much too generous relative to contributions at the time of the 1973 pension reform, especially for those close to retirement in 1973, as a result of which the lifetime benefits of older cohorts far exceed their lifetime contributions. For one thing, even those who were too old in 1973 to contribute for the required number of years were made eligible to receive fairly generous benefits as a transitional measure. Moreover, the overly generous benefits of older cohorts have necessitated cuts in the benefits of younger cohorts as well as increases in their contribution rates, causing their lifetime benefits to fall far short of their lifetime contributions. Second, Japan's population is aging at the fastest rate in human history and will become the most aged population in the world by the year 2010. (See Mason and Ogawa, Chapter 2 this volume, and Section 4.8 for more details.) Given the pay-as-you-go structure of the Employees' Pension system, in which the benefits of current retirees are financed primarily by the contributions of current workers, population aging (increases in the retiree-to-worker ratio) has necessitated further increases in the contribution rates of younger cohorts, and this, in turn, has caused the lifetime benefits of younger cohorts to fall even farther short of their lifetime contributions. Incidentally, the aging of the population in Japan is partly a permanent phenomenon caused by increases in life expectancy and declines in the birth rate and partly a temporary phenomenon caused by the aging of the postwar baby boom generation born in 1947–9. One reason why the lifetime benefits of younger cohorts will fall far short of their lifetime contributions is that, given the pay-as-you-go structure of the Employees' Pension system, they will have to pay large contributions to finance the benefits of the unusually large baby boom cohort.

Like the Employees' Pension system, the National Pension system has an adverse impact on intergenerational equity, with lifetime benefits exceeding lifetime contributions in the case of cohorts born before 1970 and lifetime benefits falling short of lifetime contributions in the case of cohorts born after 1970 (Hatta and Oguchi, 1999, ch. 5).

5.2. *The adverse impact on intragenerational equity*

The current Employees' Pension system has an adverse impact on intragenerational equity in at least three ways. First, as Takayama *et al.* (1990*a*) and Asō (1992) have shown, in any given cohort, the net transfer from the government arising from the Employees' Pension system is larger, the higher is the individual's income (at least for cohorts born before 1945). Thus, the Employees' Pension system has been a regressive one until recently, redistributing income from the low-income to the high-income.

Second, spouses of salaried workers who are not working or whose incomes are below a certain level are exempt from paying pension contributions, but they receive supplementary spousal benefits between the time the primary beneficiary turns 60 and the time they themselves turn 65, the Basic Pension after they turn 65, and survivors' benefits (equal to three-quarters of the primary beneficiary's earnings-related benefits) after the primary beneficiary's death without paying any corresponding contributions. This causes a redistribution of resources from single salaried workers and couples consisting of a salaried worker and a working spouse to couples consisting of a salaried worker and a dependent spouse. (See Takayama *et al.* (1990*a*), Asō (1992), Hatta and Kimura (1993), Tajika, Kaneko, and Hayashi (1996), Hatta (1997), and Hatta and Oguchi (1999).)

Third, pension contributions were, until recently, levied only on one's monthly salary, even though a considerable portion (as much as one-quarter or more) of worker compensation is paid in the form of semiannual or triannual lump sum bonuses and even though there are enormous variations across firms and industries and over time in the relative magnitude of bonuses. Exempting bonus income from pension contributions has led to a redistribution of resources from workers for whom bonuses are a relatively small proportion of their total compensation to workers for whom bonuses are a relatively large proportion of their total compensation. Moreover, a similar argument can be made for lump sum retirement payments, which are also not subject to pension contributions even though the amounts thereof are quite large (as much as three times annual income at retirement or more) and even though there is considerable variation among firms in the amounts thereof.

5.3. *The adverse impact on the labor supply of the aged and of women*

Because the pension benefits of former salaried workers are reduced or eliminated between the ages of 60 and 64 if they continue working and earn more than a certain amount, and because recent retirees can "double dip" (i.e. collect pension benefits and unemployment compensation benefits concurrently), the Employees' Pension system discourages salaried workers from continuing to work after the mandatory retirement age of 60. Company employees often have the option of continuing to work for the same company, a subsidiary of the same company, or an unrelated company after mandatory retirement, but they must accept a substantial pay cut, and as a result, they can often earn more by retiring and collecting pension benefits and unemployment compensation benefits than by continuing to work. Tachibanaki and Shimono (1985), Takayama *et al.* (1990*b*), Seike (1992, 1993), and others have found that the Employees' Pension system has, in fact, substantially reduced the labor supply of the aged.

Similarly, because the spouses of salaried workers who are not working or whose incomes are below a certain level are exempt from paying pension contributions, the Employees' Pension system also discourages dependent spouses (usually wives) from working, i.e. it encourages them to reduce their working hours so as to keep their incomes below the critical level. Higuchi (1995) finds that 11.5 per cent of wives reduce their working hours for this very reason.

5.4. The adverse impact on national saving

As pointed out by Feldstein (1974), the existence of a public pension system will reduce private saving, assuming that the wealth replacement effect is larger than the induced retirement effect, and national saving will also be reduced if the pension system is a pay-as-you-go system, meaning that government saving does not increase to offset the decline in private saving. In Japan, both the Employees' Pension system and the National Pension system are essentially pay-as-you-go systems and hence could well have an adverse impact on national saving. Empirical work on Japan has tended to find that public pensions have, in fact, reduced private saving and thence national saving. (See, for example, Takayama *et al.* (1990*b*).)

5.5 The widespread evasion of contributions to the National Pension system

It is estimated that about one-third of those who belong (or should belong) to the National Pension system do not pay contributions. Sixteen per cent are those who are legally exempt from paying contributions (for example, due to their low incomes), but 7.5 per cent are those who refuse to enroll in the National Pension system and 8.2 per cent are those who enroll but refuse to pay their contributions (Hatta and Oguchi, 1999: 81). These figures are not surprising because the government has done little about going after those who do not pay and because there is a widespread perception that the public pension system is a losing proposition (that lifetime benefits will fall far short of lifetime contributions). It is not that those who opt out of the National Pension system are not worried about their retirement; in fact, many of them *do* prepare for their retirement but do so by putting their money in banks, the postal savings system, individual pensions, etc., instead of in the National Pension system, because they believe that they can get a better return on their investment in the case of the former. Many of those belonging to the pension systems for salaried workers would also undoubtedly choose to opt out of the system if they could, but they cannot because their pension contributions are deducted from their paychecks by their employers. Thus, the widespread evasion of contributions to the National Pension system causes not only a deterioration in the finances of the public pension system but also a further intragenerational inequity (between salaried workers and the self-employed).

6. The Origins of the Defects in Japan's Public Pension System

In this section, I consider why Japan adopted the public pension system it did even though it suffers from the various defects enumerated above.

6.1. The adverse impact on intergenerational equity

In my opinion, the most serious defect in both the Employees' Pension system and the National Pension system is their adverse impact on intergenerational equity, which in turn is due to the pay-as-you-go structure of these systems as well as to the fact that benefits were made too generous relative to contributions in 1973.

Looking first at why a pay-as-you-go structure was adopted, one likely reason is that virtually all other countries had adopted a similar structure, but Tajika, Kaneko, and Hayashi (1996) identify two additional reasons. First, there was a widespread consensus that resources should be redistributed from younger cohorts who were benefiting from Japan's current economic prosperity to older cohorts who had endured many hardships during the war years and the early postwar years and who had worked hard to make possible that prosperity. Second, it was politically easier to postpone the burden of financing benefits to future generations because future generations do not yet have a vote. Tajika, Kaneko, and Hayashi (1996) argue that the Japanese Ministry of Health and Welfare was well aware of the excessive burden that future generations would have to bear.

As to why benefits improved so dramatically in 1973, Noguchi (1987) and Tajika, Kaneko, and Hayashi (1996) identified the following reasons. First, there was a growing consensus that since Japan had recovered from the devastation of the war and more or less caught up with the other developed countries, she should shift her priorities from maximizing economic growth at all costs to improving the quality of life, one important component of which is better social welfare programs. In response to this shift in priorities, the government made dramatic improvements not only in public pensions but also in health insurance, welfare programs for the poor, etc., in 1973. Second, Japan had enjoyed double-digit rates of economic growth since the mid-1950s, the Japanese government's fiscal position in 1973 was very favorable, and there was widespread optimism that these conditions would continue and that Japan could afford better social welfare programs. Few suspected at the time that the first oil crisis of 1973–4 would bring Japan's era of rapid economic growth to an abrupt end and require the government to run massive deficits.

6.2. The adverse impact on the labor supply of the aged

Another major defect in the current Employees' Pension system is the earnings test on workers aged 60 to 64, but Japan cannot be singled out regarding this provision as the public pension systems of most countries contain a similar provision and the earnings test has been gradually relaxed over time.

6.3. The adverse impact on intragenerational equity and on the labor supply of women

A third major defect of Japan's current Employees' Pension system is the favorable treatment of dependent spouses, which not only causes intragenerational inequities but also discourages women from working. Until a provision exempting dependent spouses from paying pension contributions was introduced as part of the 1986 reforms, dependent spouses had the choice of enrolling in the National Pension system or foregoing public pension coverage altogether (except for survivors' benefits), and about 30 per cent of dependent spouses chose the latter option (Hatta and Oguchi, 1999: 253). The 1986 reform package contained several unpopular provisions such as cuts in future benefit levels and increases in future contribution rates, and the government decided to include a provision providing for the exemption of dependent spouses from paying pension contributions in order to marshall support for the reform package.

6.4. The adverse impact on national saving

Both the Employees' Pension system and the National Pension system have an adverse impact on national saving as a result of their pay-as-you-go structure. See Section 6.1 above for a discussion of why a pay-as-you-go structure was adopted.

Thus, the current structure of Japan's public pension system with all its defects arose partly because Japan followed the example of other countries, partly because of political expediency, and partly because of undue optimism about Japan's future growth prospects.

7. Possible Ways of Alleviating the Defects in Japan's Public Pension System

In Section 5, I identified five defects inherent in the Employees' Pension system and the National Pension system. In this section, I discuss possible ways of alleviating or eliminating these defects.

7.1. Addressing defects in the existing pension system

The adverse impact of the public pension system on intergenerational equity could be eliminated by switching to an actuarially fair system in which the expected lifetime benefits of each cohort exactly equal its expected lifetime contributions, as recommended by Tajika, Kaneko, and Hayashi (1996), Hatta (1997), and Hatta and Oguchi (1999). This would require raising the contributions and/or lowering the benefits of older cohorts and lowering the contributions and/or raising the benefits of younger cohorts. The government has already taken some steps to contain the increase in the benefits of older cohorts and to increase their contributions. As part of the 1985 reforms, the government decided to gradually reduce benefit levels over a twenty-year period. It has also begun indexing the earnings-related component of the benefits of salaried workers to after-tax wages rather than to pretax wages. As a way of holding down benefit increases, it is gradually increasing the age at which salaried workers can begin receiving the basic pension from 60 to 65, and it has been gradually increasing the contribution rate.

These are largely piecemeal measures. I would favor more comprehensive measures and would also favor performing explicit calculations to ensure that the system is actuarially fair to all cohorts. In my opinion, the best way to achieve intergenerational equity would be to switch over immediately to an actuarially fair system and to service the government's net pension debt (the net transfers to past, current, and future beneficiaries which the government has already paid or to which the government has already committed itself) via a progressive income tax and/or the issuance of long-term government bonds; in either case, the burden of servicing the government's net pension debt should be spread out as evenly as possible over future generations in order to preserve intergenerational equity. (See Tajika, Kaneko, and Hayashi (1996), Hatta (1997), and Hatta and Oguchi (1997, 1999) for more details.)

The adverse impact of the public pension system on intragenerational equity could be alleviated or eliminated in the following ways. First, the adverse impact on equity among income classes could be alleviated by taxing pension benefits more heavily in the case of high-income households. This could be done by limiting or eliminating the pension benefit deduction for these households.[8] Second, the adverse impact on equity among household types could be eliminated by requiring the dependent spouses of salaried workers to pay their fair share of pension contributions, as proposed by Hatta (1997) and Hatta and Oguchi (1999).[9]

Third, the adverse impact on equity among workers receiving varying amounts of bonuses and lump-sum retirement payments could be eliminated by ending the exemption of these payments from pension contributions, as proposed by Hatta (1997).[10] Beginning in April 1995, salaried workers are required to pay an additional pension contribution equal to 1 per cent of their bonus income (with the burden being shared equally by employer and employee), but this contribution rate is far lower than the contribution rate applied to monthly salary (17.35 per cent since October 1996).

---

[8] Takayama (1992) advocated eliminating the favorable tax treatment of pension benefits altogether, and there is considerable merit to his argument.

[9] The inequity between salaried workers with a dependent spouse and salaried workers with a working spouse was alleviated as part of the 1994 reforms. Until then, dependent spouses were eligible to receive a survivors' benefit equal to three-quarters of the primary beneficiary's earnings-related benefit after the primary beneficiary's death, while working spouses had to choose between receiving the same survivors' benefit as dependent spouses and receiving an earnings-related benefit based on their own earnings; they could not receive both. Since April 1995, however, working spouses have an additional choice—namely, to receive half the combined earnings-related benefits of husband and wife. This reduces the inequity between salaried workers with a dependent spouse and salaried workers with a working spouse but does not eliminate it, and moreover, it introduces an additional inequity: not only salaried workers with dependent spouses but also salaried workers with working spouses are now favored vis-à-vis single salaried workers. Thus, my proposed solution appears to be the more equitable one.

[10] Takayama (1992) also advocated ending the exemption of bonus income from pension contributions.

Moreover, another problem with this reform is that contributions from bonus income are not taken into account when calculating benefits. The contribution rates on monthly salary, bonuses, and lump–sum retirement payments should be equalized immediately, and they should all be taken into account when calculating benefits.

The adverse impact of the public pension system on the labor supply of the aged and of women could be alleviated or eliminated in the following ways. First, the adverse impact on the labor supply of the aged could be alleviated by relaxing the earnings test on the pensions of former salaried workers and/or prohibiting double dipping (the simultaneous receipt of pension benefits and unemployment compensation benefits). The earnings test on the pensions of former salaried workers aged 60 to 64 has been relaxed several times (most substantially in April 1995), but there is room for further relaxation. As for double dipping, it was abolished in April 1998, and a further step has been taken to encourage those aged 60 and older to continue working. Since April 1995, salaried workers who experience a sharp decline in their salary after mandatory retirement are regarded as being quasi–unemployed and are eligible for unemployment compensation benefits that amount to as much as 25 per cent of their new salary. The pension benefits of such workers are reduced by an amount equal to 10 per cent of their new salary, but even so they are much better off than before, and, more importantly, it is now less likely that they can earn more by retiring than by continuing to work.

Second, the adverse impact of the public pension system on the labor supply of women could be eliminated by requiring the dependent spouses of salaried workers to pay their fair share of pension contributions, a measure that would also alleviate the intragenerational inequities of the current system (see above).

If adopted, these measures would eliminate distortions caused by the public pension system and also help to alleviate the serious labor shortages that are forecast to emerge as the population ages by inducing the aged and women to increase their labor supply.

The adverse impact of the public pension system on saving could be alleviated by converting Japan's public pension system from what is essentially a pay–as–you–go system to a fully funded system so that increases in government saving would fully offset any pension–induced reductions in private saving. It would be difficult to make this transition any time soon given the massive unfunded liabilities of the current pension system, but Hatta (1998) and Hatta and Oguchi (1999) show that there are a number of ways to complete the transition to a fully funded system by the year 2150.

The widespread evasion of contributions to the National Pension system could be eliminated by funding the Basic Pension out of general tax revenues or by means of an earmarked tax that would be used exclusively for the purpose of financing the Basic Pension.

7.2. Two additional recommendations

One additional recommendation is to raise the mandatory retirement age from 60 to 65 and to take other steps to enable and/or encourage those aged 60 and older to continue working. It is hard to believe, but Japan has traditionally had a mandatory retirement age of 55 despite having virtually the longest life expectancy in the world (83.82 years for females and 77.19 years for males as of 1997), and despite the fact that the pensionable age for salaried workers is 60. A mandatory retirement age of 60 was introduced in steps after 1986 but was not fully implemented until 1998. First, a law requiring firms to "strive" for a mandatory retirement age of 60 passed the Diet in 1986, but the adoption of a mandatory retirement age of 60 was a very gradual process: of companies imposing a uniform mandatory retirement age, the proportion that had adopted, or planned to adopt, a retirement age of 60 was only 71.4 per cent in 1992 and 90 per cent in 1996 (Maeda, 1997). A law prohibiting firms from adopting a mandatory retirement age earlier than 60 finally passed the Diet in 1994 and took effect on April 1, 1998.

Now that it has been decided that the age at which salaried workers can begin receiving the basic pension will soon be raised to 65, it is imperative that the mandatory retirement age be raised further to 65 as soon as possible to ensure that salaried workers have an uninterrupted flow of income. Note, moreover, that raising the mandatory retirement age to 65 and taking other steps to enable and/or encourage those aged 60 and older to continue working would also alleviate the severe labor shortages that are projected to emerge early in the next century, and thus that two birds could be killed with one stone.

My last recommendation is that all social insurance programs affecting the elderly be examined in their totality with a view toward insuring old-age security without wasteful overlap among programs and without excessive intergenerational inequities. In addition to the public pension system, Japan has a medical insurance system for the aged, and a public long-term care insurance system was introduced in April 2000. Better coordination between these three programs is badly needed.

7.3. Overall recommendation

In short, what I recommend—not only for Japan, but for all countries—is a public pension system that is actuarially fair to all cohorts and to all groups within each cohort, that does not contain perverse incentives regarding labor supply and saving decisions, that eliminates the evasion of pension contributions, that ensures retirees an uninterrupted flow of income, and that is well-coordinated with other social insurance programs affecting the aged.[11] Moreover, some of my recommendations would simultaneously ease future labor shortages as well.

8. Future Prospects for Japan's Public Pension System

Japan's population is aging at the fastest rate in human history and will become the most aged population in the world by the year 2010, surpassing even the long-time

---

[11] Tajika, Kaneko, and Hayashi (1996) also strongly advocate a public pension system that is actuarially fair to all cohorts and to all groups within each cohort.

leader, Sweden. According to projections of the National Institute of Population and Social Security Research of the Japanese Ministry of Health and Welfare, the aged ratio (the ratio of the population aged 65 or older to the total population) will increase from 16.2 per cent in 1998 to 22.0 per cent in 2010 and will rise further to 26.9 per cent in 2020, 28.0 per cent in 2030, 31.0 per cent in 2040, and 32.3 per cent in 2050. In this section, I discuss future prospects for Japan's public pension system in the face of such rapid population aging.

The rapid aging of Japan's population will cause the ratio of retirees to workers in Japan to skyrocket, and, given the pay-as-you-go structure of Japan's public pension system, this in turn will necessitate drastic reforms of the system (e.g. sizable benefit reductions and/or sizable increases in contribution rates) if the solvency of the system is to be maintained. For example, according to calculations by the Japanese Ministry of Health and Welfare, the contribution rate for the Employees' Pension would have to be doubled from the present level of 17.35 per cent to 34.3 per cent by the year 2025 in order to maintain current benefit levels. Such a high contribution rate would impose too heavy a burden on salaried workers, especially when one considers that they would also have to pay national, prefectural, and municipal income taxes and separate contributions for health insurance and long-term care insurance. Thus, some sort of reform of the public pension system is badly needed. The next section describes and evaluates two reform packages that have been proposed.

9. Two Proposals for Reforming Japan's Public Pension System

A major reform of Japan's public pension system is implemented every five years after the latest population projections have been released, and 1999 was one of those years. The Japanese Ministry of Health and Welfare finalized its 1999 reform proposal on February 26, 1999, the ruling Liberal Democratic Party approved it with some modifications on March 5, 1999, and it was passed by the Lower House of the Diet on December 7, 1999, but due to strong resistance by the opposition parties, Upper House passage was delayed until the next session of the Diet. The reform proposal was finally passed by the Upper House on March 22, 2000, and passed by the Lower House for the second time on March 28, 2000. (This was necessary because the bill was carried over to the next session of the Diet.) In addition to the Ministry of Health and Welfare/Liberal Democratic Party proposal (hereafter the MHW/LDP proposal), various individuals and groups have announced their own proposals. Both the MHW/LDP proposal and the other proposals purport to maintain the solvency of the system while at the same time keeping the peak contribution rate more manageable than under the current system. In this section, I describe the MHW/LDP proposal as well as the most promising alternative—the various proposals of Hatta and Oguchi (1999)—and evaluate each on the basis of the extent to which it solves the defects enumerated in Section 5.

9.1. *The Ministry of Health and Welfare/Liberal Democratic Party Proposal*

A major goal of the MHW/LDP proposal for reforming the Employees' Pension system is to reduce future benefit expenditures by about 20 per cent so that future increases in contribution rates can be held down. The MHW/LDP proposal seeks to reduce benefit expenditures in the following ways:

(1) It proposes a 5 per cent reduction in the earnings-related component of the benefits of former salaried workers who begin receiving benefits after April 1, 2000. The benefits of those already receiving benefits as of April 1, 2000, would not be affected.

(2) It proposes a temporary suspension of the wage indexation of benefits, effective April 2000. Benefits would be indexed to consumer prices instead of wages, which implies a lower rate of increase as long as there is productivity (real wage) growth. The suspension would be lifted after benefit levels fall below 80 per cent of the level that would have been attained if wage indexation had been maintained.

(3) It proposes gradually raising the age at which the earnings-related component of the benefits of former salaried workers are paid from 60 to 65.[12] Recall that the age at which the Basic Pension of former salaried workers is paid will be gradually raised from 60 to 65 between 2001 and 2013, pursuant to the 1994 reforms, and thus this provision implies that the pensionable age of salaried workers will be raised completely from 60 to 65.[13]

(4) It proposes applying the earnings test to those aged 65–9 and collecting pension contributions from all workers aged 65 to 69 beginning in April 2002. These provisions currently apply only to those aged 60–64.

The MHW/LDP proposal also includes the following four provisions regarding the Employees' Pension system:

(1) Raising the government subsidy to the Basic Pension from one-third to one-half as soon as a stable revenue source can be found and by the next pension reform (2004) at the latest.
(2) Suspending scheduled increases in the contribution rate until the government subsidy to the Basic Pension is raised from one-third to one-half.
(3) Taxing bonus income at the same rate as regular wages beginning in April 2003.
(4) Exempting employers from the employer share of pension contributions while employees are on childcare leave beginning in April 2000.

In my opinion, the MHW/LDP proposal is totally unsatisfactory because it is a piecemeal reform whose primary aim is to maintain the solvency of the public pension system in the face of rapid population aging. It pays little heed to intergenerational or

---

[12] The age at which the earnings-related component of the benefits of former salaried workers is paid would increase by one year every three years between fiscal 2013 and 2025 in the case of males, and by one year every three years between fiscal 2018 and 2025 in the case of females.

[13] Note, however, that the MHW/LDP proposal includes a provision for salaried workers to retire at 60 and collect benefits equal to 70 per cent of what they would have received if they had waited until age 65.

intragenerational equity, the adverse impact of the public pension system on national saving and on the labor supply of the aged and of women, or to the other issues I enumerated earlier. According to Hatta and Oguchi's (1999) calculations, the MHW/LDP proposal would further worsen the already substantial intergenerational inequity of the public pension system. With respect to older cohorts, although their benefits will be reduced by the 5 per cent cut in the earnings-related component of benefits and by the temporary suspension of wage indexation, they will escape the reduction in lifetime benefits caused by the increase in the age at which the earnings-related component of benefits is paid, because it will not be implemented until 2013 and only gradually after that. Moreover, their contributions will also be reduced as a result of the temporary suspension of scheduled increases in the contribution rate. Overall, their lifetime benefits will exceed their lifetime contributions by even more than under the current system. With respect to younger cohorts, although increases in their contribution rates would be held down, their benefits would also be reduced as a result of the 5 per cent cut in the earnings-related component of benefits, the temporary suspension of wage indexation, and the increase in the age at which the earnings-related component of benefits is paid, meaning that their lifetime benefits would fall short of their lifetime contributions by even more than under the current system.

Moreover, the MHW/LDP proposal *increases* the adverse impact of the public pension system on the labor supply of the aged by extending the earnings test to the 65–9 age group. It does nothing to alleviate the intragenerational inequities and the adverse impact on the labor supply of women that arise from exempting the spouses of salaried workers who are not working, or whose incomes are below a certain level, from paying pension contributions. Nor does it address the intragenerational inequities caused by the exemption of lump sum retirement payments from pension contributions. Furthermore, the adverse impact on national saving would not be alleviated, as the system would continue to be operated on a pay-as-you-go basis. Finally, since there are no plans to raise the mandatory retirement age from 60 to 65 anytime soon, the MHW/LDP proposal would create a five-year gap between the mandatory retirement age (60) and the pensionable age (65).

About the only good things concerning the MHW/LDP proposal are that it alleviates intragenerational inequities by taxing bonus income at the same rate as regular wages, and that it alleviates intergenerational inequities somewhat by indexing benefits to consumer prices rather than after-tax wages, at least for the time being. This will hold down the benefits received by older cohorts and reduce the amount by which their lifetime benefits exceed their lifetime contributions.

In addition to the provisions for changing the Employees' Pension system, the MHW/LDP proposal contains at least two provisions relating to the National Pension system. First, it proposes the introduction of a partial exemption option for moderately low-income individuals enrolled in the National Pension system beginning in April 2002. Under this option, moderately low-income individuals (whose incomes are not low enough to qualify them for the full exemption) would have the option of paying half of the full contribution and receiving two-thirds of the full benefit. Second, it proposes the introduction of an option for deferring for up to ten years the payment of contributions to the National Pension system for the period that one is enrolled as a student, beginning in April 2000.

These provisions are designed to reduce the evasion of pension contributions by providing incentives for those on moderately low incomes and for students to pay up, but, in my opinion, they are not nearly enough to solve the problem entirely. Moreover, they do nothing about the intergenerational inequity of the current system or about its adverse impact on national saving.

9.2. *The Hatta-Oguchi 23 per cent Proposal*

The most serious defect of both the current system and the MHW/LDP proposal is their enormous intergenerational inequity. Both systems propose to maintain the solvency of the public pension system in the face of rapid population aging by gradually raising contributions and gradually lowering benefits. Examples of the latter are the current provision to gradually raise the age at which former salaried workers can begin receiving the basic pension from 60 to 65 and the proposed provision to gradually raise the age at which former salaried workers can begin receiving the earnings-related component of benefits from 60 to 65. But gradually raising contributions and gradually lowering benefits means that older cohorts will be able to escape the higher contributions and lower benefits, and thus will make out like bandits. By contrast, younger cohorts will have to bear the full brunt of both higher contributions and lower benefits and hence will receive a double whammy. The only way to minimize the intergenerational inequities of the public pension system is to raise contributions and lower benefits (e.g. by raising the age at which benefits are paid) *immediately*, and the Hatta and Oguchi (1999) "23 per cent Proposal" does just that. The main features of this proposal are as follows:

(1) *Immediately* raising the contribution rate for the Employers' Pension system from 17.35 per cent to 23.1 per cent and keeping it constant thereafter.
(2) Suspending the wage indexation of the earnings-related component of the benefits of former salaried workers until 2030.
(3) Continuing the wage indexation of the basic pension.
(4) *Immediately* raising the age at which the earnings-related component of the benefits of former salaried workers can be received from 60 to 65 but offering salaried workers the option of retiring early (between the ages of 60 and 64) and collecting actuarially reduced benefits.

Provision (1) will lead to an *immediate* increase in contributions and provisions (2) and (4) will lead to an *immediate* reduction in benefits, and thus the "23 per cent Proposal" goes a long way toward rectifying the intergenerational inequity of the current system while at the same time maintaining its solvency. (The authors do not propose suspending the wage indexation of the Basic Pension because they feel that its purpose should be to guarantee a minimal standard of living during old age.)

Moreover, the "23 per cent Proposal" would eliminate the adverse impact of the Employees' Pension system on the labor supply of the aged because the benefits of early retirees would be reduced only actuarially, and it would also eliminate the adverse impact of the Employees' Pension system on national saving because it would achieve the transition to a fully funded system by 2150.

9.3. The Hatta-Oguchi Unification Proposal

The Hatta-Oguchi "23 per cent Proposal" described above looks at the Employees' Pension system in isolation, but Hatta and Oguchi (1999) also propose a plan (their so-called "Funded Unification Proposal" (Tōgō Tsumitate An)) to unify the various public pension schemes and to effect the transition of the public pension system as a whole to an actuarially fair, fully funded system by 2150. Its main features are as follows:

(1) It proposes reducing future per capita benefit expenditures by 20 per cent.
(2) It proposes abolishing contributions to the National Pension system and financing the Basic Pension via an earmarked 5 per cent consumption tax.
(3) It proposes reducing the contribution rate of the Employees' Pension system to 5.7 per cent.
(4) It proposes replacing the one-third government subsidy of the Basic Pension with a subsidy equivalent to a 13.4 per cent tax on labor income.

Since responsibility for collecting the earmarked consumption tax would fall on the Ministry of Finance, which has more expertise at collecting taxes than the Ministry of Health and Welfare, this proposal would hopefully largely solve the evasion problem. Moreover, the proposal to keep the various tax rates constant over time instead of hiking them gradually would greatly ameliorate the intergenerational equity of the public pension system, and the use of a consumption tax rather than the present lump-sum tax would enhance the progressivity and hence the equity of the overall tax system. Furthermore, this proposal would eliminate the adverse impact on intra-generational equity and on the labor supply of women caused by exempting the dependent spouses of salaried workers from paying pension contributions. Finally, the proposal would also eliminate the adverse impact of the public pension system on national saving because it would achieve the transition to a fully funded system by 2150. The only drawback of the proposal is that breaking the link between benefits and contributions would discourage people from working, but since the current public pension system strongly discourages the dependent spouses of salaried workers from working, and since this distortion would be eliminated by the Hatta-Oguchi proposal, it would, on balance, alleviate the disincentive effects on labor supply.

Thus, in almost every respect, the Hatta-Oguchi proposals are far preferable to the MHW/LDP proposal and should have been adopted instead of the MHW/LDP proposal. There are many reasons why the Hatta-Oguchi proposals did not receive serious consideration, one of which is that the older cohorts who have the most to lose from the Hatta-Oguchi proposals are already of voting age, whereas the younger cohorts who have the most to gain from the Hatta-Oguchi proposals are not yet born or are still not of voting age. But time is rapidly running out, so I earnestly hope that the government and the people of Japan will have the wisdom and the courage to adopt a public pension system that not only maintains its solvency in the face of rapid population aging but also meets the requirements of an ideal public pension system.

REFERENCES

Asō, Yoshibumi (1992), "Kōsei Nenkin Seido ni yoru Shotoku Iten" (Income Transfers through the Employees' Pension System), *Keizai Kenkyū* (Economic Review), 43/2 (April), 149–57 (in Japanese).
——(1995), "Kōteki Nenkin no Sedai-kan Iten" (The Japanese Public Pension System and Intergenerational Transfers), *Kikan Shakai Hoshō Kenkyū* (Quarterly of Social Security Research), 31/2 (Autumn), 135–41 (in Japanese).
Feldstein, Martin (1974), "Social Security, Induced Retirement, and Aggregate Capital Accumulation," *Journal of Political Economy*, 82/5 (Sept./Oct.), 905–26.
Hatta, Tatsuo (1994), *Shōhi-zei wa Yahari Iranai* (The Consumption Tax Is Not Needed After All) (Tokyo: Tōyō Keizai Shinpōsha) (in Japanese).
——(1997), "Nenkin Kaikaku" (Pension Reform), in Ōsaka Daigaku Kyōju Gurūpu (Osaka University Professors Collective), *Nihon Keizai no Korekara* (The Future of the Japanese Economy) (Tokyo: Nihon Hyōronsha), 37–54 (in Japanese).
——(1998), "Kōsei Nenkin no Tsumitate-hōshiki e no Ikō" (Transition of the Employees' Pension to a Fully Funded System), in Hatta, Tatsuo and Naohiro Yashiro (eds.), *Shakai Hoken Kaikaku: Nenkin, Kaigo, Iryō, Koyō Hoken no Saisekkei* (Social Insurance Reform: Restructuring Pension, Long-Term Care, Medical, and Employment Insurance) (Tokyo: Nihon Keizai Shinbunsha), 19–52 (in Japanese).
——and Yōko Kimura (1993), "Kōteki Nenkin wa Sengyō Shufu wo Yūgū Shiteiru" (The Japanese Public Pension System Favors Households with Nonworking Wives), *Kikan Shakai Hoshō Kenkyū* (Quarterly of Social Security Research), 29/3 (Winter), 210–21 (in Japanese).
——and Noriyoshi Oguchi (1997), "The Net Pension Debt of the Japanese Government," in Hurd, Michael D. and Naohiro Yashiro (eds.), *The Economic Effects of Aging in the United States and Japan* (National Bureau of Economic Research Conference Report) (Chicago: University of Chicago Press), 333–51.
————(1999), *Nenkin Kaikaku-ron: Tsumitate Hōshiki e Ikō Seyo* (The Theory of Pension Reform: Switch to a Funded System) (Tokyo: Nihon Keizai Shinbunsha) (in Japanese).
Higuchi, Yoshio (1995), "Sengyō Shufu Hogo Seisaku no Keizai-teki Kiketsu" (The Economic Consequences of Policies to Protect Full-time Housewives), in Hatta, Tatsuo and Naohiro Yashiro (eds.), *Jakusha Hogo Seisaku no Keizai Bunseki* (Economic Analysis of Policies to Protect the Weak) (Shirīzu Gendai Keizai Kenkyū (Contemporary Economic Study Series) no. 10) (Tokyo: Nihon Keizai Shinbunsha), 185–219 (in Japanese).
Horioka, Charles Yūji (1997), "Kōreika to Chochiku/Koyō/Sedai-kan no Fukōhei" (Aging and Saving/Employment/Intergenerational Inequity), in Ōsaka Daigaku Kyōju Gurūpu (Osaka University Professors Collective), *Nihon Keizai no Korekara* (The Future of the Japanese Economy) (Tokyo: Nihon Hyōronsha), 23–35 (in Japanese).
——(1999), "Japan's Public Pension System: What's Wrong with It and How to Fix It," *Japan and the World Economy*, 11/2 (April), 293–303.

Kenkō Hoken Kumiai Rengōkai (National Federation of Health Insurance Societies) (ed.) (1997), *Shakai Hoshō Nenkan* (Social Security Yearbook, 1997 edn.) (Tokyo: Tōyō Keizai Shinpōsha) (in Japanese).

Kōsei Tōkei Kyōkai (Health and Welfare Statistics Association) (ed.) (1996), *Hoken to Nenkin no Dōkō* (Trends in Insurance and Pensions, 1996 edn.), *Kōsei no Shihyō* (Rinji Zōkan) (Welfare Indices, Special Expanded Edition) (Tokyo: Kōsei Tōkei Kyōkai) (in Japanese).

Kotlikoff, Laurence J. (1992), *Generational Accounting: Knowing Who Pays, and When, for What We Spend* (New York: Free Press).

Maeda, Nobuo (1997), "Kōreika Shakai: Yōgo no Kaisetsu" (An Aging Society: An Explanation of Terms), in *Gendai Yōgo no Kiso Chishiki* (Basic Knowledge of Contemporary Terms) (Tokyo: Jiyū Kokumin-sha), 986–1007 (in Japanese).

Niwata, Noriaki (1983), "Pensions," in *Kodansha Encyclopedia of Japan* (Tokyo: Kodansha Ltd.), vi. 172–3.

Noguchi, Yukio (1987), "Public Finance," in Kozo Yamamura and Yasukichi Yasuba (eds.), *The Political Economy of Japan*, i: *The Domestic Transformation* (Stanford: Stanford University Press), 186–222.

Seike, Atsushi (1992), *Kōreisha no Rōdō Keizai-gaku: Kigyō/Seifu no Seido Kaikaku* (The Labor Economics of the Aged: Systemic Reform of Business and Government) (Teigen Shirīzu (Proposal Series)) (Tokyo: Nihon Keizai Shinbunsha) (in Japanese).

——(1993), *Kōreika Shakai no Rōdō: Shijō Shūgyō Kōdō to Kōteki Nenkin* (The Labor Market in an Aging Society: Employment Behavior and Public Pensions) (Tokyo: Tōyō Keizai Shinpōsha) (in Japanese).

Tachibanaki, Toshiaki and Keiko Shimono (1985), "Labor Supply of the Elderly: Their Desires and Realities about Full-time Jobs, Part-time Jobs, Self-employed Jobs or Retirement," *Keizai Kenkyū* (Economic Review), 36/3 (July), 239–50.

Tajika, Eiji, Yoshihiro Kaneko, and Fumiko Hayashi (1996), *Nenkin no Keizai Bunseki: Hoken no Shiten* (Economic Analysis of Pensions: An Insurance Perspective) (Tokyo: Tōyō Keizai Shinpōsha) (in Japanese).

Takayama, Noriyuki (1992), *Nenkin Kaikaku no Kōsō: Daikaisei e no Saishū Teigen* (A Plan for Pension Reform: Final Recommendations for a Major Reform) (Tokyo: Nihon Keizai Shinbunsha) (in Japanese).

——(1996), "Possible Effects of Aging on the Equilibrium of the Public Pension System in Japan," *European Economy: Reports and Studies*, 3 (Aging and Pension Expenditure Prospects in the Western World), 155–94.

——Fumio Funaoka, Fumio Ohtake, Masahiko Sekiguchi, Tokiyuki Shibuya, Hiroshi Ueno, and Katsuyuki Kubo (1990*a*), "Jinteki Shisan no Suikei to Kōteki Nenkin no Saibunpai Kōka: Futari Ijō no Futsū Setai-bun, 1984-nen" (The Estimation of Human Capital and the Redistribution Effects of Public Pensions: The Case of Regular Households with Two or More Persons, 1984), *Keizai Bunseki* (Keizai Kikaku-chō (Economic Planning Agency)), 118 (March), 1–73 (in Japanese).

——Fumio Funaoka, Fumio Ohtake, Fumiko Arita (Uno), Hiroshi Ueno, and Katsuyuki Kubo (1990*b*), "Kakei no Chochiku to Shūrō-tō ni kansuru Keizai Bunseki: Kōteki Nenkin to no Kankei ni Shōten wo Atete" (Economic Analysis of the Saving, Employment, etc., of Households: With Emphasis on the Impact of Public Pensions), *Keizai Bunseki* (Keizai Kikaku-chō (Economic Planning Agency)), 121 (Nov.), 1–159 (in Japanese).

Ushimaru, Satoshi (1996), *Kōteki Nenkin no Zaisei Hōshiki* (The Financing Method of Public Pensions) (Tokyo: Tōyō Keizai Shinpōsha) (in Japanese).

5 Japanese Labor Markets:
Can We Expect Significant Change?

MARCUS REBICK

1. Introduction

The dramatic rise in the value of the yen after 1985 has made Japanese firms much more conscious of labor costs, especially those that produce goods traded in the international market. The boom of the late 1980s bought some time for these firms, but the slump of the 1990s with the unemployment rate rising to 5 per cent in 1999, combined with the yen reaching a peak of 80 yen to the dollar in the Spring of 1995, has created a much stronger sense of urgency. In addition, the slump has hit the service sector, and calls for deregulation in the financial sector in the wake of the Japanese debt crisis have also put pressure on the nontraded goods sector to reexamine labor practices. Throughout the 1980s and 1990s Japanese firms have also been struggling with the rapid aging of their personnel. The tacit commitment on the part of large Japanese firms to employ their personnel for life along with steeply rising earnings with age and seniority has led to a rapid increase in the wage bill facing firms. At the same time, the number of management posts available for older employees has remained fixed as the growth of firms has slowed, and this has resulted in morale problems for older employees. It is not surprising, therefore, that the last few years have seen an upsurge in reports of fundamental changes in personnel policy in leading Japanese firms as well as greater attention by the government. The theme of the Labor White Paper of 1996 was the introduction of measures to develop human resources and ability while the White Paper of 1997 concerned itself with changes in employment and wages and prospects for older workers.

Despite all of the attention given to reform by the media, government reports, employer associations and trade unions, there is still a great deal of skepticism (at least outside of Japan) about the extent to which reforms are taking place (Yamamura, 1997, Androchorguy, 1997). The reform skeptics frame their arguments along a number of lines. First, they see little evidence of change taking place. For example, the work of Chuma (1997) and others shows that employee tenure has actually continued to rise in Japan through to the 1990s and although the age–earnings profile for men flattened considerably in the late 1970s and early 1980s, the flattening of the profile has slowed since then (except for workers over the age of 55). A second type of argument is more

I would like to thank Giorgio Brunello for providing me with an advance draft of Ariga, Brunello, and Ohkusa (2000), and Koichiro Imano for advice. I also thank Roger Goodman, Howard Gospel, Mary Gregory, Alex Roy, participants at the Conference on Japan's Economy in the Twenty-First Century, the 1999 CEPR European Network on the Japanese Economy Conference, and the Nissan Centre Seminar for comments on an earlier draft.

theoretical. In this view the Japanese economy is characterized by a number of complementary institutions in financial, labor and goods markets that are characterized by long-term relational contracts, internal reward structures based on tournaments, and decentralized control over operations (Aoki, 1994). Attempts to modify some of these institutions in a piecemeal fashion are not likely to succeed, and strong pressures will tend to push these institutions back in place. This argument is backed up by a third, political argument that Japan lacks the leadership and cohesive ideology-based party politics that would allow for major reforms such as those undertaken by Thatcher in the UK. In short, any reform is likely to be piecemeal and compromised by the various interest groups that hold considerable power in Japanese political life.

This essay will look in detail at the first of these issues—the extent to which Japanese labor markets and institutions are changing in the 1990s. Evidence will be gathered from statistical sources and from accounts of actual reforms that are being implemented in leading Japanese firms. Many reforms cannot be implemented in the short run because of long-term commitments of Japanese employers to their employees. Therefore, evidence of gradual change, or change at the margins will get extra attention. Sections 2 through 5 of the essay will look at labor mobility, male and female career patterns and compensation systems in the Japanese labor market. I will then turn to some macroeconomic issues such as the increasing rate of unemployment and the changing nature of wage bargaining in Sections 6 and 7. Conclusions will be offered in Section 8.

2. Labor Mobility and Employment Security

Labor mobility and employment security is one area where there appears to be little change at present. Japanese men continue to enjoy high and even rising levels of job tenure (Chuma, 1997).[1] There is one sense, however, in which change is taking place. Table 5.1 reports on the rate of involuntary job loss broken down by age and gender between 1987 (an economic trough for the labor market) and 1996 (a second trough). While the rates for individual age groups don't show any increase over the intervening nine years, the aggregate rate has increased: population aging has increased the relative weight of older men who have higher separation rates due primarily to mandatory retirement. This trend will continue until the baby boom generation reaches retirement age. At the opposite end of the age scale, the market for new school graduates has suffered in the past few years. Figure 5.1 shows the rate at which new graduates had found jobs by the date of graduation, broken down by schooling and gender. All groups have suffered, but women have suffered the most, especially those with higher education. Companies have decided to reduce the numbers of "core" employees that they employ, but at this point it is difficult to know if this is really

[1] "Lifetime employment" has never been as important as the stereotypic view suggests. Even for those 10 per cent of Japanese men who work for one company from school graduation until the age of mandatory retirement at 60, many will take a "post-career" job with one or more different companies, or work as self-employed until they eventually retire.

TABLE 5.1. *Involuntary separation rates by gender and age in Japan, 1987–1996*

	1987	1988	1989	1994	1996
Men					
All	2.5	2.5	2.5	2.9	3.1
<20	2.2	2.8	3	8.9	1.8
20–29	1.4	1.8	1.7	1.4	1.8
30–44	1.1	1.1	1.2	1.3	1.3
45–54	1.9	1.7	1.6	1.4	1.9
55–64	12.5	11.4	10.8	10.1	12.2
Women					
All	3.4	2.4	2.3	2.4	2.7
<20	1.8	3.3	2.7	4.3	2.5
20–29	2.5	1.9	1.4	1.7	2.1
30–44	2.8	1.7	1.9	1.8	2
45–54	3.6	2.2	2.3	1.9	2
55–64	10.6	6.8	6.9	5.8	7.5

Source: Ministry of Labour, *Employment Trends Survey*, 1987, 1988, 1989, 1994, 1996.

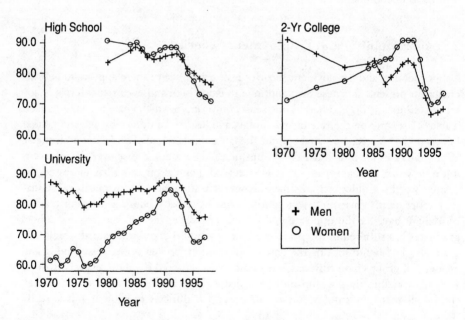

FIGURE 5.1. *Percentage of noncontinuing graduates employed at graduation by education level, 1970–1998*

Source: Ministry of Education, *Gakkō Kihon Chōsa* (Basic Survey of Schools).

just a cyclical phenomenon. Nevertheless, many new graduates may have to revise their expectations downward if they are to find work. One trend that does seem to be long term is a drop in the number of women hired into secretarial positions, especially those with two-year college degrees, as increased office automation replaces some of their functions.

One of the institutions that is said to impede the development of external labor markets and increased mobility in Japan is the secondment (*shukkō*) of employees to other firms, usually the subsidiaries of larger firms. There are several reasons why firms rely on this secondment of workers. On the positive side, there is the desire to strengthen ties within enterprise groups, and the need to provide training to suppliers of inputs for the larger firms. (This can also be accomplished by the secondment of employees of subsidiaries to parent firms.) On the negative side, subsidiaries (including foreign subsidiaries) often provide employment for redundant employees, especially in the managerial ranks. The usual contractual arrangement is for the host firm to pay the salary of the seconded employee and for the sending firm to compensate the employee for at least part of any drop in salary that comes with the move. Since larger firms typically pay higher salaries, some compensation is usually required.[2] This kind of labor mobility is managed without the use of the external labor market and therefore acts as a barrier on its development. There are limits to how far the parent firm can go, however, as the imposition of managers on subsidiaries impedes the promotion opportunities for the smaller firm's own employees and is demoralizing to the work force.[3] In 1986, 568,000 employees, or just over 1 per cent of employees were on secondment, while in 1996 both the absolute numbers and the percentage had fallen slightly (Japan Productivity Center (JPC), 1988: Table E-19, 1998, Table E-20). This suggests that secondment had reached its limit as an institution-facilitating mobility. Secondment only represents about 5 per cent of mobility for Japanese men in the 1990s in any case, suggesting that it is not that great a hindrance to the development of open labor markets.

The situation is somewhat different for older employees, however. Workers on secondment make up around 3 per cent of male employees between the ages of 50 and 69 (JPC, Table E-25), so the institution of secondment is roughly three times as important. In addition to secondment, some other distinctive institutions for moving older employees exist in Japan. There are a variety of personnel firms which act as go-betweens in the labour market by contracting with the employee's former and future employers rather than with the employee himself.[4] Again, this practice serves to protect the employment guarantees of larger firms and impedes the development of other, more open labor market institutions. The Ministry of Labour itself promotes a policy of "Changing Jobs Without Unemployment," and not only provides

---

[2] In some 25 per cent of cases, however, the receiving firm makes up the difference (Ministry of Labor (MOL) 1995, Table E-22-5).
[3] In addition, recent changes in the requirements for company accounting, particularly the requirement to provide consolidated accounts for companies and their subsidiaries will dampen any incentive to move employees out of the company for purely cost-accounting purposes.
[4] An example of one of these is the Global Brain Corporation.

its own employment brokers, but also provides subsidies to firms in designated industries that practice secondment or otherwise assist employees to find other jobs without a spell of unemployment (Ministry of Labour (MOL*c*), 1998: 25). As Rebick (1995) shows, older workers who attempt to seek new employment on their own may actually be stigmatized in the open labor market.

In conclusion, there is little evidence that Japanese firms are about to do away with the long-term employment contract in the broader sense. It may be that a prolonged slump will make some of the larger enterprises insolvent, but with takeovers and restructuring most of the employees should be able to keep their jobs.[5] The institution of secondment of employees to other companies also makes it likely that much of the mobility of older employees will be managed by firms and this in turn will make it more difficult for external labor market institutions to develop for these employees of large firms.

3. Male Career Patterns

The stylized view of the career of the employee (both blue- and white-collar) in the large Japanese firm is one of the development of wideranging skills through frequent job rotation and the discouragement of specialization. Instead, the employee develops sets of skills and personal connections that are specific to his firm and not transferable to other firms (Koike, 1988; Hashimoto, 1990). This, along with job guarantees, is held to be the main reason why mobility has been so low in Japan. Smaller firms also attempt to follow this pattern, although their ability to guarantee employment, and the extent to which firm-specific sets of skills and interpersonal relations can develop is not as pronounced (Koike, 1988). The exceptions to this pattern, however, are nonregular or temporary workers, and women. Temporary workers may only be hired for a period of one year (lest they be exploited), while women, who mainly work part-time, are not given the same kind of implicit guarantees of continuing employment as men. Consequently, any trend towards the increased use of women and/or men on temporary contract would suggest that Japanese firms are looking for ways to increase mobility. Similarly, moves toward increased employment in smaller firms (through outsourcing and spinoffs) would also tend to increase mobility for the reasons given above. Finally, moves towards increased development of specialists rather than generalists would also suggest a movement towards greater interfirm mobility as specialist skills might well be more useful in many different firms and specialists might develop a stronger occupational identity.

Table 5.2 shows that the proportion of regular employees among men fell by 3 percentage points between 1986 and 1998. Most of this drop was related to an increase in the employment of student or recent graduate part-time employment (*arubaito*) which reflects the downturn in employment prospects for recent graduates in the

---

[5] For example, after the collapse of Yamaichi Securities in 1997, some two-thirds of the employees were rehired by Merill Lynch who took over the firm's retail network.

TABLE 5.2. *Percentages of employees by firm size and status categories for 1985 and 1997–98*

	Men and women			Men			Women		
	1985	1997	Change	1985	1997	Change	1985	1997	Change
Firm size									
1,000+ employees	21.5	19.9	−1.6	24.4	22.1	−2.3	16.5	16.5	0.0
100–999 employees	22.6	25.3	+2.7	23.2	25.6	+2.4	21.4	24.9	+3.5
1–99 employees	55.9	54.8	−1.1	52.4	52.3	−0.1	62.1	58.6	−3.5
	1986	1998	Change	1986	1998	Change	1986	1998	Change
Employee status									
Regular	83.4	76.4	−7.0	92.6	89.7	−2.9	67.8	57.1	−10.7
Part-time	9.4	13.2	+3.8	0.7	1.2	+0.5	24.2	30.7	+6.5
Student/new graduate part-time employment	3.5	6.6	+3.1	2.9	5.5	+2.6	4.6	8.3	+3.7
Other temporary	3.7	3.8	+0.1	3.8	3.7	−0.1	3.4	3.8	+0.4

Sources: Japan, *Labor Force Survey* for 1985 and 1997; *Special Survey of the Labor Force Survey*, 1986 and 1998.

1990s. Table 5.2 also shows that there is a 2-point shift towards employment in medium-sized firms from large firms for men over the period 1985 to 1996. To some extent this may reflect the reclassification of entire firms from large to medium-sized with downsizing and spinoffs.

It is more difficult to document trends towards specialist careers in medium-size and large Japanese firms. Ariga, Brunello, and Ohkusa (forthcoming) survey reports from the human resource management magazine *Rōsei Jihō* and find that the development of "multiple career tracks" has been an important development of the 1990s. Under this system, after an initial period in which all management track employees follow the same career path, there are several different career paths that one can take in the firm, rather than just the single career path offered by the ability-qualification system. For example, one could specialize in accounting, law, engineering, or one branch of the firm's operations. While this offers both greater flexibility and the opportunity for specialization, Ariga *et al.* note that firms adopting this system are still hiring new graduates into a common career path for an initial period and are not really opening up an external labor market for specialists. They suggest that the new system is mainly a way of creating more opportunities for promotion, particularly for the most capable employees. Other researchers such as Imano (1998) are not as skeptical, suggesting that the multiple career track systems really are a more efficient way of training employees. Whichever view turns out to be justified, the development of multiple career track systems does have an effect on the system of compensation and also, by dividing nonmanagerial employees into different groups, acts to weaken the cohesion of labor unions. Finally, it is possible that by developing a large labor pool of specialists, the multiple career track system will open the way for the development of greater mobility in the future. I will turn to these subjects later in the paper after discussing changes in the career patterns for women.

4. Female Career Patterns

Women in Japan typically work full-time after leaving school until either their marriage or until the birth of their first child. At this point their labor force participation rate falls from 75 per cent to 50 per cent. As their children get older, women typically reenter the labor force as part-time workers and the participation rate rises again to some 70 per cent.[6] Married women often prefer to work part-time as there are tax disadvantages for higher earnings (see Mason and Ogawa, Chapter 2 this volume) and also because their husband's fringe benefits usually cover family needs. Although attitudes towards equal opportunity for women are changing, a majority of Japanese women believe that a mother should look after her children until age three (Ministry of Welfare (MOW), 1998: 85–7). For a two-child family this entails withdrawal from the labor force for at least five years, and so far, this has been a major barrier for women's career development.

In general the status of women employees in Japan is not high and only 2–3 per cent of managers are women (MOL, 1990, Appendix Table 85). The educational attainment of women who are new school graduates has risen dramatically since the passage of the Equal Employment Opportunity Law (EEOL). The percentage of women with a high school education (98 per cent in 1997) who went on to higher education rose from 34 per cent in 1986 to 47 per cent in 1997 with almost all of that rise accounted for by increasing rates of enrollment in 4-year university degree courses (Japan Ministry of Education, 1998: 36–9). The labor force participation rates for women aged 25–9 and 55–9 have also risen by some 10 percentage points. Nevertheless, the quality of the employment prospects for women have not improved as dramatically. I have already shown that women graduates have suffered more under the current slump than men. Large firms have typically offered two different career tracks for new graduates since the passage of the EEOL in 1986—general track (*ippan shoku*) and management track (*sōgō shoku*).[7] Although virtually all men enter firms on the management track, the proportion of women entering in the management track has been lower than 10 per cent overall, rising only as high as 50 per cent for university graduates (Wakisaka, 1997: 257–8). Table 5.2 shows that the percentage of women who are employed as part-time workers or casually has dramatically increased over the past decade. Although older women with families are far more likely to be employed part-time, this trend can only be partly explained by the aging of the population. Nevertheless, the passing of the EEOL undoubtedly was taken seriously by young Japanese women and is responsible for much of the growth in their educa-

[6] Women are classified as part-time employees by companies if they work fewer hours than men in the company, even though they may be working up to forty hours per week.
[7] Many companies also offer a middle course that is a limited management track that doesn't require posting to different parts of Japan. This is much easier for women employees to accept.

tional attainment (Edwards and Pasquale, 1998). A recent survey of women's attitudes to returning to work after childbearing shows clearly that university-educated women have a much stronger tendency to want either specialist or highly skilled careers (MOL, 1998). There is no indication that this trend is about to be reversed, and consequently there is a growing pool of women with higher career aspirations in Japan.

Since there is every reason to believe that aging of the population will create labor shortages in the future, it is reasonable to expect that there will be continued pressure brought to bear on firms to provide better employment opportunities for women, including arrangements for reemployment with the same firm after taking leave to look after young children. It is likely, however, that women will find themselves directed into more specialized occupations, rather than into more general line management. Even among university graduates, almost half of the women who have left the labor force to raise children would prefer to work part-time, making managerial careers difficult without major changes to Japanese organizations (MOL, 1998).

5. Compensation

Compensation in Japan is characterized by the steep rise in wages with seniority for blue-collar workers as well as white-collar workers. There is a debate among economists about the extent to which this reflects high levels of training that raise marginal productivity, long-term implicit contracts that encourage employee effort, or the vestiges of postwar wage settlements that paid older workers according to their lifecycle consumption requirements at a time when capital market institutions were not as well-developed and most people had little or no wealth. Whatever the case, two trends have been observed over the period since the 1950s. The first is that the steepness of the rise in wages with seniority has fallen with time. The second is that the direct connection between wages and seniority has weakened over time.

For most of the postwar period, compensation in Japan has had several different components that are common to all firms. These are illustrated in Table 5.3. Roughly four-fifths of current cash compensation for regular employees comes in the form of wages paid monthly (including overtime payments). The remaining fifth comes in the form of two semiannual bonuses paid in June and December. These bonuses are generally expressed in terms of a number of months of monthly pay, and so are directly linked to the determinants of monthly pay. In the monthly wage package (leaving overtime pay aside), some four-fifths of pay is "basic pay" (*kihonkyū*) while the remainder comes as allowances including family allowances, housing, and commuting allowances. Family allowances typically account for 3–5 per cent of monthly compensation (not including bonuses).[8] Some 80 per cent of firms in Japan have some form of family allowance and the ratio rises to 90 per cent for large firms with more than 1,000 employees. If anything, these ratios have risen over the past ten years

---

[8] Data from the Japanese Yearbook of Labour Statistics (MOL) and the Japan Productivity Handbook (JPC) for recent years.

TABLE 5.3. *Components of compensation for Japanese firms in 1995–1996*

	Total cash compensation (%)
Component of compensation	
Monthly cash payments:	75.3
Basic pay	60.3
Allowances:	7.5
Holding a management post	1.0
Entertainment	0.7
Family	2.4
Commuting	0.7
Housing	0.7
Regional	0.5
Other	1.7
Overtime	7.5
Semi-annual bonuses	24.7
Total cash compensation	100.0
Other expenses borne by firm	
Retirement and other severance payments	5.1
Employer's share for national health insurance	3.4
Employer's share for national pension	5.6
Employer's share for employment insurance	0.7
Employer's share for accident/injury insurance	0.8
Total other expenses	15.6

Sources: Ministry of Labour (MOLa), *Yearbook of Labour Statistics*, tables 108, 127, 128. Figures for allowances are taken from JPC (1998), *Japan Productivity Handbook*, table C-38-1 and are based on a survey of the Central Labor Commission for firms with more than 1,000 employees and more than 500 million yen in capital.

suggesting that the idea of compensating employees according to their needs is still a solid fixture of Japanese enterprise policy.[9] The firm also provides compensation in the form of paying one-half of the charges for national health insurance, unemployment insurance, and the national pension. These charges are expressed as a percentage of monthly pay. Finally, firms generally pay several years of severance pay at the age of mandatory retirement and these payments are also based on the final year's wages of the employee. Since most of the noncash compensation and bonuses are directly related to the levels of basic pay, much of the remainder of this section will discuss the determination of basic pay (wages).

Wage payments in large firms were made primarily on the basis of age and seniority in the 1950s, but through the 1960s and 1970s almost all firms adopted the ability-qualification wage payment system (*shokuno-shikaku seido*) whereby individuals in

---

[9] The allowances have been eliminated, however, for upper management who are paid by an annual salary scheme (Imano, 1998).

the firm are paid according to qualifications that they receive for developing skills. Payments in this system are based primarily on these qualification rankings and not on the actual post held on the factory floor or in line management. The qualification rankings themselves are common to all employees in the firm and tend to be acquired with seniority so that wages are still essentially linked to seniority, although there is some variance introduced in the speed with which employees acquire the qualifications. Although earnings dispersion increases with age, seniority and age still have the largest effect on earnings in the Japanese firm, often acting as a prerequisite for promotion (Tachibanaki, 1996). The problem with this system is its emphasis on the acquisition of general skills. Although there are many good reasons for acquiring a wide set of general skills, firms are increasingly interested in the development of specialist skills as the previous section indicated. As a result, many firms are moving away from the ability-qualifications system to wage determination based on job content or on ability as shown through actual performance on the job, rather than potential performance on the job. Since the number of managerial posts is limited, another way in which individuals can demonstrate ability is through the acquisition and use of more intensive, specialist knowledge.

Many firms have started to announce changes to their system of evaluation. Table 5.4 lists some of the changes that are taking place and planned for the immediate future. It is evident that job-based performance evaluation and the introduction of an annual salary system (with pay based on job performance) that would bear closer resemblance to practices in the United States have become popular, especially with large firms in Japan. In 1984 43 per cent of large firms and 38 per cent of all firms were basing at least some of the basic wage (*kihonkyū*) on job-related pay. By 1992 this had risen to 50 per cent of large firms and 41 per cent of all firms. The extent to

TABLE 5.4. *Percentage of firms with changes or planned changes to their wage and salary system*

Type of change	All firms		Large firms	
	Implemented in the last 3 years	Planned for the next 3 years	Implemented in the last 3 years	Planned for the next 3 years
Increase in the range of salary increases	11.9	12.2	15.7	13.8
Decrease in the range of salary increases	23.3	16.3	18.4	11.6
Abolition of the regular salary increase	3.8	5.3	6.3	7.5
Increase in job content-related pay	12.1	19.8	12.8	26.9
Increase in functional ability-related pay	15.7	27.2	24.5	37.0
Increase in results-related pay	15.0	27.2	28.2	42.3
Decrease in allowances	4.9	5.3	8.7	10.7
Revision/Introduction of annual salary system	3.0	8.8	9.1	22.3
Increase in weight of the bonus	3.5	8.3	3.5	9.1

Source: Survey of the Wage and Working Hours System, 1994 as reported in Ministry of Labour (1994), *Yearbook of Labour Statistics* table 127, pp. 221–2. Large firms have more than 1,000 employees.

which Japanese firms have been using bonuses as a means of sharing profits has been debated, but Imano (1998) reports that there are clear signs that firms are increasing the explicit linkage between firm performance and bonus payments. Many firms are also linking bonuses to group performance within firms or to individual performance. Although the annual salary system introduced by many firms for upper-level management and for specialists within the firm dispenses with bonuses (and most allowances), the part of the annual salary that is comparable to the old base wage usually remains unchanged, while it is the part comparable to the semiannual bonus that is subject to greatest variation according to individual and firm performance (Imano, 1998). In this sense, the introduction of the annual salary system is primarily a means of individualizing the bonus portion of compensation. While the tying of bonuses or annual salaries more closely to firm and individual performance won't necessarily affect the steepness of the age–earnings profile, the introduction of greater incentives for performance may make it easier to flatten this profile without adversely affecting employee incentives.

Despite the evidence that firms are formally changing their compensation systems it is not clear whether these new systems are, as skeptics would maintain, merely changes in the name of old practices that firms use to make themselves look progressive, or whether they will result in substantial changes in the actual wage received or in individual behavior within the firm. I turn to this subject in the remainder of this section, first by looking at the flattening of the age–wage profile and second by looking at the increased dispersion of wages within age groups. It should be noted, however, that an increase in the weight of performance-based pay alone is not necessarily as important as changes in the criteria used to assess performance and incentives, as these will eventually have an impact on productivity in the workplace.

5.1. Flattening of the age–wage profile

Figure 5.2 shows the earnings differential for basic monthly pay between 20–4 year-old and 50–4 year-old men in manufacturing who have worked for one firm since school graduation between 1967 and 1996. Separate curves are shown for large and small firms and for high school and university graduates. The figure shows a substantial drop in this differential between 1967 and 1979 with a gentler decline afterwards. Since employees who have only worked for one firm are an unrepresentative group, it is better to look at evidence of changing rates of return to age and tenure using a broader sample. Clark and Ogawa (1992a,b) have done this and their findings are roughly in accord with Figure 5.2 although they find greater flattening after 1980. More specifically, they provide cross-industry evidence that aging of the work force and the increase in the age of mandatory retirement have led to flatter wage profiles, and this is consistent with the implicit contract model of Lazear (1979) that suggests that late payment of rewards can act as a disciplinary device.[10] As a corollary of this,

---

[10] In Lazear's model employees are paid less than their marginal product in their early years with the firm and paid more than their marginal product in their final years with the firm in order to make the threat of dismissal for poor performance have serious financial consequences for the employee. Mandatory

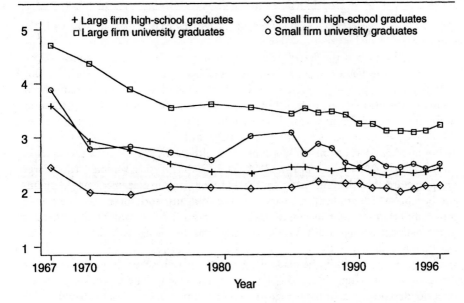

FIGURE 5.2. *Older/younger wage differential for men with maximum seniority: manufacturing, 1967–1996*

we might expect that extension of the mandatory retirement age to 65, a goal of the government, would induce further flattening. It is likely that extension of employment guarantees to 65 would be accompanied by agreements to cut wages after age 60 (or even earlier) in a similar manner to what already occurs under existing employment extension programs (Rebick, 1992).

There are other reasons, however, why we might expect the seniority–wage or age–wage profile to flatten in the future. If new systems of personnel evaluation such as those mentioned above are increasingly used as a motivating device, there may be less need to rely on long-term implicit contracts and we might expect that the profile would gradually flatten over time. Okunishi (1998) using a survey of 450 firms in the Tokyo area finds that firms with steeper age–earnings profiles also tend to be firms that are most likely to use secondment and early retirement incentive schemes to encourage or force older employees to leave the firm. They are also more likely to be instituting policies to deliberately flatten the age–wage profile. What he doesn't find, however, is evidence that the steepness of the age–earnings profiles is correlated with the use of any particular payment system. It is neither obvious that the new compensation systems are dramatically changing incentives, nor that the steepness of the

retirement is necessary in order to limit the extent of overpayment in later years. If the age of mandatory retirement is increased, then the wage profile must become flatter, other things equal. Although Japanese firms ordinarily find it difficult to dismiss employees, they are able to pressure employees to leave the firm by assigning them to intolerable work or by social ostracism.

age–earnings profile has a great effect on incentives (other than to stay with the same firm).

One other aspect of the flattening of age–earnings profiles relates to noncash compensation in the form of health insurance and both public and company pension contributions. The rate of premiums that firms must pay for public health insurance and the national pension scheme is increasing over time and this is adding to the pressure felt by firms on their wage bill. The rate of return experienced by the employee on these payments is declining with the aging of the work force as the number of claimants of pensions or health services rises with the aging of the Japanese population (Horioka, 1999, and Chapter 4 this volume). Most large firms operate their health insurance through company management of premiums and benefits which are kept in balance. As the company work force ages, the cost of providing health care for its employees rises. For smaller companies that participate in the national public health insurance, premiums are rising with the aging of the population.

Finally, mention should be made of company pension schemes which often take the form of lump-sum severance payments at retirement. These pension plans are typically designed benefit plans that pay a lump-sum or annuity that is based on the monthly wage of the employee just prior to retirement. In 1993 these averaged around 45 months of such pay.[11] Although there is a great deal of discussion of the need to reduce the level of company pensions as the company work force ages, there is little evidence so far of changes in the number of months of pay being used for severance payments.[12] However, as the age–wage profile flattens, company pensions will automatically fall in size relative to starting wages, even if the number of months of final wages remains unchanged. This too will have the effect of making the overall compensation profile flatter.

One other way in which changes in the design of company pensions may affect the incentive to stay with the same company would be moves from defined benefit plans toward defined contribution plans or private insurance policies. Matsushita Electric has attracted a great deal of attention with its offer of current cash compensation rather than future pension benefits (or lump-sum retirement benefits) to incoming employees (Strom, 1998). Matsushita has aimed the most radical parts of this offer to specialists in law or engineering, employees who are most likely to benefit from the mobility offered by a private pension plan or a defined contribution plan. In general, most employers will find it difficult to match Matsushita's offer because there are tax incentives for offering a defined retirement benefit under Japanese tax law. The Japanese government is considering altering the pension law to allow for defined contribution plans, however, and the possibility of portable pensions may, along with flattening of the wage profile, lead to greater mobility, especially for employees with skills that are not firm-specific.

---

[11] Ministry of Labour (MOL), 1995, Table E-39.

[12] Evidence that the number of months of final wages has remained unchanged may be found in Rōmu Gyōsei Kenkyūsho, *Rōsei Jihō*, No. 3356, June 26, 1998, p. 41, Table 15. For an example of a proposal to cut the number of months see the same issue, p. 30.

5.2. Increased dispersion in wages

Okunishi (1998) using data from the Japanese Wage Census finds that there has been a marked increase in the dispersion of wages for given age groups of employees who work in large firms of more than 1,000 employees in Japan between 1980 and 1997. He finds that the standardized interdecile range of monthly wage payments has increased from the level of .27–.29 to .30–.35 over this period for groups over age 35.[13] This is roughly equivalent to a 15–20 per cent increase in the standard deviation of earnings. Whether this is primarily due to increases in within firm variance or due to increased dispersion of pay between firms is an issue that I will take up in the section on national wage bargaining. Okunishi, using a sample of 450 firms in the Tokyo area finds that firms that primarily use age and seniority as determinants of basic pay tend to have the lowest variance of wages within age groups while those that use performance as a determinant tend to have the highest variance within age groups.[14] This suggests that changes in the formal method of wage determination have a real effect on the dispersion of wages and consequently are likely to affect incentives. Okunishi also finds that the separation of younger employees in their twenties and thirties is higher in firms with greater dispersion in within-age group earnings. This suggests that moves to link pay more closely with performance may act to increase labor market mobility.

In conclusion, there is evidence of change in the structure of basic cash compensation and the criteria on which bonuses are paid. There is also some evidence that the flattening of the seniority–wage profile will continue in the future, with peak earnings being reached at an earlier age by the majority of employees. Accompanying this are changes in the way in which performance is being evaluated. It is possible that employees will be encouraged to acquire more specialist skills that will allow them to adapt to the changing needs in the workplace in the future. This may increase the share of investment in general human capital relative to firm-specific capital.

6. Unemployment

I now turn to consideration of Japan's employment performance in the wake of the recession of the 1990s. The rise of the unemployment rate to a high of 4.9 per cent in June 1999 has created great consternation in Japan and has made it difficult for the government to achieve much with stimulus packages, given the high levels of uncertainty and rising household savings rates. If we look at trends in the unemployment rate broken down by gender and age group in Figure 5.3 we see that the increase in unemployment is concentrated among men age 55–64 and women age 25–34. By contrast, the unemployment rates for prime-age men who carry most of the responsibility for family well-being has increased, but is still below 2 percent. This suggests that even if the unemployment rate rises much further, the stability of Japanese society is

---

[13] This is defined as (9th decile–1st decile) / (median * 2).

[14] Okunishi's results have only weak statistical significance, largely due to the small sample size. Future research with larger samples should help to clarify these findings.

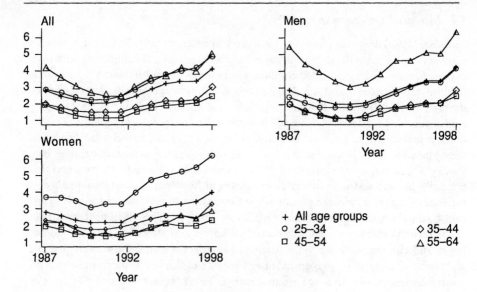

FIGURE 5.3. *Unemployment rate by age and gender*
Source: Management and Coordination Agency, *Labour Force Survey*.

not under any grave threat. Rebick (1994) shows that the unemployment rate of older men is highly sensitive to economic fluctuations and that this sensitivity has not been greatly affected by the generosity of social security programs. Older Japanese men continue to show very high participation rates by OECD standards, and this is responsible for much of the increase in Japan's unemployment rate at the same time that this growing group provides a safety valve for Japanese companies looking to reduce their numbers of employees.

It is sometimes suggested that Japanese unemployment rates are underestimated and that the rates would be much higher either because of technical differences in the definition of the unemployed (Taira, 1983) or because there is a large discouraged workers effect, especially for older men who have lost their jobs in their fifties (Nakamoto, 1999). The argument about technical differences made by Taira (1983) has been convincingly refuted (Kurosaka, 1988; Sorrentino, 1984), but the existence of a discouraged worker effect suggests that examination of the employment/population ratio (employment rate) would be useful. Table 5.5 shows the employment rates by gender for 1988, 1992 (the peak year in the labor market) and for 1998. Although employment rates have dropped in most cases from the peak year of 1992, most of the drops have not been much larger than the increases in the unemployment rate over the same period shown in Figure 5.3. What is really striking in this table is the increase in the employment rates of women aged 25–34 and over the age of 45 over the past decade, consistent with the rising aspirations of women mentioned previously. The other notable feature in the table is the high employment rate for older

TABLE 5.5. *Employment rates by year and gender*

Gender	Year	Age group			
		25–34	35–44	45–54	55–64
All	1988	73.7	79.6	80.1	60.7
	1992	76.1	81.4	82.6	64.6
	1998	76.0	79.8	81.6	63.8
Men	1988	94.6	96.0	95.0	78.7
	1992	95.3	96.9	96.4	82.2
	1998	92.8	95.1	94.8	79.8
Women	1988	52.4	63.1	65.2	44.3
	1992	56.5	65.7	68.8	47.9
	1998	58.7	64.0	68.5	48.5

Sources: Japan, *Labour Force Surveys*.

men by OECD standards. While it is undoubtedly true that Japanese unemployment rates would be higher if discouraged workers were considered, other OECD countries have the same problem to an even greater extent.

Government policy in Japan is unlikely to do much to alleviate the misery of older men or younger women who are unemployed. The government is determined to keep public welfare expenditure at a minimum and is encouraging the further development of private pension systems and life insurance to replace some of the government provision in the future (Shinkawa and Pempel, 1996). At the same time, however, the levels of underutilized labor within firms are now quite high, and there is considerable interest in the provision of training to enable employees to become usefully employed at new jobs within their companies or subsidiary enterprises.

Finally, mention should be made of one other route by which changes in personnel management and compensation systems are affecting macroeconomic employment. Changes in management practice have a high visibility in the Japanese media and have undoubtedly contributed to a feeling of insecurity in the workplace about future employment prospects and the level of future earnings. Under these circumstances it is understandable that households would increase precautionary savings, lowering consumer demand. This in turn would contribute to a higher unemployment rate, at least in the short run.

7. The Changing Nature of the Spring Bargaining Offensive (*Shuntō*)

Changes in the compensation system are beginning to have an effect on the nature of economy-wide bargaining in Japan. Although Freeman and Weitzman (1987) claimed that bonuses represented profit sharing within firms, their data was at the industry level, and follow-up studies (Brunello and Ohtake 1987; Koshiro 1992) were much more cautious in their conclusions. Whatever the truth about the past, it is now apparent that bonuses are much more sensitive to company performance and the introduction of the annual salary system is one manifestation of that (Imano, 1998).

To some extent solidarity in the Spring Bargaining Offensive (*Shuntō*) is made more difficult as management links pay more closely to firm performance rather than industry conditions. So far there is little statistical evidence of a major increase in the variance of wage settlements. An annual survey of some 300 large, unionized firms by the Ministry of Labor shows that the standardized interquartile range of wage settlements across firms has actually declined since the volatility of the late 1980s. This also suggests that Okunishi's findings of increased variance in wages within age groups has more to do with increased variance within firms rather than increased variance between firms. The consequence of greater emphasis on individual performance is undoubtedly contributing to the weakening of the labor movement. Union membership has declined from 35 per cent in 1970 to 22 per cent in 1998 for a number of reasons including demographic changes and changes in industrial structure. What is very striking, however, is the drop in the birth rate of new unions (Freeman and Rebick, 1989) as well as the sharp drop in the percentage of organized workers in large firms (from 68 per cent to 57 per cent). It is not surprising that there should be less interest in unions if individuals believe that their future earnings are more likely to be affected by their own performance rather than the bargaining strength of their union. Ishida (1998) argues that unions must shift their focus from the achievement of wage settlements to pushing for greater involvement in the management of work in the workplace if they are to maintain a useful role in the future.

8. Prospects for the Future and Conclusions

What then can be made of the view, commonly expressed in the press, that the Japanese employment system is breaking down? We should start by noting that Japan is experiencing its worst recession since the 1950s, but that does not imply that major structural change is required for the Japanese economy to recover (see Weinstein, Chapter 1 this volume). Japanese employees (especially blue-collar workers) were dismissed in large numbers during the recession of the mid-1970s and many observers at that time also forecast the end of employment guarantees. Press accounts naturally focus on the most dramatic stories, but the statistical evidence of this paper shows that this focus can be misleading. Finally, even the press accounts suggest that change is not that rapid. Articles often begin by giving the most dramatic examples of change in company policy but end with more sobering thoughts about the "glacial" pace of change in Japanese practices. Press accounts of Matsushita Electric have mostly been concerned with Matsushita's changes in pension policy that could promote greater interfirm mobility. At the same time, however, back-page reports in the Japanese business press tell us that Matsushita now provides employment guarantees up to the age of 65 for all of its employees. In other words, if we ignore the main headlines, the conclusions of this paper are not inconsistent with the factual information provided by the press.

First, it appears unlikely that Japan is about to move abruptly towards an Anglo-American type of open labor market. It is much more likely that firms will attempt to maintain job security for their employees (including employment with affiliated companies), and will continue to be concerned about the role of the firm in family support for prime-age men. However, it is likely that there will continue to be a gradual increase in the use of contingent labor and outsourcing will be used to accomplish certain specialized tasks. Second, there is likely to be a change in the nature of assessment and rewards within the Japanese firm. Some of these changes may lead to a greater dispersion in pay, and there are signs that this is already taking place. It is also likely that general human capital that is transportable between firms may become more important. The importance of personal contacts and detailed knowledge about specific markets and products may decline if companies' activities become more varied and economic conditions become more volatile. In this sense, the Japanese firm may converge towards Anglo-American practice.

The evidence suggests that large firms will continue to be reluctant to hire women into line-management positions, and women will continue to dominate the contingent work force in Japan, as in many other countries. The higher aspirations of women with better educational credentials may however be satisfied to the extent that they become technical specialists. Will Japanese policymakers endeavor to change this situation? Much of the policymaking discussion about the future of women in the Japanese labor market has been concerned with the recent collapse in the fertility rate in Japan along with the rise in the mean age of marriage and with the provision of care for the rapidly growing elderly population (Mason and Ogawa, Chapter 2 this volume). Government policy has aimed to make it easier for women to continue working while having children. Nursery, daycare, and kindergarten provision in Japan is already well-developed and low-cost as it is subsidized by the state.[15] Since 1995 Japan has had mandated maternity leave with benefits and take-up rates that are about average for the OECD (OECD, 1995: 175–88; Ministry of Welfare, 1998: 200–3). Recent policy has introduced subsidies for homecare leave to enable employees to take time off to care for relatives and small subsidies to encourage employers to rehire employees who have left to take care of young children or family (MOL, 1998: 339–40). The Japanese government implemented a revision of the EEOC in 1999, but outside of some minor regulatory changes, the revised law, like the original, relies mainly on administrative guidance to encourage the cooperation of firms (MOL, 1998: 332–6). Although the status of women in Japan remains low, outside of consciousness-raising, the government's direct action to change this situation will remain limited to its own hiring policies.[16]

---

[15] There is overall some 15 per cent overcapacity in provision of daycare, although there is roughly 15 per cent undercapacity for the youngest children in urban areas. Monthly fees range from US$0–800 depending on income level, but a family with income of US$40,000 would pay about US$250 (MOW, 1998: 156–7).

[16] It should be noted that any measures taken such as revision of the tax code to directly encourage the movement of women into jobs with higher pay may have adverse consequences for the fertility rate that make them unattractive. (see Mason and Ogawa, Chapter 2 this volume).

It is too early to tell how much of an effect changes in Japanese financial markets including the decline of the main-bank system and the increase in direct foreign investment (Blomström, Konan, and Lipsey, Chapter 11 this volume) will have on the speed of the changes just mentioned. According to Aoki (1994) and other theories of complementary institutions, a move away from the main-bank system of corporate governance towards direct governance by shareholders would push managers to pay more attention to short-run profitability and lead to a weakening of the long-term labor contract. The growth in shareholding by institutional investors such as life-insurance companies and pension funds (through trust banks), along with changes in accounting practices may lead to greater pressure for reforms in employment practices. At present, however, Japanese law does not allow pension funds to hold shares directly, and there is no evidence so far of these investors exerting direct pressure on Japanese companies through financial intermediaries (Suto, 1999). Some economists suggest that the increased presence of foreign-owned firms in Japan may lead to more rapid change, especially in the treatment of women (Blomström, Konan, and Lipsey, Chapter 11 this volume). Foreign-owned firms do have the reputation of offering better opportunities to women (Tōyō Keizai, 1996: 65), but these companies make up just 0.5 per cent of private-sector employment in Japan (ibid. 47) and even with expansion, it will be a long time before they have much of an overall impact.

Turning to macroeconomic issues, higher unemployment may be tolerable if it affects groups that are more marginal to the labor force, and it is unlikely that the government will respond by providing more generous benefits other than subsidies for job retraining. The growing divergence of company performance along with slower growth makes the *Shuntō* less attractive as a mechanism for wage determination and Japan may move towards a more decentralized system such as that found in the United Kingdom or United States. Japanese labor market institutions can be expected to converge towards Anglo-American practice in some areas, although the convergence is likely to be slow and piecemeal. It is unlikely that Japanese firms will give up their guarantees of job security for prime-age men, even if there is some private loss to be borne and underemployment of labor within the enterprise.

REFERENCES

Anchordoguy, M. (1997), "Japan at a Technological Crossroads: Does Change Support Convergence Theory?," *Journal of Japanese Studies*, 23/2: 363–98.
Aoki, M. (1994), "The Japanese Firm as a System of Attributes: A Survey and Research Agenda," in Aoki, M. and R. Dore (eds.), *The Japanese Firm: The Sources of Competitive Strength* (Oxford: Oxford University Press), 11–40.
Ariga, K., G. Brunello, and Y. Ohkusa (2000), *Internal Labor Markets in Japan* (Cambridge: Cambridge University Press).

Brunello, G. and F. Ohtake (1987), "Bonasu, Chingin no Kettei Mekanizumu to Koyō: Kigyōbetsu Dēta ni yoru Saikō," (Bonus, Wage Determination Mechanisms, and Employment: A Reconsideration Based on Firm-level Data) *Osaka Daigaku Keizaigaku*, 37/1: 28–41.

Chuma, H. (1997), "Keizai Kankyō no Henka to Chūkō Nensō no Chōkinzokuka," (Change in the Economic Environment and Lengthening of Tenure for the Middle and Older Age Groups), in *Koyō Kankō no Henka to Josei Rōdō* (Change in Employment Practices and Women's Labor), in Chuma, H. and T. Suruga (eds.), (Tokyo: Tokyo Daigaku Shuppankai), 47–114.

Clark, R. L. and N. Ogawa (1992*a*), "The Effect of Mandatory Retirement on Earnings Profiles in Japan," *Industrial and Labor Relations Review*, 45/2: 258–66.

——(1992*b*), "Employment Tenure and Earnings Profiles in Japan and the United States: Comment," *American Economic Review*, 82/1: 336–45.

Edwards, L. N. and M. K. Pasquale (1998), "Equal Employment Opportunity and Women's Higher Education in Japan," unpub. MS, Japan Economic Seminar, East Asian Institute, Columbia University, NY.

Freeman, R. B. and M. B. Weitzman (1987), "Bonuses and Employment in Japan," *Journal of the Japanese and International Economies*, 1/2: 168–94.

——and M. E. Rebick (1989), "Crumbling Pillar: Declining Union Density in Japan," *Journal of the Japanese and International Economies*, 3/4: 578–605.

Hashimoto, M. (1990), *The Japanese Labor Market in a Comparative Perspective with the United States*, (Kalamazoo, Mich.: Upjohn).

Imano, K. (1998), *Kachinuku Chingin Kaikaku* (The Success of Wage Reform) (Tokyo: Nihon Keizai Shinposha).

Ishida, M. (1998), "Jinji Shōgu no Kōbetsuka to Rōdōkumia Kinō," (What Scope does the Individualization of Remuneration Give the Enterprise Union?), *Nihon Rōdō Kenkyū Zasshi*, 22: 10 (Oct.), 40–8.

Japan Institute of Labour (1998), "Kanrishokuso no Koyōkanri Shisutemu ni kansuru Sōgōteki Kenkyū (shita)—Hiseizōgyō Ankeeto Chōsa Sōkatsuhen," (General Research on the Employment Management System for Managers—Summary of a Questionnaire Survey of Nonmanufacturing Industries), Chōsa Kenkyū Hōkokusho, No. 107 (Survey Research Report No. 107) (Tokyo: Japan Institute of Labour).

Japan Ministry of Education (MOE) (1998), *Monbu Tōkei Yōran* (Handbook of Education Statistics) (Tokyo: Ministry of Finance).

Japan Ministry of Labour (MOL*a*) (Annual), *Yearbook of Labour Statistics*, (Tokyo: Ministry of Finance).

——(MOL*b*) *Rōdō Tōkei Yōran* (Handbook of Labor Statistics) (Tokyo: Ministry of Finance).

——(MOL*d*) *Hataraku Josei no Jitsujō* formerly *Fujin Rōdō no Jitsujō* (Conditions of Working Women) (Tokyo: Ministry of Finance).

——(MOL*c*) (1998), *Nihon no Rōdō Seisaku* (The Labor Policy of Japan) (Tokyo: Labour Standards Survey Association).

Japan Ministry of Welfare (MOW) (1998), *Kōsei Hakusho* (White Paper on Welfare) (Tokyo: Kōsei Mondai Kenkyūkai).

Japan Productivity Centre (JPC) (Annual), *Katsuyō Rōdō Tōkei* (Useful Labor Statistics) (Tokyo: Japan Productivity Centre).

Koike, K. (1988), *Understanding Industrial Relations in Modern Japan* (London: Macmillan).

Koshiro, K. (1992), "Bonus Payments and Wage Flexibility in Japan" in Koshiro, K. (ed.), *Employment Security and Labor Market Flexibility* (Detroit: Wayne State University Press), 45–77.

Kurosaka, Y. (1988), *Makuro Keizaigaku to Nihon no Rōdō Shijō: Kyōkyūsaido no Bunseki* (Macroeconomics and the Japanese Labour Market: A Supply-Side Analysis) (Tokyo: Tōyō Keizai).

Lazear, E. (1979), "Why is There Mandatory Retirement?," *Journal of Political Economy*, 87 (Dec.): 1261–84.

Nakamoto, M. (1999), "Leaving the Fold," *Financial Times*, March 15, comment and analysis.

OECD (1995), *Employment Outlook* (Paris: OECD).

Okunishi, Y. (1998), "Kigyōnai Chingin Kakusa no Genjō to sono Yōin," (In-house Wage Differentials and Determining Factors), *Nihon Rōdō Kenkyū Zasshi*, 22: 10 (Oct.), 2–16.

Ono, A. (1997), "Haenuki Tōyō no Kōtai to Naibu Rōdō Shijō no Henshitsu" (Changing Internal Labor Markets and the Narrowing of the Gap in Promotion Rates Between Lifetime Employees and Mid-career Hires), in Chuma, H. and T. Suruga (eds.), *Koyō Kankō no Henka to Josei Rōdō* (Change in Employment Practices and Women's Labor) (Tokyo: Tokyo Daigaku Shuppankai), 83–114.

Rebick, M. E. (1992), "The Japanese Approach to Finding Jobs for Older Workers," in Mitchell O. S. (ed.), *As the Workforce Ages: Costs, Benefits and Policy Challenges* (Ithaca, NY: ILR Press), 103–24.

——(1994), "Social Security and Older Workers' Labor Market Responsiveness: The United States, Japan, and Sweden," in Blank, R. M. (ed.), *Social Protection and Economic Flexibility: Is There a Trade-Off?* (Chicago: University of Chicago Press), 189–222.

——(1995), "Rewards in the Afterlife: Late Career Job Placements as Incentives in the Japanese Firm," *Journal of the Japanese and International Economies*, 9/1: 1–28.

——(1998), "The Japanese Labour Market for University Graduates: Trends in the 1990s," *Japan Forum*, 10/1: 17–29.

Sako, M. and H. Sato (eds.) (1997), *Japanese Labour and Management in Transition: Diversity Flexibility and Participation*, (London: Routledge).

Shinkawa, T. and T. J. Pempel (1996), "Occupational Welfare and the Japanese Experience," in Shakev, M. (ed.), *The Privatization of Social Policy?* (London: St Martin's Press), 280–367.

Sorrentino, C. (1984), "Japan's Low Unemployment: An In-depth Analysis," *Monthly Labor Review*, 107/3: 18–27.

Strom, S. (1998), "Rethinking Lifetime Jobs and Their Underpinnings," *New York Times*, June 17, section D, p. 1.

Suruga, T. (1997), "Nihon Kigyō no Koyō Chōsei," (Employment Regulation in Japanese Firms), in Chuma, H. and T. Suruga (eds.), *Koyō Kankō no Henka to Josei Rōdō* (Change in Employment Practices and Women's Labor) (Tokyo: Tokyo Daigaku Shuppankai), 13–46.

Suto, M. (1999), "Shisan Kanri Sangyō no Daitō to Cōporēto Gabanansu," (The Growth of the Financial Management Industry and Corporate Governance), in Hanawa, T. (ed.), *Kinyū Shisutemu no Kōzō Henka to Nihon Keizai* (Structural Change in the Financial System and the Japanese Economy) (Tokyo: Chūō Daigaku Shuppanbu), 141–79.

Taira, K. (1983), "Japan's Low Unemployment: Economic Miracle or Statistical Artifact?," *Monthly Labor Review*, 106/7: 3–10.

Tachibanaki, T. (1996), *Wage Determination and Distribution in Japan* (Oxford: Oxford University Press).

Tōyō Keizai (1996), *Kaisha Shikihō: Joshi Gakusei Shūshokuhan* (Quarterly Report on Firms: Women Students' Job Search Edition) (Tokyo: Tōyō Keizai Shinpōsha).

Wakisaka, A. (1997), "Kōsu-betsu Jinji Seido to Josei Rōdō," (Course-based Personnel Systems and Women's Labor), in Chuma, H. and T. Suruga (eds.), *Koyō Kankō no Henka to Josei Rōdō* (Change in Employment Practices and Women's Labor) (Tokyo: Tokyo Daigaku Shuppankai), 243–78.

Yamamura, K. (1997), "The Japanese Economy after the 'Bubble': Plus Ça Change?," *Journal of Japanese Studies*, 23/2: 291–332.

Yashiro, N. and Y. Harada (eds.) (1998), *Nihonteki Koyō to Kokumin Seikatsu* (Japanese-style Employment and the Life of the Citizenry) (Tokyo: Tōyō Keizai Shinpōsha).

Part II

THE REGULATORY REGIME AND INDUSTRIAL RESTRUCTURING IN JAPAN

6 Central Banking, Financial, and Regulatory Change in Japan

THOMAS F. CARGILL

1. Introduction

Japan's central banking, financial, and regulatory institutions evolved slowly from the start of industrialization in the second half of the nineteenth century, reaching maturity in the 1950s. In the 1950s and 1960s they supported an impressive record of economic growth and macroeconomic stability that elevated Japan to the second largest economy in the world. Financial and monetary institutions began to change in the second half of the 1970s in response to new economic, political, and technological forces, both internal and external to Japan, calling for a more open, competitive, and internationalized financial system. The changes during the subsequent fifteen years were gradual and appeared successful, but in hindsight they did not meet the requirements of the new environment. Japan's impressive growth after 1975 continued through the 1980s but masked fundamental flaws in its financial and monetary institutions.[1] Institutional change accelerated in the 1990s in response to widespread and deep economic and financial distress in Japan. All indications are that further change will continue. The elements of continuity with Japan's past financial and monetary institutions, however, will pale in comparison to the new institutions and attitudes that will define Japan's financial and monetary affairs in the first part of the new century.

This chapter provides a past, current, and future perspective on financial and monetary institutional change in Japan.[2] The perspective is developed in three stages. First, the chapter discusses the evolution of financial and monetary institutions that reached maturity in the early 1950s. These institutions supported Japan's impressive postwar growth through the 1980s and served as a model for other Asian countries, especially South Korea. Second, the chapter discusses four phases of institution change in Japan's financial and monetary institutions: 1976–89; 1990–November 1997; November 1997–October 1998; and October 1998 through 1999. Third, the chapter discusses three challenges facing the new financial and monetary institutions emerging in the first part of the twenty-first century. A short concluding comment ends the chapter.

---

[1] The early 1970s were an exception to Japan's postwar record through 1989. The period was characterized by high rates of inflation referred to as "wild inflation," appreciation of the yen, and oil-price shocks. The economy recovered by 1975 largely due to policies set by the Bank of Japan. See Cargill, Hutchison, and Ito (1997) for a general overview of financial and monetary development in postwar Japan.

[2] This chapter draws on material in Cargill (1999 and 2000); Cargill, Hutchison, and Ito (1997, and forthcoming); and Cargill and Yoshino (forthcoming).

2. Financial and Monetary Institutional Development Through the 1970s

Japan's financial and monetary institutions began development after the Meiji Restoration in 1868, when the political decision was made to transform the economy from a feudal-agricultural to a market-based industrial structure. The goal of the transformation was to first achieve industrial and military parity with the West, and then surpass the West. The goal required financial and monetary institutions that did not previously exist, and as a result Japan looked to other countries for guidance.

A national banking system was established in 1872 based on the US model. Like the US system, Japan did not establish a central bank that could provide a flexible bank-note system and limit bank-note expansion. Excessive bank-note expansion and inflation led to revision of the banking system and the establishment of the Bank of Japan in 1882 as the sole issuer of bank notes. The Bank of Japan was based on the Belgian model (Goodhart, 1991). In 1875, Japan established a postal savings system based on the UK model as part of a network of post offices to bring deposit services to all parts of the country, and by the early 1900s the postal savings system added life insurance services. Postal savings and life insurance eventually formed the foundation of an extensive system of government financial intermediation currently known as the Fiscal Investment and Loan Program or FILP System.

Financial and monetary institutions played an important part in Japan's emergence as an industrial and military power by the first part of the twentieth century. By that time, these institutions exhibited well-defined characteristics, many of which would become prominent in postwar Japan. First, direct finance through money and capital markets played an insignificant role in the transfer of funds from surplus to deficit units. Second, competition in one sense was restricted by cartels of large banks with implicit government permission, in which banks individually formed long-term customer relationships with nonfinancial business entities. This became the forerunner of the *keiretsu* or main bank system. Third, in another sense, there existed substantial competition in the banking system, as there were a large number of small but poorly capitalized banks. Fourth, government financial intermediation became an important component of the financial system as funds from the postal savings system were transferred to the government to finance various projects and fund government sponsored banks. Fifth, the Bank of Japan was essentially an extension of the Ministry of Finance designed to regulate international capital flows, maintain a fixed rate of exchange, support large banks, and provide price stability.

Institutional development was modified in response to the collapse of the banking system in 1927, war mobilization in the 1930s, and war in the first half of the 1940s. The government assumed a more explicit influence over the financial system and aggressively pursued a consolidation policy to transform the banking system into a small number of institutions segmented by type of lending and sources of funding.

The second half of the 1940s was a turbulent period for Japan. Japan's financial and monetary institutions slowly recovered from the war. Under the influence of the Dodge Plan in 1949, Japan adopted an austerity policy to restore financial and economic stability.[3] The Dodge Plan was designed to bring inflation under control by reducing the growth of the money supply, stabilize the yen at 360 yen to the dollar, reduce government deficits, and limit the ability of the government to use the central bank as a means to finance government spending. The Dodge Plan policies would have caused a sharp slowdown in economic growth, but the start of the Korean War in June 1950 provided a stimulus that allowed Japan to reestablish stable financial and monetary institutions and set the foundation for sustained economic growth for the next two decades.

In the early 1950s Japan's financial and monetary institutions were restored. While the Allied occupation had some influence on these institutions, by and large the set of institutions that emerged in the early 1950s were a continuation of prewar developments and objectives. The financial regime, as it existed in the postwar period and prior to the start of financial liberalization in the second half of the 1970s, was designed to support industrialization and economic growth by reducing the cost and risk of investment in both the nonfinancial and financial sectors.[4] This was achieved through a highly regulated and nontransparent bank-finance model designed to transfer funds from the household to the business sector, limit household access to the financial system for consumer and mortgage credit, and encourage high rates of household saving. Interest rates, with a few exceptions, were administered and regulated by the Ministry of Finance and the Bank of Japan.

Economic growth was supported by high rates of domestic investment and exports. Manufacturing industries were encouraged to compete for foreign markets and capital, but the government did not relax constraints on capital inflows and continued to limit foreign presence in domestic markets. Regulation and tax policy encouraged high rates of household saving by limiting household access to the financial system as a source of funds and limiting taxes on interest income.

The financial and monetary institutions that dominated Japan's economy through the 1970s were successful by any reasonable standard. First, they met their objectives and played an important role in Japan's emergence from complete devastation in 1945 to become the second largest economy in the world by the 1980s. Second, financial regulation and supervision were able to achieve a high degree of financial stability in which, other than a few isolated cases, such as the failure of Yamaichi Securities Company in 1965, there were no official failures of financial institutions. In the nonfinancial sector, bankruptcies among companies, especially large companies, were rare. Third, the Bank of Japan, formally one of the world's most dependent central banks, achieved a record of moderate price inflation despite almost two decades of 10 per cent annual growth in real GDP from 1950 to 1970. Fourth, the household sector that

---

[3] The Dodge Plan refers to policies advocated by Joseph Dodge, an American banker who came to Japan in 1949 to serve as an economic advisor to the Supreme Commander of the Allied Occupation and help stabilize the economy. Dodge had previously assisted West Germany in bring inflation under control and is highly regarded in Japanese postwar history as providing the basis for industrialization and rapid economic growth after 1950.

[4] Aoki and Patrick (1994); Cargill (1999); Cargill and Royama (1988); Hamada and Horiuchi (1987); Patrick (1994); and Suzuki (1980 and 1987) provide detailed discussion of the Japanese financial regime in the postwar period.

provided the savings to drive the economy was compensated by high rates of real income growth as well as some access to the financial system through government banks for small business and mortgage credit.

The success of the Japanese financial and monetary regime influenced institutions throughout Asia, as other developing economies sought to duplicate Japan's economic performance. Asian countries adopted the Japanese regime in different ways, while maintaining the essential elements of financial repression, bank finance, and non-transparency.[5] These include differences in the organization of nonfinancial businesses, the degree of credit allocation, the amount of financial repression, and the degree of central bank independence. South Korea was the most transparent example of the Japanese regime.

3. Financial and Monetary Institutional Change: Four Phases

The financial and monetary regime reached maturity in the 1970s, but new economic, political, and technological forces were calling for institutional change in Japan and throughout the world. Starting in the 1970s, a wide range of developed and developing countries initiated a process of financial liberalization. Japan's financial liberalization process officially began in 1976 when the Ministry of Finance recognized a repurchase market in government bonds (*gensaki* market) which had been permitted to operate unofficially since the late 1960s.

Institutional change from the 1970s to the present can be considered from the perspective of four periods or phases: 1976–89; 1990–November 1997; November 1997–October 1998; October 1998 through 1999. Each period represents a distinct phase in terms of how institutional change was perceived in Japan and the quality and quantity of institutional change accomplished.

3.1. Institutional change: 1976 to 1989

The Japanese government adopted an official liberalization policy in 1976 in response to a variety of internal and external forces (Cargill and Royama, 1988; and Feldman, 1986). Japan's approach to liberalization during the 1976–89 period was gradual, administratively directed, and lacked the financial disruptions that characterized the United States and Scandinavian countries in the late 1980s. This was a remarkable achievement, especially since this period included the second series of oil price shocks in 1979 and 1980. Unlike most of the other industrial countries Japan was able to avoid a long period of inflation and disinflation in the early 1980s. By the mid-1980s, Japan attracted considerable attention because, unlike many industrial countries, Japan appeared to have achieved a smooth process of financial and monetary institutional change despite structural changes, internationalization, and macroeconomic shocks.

---

[5] See Cargill (1999), Cargill and Parker (forthcoming); and Huh and Kim (1994).

Two sets of institutional change can be identified during this period. The first was nontransparent, but nonetheless important, and the second was transparent and as a result, received most of the attention. The first concerns the Bank of Japan, and the second the structure of the financial system.

The Bank of Japan

The Bank of Japan was established in 1882 with renewed charters in 1912 and 1942. The legal framework of the Bank of Japan throughout the 1976–89 period was the 1942 Bank of Japan Law or, as it was frequently called, the "wartime" Bank of Japan Law.[6] The only significant institutional change to the 1942 Bank of Japan was the addition of a Monetary Policy Board in 1949 as part of the Dodge Plan reforms. The Policy Board was not an effort to provide legal independence to the Bank of Japan, but rather to broaden the influence on the Bank of Japan to reduce the potential for using monetary policy to finance government deficits.

A key characteristic of the 1942 Bank of Japan was its formal dependence on the Ministry of Finance. Articles 25 and 43 of the 1942 Law clearly express this formal dependence:

The Bank of Japan may, with the permission of the competent Minister, undertake such businesses as are necessary for the maintenance and fostering of the credit system. (Article 25)

The Bank of Japan shall be under the supervision of the competent Minister. (Article 43)

The Monetary Policy Board addition in 1949 did not change the legal relationship between the Bank of Japan and the Ministry of Finance. In fact, the Board within a short period of time evolved into a passive, rather than an active, component of Bank of Japan monetary policy.

The formal dependence of the Bank of Japan was verified by several well-known studies that ranked central banks by the degree of their dependence on the government.[7] The most extensive effort to measure central bank independence based on the parameters of the enabling legislation was provided by Cukierman, Webb, and Neyapti in 1992. According to their ranking of 72 countries for the 1980–9 period, only Belgium, Morocco, Poland, Norway, and Yugoslavia had more dependent central banks than Japan, and only Nepal was tied with Japan.

These rankings however, were misleading from two perspectives. First, with the exception of the "wild inflation" of the early 1970s, the Bank of Japan achieved a

---

[6] The wartime conditions of the 1942 Law are frequently exaggerated. Comparison of the 1882 Law and the 1942 Law reveals little difference in the expressed relationship between the Bank of Japan and the government.

[7] See Alesina and Summers (1993); Burdekin and Willett (1991); and Cargill (1995) for a discussion of the various indexes. The studies are not consistent in their ranking of the Bank of Japan, though in general, the Bank of Japan is regarded as one of the more formally dependent central banks among the industrialized countries. Cukierman, Webb, and Neyapti (1992) regard the Bank of Japan as one of the least independent central banks in the world. In contrast, the Bade–Parkin–Alesina index (modification and extension of the original Bade and Parkin (1982) ranking and reported in Alesina and Summers (1993)) assigns the Bank of Japan a relatively high level of independence, in fact the same as the Federal Reserve System. Burdekin and Willett (1991) and Cargill (1995) specifically criticized Japan's high independence ranking based on the 1942 Law.

record of price stability that is impressive by any standard. During the High Growth Period from 1950 to 1970 the inflation rate averaged 4 to 5 per cent, but in the context of real GDP growth of 10 per cent per annum. More important, after 1973 the Bank of Japan was able to bring the inflation rate down and after 1975 achieved price stability in spite of oil price shocks in 1979 and 1980. The Bank of Japan's performance contradicted the empirical evidence that there existed a statistically robust and inverse relationship between inflation policy outcomes and central banking independence as measured by indexes constructed by Cukierman, Webb, and Neyapti, and others (Cargill, 1995).

Second, the low independence rankings based on the 1942 Bank of Japan Law fail to recognize a subtle institutional change in monetary policy that occurred in the first half of the 1970s. The Bank of Japan had been constrained by two factors prior to the early 1970s. Monetary policy was focused on maintaining the fixed exchange rate of 360 yen to the dollar, and the Ministry of Finance played a major role in formulating monetary policy. The end of the fixed exchange rate system in 1973 provided the Bank of Japan with operational independence, and the high rates of inflation experienced in the early 1970s as a result of government-directed monetary policy provided the Bank of Japan with de facto political independence to pursue price stability.

Thus, institutional change in the Bank of Japan was significant, but nontransparent. The Bank of Japan during the 1976 to 1989 period became increasingly politically independent from the Ministry of Finance. In terms of policy outcomes, the Bank of Japan achieved a record of price stability superior to the more formally independent central banks of the world such as the Federal Reserve System.

The structure of finance

The Japanese financial system in 1975 was one of the most rigidly regulated and administratively controlled among the industrialized countries of the world. The financial system was designed to achieve rapid industrialization, export-led economic growth, international isolation, and high rates of household saving. In 1976 Japan adopted an official policy of financial liberalization that was carried out in a series of gradual steps over the next fifteen years.

Interest rate controls on deposits were phased out gradually by first permitting unregulated interest rates for large CDs, introduced in 1979, and then phasing out ceilings on first, large denomination deposits, and then smaller denomination deposits by 1993. Bank lending rates were liberalized in the early 1980s. Financial institutions were provided with enhanced portfolio diversification powers, and the domestic financial system became less segmented. Money and capital markets were expanded. Foreign financial institutions were granted greater access to the domestic market. Households were granted greater access to consumer and mortgage credit. Greater competition was permitted between banks and securities companies. Inflows and outflows of capital were gradually liberalized after 1980. Japan's short-term money markets, for example, were integrated with the international financial system by the early 1980s.

These institutional changes compared to the financial system of 1975 were significant, but, on a more fundamental level, paled in comparison to the institutional changes required to render Japan's financial and monetary regime compatible with the new economic, political, and technological environment. Despite an official policy of liberalization and institutional change, the essential elements of the old regime remained firmly in place through 1989. In particular, Japan continued to rely on a bank-finance model with pervasive government deposit guarantees maintained by Bank of Japan lending, administrative guidance by the Ministry of Finance, non-transparency, and a mutual support system referred to as the "convoy" system.

Japan's gradual and reluctant liberalization process proceeded at a slow, steady pace with few disruptions to the real or financial sectors, especially when compared to the financial disruptions in the United States (Cargill and Royama, 1988). This approach and outcome were made possible by the price stability policies of the Bank of Japan. Low and stable inflation rates resulted in small gaps between regulated and unregulated interest rates. What started as a smooth transition, however, changed dramatically in the second half of the 1980s with the sharp run-up in asset prices and booming economic and monetary growth that characterized the "bubble economy" (Cargill, Hutchison, and Ito, 1997).

The collapse of asset prices in 1990 and 1991 set into motion a series of events that resulted in significant institutional change in the 1990s, but, again, the institutional change was constrained by an unwillingness to depart from the old regime.

3.2. Institutional change: 1990 to November 1997

The bubble economy followed the pattern of a classic speculative bubble until it began to unravel in May 1989, when the Bank of Japan, in opposition to the Ministry of Finance, raised the discount rate. The subsequent fall in asset prices in the early 1990s, and associated recession, adversely impacted bank balance sheets. Financial institutions were saddled with a massive nonperforming loan problem estimated even in the early 1990s to exceed US$500 billion.

The banking crisis and nonperforming loan problem in Japan was aggravated by regulatory inertia, forbearance, and forgiveness. The piecemeal and tentative approach initially followed by the Ministry of Finance in dealing with the banking crisis exhausted the limited resources of the Deposit Insurance Corporation without confronting the underlying problems. Economic growth in the first half of the 1990s stagnated, and financial distress increased each year, as Japan was forced for the first time in its postwar history to officially declare a depository institution insolvent. A total of eleven small cooperatives and banks failed from 1991 to 1995.

The regulatory approach rooted in the old financial and monetary regime was not able to resolve the growing financial distress. Starting in 1995, Japanese authorities took more decisive financial and monetary institutional reform.

Deposit insurance reform, Prompt Corrective Action, and a complete deposit guarantee
In December 1995 the decision was made to restructure the Deposit Insurance Corporation and to adopt a new approach to dealing with troubled financial institutions, referred to as Prompt Corrective Action. To maintain public and international

confidence in the financial system, the government announced in late 1995 a complete deposit guarantee effective to March 2001 and assured the public that the financial distress had not reached the center of the financial system but was confined to specialized and smaller financial institutions. The government's decision to guarantee all deposits was also a reaction to the "Japan premium" in international bank markets during summer 1995. The Japan premium is the additional basis points that Japanese banks were required to pay in the international market. Figure 6.1 presents the Japan premium from 1994 to 1999 calculated as the difference between the quoted interest rate of TIBOR (in the Tokyo offshore market where most banks are Japanese) and the quoted interest rate of LIBOR (in the London offshore market where most banks are western). The premium presented in Figure 6.1 is provided by Ito and Harada (2000).

Resolution of the jusen problem
The *jusen* companies were created in the mid-1970s as subsidiaries of banks, securities firms, and life-insurance companies. They originally focused on consumer lending, but as banks became aggressive competitors in the consumer lending market in the 1980s, the *jusen* companies turned to real estate lending. During the 1990–1 period, *jusen* lending was supported increasingly by funds from a large number of small agricultural cooperatives. Concerns over the asset quality of the *jusen* industry were raised as early as 1992, but the Ministry of Finance essentially ignored and covered up the problem. The *jusen* problem by 1995, however, loomed even larger than the bank nonperforming loan problem. An August 1995 audit revealed that 74

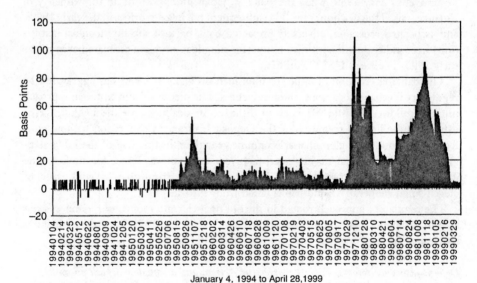

January 4, 1994 to April 28, 1999

FIGURE 6.1. *Japan premium*
Source: Ito and Harada (2000).

per cent of *jusen* loans were nonperforming and 49 per cent of *jusen* loans were considered unrecoverable. At that time the political decision was made to close the insolvent *jusen* industry.

Disposal of nonperforming loans
In 1992, 162 private banks established the Credit Cooperative Purchasing Company with the encouragement of the Ministry of Finance. The Company was designed to purchase nonperforming loans from the member banks, financed by the banks. The difference between the purchasing and selling price of the collateral would then be charged against the bank that sold the loan to the Company.

In 1995, two new government-loan disposal agencies were established. To assist in disposing of assets of troubled cooperatives, the government established the Resolution and Collection Bank to liquidate the assets of failed credit cooperatives. This was a supplement to the Credit Cooperative Purchasing Program. The Housing Loan Administration was established to assume the assets of the *jusen* industry.

Big Bang announcement of November 1996
By late 1996, financial distress was considered under control from several perspectives. The economy appeared to be in a recovery stage in terms of real GDP growth (Figure 6.2), and estimates of nonperforming loans declined. The government had completed significant institutional change by reforming the Deposit Insurance Corporation, establishing the Resolution and Collection Bank, and closing the *jusen*

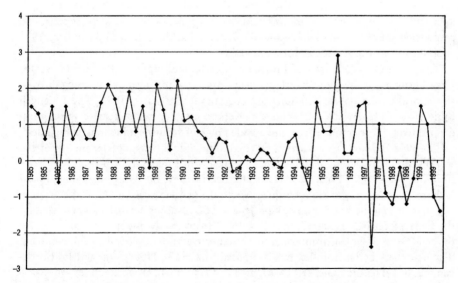

FIGURE 6.2. *Quarterly growth of real GDP*

154 Thomas F. Cargill

industry. The Japan premium remained positive, but declined from the highs reached in the second half of 1995. The complete government deposit guarantee provided a window of opportunity for banks to more aggressively improve their balance sheets. The Liberal Democratic Party was returned to a majority position in the Lower House in October 1996 on a platform of economic reform.

Confidence that financial and economic distress were under control was manifested by the new Prime Minister Hashimoto's Big Bang announcement of November 1996 (see Ito and Melvin, Chapter 7 this volume). The Big Bang represented a bold and accelerated approach to liberalization that assumed financial distress was under control and would be shortly resolved. Rather than a specific list of policies, the Big Bang announcement emphasized the need for a new financial structure by 2001 based on the principles of free, open, and internationalized financial markets. The Big Bang envisaged significant institutional change that would include transparent and enforced rules of conduct as well as accounting, legal, and supervision reforms consistent with international standards.

Institutional change and the Big Bang

The first implementation of the Big Bang was taken in April 1998 by deregulating the Foreign Exchange Law. Brokering of foreign exchange transactions was no longer restricted to authorized banks, and for all practical purposes anyone could conduct foreign exchange operations without permission or informing the Ministry of Finance. The next implementation of the Big Bang was a series of legislative changes in the spring and early summer of 1997 (Cargill, Hutchison, and Ito, 1998). Establishment of the Financial Supervisory Agency and revision of the 1942 Bank of Japan Law were the two most significant legislative events in 1997. Both changes significantly reduced the influence of the Ministry of Finance in Japan's financial supervision and regulation framework. The Ministry's policies were widely regarded as responsible for the financial and economic distress that characterized Japan from 1991 to 1996, and its reputation was at a low point.

The power of the Ministry of Finance to monitor and supervise the financial sector was transferred to the Financial Supervisory Agency, a new agency reporting directly to the prime minister that commenced operations on April 1, 1998. The Financial Supervisory Agency also was granted powers to monitor and supervise agricultural cooperatives, labor cooperatives, and a wide range of finance and leasing companies.

The 1942 Bank of Japan Law was revised to provide the Bank of Japan, one of the world's most formally dependent central banks, with enhanced formal independence from the Ministry of Finance. First established in 1949, the Monetary Policy Board had become passive over the subsequent years; the new law reinstated it as the primary decision-making body of the Bank of Japan. The resulting formal independence of the Bank of Japan was significant. Table 6.1 illustrates the independence index for the new Bank of Japan in international perspective with other industrial countries. The new Bank of Japan index was computed by Cargill, Hutchison, and Ito (forthcoming) based on the same framework used by Cukierman, Webb, and Neyapti. Revision of the Bank of Japan Law elevated Bank of Japan independence from near the

TABLE 6.1. *Central Bank legal independence: The Bank of Japan in international perspective*

	Index
Germany	0.69
Switzerland	0.64
Austria	0.61
Denmark	0.50
United States	0.48
Canada	0.45
Ireland	0.44
Netherlands	0.42
New Bank of Japan as of April 1, 1998	0.39
Australia	0.36
Iceland	0.34
Luxembourg	0.33
Sweden	0.29
Finland	0.28
United Kingdom	0.27
Italy	0.25
New Zealand	0.24
Spain	0.23
Old Bank of Japan	0.18
Norway	0.17
Belgium	0.17

Sources: The indexes of legal independence, with exception of new Bank of Japan, are from Cukierman, Webb, and Neyapti (1992: 362) and represent the period from 1980 to 1989; however, the indexes are considered reasonable through 1996. The new Bank of Japan index is from Cargill, Hutchison, and Ito (forthcoming, ch. 4).

bottom to the top half. This represents a major institutional change in Japan's financial and monetary system.

3.3. Institutional change: November 1997 to October 1998

Optimism ended in late 1997 in response to external and internal shocks to the Japanese economy. Banking problems and general financial distress became a common feature of many Asian economies, and by November 1997 had reached South Korea, widely regarded as Asia's next giant. The regional problems adversely impacted Japan's economy and exposed Japanese financial institutions to further loan losses.

The most dramatic events in late 1997, however, were internal. The failures of Hokkaido Takushoku, one of Japan's city banks and nineteenth largest bank, and

Yamaichi Securities Company, Japan's fourth largest security company, in November 1997 indicated that financial distress was not confined only to Japan's smaller institutions. The market responded dramatically to the two failures. Bank stock prices declined relative to the market and the "Japan premium" increased 100 basis points on the international market. (Figure 6.1).

The hesitant recovery that started in the latter part of 1996 and first part of 1997 was replaced by declining output and increasing unemployment, which in turn, further increased the size of the nonperforming loan problem and elevated financial distress. A sense of crisis emerged.

On January 12, 1998, the Ministry of Finance, in an effort toward greater transparency, officially acknowledged that the nonperforming loan problem was more serious than previously reported and indicated a willingness to provide more candid estimates of the condition of the financial system. In December 1997, the Ministry of Finance recommended 30 trillion yen of public funds be raised and committed to protecting depositors and injecting new capital into the banking system. Of the 30 trillion yen, 13 trillion was to be used to inject capital to solvent but thinly capitalized banks, while the remaining 17 trillion was to be used to protect depositors of failed banks.

The first allocation of the 30 trillion yen in March 1998 revealed that the old mutual support system was still in place. The government provided an across-the-board capital injection of 1.8 trillion yen to twenty-one banks (eighteen large banks and three regional banks) irrespective of their individual condition and without the prior commitment to restructure, despite assurances that prior conditions would be obtained. Regulatory authorities had not yet reached a point where they were willing to abandon the convoy system and differentiate between nonviable and weak but viable institutions. The capital injection had no meaningful effect on bank stock prices or the Japan premium.

The financial distress worsened. Nonperforming loans at the top nineteen banks (including the Long Term Credit Bank and Nippon Credit Bank, which were subsequently nationalized) were estimated at 57.3 trillion yen as of March 1998, representing 15.7 per cent of outstanding loans or 18 per cent of real GDP. In the summer of 1998 the Long Term Credit Bank and Nippon Credit Bank were declared nonviable, though, again, the declarations were a belated announcement.

3.4. Institutional change: October 1998 to 1999

The Liberal Democratic Party lost the majority in the Upper House and Prime Minister Hashimoto resigned in July 1998. The new Prime Minister Obuchi announced a series of more aggressive policies in October 1998. The Long Term Credit Bank and Nippon Credit Bank were nationalized. Committed government funding was raised from 30 to 60 trillion yen to protect depositors of failed banks and to inject capital into banks that could survive, either on their own or with a merger partner. Regulatory authorities adopted a more liberal view toward foreign capital and foreign institutions in dealing with the financial distress; for example, Merrill Lynch was permitted to purchase Yamaichi Securities Company. A new coordinating agency, the Financial Reconstruction Committee, was established as part of the prime minister's office to manage the resolution of failed institutions, manage the financial crisis in general, audit and inspect financial institutions, and oversee the operations of the Financial Supervisory Commission. The Resolution and Collection Bank and the Housing Loan Administration were consolidated into a US-type resolution trust corporation called the Resolution and Collection Organization.[8] Evidence of the change in attitude and policy occurred with the second capital injection of public funds into the banking system in March 1999. The March 1999 injection was based on the same framework as March 1998; however, the implementation was significantly different. The Financial Reconstruction Commission, in charge of the capital injection, raised the standards for securing public funding. The definition of net worth was made more rigorous, higher standards were applied to classifying loans into performing and non-performing categories, and banks were required to submit detailed and meaningful restructuring plans (International Monetary Fund, 1999, Annex II). In addition, the March 1999 injection totaled 7.5 trillion yen, compared to 1.8 trillion yen in March 1998. The majority of injections to any one bank was in the form of convertible preferred shares with a "grace period" condition attached that gave the government considerable control over the receiving bank for up to five years.

The March 1999 capital injection was followed by continued progress to implement the goals of the Big Bang. The fixed brokerage commission system, long an institutional feature of Japan's equity markets, was completely abolished on October 1, 1999, for all transactions, completing a process started in April 1998 when the fixed system was abolished on trades of 50 million yen or more. Access to the securities industry was simplified, the established exchanges' monopoly on stock trade was abolished so that equity trade could take place outside of the established exchanges, and the financial services industry now appears ready to undergo an "internet" revolution.

Consolidation is occurring rapidly in the financial services industry. In the past consolidation was encouraged by the government as a method for dealing with financial distress; however, there appears to be less pressure by the government to force "white knight" acquisitions. The most dramatic example of this occurred in August 1999 when Dai-Ichi Kangyo Bank, Fuji Bank, and the Industrial Bank of Japan announced plans to merge. The new institution would be the largest bank in the world.

4. Challenges to Future Institutional Change

Japan's financial and monetary institutions are in transition toward ones that will enable Japan to achieve the goals of the Big Bang announcement, which remains the operating financial map for institutional change. At the same time, a number of issues remain whose resolution is not clear at this time. Three can be identified: central bank

---

[8] The Resolution Trust Corporation was established in 1989 to liquidate assets of failed S&J.s.

policy; regulatory institutions and the bank-finance model; and government financial intermediation.

4.1. Bank of Japan policy

The newly independent Bank of Japan encountered a variety of problems. Some were short term such as scandals in the Bank Examination Bureau that led to the resignation of the governor and deputy-governor in 1998. Others were more serious and concerned problems of conducting monetary policy in a near-zero interest rate environment and whether the Bank of Japan's independence would be challenged despite the new Bank of Japan Law.

A lively debate ensued in 1999 over whether the Bank of Japan was sufficiently stimulative. A number of observers regarded the Bank of Japan's policy as not sufficiently stimulative as evidenced by price deflation in the late 1990s (Cargill, 2000; Cargill, Hutchison, and Ito, forthcoming; and Posen, 1998 and 1999). The debate highlighted the importance of preventing deflation as well as inflation. There were also concerns raised about the ability of the Bank of Japan to maintain its new independence in the context of changes in Japan's political institutions. The Bank of Japan, while removing itself from the Ministry of Finance's influence, may become more dependent on politicians. Political institutions are changing in Japan, as politicians increasingly realize they will be punished for poor economic performance. A reduced national consensus for economic growth and a more politically active household sector are generating fractionalized political institutions willing to use monetary policy to enhance political power. Thus, the Bank of Japan could become more sensitive to political influences, especially since the Cabinet with consent of the Diet selects six of the nine members of the revised and enhanced Monetary Policy Board.

A number of observers have suggested that further institutional change is required that would assist the Bank of Japan in preventing deflation as well as inflation and in remaining politically independent. Specifically, the Bank of Japan should adopt an explicit inflation target. Explicit inflation targeting would have prevented the policy mistakes of 1998 and 1999 and would go a considerable distance to ensuring that monetary policy does not become an instrument of political manipulation to maintain and enhance political power.

There is also a relatively minor institutional issue with regard to the role of the Bank of Japan in bank supervision. Currently the Bank of Japan conducts bank audits, which were once shared with the Ministry of Finance. The new Financial Supervisory Agency has taken over the function of bank supervision from the Ministry, and there remains an issue of whether the current Bank of Japan role in bank supervision needs to be transferred to the Financial Supervision Agency. Arguments can be made in both directions.

4.2. Decline of the bank-finance model and dealing with financial distress

The most immediate problem of the new financial and supervisory institutions is to resolve the large volume of nonperforming loans. The committed financial resources

(60 billion yen) are sufficient, the institutional framework has been put into place, but it is not entirely clear whether Japan is ready to consolidate its banking system and permit a greater flow of funds through money and capital markets. Two problems can be identified.

First, Japan imposed a complete deposit guarantee in 1995 intended to end March 1, 2001. At that time, the insurance limit of 10 million yen per deposit will be reimposed and the resources of the Deposit Insurance Corporation will become the foundation for public confidence in deposit money. In late 1999, politicians were calling for an extension of the deposit guarantee because of fear the banking system has not sufficiently recovered. The deposit guarantee was extended for an additional year to March 31, 2002.

Second, and of longer-run concern, the new financial regulatory institutions like the old ones are based on the bank-finance model. But banks have lost and will continue to lose market share as new financial channels develop. According to Hoshi and Kashyap (1999), bank loan demand in Japan could decline by more than 20 per cent in the next decade using the United States as a benchmark and focusing only on demand for funds by large businesses. It remains an open question as to how well the new institutions will oversee the declining role of the banking system, which has stood at the center of Japan's financial system since the start of industrialization.

Like the Bank of Japan, the new regulatory institutions are more dependent on the prime minister's office and politicians. The decline in the influence of the Ministry of Finance is offset by an increase in the influence of politicians. Thus, there is as much concern that the new regulatory institutions retain independence as there is that the Bank of Japan retain its newly acquired independence.

4.3. Government financial intermediation

Japan's financial institutions include a multidimensional and complex institutional arrangement of postal savings offices and government financial institutions designed to transfer funds from the public to designated sectors of the economy. The system is referred to as the Fiscal Investment and Loan Program system (FILP) and is under the control of the Ministry of Finance, receiving and distributing funds through its Trust Fund Bureau. In terms of deposit size, the postal savings system is the world's largest financial institution with 240 trillion yen in deposits representing 36 per cent of total deposits in 1998 and a significant share of life insurance (31 per cent in 1998). There has also been a shift in lending activity as a greater proportion of loans are being made to business and housing in an effort to offset the late 1990s credit crunch at private banks.

The postal savings system and the FILP have resisted reform during the past two decades (Cargill and Yoshino, 2000). The Big Bang announcement in November 1996, despite its broad agenda, did not mention the postal savings system or make any meaningful reference to FILP reform. Their omission from the announcement suggested official reluctance to deal with one of the most important constraints on financial modernization. In fact, the postal savings system at the time was being held up as a model for other Asian countries (*Wall Street Journal*, 1997).

The FILP system has recently become the object of reform, however. As part of the Laws to Reform Central Government Ministries and Agencies passed in June 1998, the structure of government budgeting was fundamentally changed (Cargill and Yoshino, 1998). Starting March 2001, the government will no longer receive funds from the postal savings system. Government financial institutions will then be required to develop new sources of funding. The future roles of the postal savings system and government financial institutions, however, are left unresolved at this time.

5. Concluding Comment

Japan's financial and monetary institutions broke down in the 1990s. Failure to recognize the new economic, political, and technological environment, and the past success of the existing financial and monetary institutions, led regulatory authorities to believe that the old regime could continue into the twenty-first century. The 1990s, and especially the late 1990s, were a critical turning point. New institutions and new attitudes have emerged that if successfully implemented will help Japan achieve the goals of the Big Bang announcement and render Japan's financial and monetary system an important and stable part of the world economy.

REFERENCES

Alesina, Alberto and Lawrence H. Summers (1993), "Central Bank Independence and Macroeconomic Performance: Some Comparative Evidence," *Journal of Money, Credit, and Banking*, 25: 151–62.

Aoki, Masahiko and Hugh Patrick (eds.) (1994), *The Japanese Main Banking System* (Oxford: Oxford University Press).

Bade, Robert and Michael Parkin (1982), "Central Bank Laws and Monetary Policy," unpub. MS., University of Western Ontario, Canada.

Burdekin, Richard C. K. and Thomas D. Willet (1991), "Central Bank Reform: The Federal Reserve in International Perspective," *Public Budgeting and Financial Management*, 3: 619–49.

Cargill, Thomas F. (1995), "The Statistical Association Between Central Bank Independence and Inflation," *Banca Nazionale Del Lavoro: Quarterly Review* (June): 159–72.

——(1999), "Korea and Japan: The End of the 'Japanese Financial Regime'," in George Kaufman (ed.), *Bank Crisis: Causes, Analysis and Prevention* (London: JAI Press).

——(2000), "Monetary Policy, Deflation, and Economic History: Lessons for the Bank of Japan," *Monetary and Economic Studies* (Dec.): 1–22.

——(2000), "What Caused Japan's Banking Crisis?," in Takeo Hoshi and Hugh Patrick (eds.), *Crisis and Change in the Japanese Financial System* (Boston: Kluwer Academic Press).

——and Elliott Parker (forthcoming), "Financial Liberalization in China: Limitations and Lessons of the Japanese Regime," *Journal of the Asia–Pacific Economy*.

——and Shoichi Royama (1988), *The Transition of Finance in Japan and the United States* (Stanford: Hoover Institution Press).

——and Naoyuki Yoshino (1998), "Too Big for its Boots," *The Financial Regulator*, 3 (Dec.): 39–43.

————(2000), "The Postal Savings System, Fiscal Investment and Loan Program, and Modernization of Japan's Financial System," in Takeo Hoshi and Hugh Patrick (eds.), *Crisis and Change in the Japanese Financial System* (Boston: Kluwer Academic Press).

——Michael M. Hutchison, and Takatoshi Ito (1997), *The Political Economy of Japanese Monetary Policy* (Cambridge, Mass.: MIT Press).

————(1998), "The Banking Crisis in Japan," in G. Caprio, Jr., W. C. Hunter, G. G. Kaufman, and D. M. Leipziger (eds.), *Preventing Bank Crises: Lessons from Recent Global Bank Failures* (Washington: World Bank).

————(forthcoming), *Financial Policy and Central Banking in Japan* (Cambridge, Mass.: MIT Press).

Cukierman, Alex, Steven B. Webb, and Bilin Neyapti (1992), "Measuring the Independence of Central Banks and its Effect on Policy Outcomes," *World Bank Economic Review*, 6: 353–98.

Feldman, Robert Alan (1986), *Japanese Financial Markets: Deficits, Dilemmas, and Deregulation* (Cambridge, Mass.: MIT Press).

Goodhart, Charles (1991), *The Evolution of Central Banks* (Cambridge, Mass.: MIT Press).

Hamada, Koichi and Akiyoshi Horiuchi (1987), "The Political Economy of the Financial Market," in K. Yamamura and Y. Yasuba (eds.), *The Political Economy of Japan*, i. (Stanford: Stanford University Press).

Hoshi, Takeo and Anil Kashyap (1999), "The Japanese Bank Crisis: Where Did it Come From and How Will it End?," in Ben S. Bernanke and Julio Rotemberg (eds.), *NBER Macroeconomics Annual 1999* (Cambridge, Mass.: MIT Press).

Huh, Chan Guk and Sun Bae Kim (1994), "Financial Regulation and Banking Sector Performance: A Comparison of Bad Loan Problems in Japan and Korea," *Economic Review* (Federal Reserve Bank of San Francisco), No. 2.

International Monetary Fund (1999), *International Capital Markets* (Washington: International Monetary Fund).

Ito, Takatoshi and Kimie Harada (2000), "Japan Premium and Stock Prices: Two Mirrors of the Japanese Banking Crisis," draft manuscript.

Patrick, Hugh (1994), "The Relevance of Japanese Finance and its Main Bank System," in Masahiko Aoki and Hugh Patrick (eds.), *The Japanese Main Banking System* (Oxford: Oxford University Press).

Posen, Adam S. (1998), *Restoring Japan's Economic Growth* (Washington: Institute for International Economics).

——(1999), "Nothing to Fear but Fear (of Inflation) Itself," *International Economics Policy Briefs* (Washington: Institute for International Economics (Oct.).

Suzuki, Yoshio (1980), *Money and Banking in Contemporary Japan* (New Haven: Yale University Press).

Suzuki, Yoshio (ed.) (1987), *The Japanese Financial System* (Oxford: Clarendon Press).

Wall Street Journal (1997), Masayoshi Kanabayashi, "Postal Savings may Prove Popular Throughout Asia", April 18.

7 Japan's Big Bang and the Transformation of Financial Markets

TAKATOSHI ITO AND MICHAEL MELVIN

1. Introduction

The "Big Bang" of Japanese financial markets was proposed in November 1996 by the Hashimoto government. This was the beginning of the end to the "convoy" system—no failure and regulatory protection—that had ruled the Japanese financial markets since the end of the Second World War. It is a bold idea to deregulate and liberalize the financial sectors, if not belatedly.

There were three main objectives. First, the Big Bang aims at making the Japanese market more efficient and internationalized. The market will become more active and competitive, and users, such as the Japanese corporations and retail consumers, will be beneficiaries. Second, the Japanese institutions, with competitive pressures from foreign institutions, become more efficient. Third, it will deflect the political pressures, representing vested interest, on the Ministry of Finance.

After the bubble burst, the Tokyo financial markets have been losing steam. The Tokyo Stock Exchange has lost more than half of its capitalization since the peak of the bubble (December 1989). There had been a mass exodus of foreign stock listings from the Tokyo Big Board. The trading volumes of the Tokyo foreign exchange market had not been growing in the 1990s, and Hong Kong and Singapore were catching up fast. The usage of the yen in Asia had not grown as some economists had predicted, partly because of the cumbersome rules and regulations in Tokyo. The first motivation of the Big Bang was to stop the skidding of Tokyo as an (if not "the") Asian financial center.

Making the Tokyo markets efficient does not necessarily mean that the Japanese institutions will flourish. If foreigners have a competitive advantage in financial products, then they will take greater market shares in Tokyo. It must be endured, the policymakers argued. However, it was hoped that intensified competition would make Japanese institutions more efficient and stronger. The second objective, which derives from the first one, was more nationalistic, but tried to force Japanese financial institutions to try harder.

Although the objectives were unanimously hailed as appropriate and desirable, the timing of the announcement was not so obvious. The Ministry of Finance was heavily criticized for its role in first creating and then bursting the bubble and not guiding the banking industry through the sea of nonperforming loans. First, the Ministry tried to maintain the "convoy" system, i.e., forcing healthy banks to share the burden of failing banks and allowing banks to postpone provisioning and sales of bad assets, and then abandoned it without a sufficiently funded safety net (deposit insurance system). The Big Bang is a constructive way to steer attention away from the sorry past to a bright future.

The rest of this paper will examine the contents of the Big Bang, discuss its likely effects, and present some econometric analysis of early indications in the foreign exchange market.

2. What is the Big Bang?

The Ministry described the spirit of the Big Bang as "fair, free, and global." Obviously, the main objectives of the Big Bang are to make the Japanese financial markets more competitive and to provide Japanese institutions with more opportunities than fetters. When the Big Bang is implemented, transaction costs will be substantially reduced, and those who are using the Tokyo markets, mostly institutions in Japan, will benefit from deregulation. However, many observers point out that there may be more political (or political economy) objectives. First, the Big Bang is sequenced so that it will take some time to complete it, but will be carried through to the end. The foreign exchange controls were effectively eliminated on April 1, 1998. Nonfinancial institutions in Japan can deal in foreign exchange without banks' intermediation. Moreover, Japanese investors are now allowed to open and maintain accounts with financial institutions in foreign countries. Without change, Japanese banks will lose a large chunk of formerly protected businesses to New York and London. The Big Bang starting with the foreign exchange deregulation will ensure that the rest of the reforms will be carried through.

Politically, the Big Bang may have been a response to various scandals among the Ministry officials. The revelation that some high-ranking officials were caught in near-bribery scandals put the Ministry on the defensive. Proposing and carrying out a high-profile project like the Big Bang may deflect media attention. (Despite the effort, the Ministry of Finance continued to be criticized in the media, since new scandals erupted in 1997.)

The name Big Bang is misleading as the proposal is not a sudden change. The foreign exchange control was effectively eliminated in April 1998. But, other reforms in banking, securities, and insurance sectors are scheduled to follow. The accounting standard will also be changed, but that will take time, as public accountants have to be educated on the change first. Economic benefits from the Big Bang will extend to an entire financial sector and the economy in general when the reforms are completed.

Traditionally, domestic deregulation has been stalled by vested interests of segmented financial markets. The Big Bang is a final answer to deal with the crush of vested interests. Several examples will give a good picture of the financial markets problem and the proposed solution.[1]

First, banks and securities firms are at odds. Banks opposed securities houses' desire to make customers' securities accounts more like bank accounts (automatic deposits,

---

[1] For the market structure before deregulation, see Ito (1992, ch. 5)

demand deposits, and automatic payment services)—this was removed at the beginning of the 1990s.

Second, securities houses opposed the banks' plan to sell mutual fund products at bank tellers' windows—this was removed in December 1998.

Third, ordinary banks and long-term credit banks were squabbling over the ordinary banks' product line. Long-term credit banks opposed the ordinary banks' proposal to offer time deposits exceeding two years—this was removed in the mid-1990s.

In general "holding companies" are prohibited in Japan. Under the Big Bang, the establishment of financial holding companies will be permitted, so that banks, securities firms, and insurance companies may be controlled and coordinated by a single headquarters.

Insurance companies are segmented into three categories: life insurance, non-life insurance, and the "third" category—such as cancer insurance. This segmentation will be lifted in March 2001, under the Big Bang.[2] Insurance premiums have been regulated and controlled. Under the Big Bang, companies can charge different premiums to different kinds of customers, e.g. nonsmoker life insurance, drivers without accident records.

Among the changes in the foreign exchanges on April 1, 1998, the elimination of the exclusive dealing by banks is most prominent. Foreign exchange had been exclusively exchanged in banks that are licensed to do dealings. Securities firms, trading houses, and other large nonfinancial companies regularly receive both buying and selling orders of foreign exchange. However, they cannot offset (marry) their buy and sell positions, but must ask banks to carry out the transactions. Then the banks automatically receive commissions. This restriction was removed on April 1, 1998 as a part of the Big Bang. In addition, investors are now allowed to hold accounts at financial institutions abroad. These changes have put additional competitive pressure on Japanese banks.

In order to disentangle the vested interest turf claims, the Big Bang—simultaneous, or at least committed schedule of, deregulation—is the answer.

3. Political Economy

The Big Bang idea was an attempt of the Hashimoto government, with help from some quarters of the Ministry of Finance, to pursue structural reforms in domestic and international economic policymaking. The domestic politics needed some banner for the Hashimoto government (since January 1996). Public opinion had turned against the Ministry of Finance, as the final resolution of the insolvent *Jusen* (housing loans companies) required an injection of 685 billion yen, and some Ministry officials were alleged to have accepted cash and lavish entertainment.

[2] US pressure has been instrumental in much deregulation in Japan in the 1980s. However, it is ironic that the US is now opposing deregulation of insurance segments in Japan, because AIG (a US company) has a vested interest in the "third" market.

During the summer of 1996, it was proposed to reform the Bank of Japan to make it more independent from the Ministry. This was considered to be a deflection of criticism.

The Big Bang had several additional political advantages. First, domestic resistance toward deregulation and liberalization would decline when a "declaration" for the big deregulation was made internationally. Second, it helped international negotiations. The US had pressured Japan to "open up" the insurance market. In fact, the US demands were aimed at keeping the Japanese insurance market under regulation. The so-called third market (for non-life insurance) was dominated by the US insurance companies. As a result, the US opposed the deregulation of that market. The Big Bang basically set the deadline for allowing such vested interests.

Immediate impacts on various groups of consumers are unclear. Wealthy individuals will benefit from the wider range of choices in their asset portfolios. However, small savers including pensioners may suffer from deregulation as the various rates (brokerage commissions, insurance premiums, bank monthly fees) will be differentiated for different types of customers.

We now turn to the statistical evidence on how the first step of the Big Bang, namely the foreign exchange market deregulation, is affecting the yen–dollar exchange market.

4. A First Look at the Deregulation of the FX Market

On April 1, 1998 the revised Foreign Exchange and Foreign Trade Control Law ended the monopoly of Japanese banks in Japanese foreign exchange (FX) trading. Now other firms, such as general trading firms, and individuals could freely buy and sell foreign currencies. The law extends down to the retail level, where shops and restaurants may exchange foreign money for yen. The revised law also permits individuals to open and maintain foreign currency-denominated bank and securities accounts in foreign countries.[3] At first thought, it seems reasonable that the deregulation should generate a yen depreciation, as the interest rate in Japan was so much lower than in other countries. However, the expected effect on the volatility of the yen/dollar exchange rate is unclear.

In the weeks before the deregulation went into effect, market participants expressed the opinion that the yen should weaken as it would be easier for Japanese agents to sell yen for dollars. However, there were persistent rumors of central bank interventions, selling dollars to prevent the dollar appreciation, so it is possible that the effect of private market yen sales was offset by central bank purchases. There were also confounding factors, as the time of the deregulation was one where other important events were occurring. For instance, on April 3, Moody's Investors Service

---

[3] Even before the Big Bang, foreign currency-denominated deposits could be made with Japanese or foreign financial institutions that were located in Japan.

downgraded to "negative" from "stable" its outlook for Japan's government obligations. This news resulted in the yen/dollar exchange rate dropping to 135 for the first time in over six years. In the same week, the Bank of Japan's Tankan report indicated that the outlook had turned more negative among Japanese firms. So, it is clear that there was plenty of news to motivate yen selling around the time of the deregulation, so that one must be careful when making claims about the effects of the April 1 change. We will now turn to a first look at the empirical evidence related to the FX market Big Bang.

4.1. Yen/dollar exchange rate

With the lifting of restrictions on dollar-denominated deposits in foreign countries, we expect that pressures from abroad will force the Japanese and foreign institutions in Tokyo to offer better products. This may cause a shift to dollars from yen and a consequent yen depreciation. In a real sense, any such depreciation is reflecting expectations regarding the Japanese economy and financial market differences between Japan and the United States (like interest differentials and stock market performance). The deregulation should simply allow more Japanese firms and households to diversify their portfolios at lower cost. To see whether there was any discernible effect of deregulation on the yen/dollar exchange rate, we first plot the daily data in Figure 7.1. The figure indicates that in the week containing the deregulation, the yen depreciated against the dollar from about 130 to 135. However, there was a sharp appreciation in the following week which appears to have been a result of two factors. The Bank of Japan intervened in support of the yen and, reportedly, sold US$12 billion in exchange for yen on Thursday and Good Friday. At the same time, US Treasury Secretary Rubin stated that he supported the Bank of Japan action and was concerned about recent weakness in the yen. There was also an expectation among market participants of a coordinated intervention to support the yen following the G7 meeting scheduled for April 15. All of these factors contributed to the yen appreciation below 130 in the second week of April. However, as Figure 7.1 shows, by the third week of April, following no action by the G7, a steady yen depreciation began that peaked in June.

Aside from the yen appreciation prior to Easter weekend, it is clear that the yen depreciated over most of the period starting in mid-February. While this could have been due to expectations and the consequent realization of portfolio rebalancing following April 1, there was also plenty of bad news related to the Japanese economy that occurred at the same time.

4.2. Transaction costs

One would expect that deregulation increases efficiency as banks face greater competition so that spreads and commissions on trading fall. There was anecdotal evidence that this occurred. Banks cut the foreign exchange commission charged to

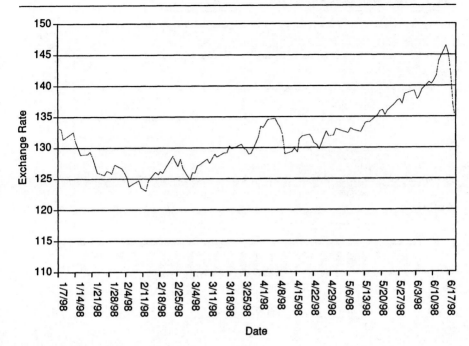

FIGURE 7.1. *Yen/dollar spot exchange rate*
Sources: Own calculations based on data from Olsen & Associates, Zurich.

retail customers.[4] Securities firms cut exchange rate commissions for preferred customers who purchase foreign-currency denominated bonds. Aside from such anecdotal evidence from the retail level, what do the data say about the wholesale interbank market?

We examine tick-by-tick data on the yen/dollar exchange rate for evidence regarding spreads.[5] First, we plot the average daily quoted bid-ask spreads for Japanese banks and all banks in Figure 7.2. It is interesting to note that the Japanese quoted spreads exceed the rest of the market. There may be several reasons why Japanese banks' spreads are wider. First, they may be just inefficient. Second, Japanese banks' reputation was categorically damaged when one of the 20 large banks failed in November 1997, and many others had been downgraded. The Japanese banks were charged a "Japan premium" by American and European banks. Credit lines were severely cut. Unless the Japanese banks offered a higher rate, they could not borrow. A look at Figure 7.2 does not provide obvious evidence that the spreads narrowed

[4] For instance, at the end of March, Daiwa Bank reduced its exchange commissions so that it charges 28,000 yen to purchase US$10,000. This was 2,000 yen below the other Tokyo city banks. On April 6, Sanwa Bank cut its foreign-currency wiring fee by up to 2,300 yen.
[5] The data were obtained from Olsen & Associates in Zurich and include the intradaily quotes over the first half of 1998.

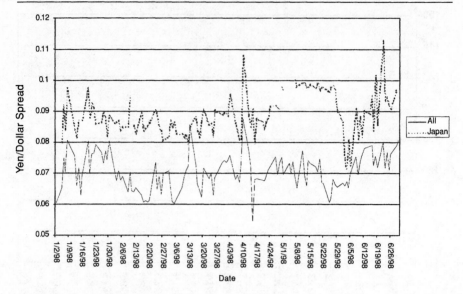

FIGURE 7.2. *Average daily bid-ask spread of yen/dollar*
Sources: As Figure 7.1.

following the April 1 deregulation. Neither the spreads of all quoters nor those of Japanese quoters systematically fell after April 1. Furthermore, it is not obvious that the spreads quoted by Japanese banks converged to those quoted by others following April 1.

The two spikes in the spread series for all quoters are related to specific events. The first spike occurring on March 13 coincides with the arrest of a senior BOJ official for leaking sensitive information and the ensuing corruption scandal. The second peak occurred on Good Friday (April 10). This was to be expected as there was heavy BOJ intervention on this day and the Easter weekend is a 3-day holiday weekend in many countries. With much uncertainty regarding action by the G7 the next week and an extended market closing, we should expect the widening spreads. Note that spreads fell sharply the next week, following the lack of action by the G7.

To more formally examine the effect of the deregulation, we estimated econometric models of the spread. Microstructure models suggest that volume and volatility should both be important determinants of the spread.[6] In addition, a dummy variable was added to estimate the impact of the April 1 deregulation. The dummy switches from zero to one on April 1. The model is estimated twice. First, we estimate the effect of volume, volatility, and deregulation on the average daily spread quoted by Japanese banks. Then the model is reestimated using the difference between the average daily Japanese quoted spreads and the average daily quoted spreads across

[6] See Hartmann (1998) for an analysis of the relationship between the tick-by-tick spread and trading volumes.

all banks. The independent variables used in the estimation are as follows: (a) volume, the sum of daily volume in the spot and swap markets in Tokyo; (b) volatility, the absolute daily change in the yen/dollar spot rate; and (c) the dummy for deregulation. To account for the simultaneity in the data, an instrumental variables estimation was employed where the instruments included two lags of volume and volatility and a dummy variable for the April 10 intervention by the BOJ. A specification search revealed that a parsimonious representation of the data required a first- and second-order autoregressive term be included to account for the autocorrelation in the residuals.

The results are reported in Table 7.1. Volume seems to have no statistically significant effect on either dependent variable. Volatility has a statistically significantly positive effect on the Japanese quoted spread and no effect on the difference between Japanese and all spreads. The April 1 dummy has a negative and statistically significant effect in both cases. So taking account of the volume and volatility effects on the spread, one can estimate a negative effect of deregulation on the quoted spread of Japanese banks. In addition, it appears that, holding constant the effects of volume and volatility, the deregulation was associated with a convergence of Japanese quoted spreads toward those of other banks.

The efficiency gains associated with FX market deregulation in terms of lower transaction costs, appears to extend beyond the retail level. The evidence presented here is supportive of a structural change in the wholesale exchange rate quotes consistent with lower transaction costs in Japan.

4.3. Volatility

The net effect that deregulation should have on FX volatility is unclear. On the one hand, the entry of more participants might add depth and larger liquidity trades, so

TABLE 7.1. *Yen/dollar spreads*

Independent variable	Japanese quotes	p-values	Japanese-all quotes	p-values
Constant	0.0836	0.00	0.0006	0.97
Volume	1.6×10^{-7}	0.69	7.8×10^{-7}	0.13
Volatility	2.657	0.00	−0.947	0.24
Dummy (deregulation)	−0.008	0.00	−0.009	0.00
AR (1)	0.2990	0.00	0.3376	0.00
AR (2)	0.4376	0.00	0.3464	0.00
F	4.49	0.00	7.06	0.00
SSR	0.0055	—	0.0061	—
Q (24)	18.90	0.65	23.34	0.38

Source: Daily data for January 1998 to June 1998.

that that discrete price jumps occur less frequently. The usual case that volume and volatility are positively correlated is, at least in part, a result of both being driven by news. It is not necessary that the deregulation will increase trading volume as firms can now take positions internally that were previously accomplished through bank trading-rooms. This could result in thinner trading. The next section will examine the evidence on volume, so here we look directly at volatility. Figure 7.3 plots the daily (9 a.m. to 4 p.m., Tokyo) return on the yen/dollar exchange rate. There is no clear pattern of volatility after April 1 compared to before. The negative spike on April 10 is associated with BOJ intervention. Since the table does not reveal any obvious effect of deregulation, we will examine more formal evidence.

It is well known that high-frequency exchange rate data exhibit GARCH effects. As a result, we do not want to simply look at the pattern of the unconditional volatility to make inferences regarding the path of volatility around April 1. Instead, we report estimates of GARCH models.

We constructed a data set of 15-minute returns for the yen/dollar spot rate during Tokyo business hours, ensuring that no overnight or weekend returns were included. This is the dependent variable in the mean equation. As is usually the case in high-

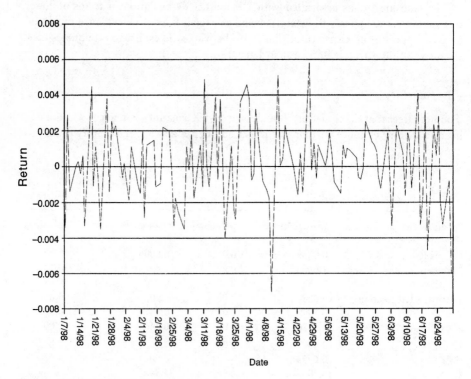

FIGURE 7.3. *Daily yen/dollar return*
Sources: As Figure 7.1.

frequency exchange rate applications, a GARCH(1,1)–MA(1) model represents the data well. To test the hypothesis that the April 1 deregulation resulted in lower volatility, we include a dummy variable that switches from zero to 1 on April 1 in the conditional variance equation. To account for the volatility associated with the BOJ intervention, an additional dummy variable is added that takes on the value of one for April 10.

Estimation results are reported in Table 7.2. The diagnostics indicate that the model represents the data well. The deregulation dummy is negative and statistically significant at the 4 per cent level. Thus, accounting for the persistence that exists in intradaily exchange rate quotes, we find evidence consistent with the deregulation reducing volatility.

4.4. Volume

Since nonbank firms could hold dollar deposits after April 1, 1998, they could circumvent the bank exchange services and finance dollar deals directly. For this reason, we might expect that the volume of foreign exchange trading in Tokyo would fall with the April 1 deregulation. To explore the pattern of FX trading volume we examine the Bank of Japan data on daily volume. The BOJ collects daily data from brokers and dealers on interbank foreign exchange transaction volume. Spot volume for the first half of 1998 is plotted in Figure 7.4. Forward and swap volume is plotted in Figure 7.5. The spot volume data in Figure 7.4 indicate a clear outlier associated with the pre-Easter intervention. Aside from this, there appears to be an uneven decline in volume for about a month, after which volume starts to climb

TABLE 7.2. *Yen/dollar conditional volatility*

Independent variable	Coefficient	p–value
Mean equation:		
Constant	0.1117	0.04
MA (1)	−0.819	0.01
Conditional Variance equation:		
Constant	3.3402	0.00
ARCH (1)	0.2654	0.00
GARCH (1)	0.6216	0.00
Dummy (deregulation)	−1.062	0.04
Dummy (intervention)	26.12	0.09
SSR	4.448	
Log Likelihood	−11126	
Q (24)	29.24	0.17

Source: 15-minute data from January 1998 to June 1998.

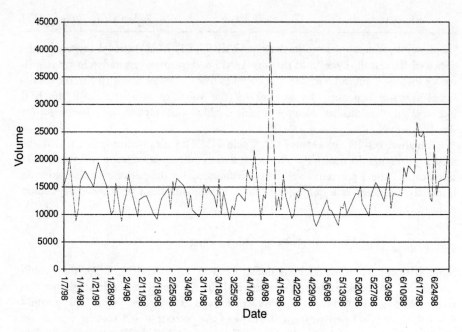

FIGURE 7.4. *Daily spot market volume (million yen)*
Sources: Own calculations based on data from the Bank of Japan.

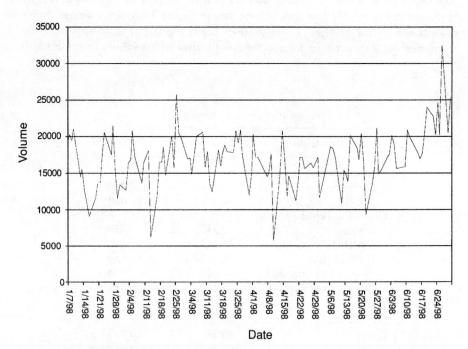

FIGURE 7.5. *Daily swap market volume (million yen)*
Sources: As Figure 7.4.

again. The swap market volume indicates a similar upward trend near the end of the sample.

To isolate the effect of deregulation on volume, we would ideally need to account for information flows as volume (and volatility) is driven by public and private information disclosure. Lacking data on such information flows, we experimented with alternative models of volume being driven by volatility and a dummy for the April 1 deregulation. There were no robust results linking volume to the deregulation. It appears that other factors dominate the volume effect.

4.5. Overall effects of deregulation on the FX market

Based on our look at the wholesale interbank FX market, we can discern the following:

(1) There is evidence of lower transaction costs associated with yen/dollar trading. The data suggest that, holding constant the effects of volume and volatility, the bid-ask spread drops on yen/dollar quotes. In addition, the difference between spreads quoted by Japanese and non-Japanese quoters narrows after the deregulation.

(2) There is evidence that the deregulation lowers conditional volatility. While the *direct* effect of deregulation on volatility is unclear, the data indicate that a GARCH framework that takes account of the persistence in volatility and intervention captures a negative effect.

We urge caution in interpreting these results as there were many factors affecting the exchange rate over this period and deregulation was but one. Nevertheless, it is useful to know that the effects of deregulation extend beyond the retail level of FX that has been discussed in the popular press.

5. Concluding Remarks

The Big Bang alone will not be enough to put the Tokyo financial markets at par with New York and London, or to make the yen an international key currency.[7] However, it is an important first step. When accompanied by tax law changes and improvement in financial infrastructure, complete deregulation on business activities, known as the Big Bang, will increase financial activities in Tokyo (by both Japanese and non-Japanese institutions), and will boost the use of the yen. However, it remains to be seen whether these changes are made in time.

This paper examined how the bid-ask spread and conditional volatility in the yen/dollar exchange market changed at around the time of deregulating the foreign exchange law. Some evidence of an impact of deregulation on the market activities was detected. However, whether the econometric evidence can be translated into more

---

[7] For steps toward internationalization of the yen, see Ministry of Finance (1999).

tangible results in the long run is not obvious. The answer partly depends on the success of the remaining changes scheduled under the Big Bang.

REFERENCES

Andersen, Torben and Tim, Bollerslev (1997), "Intraday Periodicity and Volatility Persistence in Financial Markets," *Journal of Empirical Finance*, 4: 115–58.
Hartmann, Philipp (1998), "Do Reuters Spread Reflect Currencies' Differences in Global Trading Activity?," *Journal of International Money and Finance*, 17: 757–84.
Ito, Takatoshi (1992), *The Japanese Economy* (Cambridge, Mass.: MIT Press).
Ministry of Finance, Council on Foreign Exchange and Other Transactions (1999), *Internationalization of the Yen for the 21st Century: Japan's Response to Changes in Global Economic and Financial Environments*, April 20 (Tokyo: Ministry of Finance).

8 Has Japan Specialized in the Wrong Industries?

EDWARD N. WOLFF

1. Introduction

Japan has slipped from being one of the fastest growing economies in the world to one of average growth. During the 1960s, labor productivity was growing at an average annual rate of 9 per cent; in the 1990s, it was growing at only 3 per cent per year. Part of this slowdown reflects the transition from being a converging economy to a "frontier economy." Indeed, most of Japan's phenomenal productivity growth from 1960 to 1980 can be traced to technological catch-up combined with an extremely high investment rate (see Wolff, 1996). However, the anemic performance of the Japanese economy during the 1990s has generated a slew of articles and books, proclaiming the end of the Japanese "economic miracle" (see Katz, 1998, for example).

One of the unique features of Japan's growth trajectory over this period is a dramatic change in industrial structure. Whereas other OECD countries have maintained their specialization in particular industries over long periods of time, Japan is notable among OECD countries in substantially changing its pattern of specialization and industrial composition. The main focus of the paper is to investigate changes in industries of specialization and examine the implications of these changes for the slowdown of productivity growth within Japan. The major question of interest is whether Japan may have specialized in the "wrong" industries. In particular, during the 1970s and 1980s, Japan specialized in a range of mid-tech industries such as iron and steel, motor vehicles, shipbuilding, motorcycles and bicycles, and other transport equipment, which may have turned out to be the low productivity growth industries of the 1990s.

The period of analysis will be from 1970 to 1995. The primary data source is the OECD STAN (Structural Analysis) database, which provides statistics on value added and employment for 33 manufacturing industries in 14 OECD countries. A secondary source is the OECD ISDB (International Intersectoral) Database, which provides similar data, as well as gross capital stock, for ten major sectors and nine manufacturing industries in 14 OECD countries. I will also use Balassa's Revealed Comparative Advantage (RCA) index to measure specialization. Comparisons of Japan with the US and Germany will be featured.

The paper is organized as follows. Section 1 provides comparative data on Japan's aggregate performance with that of Germany and the US. Section 2 provides details on patterns of industry specialization and comparative productivity performance for manufacturing industries. Section 3 presents a similar set of statistics by major sector of the economy. Conclusions and speculations about future performance are presented in the last section.

2. Comparisons of Aggregate Performance

Part I of Table 8.1 shows the basic statistics for the entire economy from the period 1950 to 1989, based on data from Maddison (1991 and 1993). Output is measured by GDP in 1985 US relative prices, the labor input by hours worked, and the capital input by gross nonresidential fixed plant and equipment in 1985 US relative prices. Capital stock estimates are standardized across countries by using the same service lives (a 39-year life for nonresidential structures and a 14-year life for machinery and equipment), as well as the same (US) prices.

Total factor productivity (*TFP*) here is defined as

$$LnTFP^h_t = Ln Y^h_t - \alpha LnL^h_t - (1 - \alpha)LnK^h_t, \tag{1}$$

where Y^h is the total output of country h, L^h is its labor input, K^h its capital input, and α is the international average wage share. *TFP* growth, *TFPGR*, is then defined as:

$$TFPGR^h_t = Y^{*h}_t - \alpha L^{*h}_t - (1 - \alpha)K^{*h}_t, \tag{2}$$

where an asterisk (*) indicates the rate of growth. The actual calculation of *TFP* growth uses the average wage share over the period of estimation (referred to as the Tornqvist–Divisia approximation).

Annual *TFP* growth in Japan averaged 4.9 per cent in 1950–60 and 4.0 per cent in 1960–70, the highest among the three countries. It then fell off precipitously to 0.1 per cent in 1973–9 but recovered to 1.2 per cent in 1979–89, again the highest among the three countries. Over the whole 1950–89 period, Japan led the three countries in terms of *TFP* growth. These *TFP* estimates, by the way, are quite a bit higher than those made by Young (1993), who argued that *TFP* growth in Japan had been low relative to other OECD countries in the postwar period.

Also shown in part IA of Table 8.1 is the ratio of Japan's *TFP* level to the US *TFP* level. There was substantial catch-up on the US level between 1950 and 1973, with the ratio rising from 0.34 to 0.65, no change between 1973 and 1979, and then a moderate gain from 1979 to 1989. However, still in 1989, Japan's *TFP* was only 69 per cent of the US level according to the Maddison data.

The growth in capital intensity (the ratio of gross capital to hours worked) in Japan surged from 1.5 per cent per year in the 1950s to 11.7 per cent per year in 1960–73, then declined to 7.5 per cent per year in 1973–9, and further to 5.0 per cent per year during the 1980s. Japan was the leading country in all periods except 1950–60, though its lead on the other two countries was much greater in the 1960s than in the 1980s. In terms of the actual level of the capital–labor ratio, Japan was way behind the US in 1950 (only one-seventh of the US level) but by 1989 it had reached 83 per cent.

A somewhat different pattern is evident for labor productivity growth, in comparison to *TFP* growth, as shown in part IC. Japan's labor productivity growth increased from 5.5 per cent per year in the 1950–60 period to 8.7 per cent per year in 1960–73,

TABLE 8.1. *Average annual growth in TFP, labor productivity, and the capital–labor ratio, in the total economy for Japan, Germany, and the United States, 1950–1994 (growth rates in per cent per annum)*

	1950 –60	1960 –73	1973 –79	1979 –89	1989 –94	1994	1950 –89	1973 –94
I. Maddison data[a]								
A. TFP growth								
Japan	4.92	4.01	0.11	1.21			2.82	
Germany	4.82	2.09	1.60	0.60			2.23	
US	1.56	1.65	0.00	0.75			1.07	
Japan/US level ratio[c]	0.34	0.48	0.65	0.65	0.69			
B. Growth of the ratio of gross capital to hours								
Japan	1.53	11.65	7.54	4.97			6.71	
Germany	4.53	7.46	5.02	3.55			5.33	
US	2.18	1.91	1.89	1.50			1.87	
Japan/US level ratio[c]	0.13	0.12	0.42	0.59	0.83			
C. Labor productivity (GDP/hours) growth								
Japan	5.54	8.70	3.14	3.21			5.63	
Germany	6.65	5.09	3.62	2.03			4.48	
US	2.44	2.42	0.76	1.35			1.90	
Japan/US level ratio[c]	0.15	0.20	0.46	0.53	0.64			
II. ISDB 1997 data[b]								
A. GDP growth								
Japan		na	3.33	4.00	2.11			3.36
Germany		4.29	2.45	1.87	2.47			2.18
US		3.75	2.28	2.68	1.82			2.36
B. TFP growth								
Japan		na	0.72	1.79	0.91			1.28
Germany		3.15	2.24	1.19	1.66			1.65
US		1.51	-0.21	0.47	0.57			0.30
Japan/US level ratio[c]			0.66	0.70	0.80	0.81		
C. Growth of the ratio of gross capital to hours								
Japan		na	7.62	4.89	4.17			5.50
Germany		4.97	3.64	2.19	1.86			2.53
US		1.69	0.85	0.89	1.16			0.95
Japan/US level ratio[c]			0.23	0.35	0.55	0.70		
D. Labor productivity (GDP/hours) growth								
Japan		na	3.35	3.45	2.81			3.27
Germany		5.09	3.72	2.10	2.77			2.72
US		2.15	0.12	0.68	0.98			0.59
Japan/US level ratio[c]			0.41	0.50	0.66	0.73		

[a] The data sources are Maddison (1991, 1993). Output is measured by GDP in 1985 US relative prices, labor by hours worked (employment times average hours per year), and capital by gross nonresidential fixed plant and equipment in 1985 US relative prices and with standardized service lives. Factor shares used to compute *TFP* are based on the average ratio of employee compensation to GDP for the six countries over the 1950–89 period.

[b] The source is the OECD, Intersectoral Data Base (ISDB), 1997 version. Output is measured by GDP in 1990 US dollars, labor by hours worked (employment times average hours per year), and capital by gross nonresidential fixed plant and equipment in 1990 US dollars (with individual country service lives). Factor shares used to compute *TFP* are based on the average ratio of employee compensation to GDP for the 14 countries in the data base over the 1970–94 period. Germany refers to West Germany only. Capital stock for Japan includes OECD imputations.

[c] The ratio as of the beginning of the period.

fell off sharply to 3.1 per cent per year in 1973–9 and then increased slightly to 3.2 per cent per year in 1979–89. Japan was second to Germany in the 1950s and then led both Germany and the US in the 1960s by a considerable margin. In the 1973–9 period, its labor productivity growth was again second to Germany's, while in the 1980s, it was the leading country but the margin was much smaller than in the 1960s. Over the whole 1950–89 period, it had the highest rate of labor productivity growth.

In terms of Japan's labor productivity level, there was substantial catch-up on the US level between 1950 and 1973, with the ratio rising from 0.15 to 0.46, followed by more moderate gains between 1973 and 1979 and between 1979 and 1989. However, by 1989, Japan's labor productivity was only 64 per cent of the US level, less than its relative *TFP* level.

What is surprising is that despite the marked fall-off in *TFP* growth after 1973, the rate of labor productivity growth remained relatively robust, at least compared to the US and Germany. The reason can be seen by rewriting equation (2) as:

$$LPGR^h{}_t = TFPGR^h{}_t + (1-\alpha)KLGR^h{}_t, \tag{3}$$

where $LP = Y/L$, the level of aggregate labor productivity, $LPGR$ is the rate of labor productivity growth, $KL = K/L$, the ratio of the capital stock to labor, and $KLGR$ is the rate of growth of the capital–labor ratio. The very high rate of labor productivity growth in Japan over the 1960–73 period thus emanated from both a high rate of *TFP* growth and very strong capital formation. In the 1973–9 period, when *TFP* growth went to virtually zero, labor productivity growth fell off to a respectable 3 per cent per year because of the continued high rate of investment. Labor productivity growth remained at 3 per cent in the 1979–89 period because the decline in the growth rate of the capital–labor ratio was offset by the recovery in *TFP* growth.

Part II of Table 8.1 updates these results to 1994. The source here is the OECD Intersectoral Data Base (ISDB), 1997 version. Output is measured by GDP in 1990 US dollars, labor by hours worked (employment times average hours per year), and capital by gross non-residential fixed plant and equipment in 1990 US dollars (with individual country service lives). Factor shares used to compute *TFP* are based on the average ratio of employee compensation to GDP for the 14 countries in the data base over the 1970–94 period.[1] The estimates differ between the ISDB and the Maddison data because of different data sources and methods and because of the use of standardized capital service lives in the latter. Despite these differences, the patterns of results are quite similar for the overlapping period, 1960–89.

Part IIA shows GDP growth in the three countries and highlights the sharp fall-off in output growth in Japan in the 1989–94 period. Estimates of *TFP* growth for Japan are higher on the basis of the ISDB data but still indicate a precipitous decline

---

[1] Following the ISDB convention, I measure the wage share as employee compensation in national currency at current prices multiplied by the ratio of total employment (ET) to the number of employees (EE) and then divided by GDP in national currency at current prices.

between the 1979–89 and the 1989–94 periods, falling by almost half. There is also additional catch-up on the US level of *TFP* between 1989 and 1994, though the gain is quite modest.

The growth in the capital–labor ratio remained strong in Japan in the years 1989–94, over 4 per cent per year, particularly in comparison to Germany and the US, with capital intensity in Japan in 1994 reaching 70 per cent of the US level. Labor productivity growth also stayed strong in Japan in the 1989–94 period, at almost 3 per cent per year. The main reason is the continued high rate of investment, since *TFP* growth fell off in Japan in those years. By 1994, labor productivity in Japan had reached 73 per cent of the US level, up from 66 per cent in 1989. Labor productivity growth also remained relatively high in Germany between 1989 and 1994 but the main reason in this case was the recovery in *TFP* growth in Germany during this period.

3. Patterns of Industry Specialization in Manufacturing

I next investigate patterns of specialization for Japan within the manufacturing sector. I make use of the 1997 OECD STAN database, which covers the time period 1970 to 1994.[2] This source provides statistics on value added, measured in both current and 1990 local prices;[3] total employment; employee compensation;[4] and PPP conversion factors for each country and year.[5] Data on each of these variables are provided for 33 manufacturing industries.

Comparisons of output among the countries is made on the basis of value added by industry in 1990 local currency converted to 1990 US dollars on the basis of the 1990 PPP rate for that country. Specialization is measured by the share of the total production of a given commodity made in an individual country relative to its share of GDP:

$$RELPSHR_i^h = [y_i^h / \sum_h y_i^h]/(GDP^h / \sum_h GDP^h),\qquad(4)$$

where y_i^h is the output of sector i in country h and the GDP figures, obtained from the OECD ISDB, are in 1990 US dollars. This index is analogous to Balassa's Revealed Comparative Advantage (RCA) measure (Balassa, 1965), which is used to measure trade specialization. The numerator of *RELPSHR* indicates country h's share of the total production of industry i, while the denominator measures country h's share of total GDP for these 14 countries. A value above (below) 1 indicates that country h's share of the group's total production of product i is higher (lower) than its share of the total GDP of this group. This index indicates in which product lines a country's production is concentrated, which is taken as a measure of specialization.

---

[2] Some series do extend to 1995 for a limited set of countries.
[3] The value added is exclusive of value added taxes and other indirect business taxes.
[4] This is defined as the sum of wages and salaries, social insurance taxes, and other employee fringe benefits paid by the employer.
[5] Unfortunately, PPPs are not available at the industry level.

In general, some values of *RELPSHR* for a country will be greater than 1, while others will be less than 1.[6]

The 33 industries selected are the most detailed ones available with the requisite data. They are all three-digit ISIC industries, with the exception of transport equipment, which is available on the four-digit level. These industries are divided into three technology groups on the basis of the average R&D intensity of production of these industries in OECD countries in 1985, as follows: low-tech—less than 0.5 times the mean R&D intensity; medium-tech—from 0.5 to 1.5 the mean R&D intensity; and high-tech—over 1.5 the mean R&D intensity.

Calculations of *RELPSHR* for Germany, Japan, and the US are shown in Table A8.1. In 1970, Japan accounted for 13 per cent of total manufactures of this group of 14 countries, Germany for 14 per cent, and the US for 40 per cent, and the three together two-thirds. Japan's share of total manufacturing was almost identical to its GDP share (13 per cent), accounting for a *RELPSHR* score of 1.0; Germany's share was considerably greater than its share of 14-country GDP (14 versus 9 per cent); whereas the US manufacturing share was smaller (40 versus 45 per cent).

Japan in 1970 was particularly strong in plastics, glass and glass products, and other transport equipment (all values above 1.6). The specialization of Germany in beverages, petroleum refineries, petroleum and coal products, industrial chemicals and professional goods and scientific instruments in 1970 is also apparent (all values of *RELPSHR* exceed 2.0), as well as in motor vehicles and electrical machinery (both values exceed 1.8). The major US specialization was aircraft (a value of 1.7). In 1970 Germany had the highest relative production shares among all 14 countries in total manufacturing, all the high-tech industries except aircraft, motor vehicles, and 7 low-tech industries. Japan led the 14 countries in only one industry (food products), and the US in only one (aircraft).

Between 1970 and 1994, both the German and the US share of total manufacturing production declined by 3 percentage points whereas Japan's share increased sharply, by 10 percentage points. By 1994, Japan's manufacturing output was more than double Germany's and over 60 per cent the level of the US. Germany's share of output remained the same or fell in almost every manufacturing industry. The US share likewise remained unchanged or declined in almost all industries, with the major exception of textiles, wearing apparel, plastics, and non-electrical machinery (including office and computing machinery). Japan's share, on the other hand, increased in most industries—notably, electrical machinery (including radios, TV, and communication equipment), rubber products, iron and steel, shipbuilding, motor vehicles, motorcycles and bicycles, and other transport equipment.

Japan's inroads were particularly marked in the medium-tech and high-tech industries. In contrast, Germany basically held its production shares in the medium-tech

---

[6] I have defined *RELPSHR* as a country's share of the total output of a particular industry relative to its share of total GDP rather than to its share of total manufacturing output in order to reflect the fact that some countries such as Germany and Japan have specialized production in manufacturing relative to non-manufacturing sectors. Countries with a large manufacturing sector will tend to have a large number of industries with values of *RELPSHR* exceeding one.

industries but declined in the high-tech and low-tech industries. The US made its major gains in low-tech industries, such as food, apparel, and wood products; lost share in the medium-tech industries; but retained its share in the high-tech industries. As a result, Japan was now highly specialized in iron and steel, shipbuilding, motor vehicles, motorcycles and bicycles, other transport equipment, and, especially, electrical machinery (all *RELPSHR* values above 1.6); Germany remained extremely specialized in only three industries, including motor vehicles; and the US in only aircraft. Japan now had the highest relative production share among the 14 countries in total manufacturing, and in two high-tech industries, non-electrical machinery and electrical machinery, as well as other manufactures. Germany had the highest value in three industries and the US in only one.

Part A of Table 8.2 shows the correlation and rank correlation between the relative production shares by industry between the countries. What is, perhaps, most striking is the low correlation coefficients between Japan and the other two countries—in 1970, −0.33 with Germany and −0.57 with the US, and in 1994, −0.23 and −0.42, respectively. The rank correlations are similar for 1970 (−0.34 and −0.49, respectively) but are smaller in absolute value in 1994 (−0.09 and −0.28, respectively). The fact that the correlations remain negative indicates that Japan has specialized its production in distinctly different industries than Germany or the US, though the decline in the absolute values of the correlation coefficients suggests a mild

TABLE 8.2. *Correlations between countries and over time in relative production shares* (RELPSHR*) in manufacturing industries, 1970–1994*[a]

A. Correlations between countries in RELPSHR

	Correlation coefficients			Rank correlations		
	1970	1979	1994	1970	1979	1994
Japan and Germany	−0.33	−0.29	−0.23	−0.34	−0.24	−0.09
Japan and US	−0.57	−0.50	−0.42	−0.49	−0.42	−0.28
Germany and US	0.07	0.13	−0.06	0.17	0.24	−0.01

B. Correlations over time

	RELPSHR			LN(RELPSHR)		
	1970–79	1979–94	1970–94	1970–79	1979–94	1970–94
Japan	0.84	0.84	0.58	0.88	0.92	0.71
Germany	0.96	0.87	0.76	0.96	0.92	0.82
US	0.96	0.92	0.86	0.98	0.97	0.95

[a] See equation (4) for the definition of *RELPSHR*. Correlations are based on thirty-three industries, including five transport equipment subsectors. See Table A8.1 for a listing of the industries.

convergence in industries of specialization between Japan and the other two countries (particularly with Germany) between 1970 and 1994.

One special feature of Japanese economic development over the last quarter century is that while most countries have retained their industries of specialization over time, Japan has undergone a major industrial restructuring. This is documented in part B of Table 8.2, which shows correlation coefficients of both *RELPSHR* and the logarithm of *RELPSHR* by industry. By both measures, Japan has the lowest correlation coefficients over both the 1970–9 and 1979–94 period. In contrast, these correlations remain higher over time for both Germany and the US, particularly the latter.

3.1. Labor productivity differences

I next turn to a comparison of industry labor productivity levels, also on the basis of the STAN database. Let us first define the labor productivity level, *LP*, of industry i in country h as:

$$LP_i^h = y_i^h / n_i^h \tag{5}$$

where n_i^h is total employment in industry i of country h. The (weighted) average labor productivity of industry i in the 14 countries is given by:

$$LPAVG_i = \sum_h y_i^h / \sum_h n_i^h$$

In analogous fashion to *RELPSHR*, I define

$$RELLP_i^h = LP_i^h / LPAVG_i \tag{6}$$

which shows productivity in industry i of country h relative to the average productivity in industry i of the 14 countries.

In 1970 US labor productivity in total manufacturing was about 50 per cent greater than in Germany and more than double Japan's (see Table A8.1, which for the purposes here shows labor productivity levels relative to the US rather than *RELLP*). Japan's labor productivity exceeded that of the US in 5 industries—beverages, wearing apparel, leather products, furniture and fixtures, and glass products—all low-tech industries. German labor productivity was below the corresponding US level in every industry. Its relative strengths (ratios exceeding 0.8) were in beverages, wearing apparel, leather products, petroleum refining, and nonmetal products—again, all low-tech industries.

By 1994, Japan had surpassed Germany in labor productivity in total manufacturing, but US productivity was still a third greater than Japan's and 50 per cent greater than Germany's. Japan's labor productivity now exceeded the US level in 9 industries, including 6 low-tech ones (leather products, furniture and fixtures, petroleum refineries, nonferrous metals, shipbuilding, and other manufacturing), two medium-tech ones (motor vehicles and motorcycles and bicycles), and now one high-tech industry (electrical machinery). Germany's labor productivity exceeded the US level in three industries—all low-tech.

TABLE 8.3. *Correlations between countries and over time in Relative Labor Productivity (*RELLP*) in manufacturing industries, 1970–1994*[a]

A. *Correlations between countries in* RELLP

	Correlation coefficients			Rank correlations		
	1970	1979	1994 (1994[b])	1970	1979	1994
Japan and Germany	−0.33	−0.32	−0.39 (−0.40)	−0.62	−0.67	−0.46
Japan and US	−0.54	−0.32	−0.36 (−0.41)	−0.53	−0.38	−0.35
Germany and US	0.10	−0.15	−0.22 (−0.19)	0.14	−0.26	0.16

B. *Correlations over time*

	RELLP			*LN (RELLP)*		
	1970–79	1979–94	1970–94	1970–79	1979–94	1970–94
Japan	0.74	0.72	0.48	0.72	0.79	0.44
Germany	1.00	0.98	0.97	0.96	0.93	0.88
US	0.88	0.61	0.55	0.88	0.72	0.61

[a] See equation (6) for the definition of *RELLP*. Correlations are based on twenty-nine industries, including a single transport equipment sector but excluding the five transport equipment subsectors, unless otherwise noted. See Table A8.1 for a listing of the industries.
[b] Correlations are based on thirty-three industries, including five transport equipment subsectors.

As shown in Table 8.3, the correlation coefficients and rank correlations in industry *RELLP* between Japan and the other two major economies in 1970, 1979, and 1994 are negative in every case. Moreover, Japan's strengths in terms of productivity changed markedly over time. The correlation in *RELLP* values between 1970 and 1994 is only 0.48 (0.44 for the correlation in the logarithm of *RELLP*). Germany, in contrast, displayed amazing stability in terms of its productivity strengths (a correlation of 0.97 for *RELLP* and 0.88 of the logarithm of *RELLP*). US relative productivity positions also changed substantially over time, though not as much as did Japan's. These results indicate that Japan was strong in different industries than the other two major economies not only in terms of relative production shares but also in terms of productivity performance. Its productivity strengths (and weaknesses), like its relative production shares, also changed significantly over time.

3.2. *Decomposition analysis*

I next make use of a decomposition analysis to separate out the effects of two factors on aggregate performance. The first is from growth within industry and the second is from the composition of industries (or patterns of specialization) within the country. I first consider the growth of total output in manufacturing. Define:

$$s_i^h = p_i^h y_i^h \Big/ \sum_i p_i^h y_i^h \tag{7}$$

where s_i^h shows the share of industry i's output (in national currencies at current prices) in the total output of country h. For this application, I will look at only total manufacturing. Then, it can readily be shown that:

$$Y^{*h} = \sum_i s_i^h y_i^{*h} \tag{8}$$

In other words, the growth of total output is a weighted sum of the growth of output of individual sectors, where the weight is equal to the share of that sector's output in total output.

Table 8.4 shows the effects of different output weights on aggregate output growth in manufacturing. It is first of note that manufacturing output growth in Japan took a nosedive in the 1989–94 period, from 4.4 per cent per year in the preceding two decades to only 1 per cent per year. A comparison of measured output growth rates using different output composition weights reveals that generally speaking Japan's industrial structure moved towards industries experiencing higher output growth rates.[7] The differences are particularly striking for the 1970–9 period, for which the 1994 industrial structure of Japan, together with actual industry output growth rates of the 1970–9 period, would have yielded a total annual output growth over 2 percentage points higher. A similar finding is evident for the 1979–89 period, for which the 1994 industrial structure coupled with actual industry output growth rates of the period would again have increased aggregate output growth by 2 percentage points.

In the 1989–94 period, by contrast, the overall output growth rate is insensitive to the choice of output weights. This result indicates that the slowdown in aggregate output growth over this period is due to the decline in output growth across the full range of industries in Japan, rather than to a shift in output toward slower growth industries. Interestingly, if Japan had adopted the industrial structure of Germany or the US (but had maintained the same output growth rates by industry as in actuality), aggregate output growth in Japan would have been higher. However, the differences are more marked in the earlier periods (1970–9, particularly) than in the later ones (especially 1989–94).

Comparisons with Germany and the US are revealing. In both the German and American cases, output growth in manufacturing declined rather sharply between the 1970–9 and the 1979–89 periods and then again from the latter period to 1989–94 (when it reached virtually zero in Germany and 1 per cent per year in the US). Here, too, output shares of more recent periods yield higher aggregate growth rates than those of earlier periods, though the effects are not as strong as in the Japanese case and they are mitigated over time. Moreover, in the German case, the adoption of the Japanese or American industrial structure would not have affected German aggregate growth rates very significantly. In the US case, the adoption of the

---

[7] This is not entirely unexpected since, in general, output shares in current prices will shift toward industries with higher output growth, as long as their relative prices do not decline to the same percentage degree.

TABLE 8.4. *The effects of output composition on manufacturing output growth in Japan, Germany, and the United States, 1970–1994*[a] *(rate of output growth in per cent per annum)*

Country and output (s) weights	Period			
	1970–9	1979–89	1989–94	1970–94
A. Japan				
Actual output growth	4.44	4.43	0.99	3.72
1970 output (s) weights	4.28	3.85	0.95	3.35
1979 output (s) weights	5.33	4.00	0.53	3.71
1989 output (s) weights	6.23	5.20	0.50	4.55
1994 output (s) weights	6.65	6.31	0.88	5.24
Germany[b] output (s) weights	5.40	4.69	1.05	4.11
USA[b] output (s) weights	5.15	4.57	0.62	4.00
B. Germany				
Actual output growth	2.29	0.76	0.03	1.18
1970 output (s) weights	2.13	0.47	−0.19	0.96
1979 output (s) weights	2.34	0.36	−0.29	0.97
1989 output (s) weights	2.90	0.82	−0.18	1.39
1994 output (s) weights	3.16	1.08	0.01	1.64
Japan[b] output (s) weights	2.40	0.94	−0.19	1.27
USA[b] output (s) weights	2.22	0.87	−0.06	1.21
C. USA				
Actual output growth	3.85	2.46	1.09	2.70
1970 output (s) weights	3.85	2.12	1.36	2.54
1979 output (s) weights	3.95	2.14	1.15	2.54
1989 output (s) weights	4.14	2.68	0.73	2.75
1994 output (s) weights	4.42	3.12	0.99	3.09
Japan[b] output (s) weights	3.96	2.50	2.04	2.98
Germany[b] output (s) weights	4.05	2.30	1.82	2.83

[a] The analysis, derived from equation (8), is based on actual output growth rates by industry and assumes that output shares are fixed over the period. The computations are based on 33 industries. The data source is the STAN database.
[b] Average output weights over the same time period.

Japanese or German industrial structure would not have affected overall output growth in the 1970s or 1980s but would have substantially increased growth in the 1989–94 period.

A similar kind of analysis can be used to decompose the change in aggregate labor productivity into two effects: the first from the change in the distribution of employment among the sectors of the economy and the second from the change in relative productivity levels of the various sectors of economy. It is straightforward to show that:

$$LP^h = \sum_i e_i^h LP_i^h \tag{9}$$

where $e_i^h = n_i^h / \Sigma_i n_i^h$ is the share of total employment in country h in industry i. There is no simple decomposition of aggregate labor productivity growth into sectoral labor productivity growth rates. Table 8.5 shows results for the case when employment shares e_i are fixed over time.

TABLE 8.5. *The effects of employment shares on manufacturing labor productivity growth in Japan, Germany, and the United States, 1970–1994[a] (rate of labor productivity growth in per cent per annum)*

Country and employment (e) weights	Period			
	1970–9	1979–89	1989–94	1970–94
A. Japan				
Actual labor productivity growth	5.02	3.48	0.66	3.47
1970 employment (e) weights	5.56	4.15	0.36	3.89
1979 employment (e) weights	5.37	4.05	0.05	3.71
1989 employment (e) weights	5.79	4.42	0.15	4.05
1994 employment (e) weights	5.69	4.32	0.06	3.95
Germany[b] employment (e) weights	5.85	4.17	0.18	3.94
USA[b] employment (e) weights	5.26	3.97	−0.45	3.41
B. Germany				
Actual labor productivity growth	3.58	1.12	1.83	2.19
1970 employment (e) weights	3.46	1.40	1.70	2.23
1979 employment (e) weights	3.42	1.33	1.64	2.18
1989 employment (e) weights	3.46	1.32	1.58	2.17
1994 employment (e) weights	3.43	1.27	1.54	2.14
Japan[b] employment (e) weights	3.55	1.43	1.40	2.24
USA[b] employment (e) weights	3.37	1.13	1.48	2.07
C. USA				
Actual labor productivity growth	2.87	3.23	2.11	2.86
1970 employment (e) weights	2.98	3.61	2.12	3.06
1979 employment (e) weights	2.89	3.68	2.12	3.06
1989 employment (e) weights	2.90	3.54	1.97	2.97
1994 employment (e) weights	2.93	3.52	1.90	2.96
Japan[b] employment (e) weights	3.05	3.88	2.81	3.31
Germany[b] employment (e) weights	3.10	3.86	2.69	3.34

[a] The analysis, derived from equation (9), is based on actual labor productivity growth rates by industry and assumes that employment shares are fixed over the period. The computations are based on 28 industries, including a single transport equipment sector but excluding the 5 transport equipment subsectors. The data source is the STAN database.
[b] Average employment weights over the same time period.

The slowdown in Japanese manufacturing labor productivity growth is very striking—from 5.0 per cent per year in 1970–9 to 3.5 per cent per year in 1979–89 and to 0.7 per cent per year in 1989–94. The effects of different employment shares on overall productivity growth in Japanese manufacturing is very muted. The 1989 employment weights yields the highest rate of productivity growth but the differences with the employment shares of other years are, as noted, very small. The adoption of both German and US employment weights (together with actual Japanese industry productivity growth rates) would have resulted in higher overall labor productivity growth in both the 1970s and 1980s but lower productivity growth in the early 1990s.

Both Germany and the US experienced very different patterns of labor productivity growth than Japan. In the case of the former, annual labor productivity growth in manufacturing fell by over 2 percentage points between the 1970s and 1980s but then recovered in the early 1990s. In the US, annual labor productivity growth increased somewhat between the 1970s and 1980s and then fell off by about 1 percentage point in the early 1990s. However, in the 1989–94 period, labor productivity grew at 2.1 per cent per year in the US, 1.8 per cent per year in Germany, and only 0.7 per cent per year in Japan. In the case of both Germany and the US, changing employment weights over time had little effect on aggregate labor productivity growth. In the case of Germany, adoption of either Japanese or American employment weights would have had little impact on overall productivity growth. In the US case, adoption of either Japanese or German employment weights would have actually increased annual labor productivity growth by about 0.5 percentage point.

The results clearly point out that the slowdown in both aggregate output growth and aggregate labor productivity growth in Japanese manufacturing in the early 1990s was due to across the board declines in industry output growth and labor productivity growth, respectively. Moreover, switching to the German or American industrial structure would not have offset the slowdown.

4. Patterns of Sectoral Composition of the Whole Economy

I repeat the analysis of Section 3 with two changes. First, I look at changes in the sectoral composition of total (economy-wide) output. Second, I focus on *TFP* growth, rather than labor productivity growth. The data source for this section is the 1997 version of the ISDB.

The first six columns of Table 8.6 show the output composition of the three countries (in 1990 US dollars). There are some striking differences between Japan and the US. In 1970, Japan had more than double the share of output in agriculture, though by 1994 the shares were similar (2 per cent of total output). In both 1970 and 1994, Japan had a significantly higher share of total output in manufacturing (a 6 percentage point difference in 1970 and an 8 percentage point difference in 1994); in construction (a 6 percentage point advantage in both years); and in community, social and personal services (a 4–5 percentage point difference). In contrast, US production was

TABLE 8.6. *Composition of gross value added in 1990 US dollars and TFP level relative to the USA, by major sector, 1970 and 1994[a]*

	Output composition (%)						TFP relative to US			
	1970			1994			1970		1994	
	Japan	Germany	USA	Japan	Germany	USA	Japan	Germany	Japan	Germany
Agriculture	5	2	2	2	2	2	0.45	0.32	0.31	0.60
Mining	1	2	3	0	1	2	0.41	0.53	0.56	0.45
Manufacturing	26	38	20	26	29	18	0.63	0.84	0.72	0.90
Utilities	2	2	3	3	3	3	0.82	0.52	0.89	0.75
Construction	13	8	7	10	5	4	0.69	0.51	0.84	0.90
Trade	9	10	12	13	10	16	0.45	0.66	0.78	0.81
Transportation and communications	8	5	5	6	6	7	1.00	0.70	0.72	0.72
Finance, insurance, and real estate[a]	12	9	21	17	13	26	0.79	—	1.27	—
Community, social, and personal services[b]	15	12	11	16	21	11	1.05	0.81	0.79	1.15
Government services	10	12	15	7	11	11	0.87	0.96	0.76	1.10
Total economy	100	100	100	100	100	100	0.66	0.70	0.81	0.96

Correlation with Japan	0.93	0.74	0.93	0.93	0.81
Correlation with 1970			0.93	0.90	0.94

All manufacturing	0.63	0.84	0.72	0.90
Food, beverages, and tobacco	1.29	0.86	0.79	0.95
Textiles, apparel, and leather	0.49	1.01	0.47	0.91
Wood and wood products	—	0.92	—	1.02
Paper, printing, and publishing	0.36	0.63	0.53	0.86
Chemicals and chemical products	1.40	1.17	1.13	1.10
Nonmetallic mineral products	0.86	0.89	0.73	1.17
Basic metal industries	0.76	0.58	1.06	1.05
Fabricated metal products, machinery, and equipment	—	0.82	—	0.75

^a Includes business services.
^b Includes hotels and restaurants.

Source: Own computations from the OECD International Sectoral Database (ISDB) on diskettes (1997 version). See equation (1) for the definition of *TFP* (total factor productivity).

much more concentrated in finance, insurance, real estate and business services (a 9 percentage point difference); and somewhat more concentrated in trade (a 3 percentage point difference) and government services (a 4–5 percentage point difference). Between 1970 and 1994, the output compositions of the two countries become more similar, with the correlation coefficient rising from 0.74 to 0.81.

Interestingly, Germany's output composition was more similar to Japan's than to the US. However, in 1970 Germany had a much higher share of total output in manufacturing than did Japan (38 versus 26 per cent), though by 1994 the shares were similar between the two countries (29 versus 26 per cent).

The last four columns of Table 8.6 show the *TFP* level of Japan and Germany relative to that of the US in 1970 and 1994.[8] In 1970, Japan's overall *TFP* level was 66 per cent that of the US, and it was behind the US in every sector except transportation and communications and community, social, and personal services. Between 1970 and 1994, Japan's *TFP* reached 81 per cent of the US level and gained on the US in every sector except agriculture, transportation and communications, and community, social, and personal services. In 1994 Japan's *TFP* was still far behind the US in agriculture (only 31 per cent of the US level) but it had surpassed the US in finance, insurance, real estate, and business services. In total manufacturing, Japan's *TFP* rose from 63 to 72 per cent of the US level between 1970 and 1994. In 1970, *TFP* in Japan exceeded that of the US in textiles, apparel, leather, and in chemicals; in 1994 it was ahead of the US in chemicals and basic metal industries.

Germany's overall *TFP* rose from 70 to 96 per cent of the US level between 1970 and 1994. In 1970 German *TFP* was behind the US in every sector and in 1994 every sector except in community, social and personal services, and in government services. Germany's *TFP* in total manufacturing rose from 84 to 90 per cent of the US level over this period. It exceeded American *TFP* in 2 of the 8 manufacturing industries in 1970 and in 4 of the 8 in 1994.

Table 8.7 shows the effects of different output weights on aggregate output growth in the total economy on the basis of equation (8). As with manufacturing output growth in Japan, total output growth fell off precipitously in the 1989–94 period, from over 4 per cent per year in the preceding two decades to only 2 per cent per year. As with manufacturing, Japan's overall output composition moved towards sectors experiencing higher output growth rates, but here the effects are much smaller. This is due to the high correlation of sectoral output shares over time (0.93 between 1970 and 1994). The results also show that if Japan had adopted the sectoral structure of the US but had maintained actual output growth rates by sector, aggregate output growth in Japan would have been higher in the 1970–9 period but unchanged in the later ones. In contrast, adopting the German industrial structure would have had almost no effect on aggregate growth.

For both Germany and America, total output growth declined between the 1970–9 and the 1989–94 periods but not nearly as much as in Japan. As for Japan, output shares of more recent periods generally yield higher aggregate growth rates than those

[8] The wage share calculations for each sector are based on the fourteen countries in the database.

TABLE 8.7. *The effects of output composition on economy-wide output growth in Japan, Germany, and the United States, 1970–1994*[a] *(rate of output growth in per cent per annum)*

Country and output (s) weights	Period			
	1970–9	1979–89	1989–94	1970–94
A. Japan				
Actual output growth	4.59	4.01	2.09	3.83
(1) 1970 output (s) weights	4.75	3.98	1.80	3.82
(2) 1979 output (s) weights	4.82	3.98	1.91	3.86
(3) 1989 output (s) weights	4.91	4.09	2.06	3.97
(4) 1994 output (s) weights	4.93	4.07	2.16	3.99
(5) Germany output (s) weights[b]	4.63	3.97	2.08	3.82
(6) USA output (s) weights[b]	5.06	3.99	2.00	4.04
B. Germany				
Actual output growth	2.94	1.83	2.00	2.28
(1) 1970 output (s) weights	2.89	1.56	1.42	2.03
(2) 1979 output (s) weights	3.03	1.71	1.59	2.18
(3) 1989 output (s) weights	3.21	1.96	1.88	2.41
(4) 1994 output (s) weights	3.32	2.13	2.16	2.58
(5) Japan output (s) weights[b]	3.00	1.84	2.02	2.32
(6) USA output (s) weights[b]	3.12	1.91	2.17	2.48
C. USA				
Actual output growth	3.05	2.71	1.85	2.66
(1) 1970 output (s) weights	3.08	2.67	1.88	2.66
(2) 1979 output (s) weights	3.07	2.68	1.87	2.66
(3) 1989 output (s) weights	3.24	2.76	1.84	2.75
(4) 1994 output (s) weights	3.31	2.79	1.86	2.79
(5) Japan output (s) weights[b]	3.02	2.56	1.77	2.59
(6) Germany output (s) weights[b]	2.94	2.40	1.70	2.50

[a] The analysis, derived from equation (8), is based on actual output growth rates by sector and assumes that output shares are fixed over the period. The computations are based on 10 sectors. The data source is the ISDB database. See Table 8.6 for details on the sectoring.
[b] Average output weights over the same time period.

of earlier periods, though the effects are again weak (except for Germany in the 1989–94 period). In the case of the US, the adoption of the Japanese or German sectoral structure would have somewhat lowered aggregate growth rates.

Table 8.8 shows the effects of changing output composition on aggregate *TFP* growth. Here an exact decomposition is possible:

$$TFPGR^h = \sum_i s_i^h TFPGR_i^h \qquad (10)$$

TABLE 8.8. *The effects of output composition on economy-wide* TFP *growth in Japan, Germany, and the United States, 1970–1994*[a] *(rate of* TFP *growth in per cent per annum)*

Country and output (s) weights	Period			
	1970–9	1979–89	1989–94	1970–94
A. Japan				
Actual *TFP* growth	1.34	1.79	0.91	1.44
(1) 1970 output (s) weights	1.42	1.93	0.95	1.59
(2) 1979 output (s) weights	1.26	1.83	0.95	1.49
(3) 1989 output (s) weights	1.17	1.76	0.92	1.42
(4) 1994 output (s) weights	1.00	1.62	0.90	1.29
(5) Germany output (s) weights[b]	1.29	1.60	0.76	1.29
(6) USA output (s) weights[b]	1.45	1.84	1.04	1.56
B. Germany				
Actual *TFP* growth	2.49	1.19	1.66	1.78
(1) 1970 output (s) weights	2.56	1.28	1.55	1.90
(2) 1979 output (s) weights	2.43	1.22	1.58	1.83
(3) 1989 output (s) weights	2.25	1.17	1.64	1.75
(4) 1994 output (s) weights	2.07	1.12	1.69	1.67
(5) Japan output (s) weights[b]	2.51	1.27	1.59	1.85
(6) USA output (s) weights[b]	2.21	1.06	1.64	1.66
C. USA				
Actual *TFP* growth	0.36	0.47	0.57	0.44
(1) 1970 output (s) weights	0.40	0.60	0.80	0.53
(2) 1979 output (s) weights	0.32	0.58	0.82	0.50
(3) 1989 output (s) weights	0.34	0.36	0.60	0.37
(4) 1994 output (s) weights	0.38	0.31	0.54	0.35
(5) Japan output (s) weights[b]	0.40	0.58	0.61	0.50
(6) Germany output (s) weights[b]	0.48	0.58	0.51	0.51
D. Japanese manufacturing[c]				
Actual *TFP* growth	2.67	2.03	0.16	1.88
(1) 1970 output (s) weights	2.68	1.92	0.36	1.83
(2) 1979 output (s) weights	2.65	1.73	0.17	1.71
(3) 1989 output (s) weights	2.81	2.33	0.20	2.02
(4) 1994 output (s) weights	2.72	2.22	0.13	1.93
(5) Germany output (s) weights[b]	2.51	2.03	0.22	1.74
(6) USA output (s) weights[b]	2.71	2.08	0.04	1.86

[a] The analysis, derived from equation (10), is based on actual output growth rates by sector and assumes that output shares are fixed over the period. The computations are based on 10 sectors. The data source is the ISDB database.

[b] Average output weights over the same time period.

[c] The computations are based on 8 manufacturing industries.

where $TFPGR_i^h$ is TFP growth in industry i of country h and s_i^h is, as before, the output share of industry i in country h in current prices. Table 8.8 shows results for the case when output shares s_i are fixed over time.

The effects of different output shares on overall TFP growth in the Japanese economy are quite striking in the 1970s and 1980s, with the output shares of later years resulting in much smaller rates of TFP growth than those of earlier years (a difference of $0.3 - 0.4$ percentage points per year between the 1970 and 1994 output weights). This result indicates that output shifted towards sectors with lower TFP growth, at least in those years. However, in the years 1989–94, shifting output composition had virtually no effect on aggregate TFP growth. The ostensible reason is that TFP growth differences among sectors were much less pronounced in the early 1990s than in the two previous decades. The adoption of US output weights (together with actual Japanese sectoral TFP growth rates) would have increased overall TFP growth by about 0.1 percentage point per annum but adoption of German output shares would have reduced overall TFP growth by about the same amount.

Patterns are different for Germany and the US. In the former case, changing output weights over time would have lowered overall TFP growth rather substantially in the 1970–9 period, lowered it moderately in the 1979–89 period, and increased it slightly in the 1989–94 period. In the American case, shifts in output composition over time would have had virtually no effect on overall TFP growth in the 1970–9 period but would have substantially lowered it in the later two periods.

Simulation results are also shown for Japanese manufacturing. The first line of part D highlights the tremendous fall-off in manufacturing TFP growth in the 1990s, from over 2 per cent per year in the previous two decades to virtually zero. Here, again, we see that shifting output shares (in this case, within manufacturing) would have had very modest effects on TFP growth in total manufacturing. Adopting the US or German industrial mix would also have had very limited effects on Japanese TFP growth over this period.

These results also indicate that the slowdown in both aggregate output growth and aggregate TFP growth in the Japanese economy in the early 1990s was due almost entirely to slowdowns on the sectoral level, not to output shifts. Moreover, adoption of the American sectoral mix would have improved performance somewhat but not enough to offset the slowdown, whereas the adoption of the German industrial structure would have had a negative effect on Japanese growth.

5. Conclusions

The results from these decompositions shed light on whether Japan's specialization in particular industries and sectors has retarded its overall output and productivity performance in the 1990s. The answer with regard to manufacturing is that Japan did not choose the wrong industries, it just performed badly. In other words, shifts in output or employment composition over time do not account for the slowdown in output and productivity growth. Moreover, if Japan had adopted the German or US

TABLE A8.1. *Relative production shares (RELPSHR) and labor productivity levels relative to the United States in manufacturing, 1970 and 1994*

Industry	Relative production shares (RELPSHR)					Labor productivity relative to US				
	1970		1994			1970			1994	
	Japan	Germany	USA	Japan	Germany	USA	Japan	Germany	Japan	Germany
TOTAL MANUFACTURING	1.01	1.48	0.89	1.27	1.22	0.89	0.43	0.66	0.74	0.67
Low-tech industries										
Food	1.56	0.93	0.67	1.16	0.84	0.78	0.81	0.66	0.56	0.49
Beverages	1.51	2.15	0.44	0.82	1.62	0.61	1.64	0.89	0.78	0.56
Tobacco	0.18	2.62	1.12	0.24	3.94	0.70	0.14	0.63	0.43	1.89
Textiles	1.25	1.23	0.63	0.68	0.86	0.86	0.36	0.74	0.27	0.77
Wearing apparel	1.08	1.26	0.81	1.04	0.55	0.97	1.21	0.81	0.89	0.73
Leather and products	1.15	1.47	0.48	1.12	0.86	0.48	1.26	0.83	1.18	0.85
Footwear	0.25	1.30	0.74	0.27	0.68	0.39	0.58	0.68	0.60	0.79
Wood products	0.81	0.94	1.08	0.59	0.86	1.23	0.18	0.49	0.33	0.60
Furniture and fixtures	1.21	1.84	0.71	0.85	1.31	0.82	1.06	0.17	1.14	0.87
Paper and products	0.80	0.99	1.06	0.88	0.96	1.09	0.39	0.51	0.59	0.56
Printing and publishing	1.45	0.62	1.01	1.15	0.53	0.98	0.71	0.52	0.87	0.76
Petroleum refineries	0.47	2.98	0.67	0.67	2.30	0.60	0.79	0.88	1.26	2.70
Petroleum and coal products	0.39	2.37	1.10	0.52	1.66	1.27	0.19	0.70	0.44	5.53

Rubber products	0.73	1.68	0.94	1.12	0.94	0.95	0.33	0.67	0.50	0.47
Plastic products, nec	0.72	1.28	0.74	1.31	1.31	0.92	0.57	0.57	0.70	0.74
Pottery, china, etc.	1.19	1.22	0.26	1.01	0.88	0.28	0.51	0.46	0.67	0.55
Glass and products	1.65	1.11	0.91	1.03	1.56	0.75	1.00	0.40	0.87	0.72
Nonmetal products, nec	1.27	1.58	0.65	1.22	1.50	0.69	0.49	0.89	0.63	0.93
Iron and steel	1.28	1.67	1.00	1.66	1.71	0.72	0.66	0.42	0.91	0.54
Nonferrous metals	1.28	1.25	1.01	1.41	1.65	0.70	0.78	0.45	1.29	0.76
Metal products	0.76	1.63	0.85	1.02	1.69	0.89	0.33	0.60	0.54	0.61
Shipbuilding and repair	1.26	0.54	0.77	1.73	0.72	0.71	0.29	0.29	1.49	0.92
Other manufactures, nes	1.59	0.66	0.87	2.46	0.40	0.71	0.65	0.65	2.10	0.77
Medium-tech industries										
Industrial chemicals	0.89	2.07	0.84	0.96	1.49	0.88	0.43	0.73	0.82	0.50
All transport equipment	na.	na.	na.	na.	na.	na.	0.46	0.68	0.82	0.70
Railroad equipment	0.48	0.43	0.44	0.71	0.54	0.49	na.	na.	0.78	0.22
Motor vehicles	1.38	1.83	0.85	1.64	1.82	0.76	0.50	na.	1.16	0.99
Motorcycles and bicycles	1.48	0.68	0.35	1.68	0.66	0.30	na.	na.	1.14	0.54
Other transport equipment	2.07	1.15	0.00	2.20	1.03	0.00	na.	na.	na.	na.
High-tech industries										
Other chemical products	0.85	1.57	1.09	1.13	1.19	1.03	0.49	0.59	0.80	0.45
Non-electrical machinery	0.93	1.74	0.86	1.21	1.10	1.09	0.37	0.71	0.61	0.46
Electrical machinery	0.19	1.86	1.11	2.23	1.18	0.74	0.05	0.57	1.03	0.65
Aircraft	0.11	0.30	1.66	0.15	0.40	1.76	na.	na.	0.86	0.47
Professional goods	0.38	2.29	1.20	0.66	1.35	1.34	0.18	0.69	0.44	0.52

product mix (or employment composition) in manufacturing, it would not have increased its total manufacturing output or productivity growth. If Japanese productivity growth had been the same as Germany or the US by individual industry, its aggregate productivity performance would have been much better, even with its own industrial composition. The US, in particular, outperformed Japan in terms of manufacturing productivity in the 1990s because of greater technological change.

The results are echoed on the total economy level. The slowdown in aggregate output growth and *TFP* growth seen in the 1990s is not attributable to shifts in output composition over time but rather to slowdowns on the sectoral level. Moreover, adopting the US output mix would not have materially increased either output or *TFP* growth in the 1990s, while the adoption of the German output mix would actually have lowered growth.

The results clearly point out that the problem of Japan in the 1990s lies in a slowdown in the rate of technological progress on the individual industry and sectoral level. Output growth has also declined on the industry and sectoral level, though the growth in capital intensity has not fallen off that much in the 1990s. The results of the paper do not establish that Japan has specialized in the "wrong" industries in terms of productivity performance and growth potential. Rather, they suggest that Japan's performance in these industries has been poor compared to both its previous historical performance and to that of its chief competitors, Germany and the US.

Moreover, the decline in *TFP* growth in Japan is particularly worrisome given that Japan has achieved such a high R&D intensity. Indeed, according to National Science Board (1998), Japan's R&D intensity (the ratio of R&D expenditures to GDP) has steadily grown since 1980 and by 1995 Japan had the highest R&D intensity among the G7 countries (2.78 per cent compared to 2.52 per cent in the US, 2.28 per cent in Germany, 2.34 per cent in France, and 2.05 per cent in the UK).

How is Japan to get out of its productivity slump? If we knew the reasons for the slowdown of technological progress in Japan, we might be able to propose some solutions. However, the economics profession has had difficulty explaining the protracted US slump in productivity growth, from 1973 to the present, so that finding an explanation for the Japanese slowdown may be equally difficult.

There are a couple of problems that seem peculiar to the Japanese situation. First, the banking crisis in Japan over the last decade or so may have put a damper on lending to more innovative new firms. Saddled with bad loans, Japanese banks may have been reluctant to take on high-risk new investments, and this, in turn, may have impaired development of new products or industrial processes within each industry category. The recent government bailout of the banking sector, however, may open up the economy to new credit for more innovative undertakings.[9]

Second, the decline in Japanese *TFP* relative to the United States in the transportation and communications sector from 1.00 in 1970 to 0.72 in 1994 (see Table 8.6) is worrisome because of the links between these industries and other, more inno-

---

[9] Somewhat ironically, the ISDB data, shown in Table 8.6, indicate that in 1994 Japan had a 27 per cent lead in *TFP* over the US in finance, insurance, and real estate. However, this result may reflect, in part, the reluctance of the Japanese banking system to write off bad loans.

vative sectors of the economy. This is particularly so because of the connections between telecommunications on the one hand and computers, semiconductors, software, computer and Internet services, and information technology in general on the other. This industrial nexus has been the most dynamic segment of the US economy in the 1990s.

Third, rigidities in the labor system may have led firms to retain large labor forces through the slump of the 1990s. This stands in sharp contrast with the corporate downsizing that occurred in the United States during the 1980s and 1990s. Recent newspaper reports now suggest that large Japanese corporations are beginning to rationalize their labor force by laying off redundant workers.

Finally, procyclical productivity performance is common to most economies, including the US. When there is an economic slowdown, firms do not shed labor as rapidly as output falls, so that measured productivity declines. This poor productivity performance of the Japanese economy during the 1990s may itself be, in part, a consequence of the protracted recession over this period.

Though the Japanese economy will probably never again attain the high growth of the 1960s, which was largely a result of technological catch-up and its associated high investment rate, it may attain 3–5 per cent annual growth, which would be quite creditable for a "mature" economy. This may occur once the recession is over, and output and productivity growth return to more normal levels.

REFERENCES

Balassa, Bela (1965), "Trade Liberalization and 'Revealed' Comparative Advantage," *The Manchester School*, 33 (May): 99–123.
Katz, Richard (1998), *Japan: The System That Soured* (Armonk, NY: M. E. Sharpe).
Maddison, Angus (1991), *Dynamic Forces in Capitalist Development* (Oxford: Oxford University Press).
——(1993), "Standardized Estimates of Fixed Capital Stock: A Six Country Comparison," *Innovazione e Materie Prime* (April) 1–29.
National Science Board (1998), *Science and Engineering Indicators, 1998* (Arlington, Va.: National Science Foundation) (NSB 98-1).
Wolff, Edward N. (1996), "The Productivity Slowdown: The Culprit at Last?" *American Economic Review*, 86/5 (Dec.), 1239–52.
——(1999), "Specialization and Productivity Performance in Low-, Medium-, and High-Tech Manufacturing Industries," in Heston, Alan and Robert Lipsey (eds.), *International and Interarea Comparisons of Prices, Income, and Output*, Studies of Income and Wealth (Chicago: Chicago University Press), 419–52.
Young, A. (1995), "The Tyranny of Numbers: Confronting the Statistical Realities of the East Asian Growth Experience," *Quarterly Journal of Economics*, 110/3: 641–80.

9   The *Sogo Shosha*: Finding a New Role?

ÖRJAN SJÖBERG AND MARIE SÖDERBERG

1. Introduction: Giants in Distress

Japanese postwar trade has been fundamentally different from that of other industrialized countries in the sense that it has been dominated by a handful of companies, the Japanese *sogo shosha*, or general trading companies (GTCs). As late as 1990 these companies controlled 75 per cent of all imports to and around 45 per cent of the exports from Japan. The six largest general trading companies make it into the ranks of the world's top ten non-US companies. Already this piece of information indicates that the *sogo shosha* are to be reckoned with. For, although their turnover or revenues are somewhat inflated by arcane accounting practices, it cannot be denied that the likes of Mitsubishi Corporation, Mitsui, or Itochu are heavyweight players not only in the Japanese corporate world but also on the international stage. In the 1998 Forbes International Top 800, they occupied three of the top four positions with revenues in the range of US$126–143 billion each, with Marubeni, Sumitomo, and Nissho Iwai also making it into the top ten (*Forbes*, July 27, 1998: 54). In Asia itself, the position of Japan's general trading companies is overwhelming, occupying the six top positions of the "Asiaweek 1000" list of the continent's largest companies (*Asiaweek*, Nov. 20, 1998: 66–7).

Size, however, is not necessarily an adequate predictor of good performance or bright prospects. On the contrary, signs are that the *sogo shosha* are in for an increasingly rough ride. Despite claims to the effect that they "have become the master merchants of Asia" (Hatch and Yamamura, 1996: 166), since 1990 the position of the GTCs has continued to erode. To regain the initiative, both individual *sogo shosha* and their national organization have formulated strategies for the future. These strategies all have one thing in common—they do not see general trade as their main field of business in the future.

If implemented, this has a number of implications. So does the fact that Japan, if it is to recover decisively from the recession of the 1990s, needs to push through a number of fundamental changes of a structural nature, some of which are likely to have a considerable impact on the GTCs. The question is what form and direction change will take. The aim of this paper is to provide some input towards an answer. More specifically, the present paper starts by sketching a picture of the postwar role of the trading houses, up to the 1990s. We then turn to the strategies that the general trading companies adopted in the early 1990s, strategies designed with a view to

We would like to acknowledge our debt to the editors and the participants at the Stockholm and Honolulu workshops at which earlier versions of this paper were read.

retaining their positions within the Japanese economy. Having identified the general thrust of these efforts, and the immediate results thereof, we focus on how the *sogo shosha* are restructuring for the future and what this might imply. In the concluding section we draw out some of the implications of these changes for the Japanese economy as well as for the structure of power in the country.

2. Past Strength, Present Functions

Historically, the trading companies have their origins as specialized traders focusing on some specific commodity, such as textiles or metals. Alternatively, they owe their existence to their position within prewar *zaibatsu*, serving as the trading arms for these group of companies. Specialization in trade brought experience and skills useful both in mitigating the costs of operating in foreign markets and in opening up opportunities to exploit economies of scale and scope. Although it must be pointed out that a considerable part of the activities of the GTCs, both past and present, focuses on domestic Japanese business activities, early on the general trading companies acquired experience in operating overseas. As such, they accumulated a considerable expertise in shipping, forwarding, insurance and other aspects of the logistics of foreign trade. Meanwhile, they systematically acquired and developed language and related skills in short supply within Japan itself. As they went along, they also collected valuable information on international and foreign markets; indeed, monitoring developments abroad became one of the main activities of their vast networks of representative and sales offices across the globe. Similarly, by maintaining close contact with foreign governments, bureaucrats, and local businesses, these networks alerted headquarters back home and often helped mobilize resources to exploit profitable business opportunities as they appeared. Not only were the networks of the GTCs well placed abroad but indeed also at home. Besides routine business relations they were in regular contact with bureaucrats as well as politicians. Through activities such as these they could effectively extend the reach of Japanese manufacturers in need of imported raw materials and intermediate goods, and help them find markets abroad for their products.

It comes as no surprise then that much research into the role and functions of the general trading companies have underlined their ability to reduce transaction costs, that is, the costs to conduct business. "In essence," a study commissioned by the OECD noted with respect to Japan's general trading companies, "their corporate advantage is their ability to organize, coordinate and intermediate market transactions" (Kojima and Ozawa, 1984: 14). As such, and in addition to maintaining a considerable degree of flexibility and adaptability, it also implies that the GTCs have been instrumental in mitigating the risk and uncertainty associated with overseas trade and investment. This is indeed the manner in which the *sogo shosha* are generally thought of.

More specifically, as far as trade and transactions costs are concerned, the GTCs would appear to have an edge in certain product categories, the main characteristics of which according to Roehl (1983: 123) are the following:

1. standardized;
2. handled in large lots or repetitively;
3. handled by trading company at several stages of the production chain; and
4. subject to economies of scale in trading.

The last characteristic relates particularly to products that require world markets to reach the thresholds beyond which economies of scale are present and where this can be achieved through pool trading.

That these are the activities in which the *sogo shosha* do enjoy a certain leverage is also consistent with Shin's (1989) observation that manufacturers have incentives to shun the services of trading companies should they possess specialized assets such as brand-name capital. Yet the GTCs also trade more sophisticated, less standardized products, such as machinery. By way of an explanation, Roehl (1983) points to the advantage that the trading companies, as compared especially to small and medium-sized companies, have in mitigating the cost of market development or arranging for occasional transactions. Similarly, trading companies are better placed to make use of whatever synergies over the production chain that might exist. Most importantly, they perform an arbitrage function, broadly corresponding, or so Roehl (1983: 124; 1998: 206) suggests, to Williamson's concept of "trilateral governance." That is, *sogo shosha* can organize business transactions of an occasional nature where the complexity of the governance structures needed is beyond the capacity of the producer and buyer. In this connection, it should also be pointed out that Yoshihara (1982: 198–9) has noted that GTCs have stepped in not only to organize distribution but also to help manufacturers spread risk, indeed at times taking upon themselves the shielding of producers entirely from exposure (cf. Sheard, 1989).

As with other commentators, much of Roehl's argument focuses on the ability of the GTCs to collect and process information. He further notes that in addition to busying themselves with distribution and marketing, and related information gathering, the *sogo shosha* have engaged in financial intermediation (Roehl, 1983: 130–3; also, e.g. Yoshihara, 1982: 212–18). Not only is the financing of trade—including trade credits, inventory financing, loan guarantees, and foreign exchange risk management—a logical extension of their other trade-related activities, the GTCs have engaged in what essentially amounts to financial wholesaling. By borrowing on a vast scale and then lending the money on to client firms, general trading companies earn an income from interest rate differentials. Their (at times preferential) access to information, or so it is claimed, has made this otherwise rather risky procedure a workable proposition.

Also the key role played by the GTCs in consortia of investors can be thought of as an expression of transaction costs advantages. However, this particular activity extends beyond initiating investments or alerting others to such investment opportunities as may exist. By virtue of their ability to raise finance, GTCs often end up having a sizeable stake in various ventures. These are not necessarily mere examples of backward integration or an outcome of the need to invest in trade-related activities; while at times they have an at best tenuous connection to *sogo shosha* areas of strength, less virtuous motives are also conceivable. Thus, Koerner (1998) suggests that equity participation by the trading houses in upstream activities may cause information asymmetries that can be used for contract bargaining ends.

Transaction cost theory further suggests that firms will choose the solution which minimizes the sum of search and negotiation costs and the costs of monitoring and enforcing contracts (Williamson, 1985). It is indeed telling that Roehl (1983: 128) cites the ability of GTCs to reduce these costs across the entire chain of transactions and related activities, rather than for one or other part of it, as the main reason for their resilience. Even so, at the level of principle, it is possible to distinguish a number of conditions or situations under which trading companies would seem to come especially into their own. From Williamsonian transaction costs theory, Peng and Ilinitch (1998) deduce five propositions which, they argue, apply to export intermediaries generally. These propositions, which include but extend beyond the product characteristics identified by Roehl, are:

1. The more distant and unfamiliar markets are, the more likely that export intermediaries will be selected by manufacturers.
2. The higher the commodity content of the product (the lower the value added content), and thus the more standardized, the more likely that intermediaries will be used.
3. The more knowledgeable, and thus the lower search costs, the stronger the performance of the intermediary.
4. The greater the ability to handle negotiations and lower negotiation costs, the stronger the performance of the intermediary.
5. The greater the willingness to take title to goods and thus to lower monitoring and enforcement costs, the stronger the performance of the intermediary.

Although these propositions focus on the role of trading companies as intermediaries in exports, they provide something of a set of benchmarks against which the operations of Japanese GTCs can be assessed.

3. Beyond Transaction Costs

At this juncture it should be pointed out, that a transaction costs approach to the GTCs does not quite exhaust the full range of characteristics that are associated with this peculiar Japanese type of business organization. The financial operations of the trading companies may benefit from various advantages they enjoy with respect to access to information, but they also profit from they manner in which financial markets have been regulated. Indeed, as well as deriving rents from their privileged position in these markets, they in all likelihood have remained less efficient than they would have been had they faced some serious domestic or foreign competition at home. Their importance to domestic trade and finance indicates that this is in fact the case; it would be difficult to argue that their dominant position in Japan itself derives from a much superior understanding of the local market than that which local companies command.

The importance of regulation to the standing of the GTCs, goes beyond mere coincidence. Whether a case of rent-seeking or policy capture, it is clear that the *sogo shosha* owe some of their strengths, both at home and abroad, to the manner in which the Japanese economy is traditionally organized. What we have in mind are the needs and inclinations of a government bent on intervention. Put differently, the GTCs play a role as a different sort of intermediary. Not only have the *sogo shosha* derived their position of strength from their key role within the *keiretsu*, but this position has both made possible and benefited from their function as a conduit for state intervention and guidance. This aspect deserves some measured attention, both because of its implications for the implementation of industrial policy and because of its impact on the staying power of the GTCs.

The most common way of capturing the essence of the power structure in postwar Japan is the "iron triangle." This is a set-up under which, or so it is typically argued, politicians, bureaucrats, and businessmen cooperate and are mutually dependent on each other. Together they form a Japan, Inc., the energies and resources of which are put to work for the well-being of the nation as a whole (Kaplan, 1972: 14–17; Kahn, 1972). Long unrivalled as a heuristic device, different scholars have come to emphasize the power of different parts of this triangle. Some see the policy of "economy first" as a proof of the power of the business community. The cooperation between government and business has been described as so close that the border line between "public" and "private" domains is thoroughly blurred (Tsurumi, 1976: 5–9). Others emphasize the role of the bureaucracy in and for the rapid economic growth characterizing much of postwar Japan. In his seminal work, *MITI and the Japanese Miracle*, Chalmers Johnson (1982) projects an image of a country that is not fully a market economy but which rather relies on MITI to direct Japanese private companies on fundamental aspects of where to invest and how to conduct their business.

Subsequent research has shown that the picture is not quite as simple as this, that there is considerable conflict and struggle within the main groups (Curtis, 1975) and that the amount of influence varies with the issue at hand and the level of controversy: politicians are more likely to take the reins in controversial issues (Fukui, 1977: 9; Pempel, 1982: 303). Yet, few would deny that there is a "Japanese model" for economic growth, and that it has reigned supreme throughout much of the postwar period. As Ramseyer and Rosenbluth (1997) note, in Japan politicians are important. Revolving around export-driven growth with considerable state intervention, it appears—superficially at least—to have worked well for the Japanese economy from the 1960s to the 1980s. Throughout this period MITI "offered" administrative guidance and could thus direct the growth of the Japanese industry by pinpointing in which direction to go.

In this model the *sogo shoshas* had a central role to play. They operated, as the Japanese "eyes and ears" (Hatch and Yamamura, 1996: 17) abroad and the ones taking care of most of the exports and imports. As there were only a few GTCs they could develop intimate contacts with MITI. These contacts were mutually beneficial. It made it easy for the Ministry to control trade and for the *sogo shosha* to prevent MITI from letting others join the fray. However, with the recent opening up of the Japanese market, a number of new players have entered. The same is true of the drive of Japanese manufacturers to establish themselves abroad, not least following the Plaza Accord of 1985. With part of the industry moving abroad, an increase of joint venture with foreign companies, Japanese companies turning to Eurobonds instead of domestic ones, and the general globalization of the world economy, Japanese bureaucrats as well as politicians started losing their ability to control (Ito, Takuma, and Hironori, 1998). Indeed, the long-term effects of all of this have served to hollow out not only industry but also the grip of politicians and MITI officials over it.

4. The 1990s: Going Downhill

Against this background it comes as no surprise that the standing of the *sogo shosha* is now assessed differently than in the not so distant past. Throughout the 1970s and early 1980s, the GTCs were looked upon as models for others to emulate (Ozawa, 1988). Not that they were never exposed to criticism—they were, not least on account of infringements on fair trade legislation, their alleged penchant for speculation and too cozy a relationship with influential politicians (Yoshihara, 1982: ch. 2)—but as the spearheads of industrialization they were regarded as critical to the success of Japanese manufacturing. In recent years this image has changed. The cover of a 1993 report on them from Hong Kong the brokerage firm, Jardine Fleming, in featured a cartoon Tyrannosaurus rex with a crushed cigarette clenched by its teeth. The conclusion of the report was clear: Japanese trading houses "are creatures of a bygone age."

Doomsday analysts have a point. The core business that built the trading companies—importing raw materials into Japan and exporting finished goods—has seen sluggish growth for well over a decade and since 1990 the GTCs have experienced a period of outright decline. Revenues from almost all fields of operation have fallen and as can be seen from Table 9.1, which uses the year ending March 31, 1990 as the base, total sales of the five major GTCs during the financial year ending in 1998 only amounted to 67 per cent of that of eight years earlier.

This rather dismal performance occurred at a time when foreign trade was in fact expanding (Adams and Gangnes, Chapter 3 this volume). What is more, considering the high value of the yen during the 1990s, it comes as something of a surprise that imports rather than exports would be the type of business that decreased the most. In 1994–5, when the yen was at its peak, their share of imports only amounted to 52 per cent of the 1989–90 figures. Similarly, in 1997–8 GTC imports were down to 55 per cent of the level reached in 1989–90, exports fell to 67 and offshore trade to 63 per cent. The main items of offshore trade as of 1995 were non-ferrous metals and fuel (70 per cent of the total) which mostly consisted of trade on the metal market in

TABLE 9.1. *Sales volume in the five major general trading companies, 1990–1998 (100 billion yen)*

Company	1990	1998
Itochu	205	145 (71)
Mitsui	203	140 (69)
Marubeni	182	130 (71)
Sumitomo	214	116 (54)
Mitsubishi	166	120 (72)
TOTAL	970	651 (67)

Note: Figures in parentheses indicate percentages of 1990 volume.
Source: Mitsui Trade and Economic Research Institute.

London or on the spot market for oil (Yamanaka, 1996). This implies high risks and makes future sustainability doubtful.[1] Domestic trade is still the main pillar of business and by the financial year ending in March 1998 amounted to 75 per cent of the 1990 level, thereby in effect increasing its share in the total.

There are a number of reasons for these declining trends, some of which are of a structural nature. The GTCs' main strength is in trade connected to heavy industry. Metals and machinery are the most important items traded by the *sogo shosha*. Iron and steel used to be the top item, but due to the high value of the yen and the restructuring of Japanese industry those goods have seen their share of the total shrinking. In fact, raw materials have been replaced by components and other goods with higher value added contents. Similarly, nontraded items, such as financial services, became ever more important to the Japanese economy (Adams and Gangnes, Chapter 3 this volume). As suggested by proposition 2 of Peng and Ilinitch (1998), the higher the commodity content, i.e. lower value added, the more likely that intermediaries will be used. Raw materials and basic inputs such as steel must be considered products fitting this characterization and, as Japanese trade has come to concentrate in fields where value added is a more critical concern, the role of the intermediaries has decreased.

To compensate, the GTCs have long been looking for alternatives to commodity trade. As they were losing ground during the 1990s, this search intensified, with three main alternative activities pursued. These are (a) foreign direct investment; (b) the provision of infrastructure and a concomitant emphasis on Asia, particularly Southeast Asia; and (c) finding new areas of operation, including the identification of new industries, financial services and alliances with foreign companies. This, then, comprises what is perhaps best seen as the first concerted attempt at redefining the role

---

[1] Especially in light of the arrest of Yasuo Hamanaka of Sumitomo. In October 1996, Hamanaka, once dubbed "Mr Five Percent" for the share of world copper-trading he was said to have controlled, cost his company nearly 300 billion yen in losses from unauthorized copper dealings.

of the general trading houses. As such, it was not entirely successful and precipitated yet another effort to reinvent the *sogo shosha*.

5. Changing Tracks

5.1. From low margin trade to investment

Investment has for some time been considered a prime alternative, and then not only a mere supplement, to traditional trade.[2] The appreciation of the yen following the Plaza Accord in 1985 led to a new wave of Japanese companies moving production abroad. This so-called "hollowing out" of the Japanese economy also involved the GTCs, which helped the manufacturing companies by providing some of the capital needed for restructuring. In this way the *sogo shosha* came to make joint investments with Japanese manufacturing companies in a number of production sites overseas; in some cases, these ventures also had local partners. From the point of view of the trading companies, there were several motives for such investment (Hennart and Kryda, 1998): (a) to project influence and continue to be in business with Japanese producers; (b) chances of gaining a high profit, not least through the judicious use of transfer pricing techniques, but also from dividends that accrue to owners; (c) it was a requirement for being allowed to do some types of business in certain countries.

As experience has shown, there are some dangers in this strategy. Traditionally, the employees of the GTCs have their skills in trading and not in production. This makes it even more difficult to control a number of companies of different size, across a vast range of fields and a variety of locations. A further problem with local companies is that, as they become established, they want to go on their own and pursue their own strategies and not necessarily the ones preferred by the trading companies. All of this adds up to considerable problems, particularly since their numbers are typically very large. Mitsui, for example, now has around 1,100 companies in which they have more than a 20 per cent ownership stake. Some of these ventures work well, but all certainly do not, and to the extent that this is the case they become a burden to the owners both financially and in terms of managerial capacity.

5.2. Infrastructure and the Asian market

In addition to increasingly turning their energies to investment as opposed to trade, the GTCs identified one particular geographical area, Asia, as suitable for both trade and investment activities. Indeed, the Asian market was seen as the solution of many of the problems of the trading houses in the 1990s (Söderberg, forthcoming). This was nothing peculiar for the *sogo shosha*. Asia was widely regarded

[2] *Nota bene* (investment) having been instrumental in setting up industrial ventures as early as during the opening decades of this century, is of course not entirely unknown territory to the *sogo shosha* (Yoshihara 1982: 204–208).

as the major growth market by a number of multinational companies and private capital poured into the region. Economic growth proceeded at high rates and according to a report by the World Bank around US$1.5 trillion needed to be invested in Asian infrastructure before the year 2005 if growth was to continue at the same pace. This presented unprecedented opportunities for the GTCs, or so it was thought.[3]

For one thing, in order for the Asian economies to develop, and for the Japanese manufacturers to be able to establish themselves there, physical and social infrastructure were needed. Both were areas where the GTCs had some prior experience. The trading houses had accumulated considerable experience in the art of mitigating and rectifying infrastructural deficiencies in their earlier role of securing a reliable supply of raw materials. They thus re-entered this type of activity with a measure of confidence. What is more, their interest in physical infrastructure was congruent with the priorities of the Japanese government, which at the time spent enormous amounts of foreign aid on developing Asian infrastructure.

There are several interesting aspects to this development. For instance, as the Japanese overseas development assistance in the form of yen loans gradually became less tied to Japanese suppliers, not all orders were landed by Japanese companies (Söderberg, 1996). This had the effect of shifting some of the GTCs' activities to ventures with non-Japanese firms that were often part of the consortia competing for the lucrative contracts. By the same token, public money available for infrastructure was insufficient to meet demand. A number of projects, especially in the power sector, were built by private companies on a BOT or BOO basis.[4] One example of this is the so called "Paiton project" in Indonesia where Mitsui on a joint venture basis with the American company, Edison Mission Energy, built a power plant, a contract with a value of US$2.5 billion (Malmström, 1996: 138–39). This kind of project was seen as a future niche where the *sogo shosha* had an edge in arranging finance and acting as coordinators.

As the economic crisis hit the Thai economy in July 1997, bringing about a dramatic depreciation of the *baht* that in turn had repercussions on other ASEAN currencies and led to plummeting stock markets, the situation did not seem as bright any longer. Quite a few projects were cancelled and some were left unfinished. In case it had not dawned upon them earlier, like other companies active in the region, the GTCs realized that this type of project carried considerable risk. The situation was further aggravated by the political unrest that followed in Indonesia, the country which happened to be something of a favorite spot for investment by the Japanese. How deeply involved they were became quite clear when the nine major trading companies in 1998 for the first time made public the size of their investments, loans, and loan guarantees in five Asian countries. These figures are reproduced in Table 9.2.

[3] That some of these opportunities were not merely of a traditional business character is shown by the case of Mitsui, which has been implicated in what appears to be an attempt to misappropriate overseas development assistance funds (*Financial Times*, June 10, 1998).

[4] "Build Operate and Transfer" or "Build Operate and Own." This meant that private companies were able to build and operate economic infrastructure on certain conditions agreed upon beforehand.

TABLE 9.2. *Investment, lending, and loan guarantees committed to Southeast Asia as of end of March 1998 (billions of yen)*

	Indonesia	Five Asian countries
Marubeni	158.3	258.1
Mitsubishi Corp.	109.6	246.7
Itochu Corp.	132.7	192.3
Nissho Iwai Corp.	135.5	185.2
Sumitomo Corp.	100.5	155.7
Mitsui & Co.	54.1	118.9
Tomen Corp.	59.6	84.1
Nichimen Corp.	35.0	51.7
Kanematsu Corp.	26.4	39.5

Note: The "five Asian countries" are Indonesia, Malaysia, Philippines, South Korea, and Thailand.

Source: Annual Reports by companies.

5.3. New industries, financial services, and strategic alliances with foreign companies

Other strategies embarked upon by the *sogo shosha* to improve their business performance include developing new business areas and trying to target future growth industries. Information-related business, multimedia, telecom, and space development have all at one point or other been seen as such sectors of future growth. Since the 1980s a number of subsidiaries or divisions have been created to deal with projects in these newly targeted areas. Importantly, opportunities for new business that might arise from deregulation of the Japanese market are a major target for all GTCs. By way of an example, Marubeni is planning to get into the business of selling gasoline together with Daiei. As deregulation of the financial market takes place, Marubeni also plans to set up a brokerage company to sell investment trust products jointly with foreign companies. Similarly, Nissho Iwai has also expressed interest in entering the brokerage business (*Asahi Shimbun*, March 4, 1998).

As transaction costs became less of a problem to larger companies, in the 1990s, many Japanese manufacturers avoided using the trading companies in order to cut cost and become more competitive; in like fashion, many of the *sogo shosha* left Japanese manufacturers out of the picture and joined with foreign companies when this has been more profitable or the only solution to remain competitive in spite of the high value of the yen. One attraction of foreign partners appears to be that they have different areas of strength than do Japanese companies; in other cases the wary quality of being non-Japanese might prove beneficial as host governments may occasionally be wary of the implications of Japanese dominance. Be this as it may, there are a great many cases of both informal cooperation—like the one between Marubeni and the Swedish-Swiss company ABB (Malmström, 1996: 139)—and more formal strategic alliances like the one between Mitsui and Dupont in 1993 when they jointly created Dumac, a think tank charged with identifying new business opportunities.

The new strategies include efforts to restructure the operations by recourse to other means. For instance, and in contrast to past practices, cost-cutting has also been added to the agenda. As can be gleaned from Table 9.3, in recent years the number of Japanese employees has been decreasing at a steady although not particularly dramatic rate. Indeed, in view of the significant decline in revenue the main impression is one of rather slow adjustment.

6. The Situation at the End of the 1990s: Continuing Decline

As can be seen from Table 9.4, at least two of the five general trading companies for which data are readily available—Itochu and Marubeni—posted unconsolidated net losses for the fiscal year ending March 31, 1998. Mitsui and Mitsubishi both reported only net and pretax profits. Sumitomo, on the other hand, returned to the black after huge losses in 1996 from the copper-trading scandal. That these figures are in keeping with the rather dismal performance of much of the Japanese business sector throughout the 1990s is presumably of little comfort.

TABLE 9.3. *Number of Japanese employees in five major companies, as of March 31, 1990–1998*

Company	1990	1991	1992	1993	1994	1995	1996	1997	1998
Mitsubishi	9,215	9,429	9,640	9,827	9,937	9,916	9,241	8,794	8,401
Mitsui	9,094	9,145	9,140	8,929	8,670	8,341	7,974	7,783	7,538
Itochu	7,098	7,108	7,149	7,449	7,434	7,345	7,182	6,999	6,675
Marubeni	7,185	7,179	7,194	7,218	7,190	7,064	6,702	6,386	6,041
Sumitomo	6,284	6,363	6,448	6,628	6,578	6,491	6,193	5,931	5,761

Source: Mitsui Research Institute.

TABLE 9.4. *Net profits of five major companies as of March 31, 1989–1998 (100 million yen)*

	1989	1990	1991	1992	1993	1994	1995	1996	1997	1998
Mitsui	166	220	222	226	239	152	218	240	260	211
Mitsubishi	331	411	430	403	153	32	160	203	220	214
Itochu	155	186	191	109	101	20	94	102	111	−147
Marubeni	151	163	171	174	109	63	77	118	60	−307
Sumitomo	274	351	265	333	202	102	121	163	−1,486	221

Source: Mitsui Research Institute.

The consolidated financial account balance was also in the red for all GTCs, except Mitsui and Mitsubishi (Table 9.5). Their attempt to reinvent themselves seems to have yielded meager results and in some cases can even be seen as extremely unfortunate. Infrastructure development in Asia seemed like a lucrative, growing business in the middle of the 1990s but as the Asian crises hit in 1997 it proved an unfortunate area to emphasize. To venture into new high-tech industries is not an easy task either. At the same time the deflationary environment in Japan has not served to improve the situation of the trading houses.

7. Further Restructuring?

While the above might suggest both that changes are inevitable, yet hardly anywhere to be seen, some momentum has in fact developed. With respect to structural change, an important development for the *sogo shosha* is the possibility of establishing holding companies. These have not been permitted in Japan since the end of the war when the *zaibatsu* were broken up into smaller units. Some years ago it was considered unlikely for political reasons that they would be introduced again. Japan's Foreign Trade Council (JFTC), which is the association that organizes the trading companies, has worked hard to push through a change in Japanese law to this effect. As a result, almost all the GTCs are now studying the possibilities offered by this change in legislation. A step in that direction is the so called *bunshaku*, that is, a breaking up of the companies into different divisions and subgroups that would operate independently. Arguably, Itochu has advanced the furthest in this respect; for instance, it made its American operations an independent legal entity with top management consisting of Americans.

Progress in this area has otherwise been notably slow. The main reason for this state of affairs is that paying tax in Japan cannot be done on the basis of consolidated accounts. There is therefore no strong economic incentive to move in this particular direction. The JFTC is now actively lobbying for such a change and hopes to obtain it within a couple of years. If so, at that point some further restructuring is likely.

TABLE 9.5. *Consolidated financial accounts as of 31 March 1998 (billion yen)*

	Mitsui	Mitsubishi	Itochu	Marubeni	Sumotomo	N-Iwai	Tomen	Nichimen	Kanematsu
Dividend received	20.2	29.6	12.1	6.5	6.1	5.9	1.8	2.1	1.0
Interest paid	−17.7	−15.6	−55.4	−27.4	−11.4	−13.7	−18.6	−5.0	−15.7
Balance	2.5	14.0	−43.3	−20.9	−5.3	−7.8	−16.8	−2.9	−14.7

Source: Mitsui Research Institute.

Financial deregulation as officially launched on April 1, 1998—the "Big Bang"—is also of some consequence to the trading houses (Ito and Melvin, Chapter 7 this volume). An important feature of this program is that it has a timetable attached to it, one that purports to show how the government intends to transform Japan's market. Although it is not entirely clear whether the original timetable can be kept, the reform of financial markets is beginning to take effect. As a result, the financial aspects of the business activities that the trading houses engage in is likely to change. This is especially so since financial deregulation not only provides for new opportunities, but is also likely to cut into the financial intermediation business of the GTCs. Since the latter is not only an area where GTCs have had a transaction costs edge but critically have developed under the cozy conditions created for them by the heavy hand of regulation, chances are that they will lose more than they are able to gain from deregulation. How each of the major *sogo shoshas* will tackle this may well be crucial for their future prospects and manner of operation.

In the meantime, the JFTC appointed a special study group, headed by Professor Iwao Nakatani of Hitotsubashi University, to prepare a study of the GTCs in the twenty-first century. The group's report (Nakatani, 1998) foresees a radically changed role for them. Indeed, the study does not even mention trade as a mission for the future for the companies concerned. That trade is not seen as the future can also be deduced from various statements by the presidents of the *sogo shosha*. Itochu's president, Minoru Murofushi, wants to get rid of the label "trading company" and rather become an international company operating in a number of fields. According to the president of Sumitomo Trading, Kenji Miyahara, his company should be seen as a service company that adjusts its business to the demands of its customers. In Marubeni's long-range strategy, "Vision 2000," change, speed, and risk management—not trade—are the key words (*Financial Times*, March 25, 1998).

This is in line with the findings and recommendations of the JFTC report. General trade in anything from mineral water to satellite communication is a thing of the past and not an appropriate strategy for the coming century of "mega competition." The *shosha* need to become high performing companies in order to attract attention and mobilize funds in an increasingly borderless capital market. The globalization of the economy and the revolution in information technology has led to a decrease in the cost of conducting business, and hence reduced the scope for the GTCs' traditional, transaction costs reducing role.

Instead, the report comes up with six proposals for creating the twenty-first century model of the *shosha*. In place of the "all-round generalism," trading companies should switch to "strategic generalism." Capital and human resources should be used strategically and put to use in areas where the best return is to be had. Companies should divest themselves of superfluous activities and instead build operations in promising areas. The core capabilities of the GTCs in the next century are identified as becoming "global business creators," and efforts to restructure should be conceived accordingly. Combining risk management and entrepreneurship, they should open up new markets and new business areas on a global scale.

In the future, or so it is asserted, the most important asset to the company will be the people working in it. Staff should be educated individually as specialists but also as entrepreneurs. There should be free competition and individual responsibility combined in newly created systems for human resource management and development. As a corollary, structural reforms should be carried out with a view to creating a network type of organization characterized by high flexibility and speed in decision-making. Strategic management and operating functions should be separated.

Furthermore, to be accepted as global enterprises, management should be carried out according to internationally accepted standards. Top management within the trading company should act forcefully to push through structural reforms and see to it that they train professional staff that is specialized in corporate management. In the future, speed will be important and capability of risk management will be one of the factors that separate winners from losers.

It is obvious that radical measures have to be taken if the GTCs want to maintain the scope and magnitude of operations to which they have become accustomed. Are the measures now suggested enough? Indeed, are they the right ones? Recent interviews with officials in Tokyo give few clues, except that change is said to be imperative. Whether the GTCs, their national organization, or anyone else with an influence over the *sogo shosha* will be able to change their declining fortunes and, if so, by what means, remains thoroughly unclear. This will most probably vary with the company. One thing they have in common is that they are all deeply affected by the changing patterns of Japanese trade. As is often the case, observers concluding that change is imperative does not necessarily imply that such change is imminent. If it does not take place, the GTCs' traditional role will continue to be eroded with the likely consequence that they will cease to be the main actors in Japanese trade.

8. Conclusion

The rapid decline of the amount of trade conducted by the GTCs reflects the structural changes that Japanese trade is currently experiencing. Gone are the days when the *sogo shosha* had a pivotal role within Japan's famous industrial groupings, the *keiretsu*, and when foreign trade was conducted almost exclusively through the GTCs. Referring back to some of the propositions deducted from transaction theory helps us to understand why this is the case. According to the first item on the list supplied by Peng and Ilinitch (1998), the more distant and unfamiliar the markets, the more likely that intermediaries will be used. With the revolution of the information industry and the globalization of the world economy, most foreign markets do not feel as distant and are becoming less unfamiliar to Japanese manufactures. This has in part become possible because these companies have acquired considerable knowledge about markets and export processes themselves (proposition 3) as well as the capability of handling negotiations (proposition 4).

Many of the Japanese multinational corporations (MNCs) have also become global companies in the sense that they have their own production facilities and sales organization abroad. Indeed, although it has been claimed that "Japanese MNCs are more Japanese than multinational" (Hatch and Yamamura, 1996: 69), they are, as Mair (1997) has noted with respect to Honda and other companies, increasingly apt at making use of strategic localization—including the localization of product design, R&D, manufacturing, sourcing of components, production methods, and employment—to promote their interests and market positions. While the "post-national" enterprise is yet to emerge, the level of adaptation achieved to date clearly reduces the value of an intermediary such as the *sogo shosha* for the manufacturers except when they are entering into new or insecure markets. That the GTCs try as best they can to replicate these trends and turn them in their favor (cf. Dicken and Miyamachi, 1998: 73–4), such effects do not necessarily imply success.

The same can be said about foreign manufacturers exporting to Japan. To many of them, the country does not come across as that distant and unfamiliar any more. They have acquired experience, knowledge, and marketing know-how on their own or in other cases made direct contacts with Japanese counterparts. Gradually the Japanese market has also become more open. One aspect of this is the "hollowing out" of the Japanese economy, a major feature of which is that parts and components produced abroad are exported back to production sites in Japan. In this kind of intrafirm trade, no intermediaries are needed.

Proposition 2—the lower the commodity content and the higher the value added content of products, the less likely that manufacturers will use intermediaries—can also be applied. The fact that the products exported from Japan have changed to ones with higher value added content is of some consequence. Due to the high value of the yen and the concomitant restructuring of Japanese industry, products such as iron and steel that used to be the top items for the GTCs have gradually decreased in importance. Rather, there has been a shift into products that not only are characterized by increased value added content, but also require manufacturers to develop more direct rapport with customers and suppliers. Timely feedback is critical to companies that are constantly attempting to improve their products and to develop new ones. The predictable result is that GTCs as intermediaries have become more of an obstacle than a conduit for efficient contacts with markets.

In short, as Japan has moved up the ranks of industrialized countries, old patterns do not hold any longer. World markets have become more accessible, yet also much more complex, and so has the structure and pattern of Japanese foreign trade. The model with a handful of *sogo shosha* in charge of imports and exports, operating on behalf of Japanese manufacturers, is quickly being eroded. What is more, increased competition on the world market will have implications not just for Japanese trade patterns but also for the Japanese economy as a whole. Industry has to become increasingly competitive to stay ahead. It is doubtful whether they can do this under the old Japanese model of development in which *sogo shosha* were in charge. The implications for the latter are not encouraging—and this happens at a time when other areas critical to the viability of the GTCs are severely threatened as a result of financial deregulation.

Although postwar history teaches us to be careful not to predict the immediate demise of Japan's general trading companies (Roehl 1998: 201)—their resilience cannot but impress—there is little to indicate that their most recent attempts to reinvent themselves in the face of the current challenges have met with success, or that they are likely to do so anytime soon. The chances are that some of them may be able to remain influential by virtue of pursuing new strategies or improving current areas of strength, while others may not. But as long as the future survival of the *shosha* hinges on their ability to decisively change tracks, this particular piece of the old Japanese model no longer has the pivotal role it was once successful in carving out for itself.

REFERENCES

Curtis, Gerald (1975), "Big Business and Political Influence", in Vogel, Ezra (ed.), *Modern Japanese Organization and Decision Making* (Berkeley: University of California Press).

Dicken, Peter and Yoshihiro Miyamachi (1998), " 'From Noodles to Satellites': The Changing Geography of the Japanese *Sogo Shosha*," *Transactions of the Institute of British Geographers,* NS, 23/1: 55–78.

Fukui, Haruhiro (1977), "Policy-Making in the Japanese Foreign Ministry," in Scalapino, Robert (ed.), *The Foreign Policy of Modern Japan* (Berkeley: University of California Press).

Hatch, Walter and Kozo Yamamura (1996), *Asia in Japan's Embrace: Building a Regional Production Alliance* (New York: Cambridge University Press).

Hennart, Jean-François and Georgine M. Kryda (1998), "Why do Traders Invest in Manufacturing?," in Jones, Geoffrey (ed.), *The Multinational Traders* (London: Routledge), 213–27.

Ito, Tadaaki, Kiso Takuma, and Uchibori Hironori (1998), *The Impact of the Big Bang on the Japanese Financial System* (Tokyo: Fuji Research Institute).

Johnson, Chalmers (1982), *MITI and the Japanese Miracle* (Stanford: Stanford University Press).

Kahn, Heman (1972), *The Emerging Japanese Super State: Challenge and Response* (Englewood Cliffs, NJ: Prentice Hall).

Kaplan, Eugene (1972), *Japan the Government–Business Relationship: A Guide for American Businessmen* (Washington: Government Printing Office).

Kojima, Kiyoshi and Terutomo Ozawa (1984), *Japan's General Trading Companies: Merchants of Economic Development* (Paris: OECD).

Koerner, Richard J. (1998), "The Influence of *Sogo Shosha* Companies on Contract Bargaining in the Pacific Metallurgical Coal Trade," *Resources Policy*, 24/3: 167–77.

Mair, Andrew (1997), "Strategic Localization: The Myth of the Postnational Enterprise," in Cox, Kevin R. (ed.), *Spaces of Globalization: Reasserting the Power of the Local* (New York: Guilford Press), 64–88.

Malmström, Åsa (1996), "Power and Development in Indonesia," in Marie Söderberg (ed.), *The Business of Japanese Foreign Aid: Five Case Studies from Asia* (London: Routledge), 128–50.

Nakatani, Iwo (1998), *Shosha no Miraizo* (Tokyo: Toyo Keisai Shinposha).

Ozawa, Terutomo (1988), "Nascent General Trading Companies (GTCs) in Asia: Progress and Prospects," *Rivista Internazionale di Scienze Economiche e Commerciale*, 35/2: 119–34.

Pempel, T. J. (1982), *Policy and Politics in Japan* (Philadelphia: Temple University Press).

Peng, Mike W. and Anne Y. Ilinitch (1998), "Export Intermediary Firms: A Note on Export Development Research," *Journal of International Business Studies*, 29/3: 609–20.

Ramseyer, J. Mark and Frances McCall Rosenbluth (1997), *Japan's Political Marketplace* (Cambridge, Mass.: Harvard University Press).

Roehl, Thomas (1983), "A Transactions Cost Approach to International Trading Structures: The Case of the Japanese General Trading Companies," *Hitotsubashi Journal of Economics*, 24/2: 119–35.

——(1998), "Is Efficiency Compatible with History? Evidence from Japanese General Trading Companies," in Jones, Geoffrey (ed.), *The Multinational Traders* (London: Routledge), 201–12.

Sheard, Paul (1989), "The Japanese General Trading Company as an Aspect of Interfirm Risk-sharing," *Journal of the Japanese and International Economies*, 3/3: 308–22.

Shin, Kwang-Shik (1989), "Information, Transaction Costs, and the Organization of Distribution: The Case of Japan's General Trading Companies," *Journal of the Japanese and International Economies*, 3/3: 292–307.

Söderberg, Marie (1996), "OECF and the Implementation Process," in Söderberg, Marie (ed.), *The Business of Japanese Foreign Aid: Five Case Studies from Asia* (London: Routledge), 51–71.

——(forthcoming), "Asia as Seen from the Perspective of the Japanese General Trading Houses," in Söderberg, Marie and Ian Reader (eds.), *Japanese Influence and Presence in Asia* (Richmond: Curzon).

Tsurumi, Yoshi (1976), *The Japanese are Coming* (Cambridge, Mass.: Ballinger).

Williamson, Oliver E. (1985), *The Economic Institutions of Capitalism* (New York: Free Press).

Yamanaka, Toyokunio (ed.) (1996), *Nihon no Shosha* (Tokyo: Tomei Shosho).

Yoshihara, Kunio (1982), *Sogo Shosha: The Vanguard of the Japanese Economy* (Tokyo: Oxford University Press).

10 Regulatory Reform in Japan: The Road Ahead

SUMNER LA CROIX AND JAMES MAK

1. Introduction

Since the Second World War, Japan's economy has been characterized by a high degree of formal and informal regulation in many important industries. National government ministries have regulated entry and exit, pricing, product specification, and aspects of research and development. Industry regulation was grounded in national legislation that vested broad, discretionary administrative powers in a highly educated bureaucracy that forged close ties between their ministries and regulated firms. This far-reaching regulatory regime was rarely questioned during the post-Second World War period of rapid growth. Beginning in the late 1970s, rapid technological change, rising Japanese incomes, increased international competition, and political pressure from the United States and the European Union prompted the Japanese government to begin the process of regulatory reform in several important industries, including finance, telecommunications, transportation, energy, and retailing. The economic slowdown of the 1990s has prompted new calls from politicians, academics, and the general public for more extensive and more rapid deregulation encompassing a larger number of industries. Since 1995, there has been a noticeable increase in the scope and speed of deregulatory measures already undertaken, in process, or planned.

In this paper we examine the transition from one regulatory regime to another in Japan and draw inferences concerning the possible course that deregulation could take over the next decade. Section 1 considers the state of Japanese regulation during the high growth post-Second World War period. Section 2 summarizes major deregulatory measures implemented over the last 25 years in four selected industries (airlines, electricity, telecommunications, and retailing) and briefly surveys the economics literature analyzing them. Section 3 identifies and analyzes economic, political, and social factors that paved the way for the regulatory reforms of the 1980s and 1990s. Section 4 considers the momentum currently building for more sweeping reform measures and suggests possible courses that deregulation could take in Japan over the next decade.

2. Regulation in Japan since the Second World War

Prior to the Second World War, industrial regulation in Japan followed the same pattern observed in other industrialized countries: most industries were unregulated and a few—transportation, finance, public utilities, and broadcasting—were highly regulated. As in many European countries, production was carried out by publicly owned and operated corporations. Regulation of industry increased dramatically in the late 1930s and early 1940s as Japan mobilized its economy for war. Centralization of resource allocation during the long wartime period (1935–45) led to expansion of the national bureaucracy, controls on entry, suppressed capital markets, and price controls. The American occupying authorities retained many of these controls, as they found them to be useful means for carrying out their directives. Attempts by the occupying authorities to change the locus of regulation from ministries to new independent regulatory commissions had little effect. After Japan regained sovereignty in 1952, the ministry bureaucracies acted quickly to restrict the power of the new commissions and to bring them under the supervision of national ministries.

Despite the origins of industry regulation in the control economy of the Second World War, the system quickly came to be supported by a nexus of interest groups and supporting ideologies. First, industry regulations provided protection to small firms in agriculture and retailing from the competition posed by large firms. This protection helped to cement these owner/operators into the Liberal Democratic Party (LDP) interest coalition. Second, economists and political scientists rationalized the regulations as limiting the "excessive competition" that was thought to develop in free markets.[1] The concern with excessive competition produced a tolerance by regulators for informally organized industry cartels that limited price competition and facilitated exit within declining industries, such as textiles and coal.[2] Lonnie Carlile and Mark Tilton (1998, ch. 8) maintain that another purpose of the regulatory system was to establish a "de facto 'social contract' that guaranteed the survival of every firm in the industries." This reflects a concern that the outcome of competition among firms reflect "ex post equity." Keizo Nagatani (1995; 1997: 12–13) regards this concern as the "very foundation of 'Japanese Economics'."[3] By providing social insurance against bad outcomes for individual firms, the government facilitated close cooperation between the government and the regulated industry in achieving national goals during its golden era of unprecedented growth.

Regulation was coupled with extensive public ownership in post-Second World War Japan. Between 1951 and 1985, public enterprises provided international air services, rail services, and international and domestic phone services. And regulation in these industries was all embracing. According to Uekusa (1987: 507), ". . . regulation extended to such matters as their budget and fixed accounts, investment and financial programs (including new services, issuances of securities and bonds, and borrowing), appointment of top managers, and industrial relations. The higher the degree of public ownership, the wider the range and the stronger the degree of public intervention."

---

[1] Excess entry and failure to achieve all possible economies of scale characterize many oligopolistic industries. Appropriately designed and executed regulations could, in theory, remedy these problems by limiting entry, thereby allowing remaining firms to expand and achieve all possible economies of scale. See Viscusi, Vernon, and Harrington (1995), ch. 16.

[2] Tilton (1994) has argued that cartels were organized in some industries to facilitate a secure supply of industrial inputs to major Japanese manufacturing firms.

[3] See also Kristof (1998).

Japan's industry regulation has been carried out by civil servants employed by national government ministries.[4] Typically, regulatory measures are far broader and more detailed than those called for by the enabling statutes.[5] Since Japan's anti-monopoly law limits the formal regulatory power of ministries, much of their regulation has taken the form of administrative guidance (*gyosei shido*) which is broadly derived from ministries' licensing (*kyoninka*) powers. The administrative guidance provided by bureaucrats is generally the last legal word, with almost no firms resorting to the court system to overturn capricious bureaucratic actions. However, regulated firms regularly consult with Diet members, other related ministries, and their ministry to influence ministry directives. Since regulated firms and their ministry have often had extensive prior consultations, directives have frequently accommodated industry interests. In other cases, such as when a profitable bank is pressured to merge with an unprofitable bank, the ministry's actions align closely with industry desires, even if the chosen firm is unhappy with its designation as a social insurance provider.

Japan's bureaucrats are educated at Japan's best universities and typically become highly knowledgeable of the industries they regulate. Their knowledge is a byproduct of their close interaction with industry leaders in governmentally recognized industry associations. Serving as a vehicle for the ministry to gather industry opinion concerning prospective regulatory changes and to communicate new ministry directives to the industry, the associations ensure that both parties understand each others' interests and have opportunities to discuss and resolve differences. Bureaucratic consultation with the Japanese public through public hearings or written public comment on proposed regulatory changes is rare. Academic debate rages over how much influence the Japanese Diet has over bureaucratic policies. Mark Ramseyer and Frances Rosenbluth (1993) maintained that bureaucrats have paid close attention to the demands of the governing party, while Chalmers Johnson (1982) and John Zysman (1983) argued that bureaucrats have had considerable autonomy and have used it to enhance their own interests and to establish a bureaucracy-led industrial policy.

The close relationship between regulated firms and ministry bureaucrats has been coupled with the institution of *amakudari*, in which a newly retired bureaucrat (usually 55-years old) "comes down from heaven" to take a senior executive position with a regulated firm. This close relationship between the two parties, often characterized as "Japan, Inc.," has the advantage of aligning more closely the incentives of regulators and managers in both the short and the long run. Since they will one day be responsible for the regulated firm's operations, senior bureaucrats have incentives to ensure that regulated firms remain in good financial health, responding to opportunities for cost reductions and to changes in consumer demand. On the other

[4] Except in retailing, municipal and provincial governments in Japan have had virtually no direct role in industry regulation either before or after the regulatory reforms of the 1980s and 1990s.

[5] A former Finance Ministry official observes that the enabling laws "are not 'only extremely vague and wide-ranging', they are excluded from the common Compendium of Laws, making it difficult for the public to know about and discuss them" (ACCJ, August, 1998).

hand, the more closely aligned incentives also induce regulators to design regulations to produce economic rents for the regulated industries. Not surprisingly, there is widespread public perception in Japan that economic regulations in Japan have tended to favor producers at the expense of consumers.

The post-Second World War regulatory system was able to achieve its initial objectives of fostering rapid economic growth without major tears in the social fabric. In agriculture and retailing, small firms were protected against competition from large firms. Business and government concerns about "excessive competition" were alleviated by carefully limiting (or prohibiting) entry into the regulated industry and restricting price competition.[6] By providing a measure of "ex post equity" to the losers from economic development, most industry regulation acted to temper the process of creative destruction and slow economic growth in particular industries. The effect on overall growth is surely more ambiguous.[7] By reducing the social conflicts arising from rapid growth, protective industry regulations may have helped to maintain the stability of the overall economic system during a period of rapid transition from labor-intensive to capital-intensive industries (Wolff, Chapter 8 this volume).

3. Regulation and Regulatory Reform in Selected Industries

In this section, we briefly survey both regulation and regulatory reform for a sample of important industries, including airlines, telephone services, retailing, and electricity. Table 10.1 provides a summary of major deregulatory and regulatory reform measures in selected industries since 1979. Our goal is not to be encyclopedic but rather to highlight common features of regulation and different sources of regulatory reform across industries.

3.1. Domestic airline passenger service

The air transport industry did not resume service in Japan after the Second World War until 1951.[8] Japan's Civil Aviation Law required firms to obtain a license to enter

---

[6] The regulatory focus on limiting excessive competition raises the possibility that Japanese regulation may be explained by the "capture theory." This theory postulated that regulation of natural monopolies and oligopolies in the United States had its roots in the rise of populist interest groups and a decline in confidence in capitalist institutions. However, once regulation was established, the regulated firms typically "captured" the regulatory process and used it to further their own interests. One could argue that the institution of *amakudari* facilitates regulatory capture via its close alignment of the incentives of bureaucrats and managers. Stigler (1971) and Peltzman (1976) concluded that the capture theory was too narrowly conceived and propounded a broader theory which focuses on interest groups, including consumers, using the regulatory process to redistribute wealth. Becker (1983) broadened their theory by arguing that the competition for wealth redistribution would be subject to minimizing the deadweight loss imparted by the regulation.

[7] See Ito (1996) for an excellent survey of the major economic institutions supporting Japanese development in the twentieth century.

[8] See Yamauchi and Murakami (1995), Yamauchi and Ito (1996), and Chujoh and Yamauchi (1998) for overviews of aviation regulation in Japan.

TABLE 10.1. *Major economic deregulatory initiatives, 1979–1998*

1979	Negotiable CDs gradually introduced through 1985.
1980	Deposit interest rates gradually liberalized through 1995.
1981	VAN liberalization in 1971, 1982, and 1985.
1985	KDD monopoly in international telecommunications services ended.
	NTT privatized.
	Liberalization of equipment purchasing rules.
	Two satellite carriers licensed.
	Money market funds allowed.
	Deregulation of interest rates for large time deposits.
	JAL privatized.
1986	Second and third carriers allowed to enter high demand air routes.
1987	Two Mobile Phone Consortia licensed.
	Minimum deposit amount for money-market certificates reduced.
	Japan National Railway privatized.
1991	Liberalization of Large Scale Retail Store Law begins.
1992	Entry in banking by separate subsidiary allowed.
1993–4	Restrictions on market coverage and services offered by cable TV companies relaxed.
1994	Deregulation of taxi fares in Osaka and Tokyo.
1994	Liberalization of fixed commissions in stock market begins.
	Natural gas reform bill passed.
1995	Electricity and oil industry reform bills passed.
	Formulation of Deregulation Promotion Plan (1,091 items).
1996	Revision of Deregulation Promotion Plan (1,797 items total).
1997	Second revision of Deregulation Promotion Plan (2,823 items total).
1998	"Big Bang" financial deregulations are phased in.
	First new entry into airline industry in over 40 years.
	"Type I" telecommunications market open to foreign competition.
	Non-power firms allowed to sell electricity to corporate customers.
	Cap on number of airlines serving one route is abolished.

the market, to change fares, and to adjust service on routes.[9] In the 1950s and 1960s, numerous firms entered the business, had financial difficulties, and were merged with other firms. Japan Airlines (JAL), which became the national flag carrier when it was transformed from a private into a quasi-public corporation in 1953, initially offered domestic service in 1952 and then expanded into international routes in 1953. Two private domestic carriers were licensed in 1953, ran into financial trouble, and merged into All Nippon Airways (ANA) in 1957. The government licensed six regional carriers in the 1950s, but after a series of mergers, only one carrier, Toa Domestic Airways (TDA), was still operating in 1971; its name was later changed to Japan Air System (JAS). In 1972 the government in its "Notice Regarding Airline Operations"

[9] By contrast, the US Civil Aeronautics Board (CAB) regulated airfares, entry and exit on existing routes, and establishment of new routes, but did not regulate service levels on routes, e.g. flight frequency and availability of nonstop flights. For the history and effects of airline regulation and deregulation in the US, see Bailey, Graham, and Kaplan (1985), Morrison and Winston (1986), Morrison and Winston (1995), and Viscusi, Vernon, and Harrington (1995), ch. 17.

established market niches for each airline. Each airline received access to profitable trunk routes (Sapporo–Tokyo–Osaka–Fukuoka–Naha) that would offset losses on other domestic local routes and regional services. The Ministry of Transportation maintained tight regulatory control over the three airlines and their regional affiliates in this segmented air passenger market until 1985 when the spillover effects from US airline deregulation helped to spur the Japanese government to initiate changes in the nation's aviation industry.

Foreign governments had closely watched the US experiment with domestic airline deregulation that began in 1978. What became quickly evident was that US airline deregulation brought impressive economic benefits to consumers.[10] The effects of US deregulation had the ancillary effect of increasing productivity of US airlines in international markets and weakening the competitive position of foreign carriers, including Japanese airlines (Caves *et al.*, 1987).[11] This induced foreign governments to consider deregulation for their own aviation industries.[12] For many governments, privatization of national flag carriers was required before industry deregulation could be seriously considered.[13] Without privatization, losses by national carriers due to deregulation could have been covered by national treasuries. With such subsidies, market signals to exit or adjust products could be ignored and many of the beneficial effects of deregulation lost. Faced with the threat of mounting operating deficits at JAL and rising fiscal deficits in its national accounts, the Japanese government privatized JAL in 1985.[14]

In 1985, a provisional agreement between the United States and Japan on international air transportation required Japan to change its airline policy since Japan had only one international airline (JAL). In response, the Japanese government changed its aviation policy not only in the international market by allowing ANA to enter long-haul international markets, but also by encouraging greater competition in domestic markets. The Japanese government reconfigured domestic airline route assignments among the three major carriers. In 1986, three carriers were allowed to compete on routes serving more than one million passengers annually (triple tracking) and two carriers to compete on routes serving 700,000 passengers annually (double tracking). In 1993, approximately 65 per cent of air passengers flew either on double or triple tracking routes. Market shares adjusted somewhat under these changes as both JAL and JAS gained market shares at the expense of ANA. Competition was, however, constrained by the lack of take-off and landing slots at major airports (Yamauchi and Murakami, 1995). The passenger threshold levels for double and triple tracking were rapidly reduced in the 1990s, and in 1998 the cap on the number of airlines serving one route was abolished.

[10] Morrison and Winston (1995: 82) estimated that airline deregulation in the US generates annual economic benefits to consumers of US$18.4 billion in 1993 prices.

[11] For example, Japanese airlines' share of international air passengers to and from Japan was 38.4% in 1980, 36.7% in 1985, 33.9% in 1990, and 33.6% in 1995.

[12] For an analysis of airline deregulation in Europe, see Graham (1997); in Australia, see Quiggin (1996).

[13] For example, privatization of British Airways preceded airline deregulation in Great Britain.

[14] The government had previously sold 50 per cent of JAL in 1975. See La Croix and Wolff (1995) for a discussion of the problems associated with public airlines participating in a competitive aviation market.

A zone fare system, similar to one used in the US between 1978 and 1983 and in Europe before 1993, was adopted in 1996. Under this system, airlines were permitted to adjust fares within limits. While the new pricing system allowed more discounting than the old system, prices did not fall much due to the lack of entry threats.[15] On domestic routes the average fare per mile dropped by 5 per cent between FY1994 and the first half of FY 1997.

A snapshot of the airline industry in 1996 shows the big three firms still in control of the domestic market: ANA with 52 per cent, JAL with 26 per cent, and JAS with the remaining 22 per cent. The first signs of new entry in the airline market since the 1950s surfaced in 1998. Skymark Airlines, a no-frills carrier patterned after Southwest Airlines in the United States, was granted permission in July 1998 to initiate service between Tokyo and Fukuoka. It began service in September 1998 with a regular fare (13,700 yen) half that offered by established carriers.[16] Another discount airline, Hokkaido International Airlines (also known as "Air Do"), also began service from Hokkaido in December 1998 with similar discounts. The new competition prompted the three existing carriers to lower their fares on the same routes in March 1999.[17]

The threat of new competition prompted the existing carriers to lower their fares, although Japan's long economic stagnation may be partially responsible. With full deregulation implemented in FY1999, airlines no longer need permission from the Ministry of Transportation to change fares; they need only notify the Ministry of their intention. Some analysts estimate that domestic ticket prices will fall 30 to 40 per cent in the next five years after full price deregulation.

In sum, regulatory reform in Japan's aviation industry was late getting started (1985) but appeared to be picking up steam in the late 1990s, with entrance by new carriers and liberalization of route entry and pricing. A new aviation agreement concluded between the United States and Japan in 1998 provides for a more liberal pricing policy on trans-Pacific routes and allows significant entrance by ANA and several US airlines on these routes.[18] The agreement adds further urgency to the Japanese deregulation movement. As competition on trans-Pacific route is expected to become even more intense, JAL looks to airline deregulation to enable Japanese firms to expand along more profitable domestic routes. Finally, growing concern by the domestic tourist industry over further losses of the Japanese tourist business to foreign destinations further fueled industry pressure to ease regulations in Japan's domestic airline industry.

[15] In some instances, fares actually increased and consumers were confused by the complexity of new fares and discounts.

[16] These fares are considerably less than "bullet train" fares.

[17] On the Sapporo–Fukuoka route, the big three (ANA, JAL, and JAS) filed applications for the same 13,700 yen fare charged by the two discount airlines but as a special discount with attached conditions. Interestingly, while Skymark and Air Do had load factors of 70–80 per cent when they inaugurated service in Fall 1998, by June 1999 Skymark's load factor had fallen to 31.5 per cent and Air Do's to 44.3 per cent—both below profitable levels of operation.

[18] JAS, saddled with many unprofitable local domestic routes serving small and isolated communities, is expanding its service to China.

Deregulation in Japan does not, however, mean open or free entry. Entry by new carriers still requires approval from the Ministry of Transportation. Scarcity of take-off and landing slots remains a binding constraint on the number of competitors at the major airports.[19] Deregulation also does not mean that unprofitable routes will be abandoned. Residents of many small and isolated communities are concerned they will lose their air service. The Japanese government has responded by establishing a fund to subsidize unprofitable routes to maintain service to these communities.

Transportation deregulation has not been confined to Japan's airlines. Japan National Railway (formerly JNR) was privatized in 1987 and split into six private regional railroads and one freight company. Privatization has given the new JR companies flexibility in procurement and the ability to trim employment, improve services, cut costs, and enter new businesses using their valuable land near train stations. Before privatization, JR was 37 trillion yen in debt, and consistently lost money. The new JR railroads, on average, are profitable, but performance varies greatly across the seven companies. The three companies operating on the Honshu mainline (JR East, JR West, and JR Central) are profitable while the remaining three island companies (Kyushu, Hokkaido, and Shikoku) and the freight company are not. JR's ability to compete in the domestic transportation services markets will be further tested in the next decade by growing competition from private autos, long-distance bus companies, and trucking companies as Japan continues to improve its highway system, as well as from a more competitive domestic airline industry.

Regulations in the taxi industry governing entrance and pricing were relaxed for Tokyo and Osaka in 1994. The regulatory changes appear to have had little impact. In fact, fare increases were proposed by the taxi driver associations shortly after deregulation and granted by the government (Vogel, 1998). Taxi drivers continue to strenuously oppose further deregulation.

In 1989, the Diet passed two bills that relaxed entry and fare setting requirements in the trucking industry. Hirotaka Yamauchi (1995) noted that this was an "epoch making event" in that deregulation occurred without "foreign pressure." However, trucking regulations have historically been loosely enforced. Thus, the Ministry of Transport's decision to grant trucking firms substantial freedom to enter and exit routes and to set their own prices represented more an acknowledgement of the already competitive environment than radical reform (Flath, 1995; Yamauchi, 1995).

Little or no deregulation of Japan's domestic bus system has been allowed, a sharp contrast with the extensive deregulation of local and national bus services in Great Britain (except for London) and national bus services in the United States (Klein, Moore, and Reja, 1997).

3.2. Telecommunications

The telecommunications regulatory regime in Japan remained stable from 1952 until 1985 when major reform was initiated. The established regulatory regime was very

---

[19] This is also a problem at major eastern and mid-western airports in the United States (GAO, 1996).

similar to those found in European countries. Both domestic long-distance and local telephone services were provided by a public firm, Nippon Telegraph and Telephone Corporation (NTT), with a monopoly on service provision, a group of manufacturers with exclusive rights to supply equipment, and uniform technical standards applied across the system. Cooperative research and development with a group of Japanese suppliers was the norm, followed by more competitive procurement from the same group. Kokusai Denshin Denwa (KDD), a regulated private corporation, provided international service. The Ministry of Posts and Telecommunications (MPT) regulated both NTT and KDD, both of which, however, retained considerable autonomy (Vogel, 1998, ch. 7).

Dowling, Boulton, and Elliott (1994) have argued that regulatory reform and liberalization in the telecommunications services industry in many countries, including Japan, the United States, United Kingdom, and Germany were induced by rapid technological change and changes in market demand that required more flexibility in the development and provision of new telecommunication services. Traditional customers were becoming global players demanding support services in global telecommunications. In the United States, passage of the Telecommunications Act of 1996 reflects the growing perception (right or wrong) by policymakers that telecommunications is a "strategic" sector, meaning that it is an industry that generates positive externalities to other industry groups and contributes to social welfare in excess of private returns to providers (Harris and Kraft, 1997). The objective of the Act was to

maintain and expand universal service; to promote competition and its associated benefits (price reduction, quality improvements, and new service innovations) via entry by local exchange carriers, long-distance companies and cable companies into each other's markets; and to stimulate investment in the "National Information Infrastructure" which the Clinton administration has declared essential to maintain international competitiveness in the information age. (Harris and Kraft, 1997: 93)[20]

The fear of losing international competitiveness in telecommunications was also the main reason behind Japan's regulatory reforms in this sector. Regulatory reform in Japan was also spurred by pressure from US trade negotiators for NTT and KDD to buy American telecommunications equipment as well as by the British and American examples of radical regulatory reform in telecommunications. The United States broke up the Bell System in 1982, eliminated Western Electric's monopoly status as an equipment supplier, and allowed entry into long-distance services.[21] Great Britain privatized British Telecom, established a new independent regulatory commission (Oftel) to govern the telecommunications industry, and

---

[20] For analysis of telecommunications regulatory reform in Europe see Waverman and Sirel (1997). For Australia, New Zealand, Chile, and Guatemala, see Spiller and Cardilli (1997).

[21] US telecommunications reform has clearly not produced competitive local or long-distance markets. The 1996 Telecommunications Act was structured to allow entry of long-distance carriers into local service and local carriers into long-distance service. Implementation of the Act has been delayed by court challenges and in the meantime, numerous mergers have dangerously increased concentration among the local service carriers.

allowed entrance into long-distance and local service (primarily by American cable TV companies).[22]

In December 1984, the Diet passed three laws that completely changed the telecommunications environment in Japan.[23] NTT was privatized, but not broken up as in the case of AT&T. The government opted for the less politically difficult route of regulatory reform rather than the breakup of the giant monopoly. One division of NTT was assigned provision of long-distance service while eleven Regional Communications Sectors provide local telephone services. Entrance, albeit not free entrance, was allowed in both the international and domestic long-distance markets. Since 1985, over 130 "Type I" companies—firms that provide telephone services using their own transmission lines—have entered the market. These include several satellite companies, several domestic long-distance New Common Carriers (e.g. DDI Corporation, Japan Telecom, and Teleway Japan), eleven regional phone service providers, and more than eighty wireless companies. In addition there were over 4,500 "Type II" carriers—firms that lease capacity from the Type I companies and resell the capacity. Nonetheless, NTT still controls more than 90 per cent of the local telephone services market and nearly two-thirds of the domestic long-distance calls in 1999.

Two new companies (International Telecom Japan and International Digital Communications) were allowed into the international market after 1985. The new entry reduced international and domestic long-distance charges over the next decade, although rates are still much higher in Japan than in other industrialized countries. Call-back services, which allow Japanese callers to make international calls at US rates by accessing a US dial tone, have taken 4 per cent of the overseas market, are rapidly expanding, and are providing effective pressure on regulatory authorities to continue deregulation of international services provided by Japanese companies.

Cellular phone services were initially provided by NTT and by a new group using Motorola technology. Motorola and the US Trade Representative's office complained that infrastructure development had been tilted toward NTT technology, and the MPT ordered in 1994 that investment in Motorola's technology be speeded up. Regulatory changes in 1994 that liberalized cellular phone sales and service-pricing generated more than 30 million cellular customers by mid-1997.

Under Japan's telecommunications agreement with the World Trade Organization, Japan agreed to open up its "Type I" market to foreign competition. Two major foreign telecommunication carriers—WorldCom from the United States and British Telecom (BT) from the United Kingdom—immediately applied for licenses. Moreover, the government also announced that it would break up NTT into three companies in 1999: two regional carriers to serve East and West Japan and a long-distance carrier that will be allowed to compete in the international telecommunications market. In return, KDD will be permitted to provide domestic phone services, beginning in 1999. To accomplish this, KDD has formed an alliance with the new common

---

[22] For a comparison of changes in the telecommunications industry in the US, Britain, Germany, and Japan, see the case studies in Dowling, Boulton, and Elliott (1994).

[23] The Telecommunications Business Law, the NTT Law, and the Background Law for the Telecommunications Law.

carrier, Teleway Japan. Faced with growing competition at home, NTT is developing ambitious plans to enter the telecommunications business in Asia.

3.3. Electricity

After the American occupation, Japan's power-generating companies were organized following the American model. The industry currently has ten vertically integrated private firms distributing and producing electricity. Each company has a regional monopoly in distribution, yet purchases additional electricity from fifty-six relatively small public and private wholesale utilities (Navarro, 1996). Two national companies supply power from specialty sources: the Japan Atomic Power Company (nuclear) and the Electric Power Development Company (thermal and hydraulic). As in the United States, government regulates electricity prices. In Japan the regulation comes from the Ministry of International Trade and Industry (MITI), a national ministry, rather than from independent national and state regulatory commissions as in the United States.

Identified as a key industry after the Second World War, electrical utilities struggled to meet increasing demands in the 1950s. They were more successful in building new capacity to service the enormous increases in residential and industrial demands in the 1960s and 1970s. Early warnings that the performance of the highly regulated system was deteriorating in the 1980s came from studies of industry productivity and pricing by two Japanese economists. Teruhiro Tomita (1990) found that total factor productivity for the Japanese electricity industry fell at an annual rate of 1.46 per cent between 1979 and 1987. Nayiyasu Itoh (1988) compared the total factor productivity of Japan's electricity industry with those in other industrialized countries and found that Japan's productivity was significantly lower.

Japan's tightly regulated power system survived until the early 1990s when it responded to late, but extremely rapid, worldwide deregulation of electric utilities. The spectacular deregulation of Great Britain's electricity system and a less far-reaching deregulation in the United States (Smith, 1996; and Joskow, 1997) provided MITI with a glowing model of regulatory reform and the promise of lower electricity prices for US competitors of Japanese firms. MITI responded by proposing a major reform of the industry in a June 1994 report. It proposed that regulations be modified to create a nationwide wholesale market for electricity and to liberalize a utility's ability to set and adjust prices. Electric utilities would also be allowed to buy electricity from nonutilities and would be required to distribute the electricity over their lines. The Diet passed an electricity reform bill containing these recommendations in April 1995.

Further liberalization came in March 1998 when nonpower firms were authorized to sell electricity to corporate customers.[24] Steel, oil, and auto companies that generate their own power were among firms taking advantage of the new policy by reselling

---

[24] While consumption has been rising, concern over environmental pollution and the safety of nuclear power plants have made it difficult to build new power plants in Japan. At present, private electricity producers generate about 12 per cent of the electricity consumed.

power to other large firms. In early 1999, a government advisory body was considering whether to recommend easing restrictions on retail power sales.

3.4. Large-Scale Retail Store Law

Japan's Large-Scale Retail Store Law (*Daiten Ho*) was passed in 1973 to protect Japan's small, neighborhood retail stores from competition offered by the growing number of supermarkets, and large department and discount stores. Small store owners represent a sizable political interest group in Japan and have been strong supporters of the Liberal Democratic Party (LDP). As recently as 1994, over half of the retail stores in Japan had just one or two employees; over three-quarters of them had fewer than five employees. Sole proprietorships comprise 61 per cent of all store ownership, but they accounted for only 16 per cent of total sales.[25]

Japan's Large-Scale Retail Store Law required anyone who wished to build a store larger than 1,500 square meters (or 3,000 square meters in Tokyo and eleven other large cities)[26] to obtain permission from the Ministry of International Trade and Industry (MITI).[27] MITI considered the comments and desires of neighborhood store owners before granting its permission.[28] The process of securing permission typically took many months, in some cases extending to years. The result was that owners of small and medium-sized retail store had virtual vetoes of new large stores opening in their markets. The law also regulated store hours, floor space, and even the holiday policies of large stores.

By the mid-1980s, the Large-Scale Retail Store Law posed a major obstacle to foreign imports (which large stores have a higher propensity to stock) and the entry and expansion of large-scale American retailers in Japan. The 1989 Structural Impediments Initiative discussions between Japan and the United States led to Japan's agreement to ease many of the cumbersome restrictions of the Large-Scale Retail Store Law beginning in 1991. In the same year, Toys-R-Us became the first US "category killer" to open a large store in Japan. In 1997, under the US–Japan Enhanced Initiative on Deregulation and Competition Policy, Japan agreed to repeal the Large-Scale Retail Store Law.

This brief review of the history of the Large-Scale Retail Store Law reveals that its original purpose was to protect small neighborhood retail stores from competition from large domestic stores enjoying scale economies. It was clearly never intended to keep foreign retailers out of the Japanese market. The law was reformed because US

---

[25] Flath and Nariu (1996) argue that Japan's small stores are a rational response to the density of Japan's cities, the small homes in urban areas, and the type of goods consumed by the Japanese household. They conclude that historical, cultural, and legal restrictions play only a small role in determining the size distribution of Japanese retail firms. See also Mak and Sunder (1998).

[26] Later revised to 500 square meters.

[27] The 1973 Large-Scale Retail Store Law was an amendment of an earlier (1947) law (Department Store Law) which required only department stores to seek permission from MITI before they could build or expand a store in a neighborhood.

[28] For details of the permitting process, see Ito (1992): 396.

retailers saw high prices for consumer goods in Japan and wanted easier access to the affluent Japanese consumers who have always had a strong demand for Western name-brand goods.[29] On the other side, Japanese lawmakers were willing to meet American demands due to increasing domestic political pressure from consumers at home. A strong yen from 1985 to 1995 and a weak economy in the 1990s made Japanese consumers more price conscious and created an even stronger Japanese demand for foreign-made consumer goods.[30] John Fahy and Fuyuki Taguchi (1995) argued that deregulation of Japan's distribution system has been instrumental in accelerating price discounting and stimulating imports of foreign retail products.

Our review of the regulatory case histories of selected industries allows us to identify a variety of factors that may explain the surge in regulatory reform in Japan in the 1980s and 1990s. Japan belatedly found that in a globalized world economy, a highly regulated domestic industry can face direct or indirect competitive pressure from deregulated industries in other countries. For example, Japan found that it could not maintain tight price, entry, and exit control in telecommunications and still provide competitive services to its globalized firms in the face of rapid telecommunications liberalization in other industrialized countries. Japan speeded up deregulation of its airline industry when Japanese tourists began traveling to overseas tourist destinations on foreign airlines. US political pressure was the primary reason for the dismantling of the Large-Scale Retail Store Law. Indirect competitive pressure from overseas manufacturing sites as well as positive feedback from US and British experiences with deregulation provided Japanese policymakers with the incentive to initiate deregulation of Japan's electricity industry during a period of rapid yen appreciation. In the next section we undertake a more thorough examination of the driving forces behind regulatory reform in Japan and contrast them with those in the United States and Europe.

4. The Onset and Progress of Regulatory Reform in Japan

Economists and political scientists have devoted considerable intellectual energy towards understanding the forces driving regulatory and deregulatory movements over time and across a variety of political environments. Competing explanations fall into two categories: those attributing deregulation primarily to macroeconomic forces and others focusing on microeconomic developments in specific industries and markets. Macroeconomic approaches have generally performed less well than industry-oriented theories.[31] For example, theories predicting more deregulation during periods with high government budget deficits, high inflation, or stagnant growth have had problems explaining why deregulation of numerous US industries

---

[29] Maki (1998) estimated Japanese consumer prices to be more than 30 per cent higher than in the United States, United Kingdom, Germany, and France.

[30] USTR, *Barshefsky Statement*, 1998.

[31] See Peltzman (1989) for an evaluation of how well the Chicago theory of regulation explained deregulation in the United States.

continued during periods of robust growth and low inflation in the 1980s and 1990s. If, instead, deregulation in the United States was fundamentally induced by micro-economic events, then Japanese (and European) deregulation may be posited to follow the same path but with longer lags necessary to overcome higher costs of institutional change. There may still be a role for macroeconomic explanations of deregulation in providing political "cover" to politicians enacting deregulatory measures opposed by powerful interest groups. In this section, we consider both macroeconomic and micro-economic theories of Japanese deregulation.

Analysts regularly identify the macroeconomic problems triggered by the two OPEC oil crises as a common force behind deregulation in both Japan and the United States in the 1970s. In the United States, increases in oil prices were coupled with expansionary monetary policy that produced significant increases in inflation during 1973–5 and 1978–81. Mindful that most inflationary episodes ended only after monetary policy had been tightened and a recession initiated, government officials, legislators, and economists searched for less painful policy measures to control infla-tion. Deregulation seemed to fit the bill perfectly. By stimulating price competition among previously regulated firms, it would not only reduce prices paid by consumers but also induce productivity improvements and contribute to economic growth.

Several other factors may have also triggered the wave of deregulation in the United States (Lincoln, 1998; Viscusi, Vernon, and Harrington, 1995). First, deregulation was facilitated by a change in the American intellectual climate. For several decades, economists at leading US universities had published numerous studies questioning the original justification for industry regulation, arguing that it often led to such unin-tended side effects as overinvestment, reduced technological change, and higher prices (Meyer, 1959; Kahn, 1971; Stigler, 1971). Second, consumers and business firms pur-chasing regulated products formed political action groups to lobby for deregulation. Third, changing demand and cost conditions in some industries reduced the need for regulation. For example, three decades of rising per capita incomes in the United States sufficiently increased the demand for air travel on numerous routes to trans-form many natural monopoly or natural oligopoly air routes into competitive or even contestable routes. Technological innovations in telecommunications changed the natural monopoly status of long-distance carriers. Finally, some regulated firms, e.g. United Airlines (air) and Burlington Northern (rail), lobbied for deregulation of their own industries, betting that they would have improved prospects in the new deregu-lated environment.

A somewhat different set of macroeconomic forces may have triggered regulatory reform in Japan (Carlile and Tilton, 1998, ch. 8). First, the regulatory reform move-ment was triggered in the late 1970s by the national government's fiscal crisis rather than by high inflation rates as in the United States. In response to the OPEC oil shocks, the Japanese government had chosen to increase government spending and run large government budget deficits in an attempt to offset the negative effects of higher oil prices on economic growth. When a proposal to balance the budget by increasing the value-added tax encountered unexpected resistance in 1979 and 1980, the government searched for other ways to close the gap. With the support of the

TABLE 10.2. *Major regulatory commissions and government reports on regulatory reform in Japan*

1960s	First Provisional Commission on Administrative Reform (nicknamed *rincho*) formed.
1981	Second Provisional Commission on Administrative Reform (*rincho*) formed.
1982	*Rincho* issues its final report and is disbanded in 1983.
1983	Provisional Committee for the Promotion of Administrative Reform (*Gyokakushin* I) formed to follow up on *rincho*. Disbanded in 1986.
1986	Economic Planning Agency Report on Deregulation I.
1987	*Gyokakushin* II formed. Disbanded in 1989.
1989	Economic Planning Agency Report on Deregulation II. Fair Trade Commission, Study Committee on Government Regulations and Competition Policy.
1990	*Gyokakushin* III formed. Disbanded in 1993.
1990–1	Tanaka and Horie report on privatization and deregulation issued (2 parts).
1993	*Hiraiwa* study group is formed and issues report in December.
1994	Administrative Procedures bill passed.
1996	New Administistative Reform Committee (*Gyokakui*) proposes to break up NTT and further deregulate telecommunications.
1997	EPA report on effects of deregulation.

Ministry of Finance and Keidanren (the National Association of Economic Organizations), the national government established a high-profile commission (nicknamed *Rincho*) in 1981 to provide a set of recommendations for rationalizing government (Table 10.2). Issuing a highly influential series of five reports in 1982 (in particular its *Basic Report*) *Rincho* called for privatization of several major public firms. They included such heavyweights as Japan Tobacco, Japan Airlines (JAL), Japan National Railways (JNR), and Nippon Telephone and Telegraph (NTT). The goals were to raise revenue, increase enterprise efficiency, and reduce future government borrowing requirements. The reports also called for cutting expenditures by streamlining government bureaucracies. This would be accomplished by reforming the regulatory duties of national ministries.

The regulatory reform movement initiated by *Rincho* lost steam in the late 1980s as Japan's fiscal position steadily improved. *Rincho* was followed by three far less influential government commissions: *Gyokakushin* I, II, and III (Table 10.2). *Gyokakushin* I's proposal to devolve powers to provincial governments proved to be a nonstarter, while *Gyokakushin* II and III strayed from their initial deregulatory charge by issuing reports on "election-oriented projects of Japanese prime ministers" (Carlile and Tilton, 1998, ch. 4).

Foreign governments have prodded Japan since the mid-1980s to open its markets to foreign producers and have identified industry deregulation as an important vehicle for achieving more import penetration. Frustrated by growing trade deficits with Japan, the United States has been particularly active through bilateral negotiations with Japan to deregulate and open markets in areas where the US government believes that American producers have comparative advantages. In the latest agreement (June 1997) under the first year of the US–Japan Enhanced Initiative on Deregulation and Competition Policy (Enhanced Initiative), the Japanese government pledged to lift restrictions in telecommunications, building materials, medical services/pharmaceuticals, financial services, and to abolish the Large-Scale Retail Store Law.[32]

From the US perspective, these agreements reached under threat of US punitive retaliation have produced only mixed results. A study initiated by the American Chamber of Commerce in Japan (ACCJ) rated forty-five market-opening agreements between the United States and Japan from 1980 to 1996 and concluded that only thirteen were "successful," meaning that they resulted in significantly increased sales of US products. Ten were rated as "failures" and twenty-two were rated as "partially successful."[33] Theresa Greaney (1999) found no consistent pattern of increases in Japanese purchases from the US following bilateral agreements.[34] Despite the mixed success of these agreements in opening Japanese markets, US pressure on Japan to implement market-opening deregulatory measures is likely to continue well into the next century as US trade deficits with Japan persist (Adams and Gangnes, Chapter 3 this volume).[35]

The appreciation of the yen against the dollar from 1985 (¥210/$1) to 1995 (¥85/$1) placed competitive pressures on Japanese export industries to reduce costs. One mechanism for achieving cost reductions in Japanese manufacturing was to reap lower prices of transportation, telecommunication, and energy inputs from deregulation of these suppliers. Since 1995, the yen has fluctuated widely, creating uncertainty for manufacturers but not clear incentives for deregulation.

Various actors in Japan have closely monitored regulatory reforms and its aftermath in Europe and the United States. The successful demonstration of regulatory reform in another high-income country frequently induces the Japanese government to undertake its own reforms but for two very different reasons. First, foreign reforms that allow foreign firms to gain a competitive advantage or that cause business in the regulated industry to be transacted overseas pose an immediate challenge for Japan to adopt similar reforms to maintain the competitive position of Japanese firms. Second, foreign reforms that generate large gains overseas will also likely generate large gains in Japan if they can be adapted to reflect the Japanese concern for ex post equity.

The US and the British deregulation of their telecommunications industries provide perhaps the best example of the positive demonstration effect in Japan. The Japanese quickly perceived that US and British liberalization policies would allow their telecommunications companies to take advantage of technological developments

---

[32] USTR, *Barshefsky Statement*, 1998.

[33] ACCJ, *The Journal*: 7; and Sumiya, January 20, 1997.

[34] However, she noted that they may have increased third-country exports to Japan.

[35] Adams and Gangnes (1996) and Backus (1998) have shown that neither yen appreciation nor Japanese fiscal stimulus is likely to reduce Japan's persistent trade surplus significantly.

and introduce sophisticated new services to their users. The fear among the MPT, MITI, Keidanren, and NTT was that Japanese telecommunication firms would not be competitive in exporting products and services to growing Asian markets. Steven Vogel (1998, 144) notes that

[t]he United States had allowed foreign attachments to the basic telephone set in 1968, but Japan only gradually liberalized its restrictions in 1972, 1982, and 1985. The United States had adopted its "Open Skies" policy [for communications satellites] in 1972 but Japan did not even launch a communications satellite until 1983. And the United States had allowed VAN [Value-Added Network] services in 1973, but Japan only followed in 1982.

Foreign regulatory reforms have not always provided a positive demonstration effect but rather have sometimes been plagued with problems of design, execution, and compensation of the losing parties. Bus deregulation in Great Britain was begun with a great fanfare in 1985, and Japanese regulators closely watched the experiment. Since deregulation, however, the British bus industry "has experienced reduced load factors, little fare competition, little on-the-road competition, and considerable market concentration" (Klein, Moore, and Reja, 1997: 62). "Route swamping" (scheduling service so often that a competitor cannot attract enough riders to succeed) and "schedule jockeying" (arranging for your carrier to arrive just before a second carrier, thereby "stealing" passengers) both severely disrupted service and competition in the bus industry (ibid: 69–71). The root cause behind this disappointing result was that British politicians and economists failed to recognize the importance of these market imperfections. Urban transit markets can only function effectively when they are supported by a specialized institutional framework designed to support competition in this particular market. Cautious Japanese regulators who closely monitored the British example found little reason to initiate serious regulatory reform of the Japanese bus industry.[36]

A negative demonstration effect was also generated by airline deregulation in the United States. The bankruptcy of a number of high profile airlines (including Braniff, Eastern, and Pan American), the failure of new entrants such as People's Express, and the huge losses of established carriers in the early 1990s were due in part to the industry reorganization induced by deregulation, but they were also affected by the US government's failure to enforce its antitrust laws, excess capacity during the 1990–1 recession, and poor management decisions. Nonetheless, Japanese regulators viewed the "turmoil" as a reason to avoid radical US-style deregulation of the aviation industry.[37]

The recession of the 1990s has prompted new deregulation proposals, many of which have been implemented. Some Japanese economists and political parties believe that industry deregulation can stimulate Japan's economy not just by reducing input costs for Japan's manufacturing firms but also by encouraging inward foreign direct

[36] Regulatory reform in Japan's taxi industry has proceeded relatively slowly in Japan and this may be due to the decidedly mixed record of deregulation in the US taxi industry (Teal and Berglund, 1987; Klein, Moore, and Reja, 1997).
[37] The shortage of take-off and landing slots was another reason given by Japanese regulators to delay airline deregulation (Yamauchi and Ito, 1996).

investment. The 1995 Deregulation Promotion Plan and the December 1996 Program for Structural Reform adopted by Japan's cabinet represented major breaks with past regulatory reform plans in both rhetoric and substance. The Program for Structural Reform not only proposed the "Big Bang" in Japan's financial sector (see Ito and Melvin, Chapter 7 this volume), but also proposed "drastic deregulation" in telecommunications, electricity, oil, and natural gas. Achieving parity with foreign prices was prominently mentioned as a major objective of the proposed deregulation policies.

The breakdown of the long period of LDP electoral dominance and the reform of the election system are clearly major factors behind the current proposals for regulatory reform. Electoral reform in the early 1990s redistributed seats in the Diet from rural areas that receive large benefits from government regulations to urban areas that pay high regulatory "taxes." The impact of the electoral reforms was quickly reflected in rhetoric (if not in legislation!) when, in the October 1996 general election, every major party campaigned on an agenda of regulatory reform.

Finally, and most importantly, global competitive pressure has been a critical force behind deregulation in most industries. Foreign firms participating in deregulated foreign markets have repeatedly placed direct competitive pressure on Japanese firms in the 1980s and 1990s by offering lower prices and newly differentiated final products. Japan's "Big Bang" was proposed because key industry players, bureaucrats, and politicians realized that increasing numbers of financial transactions were taking place not only in the more deregulated financial markets of Europe and United States but also in Singapore and Hong Kong. Regulatory reform in Japan's domestic airline industry is proceeding rapidly because of competitive pressure from international airlines to bring Japanese consumers to overseas vacation destinations.

International call-back services have prompted deregulation of KDD. Indirect competition from foreign firms participating in traditionally unregulated markets has also been important, albeit difficult to measure. If foreign firms competing with Japanese firms in global markets face lower costs for telecommunications services, electricity, gasoline, transportation, and other inputs produced by newly deregulated industries in their home countries, then they will have a competitive advantage against Japanese firms in international markets. Cost differentials in overseas markets could also induce Japanese firms to set up production facilities overseas rather than in Japan.

Despite the progress made with respect to privatization and deregulation in the 1980s and 1990s, Japan's transportation, public utility, and communication industries are still moderately to highly regulated. Most regulation continues to be informal and to be administered by national government ministries. Entry and price regulations have been somewhat relaxed in most industries, but are still binding constraints. In Japan "liberalized entry" typically means more competitors, not free entry. Licenses to enter are still granted on an "as needed" basis. A simple Cournot oligopoly model would predict that the additional number of competitors has the effect of lowering industry prices a little. Prices may, however, not be as low as in other countries with the same number of firms in an industry because of the higher barriers to entry in Japan. Without the competitive pressure provided by potential competitors, firms will be free to charge higher prices.

Regulatory reform has increased competition in Japan but the basic parameters of regulation have not changed in most industries.[38] Major exceptions are the repeal of the large store law and the promised Big Bang deregulation in the financial sector. In the next section, we ask whether this type of deregulation represents the wave of the future or whether liberalization within existing regulatory frameworks will reign supreme.

5. Future Regulatory Reform in Japan

In this section, we build on our earlier analysis of Japanese regulatory reform in the 1980s and 1990s and examine whether the same forces—changes in the domestic economy, competitive pressure from international markets, political pressure from foreign governments, and Japanese political reforms—are likely to create an impetus for regulatory reform over the next decade.

High budget deficits played an important role in mobilizing Japan's politicians to undertake regulatory reform in the early and mid-1980s. A decade of budget reduction in the 1980s left Japan with a nearly balanced budget in 1987, when it resumed a more expansionary fiscal policy (Okazaki, 1998). The economic stagnation of the 1990s has, however, led to ballooning budget deficits, with the FY1999 national government deficit projected at 31 trillion yen or 6 per cent of GDP. At the end of FY1999, the national debt/GDP ratio is expected to increase to 110 per cent, second only to Italy among developed countries. Japan's close-to-zero interest rates are reducing the cost of financing the debt, but an economic revival, while reducing budget deficits, could also be accompanied by increased interest rates and a rising debt burden. As Japan's work force becomes a smaller percentage of the population over the next decade and an aging population begins to drive up social service expenditures, there is likely to be intense pressure to reduce budget deficits without cutting social insurance benefits (Horioka; Mason and Ogawa, Chapters 4 and 2 this volume). Following the pattern displayed in the early 1980s, streamlining government administration and reducing the burdens of public enterprise subsidies and borrowing could become a popular political agenda. On January 26, 1999 the Cabinet adopted an administrative reform outline calling for a slimmer and more efficient government beginning in 2001. The proposal calls for the existing twenty-two ministries and agencies to be consolidated into one office, ten ministries, two agencies, and a commission overseeing public safety.

As we noted above, Japan privatized its railroads, international airlines, and telephone and tobacco companies in the 1970s and 1980s. Given the smaller portfolio of public enterprises today, are there likely candidates for privatization? Possibile candidates include the government's remaining shareholdings in Japan Tobacco, the postal

---

[38] Indeed, Carlile and Tilton (1998: 3) note that the concept of regulation differs in the English and Japanese language contexts. In the former, the term deregulation generally means "the rolling back of the state authority," but the Japanese equivalent (*kisei kanwa*) is generally understood "to be a loosening or relaxation rather than a removal of regulations."

savings bank (*Yucho*), and domestic and international airports. Selling its majority interest (two-thirds of outstanding shares) in Japan Tobacco would allow the national government to capitalize the flow of economic rents. Since Japan Tobacco already generates large cash flows and is privately managed, the divestiture would be unlikely to lead to significantly reduced public borrowings or to clearly recognized productivity increases. Moreover, since the tobacco monopoly in Japan (and in France) was originally organized as an instrument of state taxation, increased autonomy on the part of the tobacco industry could make it more difficult for the national government to regulate Japan Tobacco's prices and products (Caves, 1987: 113). If the Japanese government has paid close attention to the negative experience with US tobacco regulation, it will be reluctant to sell its majority stake.

The likelihood that the Japanese government will choose to privatize Japan's airports is enhanced by the positive demonstration effects conveyed by successful airport privatization programs carried out in Great Britain and Australia and the relatively smooth transition from public management to public regulation and private management in both countries.[39] A new pilot program involving privatization of airports in five small-medium cities in the United States could also provide a competitive stimulus to Japanese transport officials worried about falling behind developments in other countries.[40] Privatization prospects may also be enhanced by the significant regulatory responsibilities that the Ministry of Transport would retain after privatization.

Privatization of the postal saving bank has been suggested but would require a series of bold policy initiatives to accomplish.[41] First, postal savings are channeled via the Fiscal Investment and Loan Program (FILP) to government corporations, agencies, and banks for preferred investment projects. The below-market interest rates paid for these loans represent a subsidy to the government affiliates that would be lost with privatization. Privatizing the postal savings bank and curtailing the FILP subsidies was proposed by the Hashimoto government and then dropped after intense political pressure from unions, parliamentarians, and consumers. Second, although the government would lose rents appropriated via the FILP system, the network of branches within the nation's post offices is an extremely valuable asset that could produce enormous revenues for the government. Third, the opaque balance sheet of the postal savings system represents a major obstacle to privatization. Until the assets and liabilities that would be conveyed to private bidders (for regional parts of the bank) become more transparent, prospects for successful privatization will be difficult to evaluate. Fourth, many Japanese citizens today view the postal savings bank as the only truly safe bank. Until confidence in Japanese banking begins to revive, citizen opposition to privatization of postal banking could kill such efforts. In sum, despite the large potential gains from privatizing the postal savings system, a successful

---

[39] Airport privatization has been implemented or is being undertaken in forty-seven countries. See Kapur (1998).

[40] See GAO (1996). New York City has recently proposed leasing La Guardia and Kennedy Airports to private management firms.

[41] Gay (1997). One analyst estimates that a privatized and listed postal savings bank would be worth 9 trillion yen.

privatization is likely only if a number of policy measures can be successfully implemented and the public's confidence in the banking system restored.

The slow economy of the 1990s has raised both domestic and foreign voices for regulatory reform as a vehicle for reviving the economy. Japan's political parties and bureaucracy have responded with numerous proposals and reports calling for regulatory reform in virtually every industry. While rhetoric about reform is cheap, implementing such measures has provoked opposition from incumbent firms with weak balance sheets after almost a decade of poor macroeconomic performance. Opposition from incumbent firms could, however, be partially overcome in the near future by the rapid accumulation of private, public and international studies that repeatedly find extremely large gains from regulatory reforms. Such studies play the important role of changing the national consensus that industry regulation is a relatively benign way to achieve ex post equity in otherwise competitive markets.

A special Japanese government study group on the economic effects of deregulation in five sectors produced estimates of the potential gains from deregulation by sector between 1995 and 2001, and these are summarized in Table 10.3. It estimates that deregulation will increase real GDP by 6 per cent, or roughly 1 per cent per year. The largest gains are projected for the information and telecommunications sector, followed by finance and distribution. Not surprisingly, the greatest deregulatory efforts to date have been in these sectors.

The overall gains mask employment losses in individual sectors. Employment is expected to increase in the information and telecommunications sector and decrease in finance, transportation, and wholesaling. A 1994 Keidanren study predicted an increase of 177 trillion yen (or roughly 4 per cent) in real GDP between FY1995 and FY2000 if deregulation led to the elimination of price disparities between Japan and the rest of the world.[42] A more recent study by the Economic Planning Agency predicted that implementation of the deregulation measures in the March 15, 1995 Deregulation Action Program would increase real GDP by 0.9 per cent per year between FY1998 and FY2003 and reduce inflation (as measured by the CPI) by 1.2 per cent per year (Table 10.3).

The potential gains from regulatory reform rise to heightened importance once we consider the poor performance of total factor productivity in some of Japan's non-manufacturing industries between 1980 and 1993 (Weinstein; Wolff, Chapters 1 and 8 this volume). The combination of poor past productivity gains and studies showing large gains from regulatory reform clearly enhances the substantive case for regulatory reform in these industries.

Foreign demonstration effects were particularly important in stimulating regulatory reform in Japan during the 1980s and 1990s, and they are likely to remain important over the next decade. If we assume that the United States and Great Britain will continue to be first movers, then we need to explore the likely course of deregulation in these countries. In the United States, the Gramm-Leach-Bliley Act was passed in November 1999. Repealing most of the provisions of the 1933 Glass-Steagall Act,

---

[42] Keidanren (1994).

TABLE 10.3. *Estimated economic impacts of deregulation between 1995 and 2001 (percentages)*

	Overall	Logistics	Energy	Information and telecoms	Finance	Distribution
Real GDP (annual av.)	6.0	0.7	0.9	2.0	1.5	1.0
Plant and equipment investment (cumulative)	9.4	1.3	1.6	1.6	2.7	2.2
Consumer prices	−3.4					
Consumer surplus per household ('000 yen)	365	30	59	135	83	60

Notes: Assumes all deregulation measures have been implemented and the effects have emerged by 2001. The sums of the individual sectors may not add up to the overall total due to factors such as the "ripple effect".

Source: News from MITI at http://www.jef.or.jp/news/eco0609.html.

Gramm-Leach-Bliley allows the creation of holding companies capable of offering banking, securities, and insurance products. The US legislation is important for Japanese financial deregulation, as its presence provides additional incentives for Japan to carry through with its "Big Bang" program of financial deregulation, which contains similar but less far reaching reforms (Ito and Melvin, Chapter 7 this volume).

The United States has had a schizophrenic attitude towards regulating cable TV, first regulating it, deregulating it (1984), reregulating it (1992), and then deregulating it again (1996). This regulatory schizophrenia has been primarily due to persistent consumer complaints about "monopoly" pricing by cable providers. With the development of new microwave technologies, these complaints could begin to soften. Microwave technology has the potential to transform the cable TV industry from a natural monopoly into a natural oligopoly, particularly for densely populated market areas. Competition among service providers could occur with respect to the bundle of services provided as well as price. As we noted above, Japan liberalized its cable TV regulations in 1993, but cable penetration among Japanese households has only increased from 4 per cent in 1992 to just over 11 per cent in 1996. As new cable services begin to effectively compete in medium and large metropolitan areas in the United States, Japanese regulators are likely to see similar opportunities in Japan's densely populated urban areas.

Pressure from international markets and from foreign governments has been effective in inducing regulatory reform in several important industries. Pressure from foreign governments has been effective when international interests align with Japanese interests and generally ineffective in sectors where US and European companies have a competitive advantage via-á-vis Japanese producers. The United States would like Japan to further deregulate and open its markets in telecommunications equipment, housing and housing supplies, medical devices and pharmaceutical products, financial services, and in retail distribution.[43] The United States has also been

[43] USTR, *Barshefsky Statement*, 1998.

pressuring Japan to allow foreign entrance to fields of its insurance business that are currently reserved for Japanese firms. With the notable exception of housing regulations (which, among other things, severely restrict the size and height of homes in urban areas), the Japanese are likely to resist adopting the US trade agenda because of the adverse impact on Japanese firms. Progress in reforming industry regulation in these fields is likely to be slow.[44]

Perhaps the wild card in the future regulatory reform equation is the partially implemented reform of the electoral process. With urban voters given more power by the electoral reforms and with the switch from multi-member to single-member electoral districts, Japan's politicians have reorganized their political competition around a set of public policies that emphasize regulatory reform. If these policies prove to be popular with the newly empowered urban voters, then more fundamental regulatory reform could occur over the next decade, including elimination of administrative guidance, implementation of licensing reform, and a decline in the extent of subsidization of rural services by urban citizens.

6. Conclusion

Deregulation in Japan started in the 1970s and has been proceeding at different speeds in different sectors of the economy. Following the pattern observed in continental Europe, deregulation in Japan has rarely meant eliminating regulations governing exit and entrance, pricing, and service provision. Instead, it has focused on reforming and liberalizing existing regulatory regimes. While regulatory reform has been induced by changes in the domestic economy, pressure from international markets and foreign governments, and changes in ideology and political organization, competitive pressure from the global economy has been the main channel driving deregulation in Japan in the 1980s and 1990s. Ideological suspicion of the rent redistribution effects of the free market, close consultation between government ministries and regulated firms, and administrative reluctance to shed regulatory powers have slowed the pace of regulatory reform.

Despite these observations, we also believe that the pace of regulatory reform is likely to increase in Japan. With the realization that their earlier industrial policy is no longer promoting growth but rather is a handicap to growth, Japan will deregulate where it serves its "new" industrial policy and new industrial interests. While faster deregulation will be prompted by a variety of forces, including the high government budget deficit, changing technologies, and positive demonstration effects from overseas, deregulation is ultimately about responding to international competitive pressures on Japan's leading industries. Given the depth of Japan's economic difficulties at the millenium and the ongoing widening and deepening of

---

[44] Ocean shipping between ports within Japan or the United State is restricted to national carriers. Organized lobby groups in the United States have been pushing more vigorously for shipping deregulation in the late 1990s. Deregulation of domestic shipping in the United States could place pressure on Japan to relax its shipping regulations.

deregulation in other industrialized countries, it is not unreasonable to expect the pace of deregulation in Japan to quicken.

REFERENCES

Adams, F. Gerard and Byron Gangnes (1996), "Japan's Persistent Trade Surplus: Policies for Adjustment," *Japan and the World Economy*, 8: 309–33.

American Chamber of Commerce in Japan (ACCJ) (1997), *Making Trade Talks Work: Lessons from Recent History* (Tokyo: ACCJ).

——(1998), "The Underpinning of Power," *The Journal*, August, 5.

Asahi Shimbun (1997), *Japan Almanac, 1998* (Tokyo: Asahi Shimbun).

Backus, David (1998), "The Japanese Trade Balance: Recent History and Future Prospects," *Japan and the World Economy*, 10: 409–20.

Bailey, Elizabeth E., David R. Graham, and Daniel P. Kaplan (1985), *Deregulating the Airlines.* (Cambridge, Mass.: MIT Press).

Becker, Gary (1983), "A Theory of Competition Among Pressure Groups for Political Influence," *Quarterly Journal of Economics*, 98: 371–400.

Bordo, Michael D., Eugene N. White, and Claudia Goldin (1998), *The Defining Moment: The Great Depression and the American Economy in the Twentieth Century.* (Chicago: University of Chicago Press).

Carlile, Lonnie E., and Mark Tilton (eds.) (1998), *Is Japan Really Changing its Ways? Regulatory Reform and the Japanese Economy.* (Washington: Brookings Institution Press).

Caves, Douglas W., Laurits R. Christensen, Michael W. Tretheway, and Robert J. Windle (1987), "An Assessment of the Efficiency Effects Of US Airline Deregulation via an International Comparison," in Elizabeth Bailey (ed.), *Public Regulation: New Perspectives on Institutions and Policies.* (Cambridge, Mass.: MIT Press).

Caves, Richard (1987), *American Industry: Structure, Conduct, Performance*, 6th edn. (Englewood Cliffs, NJ: Prentice Hall).

Chujoh, Ushio and Hirotaka Yamauchi (1998), "Japan's Air Transport Policy at a Crossroad," in Rong-I Wu and Yun-Peng Chu (eds.), *Business, Markets and Government in the Asia Pacific: Competition Policy, Convergence, and Pluralism.* (New York: Routledge).

Dowling, Michael J., William R. Boulton, and Sidney W. Elliott (1994), "Strategies for Change in the Services Sector: The Global Telecommunications Industry," *California Management Review*, 36: 57–88.

Fahy, John and Fuyuki Taguchi (1995), "Reassessing the Japanese Distribution System," *Sloan Management Review* (Winter), 49–61.

Flath, David (1995), "Japanese Regulation of Truck Transport", paper presented at the Columbia University School of Business Conference on "Regulation in Japan."

——and Tatsuhiko Nariu (1996), "Is Japan's Retail Sector Truly Distinctive?" *Journal of Comparative Economics*, 23: 181–91.

Gay, Chris (1997), "A Life of Its Own: Would a Liberalized Japan Have Room for its Postal Bank?" *Far Eastern Economic Review* (March 27), 59–60.

General Accounting Office (GAO) (1996), *Airport Privatization: Issues Related to the Sale of U.S. Commercial Airports.* (Washington: US Government Printing Office).

Gibney, Frank (ed.) (1998), *Unlocking the Bureaucrat's Kingdom: Deregulation and the Japanese Economy.* (Washington: Brookings Institution Press).

Graham, Brian (1997), "Air Transport Liberalization in the European Union: An Assessment," *Regional Studies*, 31: 807–12.

Greaney, Theresa M. (1999), "Assessing the Impact of U.S.–Japan Bilateral Trade Agreements, 1980–1995," unpub. MS (Department of Economics, Syracuse University).

Harris, Robert G. and C. Jeffrey Kraft (1997), "Meddling Through: Regulating Local Telephone Competition in the United States," *Journal of Economic Perspectives*, 11: 93–112.

Ito, Takatoshi (1992), *The Japanese Economy*. (Cambridge, Mass.: MIT Press).

——(1996), "Japan and the Asian Economies: A 'Miracle' in Transition," *Brookings Papers on Economic Activity*, 2: 205–72.

Itoh, Nariyasu (1988), *Denki Ryokin, Hiyo Kozo no Kokusai Hikaku* (International Comparison of Electricity Rates and Cost Structure) CRIEPI Report No, Y877904 (Tokyo: Economic Research Center, Central Research Institute of Electric Power Industry).

Janow, Merit (1998), "Policy Approaches to Economic Deregulation and Regulatory Reform," in Wu and Chu (eds.), *Business, Markets and Government in the Asia Pacific*. (New York: Routledge).

Johnson, Chalmers (1982), *MITI and the Japanese Miracle*. (Stanford: Stanford University Press).

Joskow, Paul L. (1997), "Restructuring, Competition and Regulatory Reform in the U.S. Electricity Sector," *Journal of Economic Perspectives*, 11: 119–38.

Kahn, Alfred (1971), *The Economics of Regulation*, 2 vols. (New York: Wiley & Sons).

Kapur, Anil (1998), *Airport Infrastructure: The Emerging Role of the Private Sector*, World Bank Technical Paper No. 313 (Washington: World Bank).

Keidanren (1994), *The Positive Economic Effects of Deregulation and Strategies Needed to Increase Employment* Tokyo, Nov. 15. http://www.keidanren.or.jp/english/policy/pol010.html.

Klein, Daniel B., Adrian Moore, and Binyam Reja (1997), *Curb Rights: A Foundation for Free Enterprise in Urban Transit* (Washington: Brookings Institution Press).

Kristof, Nicholas D. (1998). "Japan is Torn Between Efficiency and Egalitarian Values," *New York Times International*, October 26, p. A10.

La Croix, Sumner J., and David Wolff (1995), *Civil Aviation in the Asia-Pacific Region: Prospects and Challenges* (Honolulu: East–West Center).

Lincoln, Edward J. (1998), "Deregulation in Japan and the United States: A Study in Contrasts," in Gibney, F. (ed.), *Unlocking the Bureaucrat's Kingdom*, 53–68.

Mak, James, and Shyam Sunder (1998), "Why Are There So Many Small Shops in Japan?" in Mak, James, Shyam Sunder, Shigeyuki Abe, and Kazuhiro Igawa (eds.), *Japan: Why It Works, Why It Doesn't*. (Honolulu: University of Hawaii Press), 45–50.

Maki, Atsuki (1998), "How High Are Consumer Prices In Japan?" *Japan and the World Economy*, 10: 173–86.

Meyer, John R. (1959), *The Economics of Competition in the Transportation Industries* (Cambridge, Mass.: Harvard University Press).

Morrison, Steven and Clifford Winston (1986), *The Economic Effects of Airline Deregulation*. (Washington: The Brookings Institute).

——(1995), *The Evolution of the Airline Industry*. (Washington: The Brookings Institute).

Nagai, Susumu (1994), "Japan: Technology and Domestic Deregulation," in Noam, Eli, Sisuke Komatsuzaki, and Douglas A. Conn (eds.), *Telecommunications in the Pacific Basin: An Evolutionary Approach*, Communications and Society Series (New York: Oxford University Press), 458–72.

Nagatani, Keizo (1995), "Japanese Economics: An Interpretive Essay", unpub. paper (Vancouver: University of British Columbia).

Nagatani, Keizo (1997), "Japan's Sagging Credibility: A Crisis of Self-Confidence," *Look Japan*, 43 (March), 12–14.

Nambu, Tsuruhiko (1994), "A Comparison of Deregulation Policies," in Noam, Eli, Sisuke Komatsuzaki, and Douglas A. Conn (eds.), *Telecommunications in the Pacific Basin: An Evolutionary Approach*, Communications and Society Series (New York: Oxford University Press), 32–44.

Navarro, Peter (1996), "The Japanese Electric Utility Industry," in Gilbert, Richard J. and Edward P. Kahn (eds.), *International Comparisons of Electricity Regulation*. (New York: Cambridge University Press), 231–76.

Omura, Tatsuya (1997), "Japan's Stumbling Policy for Competition in the Telecommunications Industry," *Telecommunications Policy*, 21: 127–41.

Okazaki, Tetsuji (1998), "Fiscal Policy and Macro-Economy in Japan: A Historical Perspective," *Financial Review*, 47: 56–75 (in Japanese).

Peltzman, Sam (1976), "Toward a More General Theory of Regulation," *Journal of Law & Economics*, 19: 211–40.

——(1989), "The Economic Theory of Regulation after a Decade of Deregulation," *Brookings Papers on Economic Activity*, Special Issue, 1–41.

Quiggin, John (1996), "Evaluating Airline Deregulation in Australia," *Australian Economic Review*, 30: 45–56.

Ramseyer, J. Mark and Frances McCall Rosenbluth (1993), *Japan's Political Marketplace*. (Cambridge, Mass.: Harvard University Press).

——————(1998), *The Politics of Oligarchy: Institutional Choice in Imperial Japan*. (Cambridge: Cambridge University Press).

Smith, Vernon L. (1996), "Regulatory Reform in the Electric Power Industry," *Regulation*, 1: 33–46.

Spiller, Pablo T. and Carlo G. Cardilli (1997), "The Frontier of Telecommunications Deregulation: Small Countries Leading the Pack," *Journal of Economic Perspectives*, 11: 127–38.

Stigler, George (1971), "The Theory of Economic Regulation," *Bell Journal of Economics and Management Science*, 2: 3–21.

Sumiya, Fumio (1997), "Trade Pact Success Mixed, Says Chamber," *Nikkei Weekly*, January 20.

Teal, Roger F. and Mary Berglund (1987), "Impacts of Taxi Deregulation in the U.S.A," *Journal of Transport Economics and Policy*, 21: 37–56.

Tilton, Mark (1994), "Informal Market Governance in Japan's Basic Materials Industries," *International Organization*, 48 (Autumn), 663–85.

Tomita, Teruhiro (1990), "Denki Jigyo no Seisansei Bunseki" (Total Factor Productivity Analysis of Japanese Electric Power Industry), *Information and Communications Studies*, 11.

Uekusa, Masu (1987), "Industrial Organization: The 1970s to the Present," in Yamamura, K. and Y. Yasuba (eds.), *Political Economy of Japan*. (Stanford: Stanford University Press).

Uriu, Robert M. (1996), *Troubled Industries: Confronting Economic Change in Japan* (Ithaca, NY: Cornell University Press).

US General Accounting Office (GAO) (1997), *Airline Deregulation: Barriers to Entry Continue to Limit Competition in Several Key Domestic Markets* (Washington).

US Trade Representative (USTR) (1998), *Barshefsky Statement on U.S.–Japan Deregulation*, G8 Summit, Birmingham, May 15–17.

Viscusi, W. Kip, John M. Vernon, and Joseph E. Harrington, Jr. (1995), *Economics of Regulation and Antitrust*, 2nd edn. (Cambridge, Mass.: MIT Press).

Vogel, Steven K. (1998), *Freer Markets, More Rules: Regulatory Reform in Advanced Industrial Countries*. (Ithaca, NY: Cornell University Press).

Waverman, Leonard and Esen Sirel (1997), "European Telecommunications Markets on the Verge of Full Liberalization," *Journal of Economic Perspectives*, 11: 113–26.

Winston, Clifford (1993), "Economic Deregulation: Days of Reckoning for Microeconomists," *Journal of Economic Literature*, 31: 1263–89.

——(1998), "U.S. Industry Adjustment to Economic Deregulation," *Journal of Economic Perspectives*, 12 (September), 89–110.

Yamamura, Kozo and Yasukichi Yasuba (eds.) (1987), *The Political Economy of Japan: The Domestic Transformation*, I (Stanford: Stanford University Press).

Yamauchi, Hirotaka (1995), "Regulatory Reform and Changes in the Japanese Trucking Industry," unpublished manuscript.

——and Takatoshi Ito (1996), "Air Transport Policy in Japan," in Findlay, Christopher and Gary Hufbauer (eds.), *Flying High: Liberalizing Civil Aviation in the Asia Pacific* (Washington: Institute for International Economics), 33–61.

——and Hideki Murakami (1995), "Air Transport in Japan: Policy Changes and its Evaluation," unpublished manuscript.

Zysman, John (1983), *Governments, Markets, and Growth: Financial Systems and the Politics of Industrial Change* (Ithaca, NY: Cornell University Press).

Part III

FOREIGN DIRECT INVESTMENT, TRADE, AND REGIONAL INTEGRATION

11 FDI in the Restructuring of the Japanese Economy

MAGNUS BLOMSTRÖM, DENISE KONAN, AND ROBERT E. LIPSEY

1. Introduction

Both outward and inward foreign direct investment (FDI) play an important role in restructuring economies. Outward investment is a way of maximizing the rents on the accumulated knowledge and skill of a country's firms, or preserving them as long as possible when the country itself has lost its comparative advantage in their industries, and the industries, or parts of them, must relocate. Inward investment may bring new firm-specific skills and new industries to countries that lack them or preserve the rents on workers' skills in sectors where domestic firms have lost their firm-specific advantages. In this paper we will analyze the role FDI can play in the coming restructuring of the Japanese economy.

The paper begins with a brief description of the major changes in the economic structure of Japan in the last twenty years and discusses some important factors that may influence the future development of the Japanese economy. Among the factors included here are the implications of institutional changes, such as the continuing deregulation of the Japanese economy and economic changes, such as the aging of the population, the rise in per capita income, and the increasing education and labor force participation of women. These internal forces will bring about changes in FDI patterns.

With respect to outward FDI, we will ask what types of production (e.g. labor-intensive, skill-intensive) and activities Japanese firms have moved abroad in the past and what type they are likely to move in the future. What are the motivations for these relocations? How are they related to, for instance, changes in relative production costs in Japan vis-à-vis foreign countries or in the availability of skills?

A different role is envisioned for inward investment. So far, we have seen relatively little activity by foreign multinationals in Japan, but because of gradual deregulation we expect that to change in the future. Inward FDI will bring foreign firms' skills and technologies to Japan in areas where Japanese firms, partly because of the protected environment in which they have developed, are relatively uncompetitive. These Japanese firms may be forced by the intensified competition to shrink or disappear.

We are grateful to HSFR for financial support.

2. The Japanese Economy: Recent Changes and Future Developments

Every fast growing economy goes through significant structural transformations, shifting production and employment from low to high productivity activities. The remarkable economic performance during the twentieth century, particularly between 1950 and 1990, is a testimony to Japan's ability to adapt and restructure. Japan grew rapidly after the Second World War, with an average annual growth rate of 8 per cent from 1953 to 1973 and over 10 per cent in the 1960s. As Edward Wolff documents in this volume (Chapter 8), Japan was able to transform from a mid-tech based economy in 1970 to a high-tech region by the mid-1990s. Japan's rate of transformation was much more rapid than that of its primary competitors, the United States and Germany.

Production shifted from an agricultural and light manufacturing base before the Second World War to heavy industry and, increasingly, to services. Employment trends reflect these shifts in Japan's economy. In 1954, primary sectors (agriculture and mining) accounted for 38 per cent of employment, while manufacturing comprised only 17.8 per cent. By 1970, primary production had fallen in relative terms to 17.8 per cent of the labor force and manufacturing had risen to 27 per cent of employment. As in other developed countries, the work force has continued to move sharply out of agricultural production and toward services (see Table 11.1). Manufacturing's share of overall employment has actually fallen since 1977, in spite of Japan's enormous success as an exporter of manufactured goods.

Within the manufacturing sector there were also major changes in structure. In the 1950s, manufacturing was dominated by textile and other light industry. Iron and steel production and the shipbuilding industry rose to prominence in the 1960s, followed by the chemical sector. By the 1970s, electronics and automobile production dominated manufacturing activities. Since the 1970s, electrical machinery and chemicals, particularly the former, continued to grow much faster than manufacturing production in general (see Table 11.2). Transport equipment did not even quite keep up with the average in manufacturing. Food and tobacco and iron and steel declined in importance relative to other manufacturing industries, and textiles shrank in absolute size. Although these are very broad groupings, it is tempting to see in these changes a shift to more technology-intensive sectors.

TABLE 11.1. *Employment, 1997/1977 (ratios)*

All industries	1.23
Services	1.83
Wholesale and retail trade, eating and drinking places	1.24
Manufacturing	1.08
Agriculture and forestry	0.55

Source: Bank of Japan (1997), 363; (1986), 303–4.

TABLE 11.2. *Manufacturing producer shipments, 1997/1976 (ratios)*

All industries	1.83
Electrical machinery	6.49
Chemicals	2.36
Transport equipment	1.65
Food and tobacco	1.23
Iron and steel	1.14
Textiles	0.65

Source: Bank of Japan (1997), 358; (1996), 356.

TABLE 11.3. *Shares of world exports, 1995/1977, selected groups (ratios)*

Industry Groups:	
Electrical machinery	1.76
Foods	0.77
Metals	0.75
Industries:	
Electronic components	4.27
Computer and other office equipment	3.30
Miscellaneous plastic products	2.37
Household audio and video equipment	1.66
Farm and garden machinery	0.46
Construction and mining machinery	0.52

Source: NBER World Trade Database.

Another mirror that reflects changes in the Japanese and world economies is the composition of trade. An advantage of trade data is that they are available in more detail than production or employment, especially for the world as a whole or for other individual countries with which we might wish to compare Japan.

For world trade as a whole, the major changes between 1977 and 1995, as shown in Table 11.3, were a large growth in the share of electrical machinery and large declines in foods and metals, both relatively declining industries within Japanese manufacturing production as well. World trade as a whole has been moving to computers and electrical and electronic equipment and away from primary production and from capital goods used in primary production.

The path of development of the composition of Japanese exports has been similar in many ways, but often steeper (see Table 11.4). The two predominantly primary industry groups, foods and metals, declined faster as shares of Japanese exports than for world exports as a whole. Japan already showed a revealed comparative disadvantage in exports of foods in 1977. The relative descent of metals in 1995 is

TABLE 11.4. *Shares of Japanese and US exports, 1995/1977, selected groups (ratios)*

	Japan	US
Industry Groups:		
Nonelectrical machinery	1.79	0.93
Electrical machinery	1.58	1.96
Foods	0.47	0.79
Metals	0.37	0.96
Industries:		
Electronic components	8.82	3.64
Computer and other office equipment	5.43	2.03
Miscellaneous plastic products	2.53	2.45
Drugs	1.88	1.07
Other electrical machinery	1.87	1.06
Apparel and other textile products	0.35	0.97
Other transport equipment	0.31	0.74
Primary metal industries, ferrous	0.31	0.78
Leather and products	0.21	1.22

Source: NBER World Trade Database.

particularly striking, as Japan had been a relatively strong exporter of metals, particularly steel, in 1977. It would not be surprising if the decline of metals continued in the future.

The individual industries for which the share of Japanese exports grew the most were all industries for which shares in world exports grew, but Japan seemed to be leading the way in this shift. Among the most rapidly declining industries in Japanese exports, three of the four were also declining in world exports, but not as quickly as in Japan. Thus, we can summarize the trends in trade by saying that as the world was shifting out of primary production and trade and into more technologically advanced products, Japan was doing the same, but more sharply, leading the way.

Another way to describe the shifts in Japanese trade structure is to compare them with the trade structure, and changes in it, for the United States, the highest country in per capita income and presumably the world's technological leader (again Table 11.4). The shares of the seven major industry groups in Japanese exports in 1995 were closer to those in US exports than they were in 1977 in five cases, and further away in only two. The sum of the absolute differences in shares between Japan and the US in the seven industry groups was 57.5 percentage points in 1977, but by 1995, the Japanese export shares had moved much closer to the US shares of 1977, the sum of the differences being reduced to 41.0. Thus, the distribution of exports by the US appears to serve as a leading indicator of the future changes in the structure of Japanese exports. By 1995, the total of the percentage differences was down to 33.3. Thus, the Japanese export pattern was not only catching up to the earlier US pattern, but was following some of the changes that were taking place in the US distribution.

2.1. The future

Turning to the changes that we expect in the underlying characteristics of Japan's economy in the next few decades, a closer look at demographic trends is crucial. Japanese demographics and family practices are interacting in a dramatic manner (see Mason and Ogawa, Chapter 2 this volume). Japan has recently achieved the longest life expectancy of all countries. Fully one-third of the Japanese are expected to be over 65 years of age in 2040, double the level of 1995. The size of the total population is expected to peak around 2010. Simultaneously, rates of fertility have dropped to 1.4 per woman, in part due to a delay in women's decisions to marry. These demographic influences will presumably result in a severe labor shortage early in the twenty-first century at a time when the aging population will place severe pressure on health and welfare facilities. As Mason and Ogawa point out, Japan will likely experience a slowing in the traditionally high savings rate as the population continues to age. This, in turn, implies a dramatic slowdown in investment and long-term growth rates unless offsetting increases in productivity emerge.

Yet, throughout history Japan has risen to challenges by restructuring its culture and economy. As we discuss above, Japan has rapidly adjusted its industrial activities during this century to move from agriculture and low-tech manufacturing to high-tech industries. Chapters in this volume provide details on numerous adjustments that will likely be forthcoming in the twenty-first century, many of which will have implications for inward and outward FDI. Likewise, FDI will act as an additional catalyst for adjustment to the new demands of the global information age. In this section, we highlight three of the main structural adjustments that are underway in the Japanese economy.

A major structural change is the liberalization of the labor market and the greater inclusion of women in the labor force. The conventional wisdom is that low unemployment rates and job turnover rates, attributable to a system of "life-time employment" and worker devotion to the firm, contributed to Japan's rapid growth. Firms invested heavily in costly worker education that focused on providing broad exposure to manufacturing activities, increasing productivity and firm-specific innovations. The system also acted as a type of private pension plan that essentially underpaid young workers with the promise of job security and a generous senior employee package. Ito (1996) asserts that the lifetime employment system is facing problems similar to pay-as-you-go retirement systems in other countries as the population rapidly ages. Also changing, according to Ito, is the need for very narrowly and highly specialized workers in high technology and service sectors, such as telecommunications, computer information and software, and finance. In response, the broad-based, firm-specific worker training in manufacturing will shrink. As the labor force within high-growth, high-technology sectors expands, the demand for specialized education and the job turnover rate will rise. Within the twenty-first century, labor markets will become increasingly flexible. Unemployment rates will be closer to US levels, reflecting a more competitive business environment. Labor practices will also undergo fundamental changes with performance and merit increasingly determining advancement.

In response to an increasing labor shortage, we anticipate that the twenty-first century will also bring a new role for Japanese women. Women have traditionally been underutilized given their level of education. While the increase in women's engagement in the labor force has been quite rapid, Mason and Ogawa (this volume) report a 1997 female participation rate of only 50 per cent (relative to 77.7 per cent among males). Women, especially if married, currently tend to work part-time. Yet, gender discrimination in the labor market seems to be easing in response to market conditions. Thus, a conceivable scenario would be for Japanese female participation rates to increase in response to labor shortages and more closely resemble patterns in other OECD countries.

The increasing role for women in the labor market will tend to make child-rearing even more challenging. Thus, we foresee a persistent pressure on the Japanese labor force to be highly productive and competitive in order to maintain a high living standard. Japan may seek to ease its highly restrictive immigration policies to expand the work force. More likely in our view, as we discuss in the next section of this paper, Japanese firms will increasingly relocate their less skilled labor activities overseas.

A second structural adjustment in the Japanese economy is that of regulatory reform. Twentieth-century Japan has been characterized by a high level of governmental involvement and regulation in most industries (see La Croix and Mak, Chapter 10 this volume, as well as Carlile and Tilton, 1998). Japan's postwar development strategy relied on a public–private partnership. The government sought to modernize the economic base by selecting promising industries and actively nurturing capacity by limiting competition, supporting research, development, and technology transfers, and encouraging the extension of credit. Industries with a potential to achieve economies of scale and scope were particularly favored and permitted to form horizontal and vertical cartels that cooperated on pricing, R&D, production, etc. The government also aimed to protect special interests, such as rice farmers and small retail shops, against competition through a complex system of licensing, regulation, and quality control standards.

This close partnership between business interests and the Japanese government is in direct contrast to the Western, and particularly the American, model which is grounded in a tradition of strong antitrust policy, market competition, and private ownership. Japan has viewed this approach as encouraging waste as firms may use real resources to drive others out of business or may duplicate R&D costs. Yet, in the face of a stagnant economy and an increasingly integrated global economy, Japan has been under increasing pressure to modify the existing regulatory framework and promote greater market competition.

We anticipate that the Japanese regulatory environment will increasingly converge towards the industrial policies of other advanced industrial nations, as we enter the twenty-first century. These reforms will act to create new markets, stimulate competition, attract foreign investment and technology transfer, and improve consumer welfare. While the exit of declining firms and industries will be hastened, this should eventually free resources for use in more globally competitive sectors and should promote longer-term growth and stability. Deregulation promises to be particularly valuable in nontradable services, such as insurance, travel (airlines), telecommunications, and utilities. Both business and consumers will be the ultimate beneficiaries.

Finally, global economic conditions will continue to restructure the Japanese economy. Japan has committed itself to further liberalization of its markets to trade under the WTO. While export expansion led the economic growth of the twentieth century, we anticipate that import competition and inward FDI will play a leading role in increasing productivity in Japan in the twenty-first. As Weinstein (Chapter 1 this volume) and Lawrence and Weinstein (1998) found using OECD data, productivity in Japanese import sectors has grown more rapidly than in export sectors. Imports act to create a more competitive domestic business environment. We anticipate that, as import barriers continue to fall and as domestic distribution systems become more transparent and converge to OECD standards, the import share of Japanese GDP will rise, hence improving domestic productivity.

We also anticipate that deregulation and a greater openness of the Japanese economy will generate inward FDI, as discussed below. The competitive pressure from such investment can play a role similar to that of import competition, enhancing productivity growth (see Blomström and Sjöholm, 1999).

In conclusion, while it is impossible to predict in detail the future development of the Japanese economy or any other, there is little doubt that the economy will change. In order to guess at the future role of FDI in these changes, it is necessary to make some forecast of their direction. We find it likely that Japan will continue to grow in per capita income and to move further in deregulating the economy, and will therefore become more like other economies, such as the United States.

3. The Role of Japanese Outward Direct Investment

What role has increasing outward FDI played in the restructuring of the Japanese economy? Outward FDI is not very large relative to the Japanese economy, and it showed little sign of growth, in relative terms, before the mid-1980s, despite the increases in the Japanese wage level and in the strength and size of Japanese firms (Lipsey, Blomström, and Ramstetter, 1998). After the rise in the value of the yen that began in 1985, a new trend appeared: a sharp rise in the importance of production and employment outside Japan by Japanese firms. Employment in Japanese affiliates abroad, which had been below 2 per cent of aggregate home employment since the early 1970s, rose to over 5 per cent by 1996. In manufacturing, overseas employment, 5 to 6.5 per cent of home employment before 1985, rose to 19 per cent in 1996. Value added in Japanese manufacturing affiliates abroad roughly doubled in size relative to total manufacturing value added in Japan between 1980 and 1992 (ibid.).

Within multinational corporations (MNCs), employment abroad rose from under 40 per cent of home employment in 1977 and 1980 to 55 per cent in 1992, and the affiliate share of production within Japanese manufacturing multinationals rose from 6.5 to 16.5 per cent (Ramstetter, 1991 and 1996).

While overseas manufacturing affiliates were becoming more important relative to their parents and to total manufacturing in Japan, the parents' share of Japanese manufacturing was shrinking. Value added in Japanese manufacturing parent firms fell from around 60 per cent of value added in Japanese manufacturing in 1980 and 1983 to about 50 per cent in 1992. There has apparently been a geographical reallocation of the activities of Japanese firms, and particularly those of multinational manufacturing firms. The reallocation must have changed the characteristics of the economy as a whole or it resulted from underlying changes in the economy.

Japan's share of world manufacturing exports rose over 60 per cent between 1970 and 1986 and then, by 1995, declined by a quarter. During the period of rising Japanese export shares, foreign production affiliates were small relative to aggregate Japanese employment and output, but they were of importance in some individual sectors. In mining and in three manufacturing sectors close to primary products, food products, nonferrous metals, and wood, paper and pulp, Japanese affiliates were export-oriented, usually to the extent of half or more of their sales, and were focused on exporting to the Japanese market (Ramstetter, 1991). That concentration reflected the traditional Japanese concerns about raw material and food supplies and kept at least part of import sources under Japanese control.

In foods, textiles and apparel, and wood, paper and pulp, overseas affiliates were the main sources of whatever share Japanese MNCs had of markets outside Japan. In two of those industry groups that share had traditionally been small, but textiles and apparel were a different case. Japanese exports alone had accounted for 12 per cent of world exports in 1970 and Japan had a strong export comparative advantage at that time. As Japan's share of world exports of these products fell to 7.5 per cent in 1977 and 2 per cent in 1986, and Japan lost its comparative advantage in this industry, Japanese affiliates took over part of the Japanese share in overseas markets. By 1977, they were already supplying more of those markets than their parents, and by 1986 they supplied twice as much. Thus, they helped to retain for Japanese MNCs some of the market share they might have lost if they had depended entirely on exporting from Japan.

The changes that took place in the location of the production from which Japanese MNCs served foreign markets are shown in Table 11.5. By 1977, the first year for which we have affiliate data, the affiliates had already taken over half or more of the Japanese MNCs' foreign markets in the declining industries, foods, textiles and apparel, and wood, paper and pulp. In the next decade, still in the period of Japanese trade ascendancy, the affiliate share in these industries grew still further.

In the chemicals sector, never one of Japanese export comparative advantage, and one in which Japanese parent exports hardly grew from 1977 to 1986, affiliates were initially unimportant. However, by 1986 they supplied two thirds of Japanese MNCs' foreign sales.

Most of Japanese national and MNC exports and affiliate sales are in the metals, machinery, and transport equipment groups, and affiliates accounted for less than 25 per cent of overseas markets for Japanese MNCs in 1977. That affiliate share grew in all these industries even as Japan's world export shares were growing, but the

TABLE 11.5. *Share of Japanese affiliates in total foreign sales by Japanese MNCs, 1977–1988 (percentages)*

	1977	1980	1986	1988
TOTAL	19	20	28	36
Foods	87	85	100	93
Chemicals	25	27	66	59
Metals	22	20	37	45
Nonelectrical machinery	12	13	28	23
Electrical machinery	21	21	30	35
Transport equipment	6	7	14	26
Other manufacturing:	41	42	48	52
Textile and apparel	51	57	63	67
Wood, paper and pulp	50	61	68	68
Other	27	31	38	44

Note: Total foreign sales by Japanese MNCs are the sum of manufacturing parent exports, and sales by foreign manufacturing affiliates, minus affiliate imports from Japan and affiliate exports to Japan from affiliate production, measured as total affiliate exports to Japan multiplied by the ratio of affiliate imports from Japan to total affiliate sales. Affiliate shares are derived from the difference between total foreign sales and parent exports.

Sources: Manufacturing affiliate sales in 1986 and 1989 are from Japan, ITI (1999). Other data are from Ramstetter (1991).

smallest increase in affiliate shares was in electrical machinery, the sector in which Japan's comparative advantage was greatest.

While the affiliate shares of MNC markets most closely reflect the decisions of parent firms, these decisions affect the country as a whole, outside of the MNCs. The outcome for the country can be seen in Table 11.6, which shows how all Japanese firms, including non-MNC firms, served their foreign markets. That calculation can be extended to 1995, because it does not require parent data. The period of declining Japanese export shares is most closely approximated in our data by 1986–95.

If the adjustment required by the Japanese economy in this decade was a decline in the role of manufacturing, the overseas affiliates contributed to it in every industry by supplying larger and larger shares of the foreign markets served by all Japanese manufacturing firms, MNCs and others. While the affiliate share for manufacturing as a whole grew only from 15 to 23 per cent during the high growth period, it increased from 23 to 40 per cent in the low growth era, and to 40 per cent or more in every industry except non-electrical machinery.

Even in those industries in which Japan retained its comparative advantage in 1995, the two machinery groups and transport equipment, the share of affiliates in serving Japan's foreign markets increased. The shift from exporting to affiliate production and

TABLE 11.6. *Share of Japanese affiliates in total foreign sales by Japan and Japanese affiliates, 1977–1995 (percentages)*

	1977	1980	1986	1988	1989	1995
TOTAL	15	13	23	31	33	40
Foods	44	28	59	73	74	83
Chemicals	16	16	37	52	51	51
Metals	16	14	29	39	38	46
Nonelectrical machinery	5	5	12	11	15	15
Electrical machinery	20	19	28	38	37	42
Transport equipment	4	5	16	25	29	45
Other manufacturing:	32	27	33	44	48	52
Textile and apparel	36	29	35	46	43	45
Wood, paper and pulp	46	42	46	58	50	58
Other	24	24	30	41	50	53

Note: Foreign sales by Japan and Japanese affiliates are the sum of exports of manufactured products from Japan and sales by foreign manufacturing affiliates, minus affiliate imports from Japan and affiliate exports to Japan, measured as for Table 11.5. Affiliate shares are derived from the difference between total foreign sales and Japanese exports.

Sources: Exports of manufactured products from Japan are from the NBER World Trade Database. Manufacturing affiliate sales in 1977 and 1980, manufacturing affiliate imports from Japan and exports to Japan from 1977 to 1988 are from Ramstetter (1991). Manufacturing affiliate sales from 1986 to 1995 are from Japan, ITI (1999). Manufacturing affiliate imports from Japan in 1989 and 1995 are adjusted from MITI (1998). Manufacturing affiliate exports to Japan in 1989 and 1995 are adjusted from MITI (1998) and Japan, ITI (1999).

sales was particularly large in transport equipment: from an affiliate share of 16 per cent in 1986 to 45 per cent in 1995. The move to affiliate production in this case sustained Japanese exports. Of the increase of US$36 billion in exports from Japan, US$31 billion were imports from Japan by manufacturing affiliates in the transport equipment industry, presumably mostly components for production there. Of the total growth in foreign market sales in this industry of US$148 billion, exports from Japan accounted for only the US$36 billion mentioned above; the rest came from affiliate sales net of their imports from Japan. Thus, the affiliates expanded the total Japanese market share in the industry, sustained exports from Japan, and permitted a shift in Japanese home production to inputs into the production process.

    Table 11.7 describes, for the whole range of manufacturing industries, the role of affiliate production and sales in the period of decline in Japanese home country export shares. More than half the growth in Japanese firms' sales in foreign markets, whether from exports from Japan or Japanese production abroad, came from the foreign production. The foreign production share was close to or above half in all industries but one, non-electrical machinery. The home country share was highest in the industry groups that contained the more sophisticated or research-intensive industries, but not by a huge margin.

TABLE 11.7. *Share of affiliate production in the growth of Japanese firms' sales of manufactures in foreign markets, 1986–1995 (percentages)*

TOTAL	51.2
Foods	93.0
Chemicals	55.7
Metals	64.9
Nonelectrical machinery	17.4
Electrical machinery	49.6
Transport equipment	67.0
Other manufacturing:	65.2
Textile and apparel	67.3
Wood, paper and pulp	67.7
Other	64.6

Note: The growth of Japanese firm's sales of manufactures in foreign markets is the difference between the growth of exports from Japan from 1986 to 1995 and the growth of Japanese sales to foreign markets in the same period.

Source: The data are those underlying Table 11.6.

As was the case for older industries in the period of rising Japanese export share, before 1986, the affiliates were helping Japan to sustain foreign market shares at a time when Japan's market shares were declining, and especially in Japan's less competitive industries.

Another area where we find significant Japanese outward FDI is in banking, but here we find some interesting differences from manufacturing. Overseas branches of Japanese banks have been much more important than foreign banks in Japan. The total assets of overseas branches of Japanese banks reached a peak, in absolute terms, in 1990, after much more than doubling in the previous eight years (Bank of Japan, 1997: 94–8). After 1990, these assets declined by almost a third, and then recovered somewhat, but they remained, in 1997, well below the 1990 level. Until 1990, Japanese banks were growing at home, as well as abroad, and even faster, so that the assets abroad were declining relative to those at home during the latter part of the 1980s. After 1990, the rate of decline was faster abroad than at home, so that the ratio of foreign to domestic assets fell by almost half from 1985 to 1997.

That process, first of rapid expansion abroad, and then of contraction, is illustrated by the changes in the position of Japanese banks in the United States, as reported in the US Federal Reserve Board's Reports of Conditions and Income. From 1985 to 1990, assets of US offices of Japanese banks more than doubled, and grew from 6.6 to almost 12 per cent of total assets of all banks in the United States. This share of business loans grew even faster, from about 8.5 per cent in 1985 to 19 per cent in 1990. The expansion was fed by high Japanese saving rates and restrictions on competition by foreign institutions for Japanese saving rather than by any technological superiority or high operating efficiency on the part of Japanese banks. After 1990, the absolute amount of Japanese bank assets in the United States fell sharply, and their share in total assets even more rapidly, falling to about 5.5 per cent in June 1998, well below the 1985 level. The firm comparative advantage of Japanese banks apparently disappeared with the decline in their domestic assets and the need to restore capital at home.

3.1. Future trends

A continuation of the trends of the last twenty years in the Japanese economy would point to continued relative decline of manufacturing and growth in service industries. However, a larger share for foreign firms in the somewhat liberalized finance and trade sectors might produce reductions in employment in these areas even as output grows, if these sectors are presently as inefficient as is often said.

Within manufacturing, and therefore in commodity trade, the declines in Japanese export shares and the growth in affiliate shares in many old industries, such as foods, textiles and apparel, and metals, do not have much further to go. One exception is the iron and steel industry, although foreign affiliates have not sustained Japanese MNC shares much in that case.

Manufacturing exports are, and will probably be in the future, increasingly concentrated in machinery and in transport equipment, mainly motor vehicles. Even if these remain the bulk of Japanese exports, the trend in electrical machinery and transport equipment has been, and will probably continue to be, toward supplying more of foreign markets from affiliate production. That trend has hardly begun for non-electrical machinery so far.

A comparison of Japanese affiliates with US majority-owned foreign affiliates points to some differences that suggest directions for the future evolution of Japanese FDI. One is the much smaller involvement of the Japanese affiliates in non-electrical machinery, which includes computers and parts, despite Japan's comparative advantage in that industry. The revealed comparative advantage ratio for Japanese affiliates in this industry is 0.48, as compared to 1.40 for US affiliates, although the ratios for the two home countries are close, from 1.32 to 1.42. The likely future path is a rapid growth for Japanese affiliates in this industry.

The second difference is that in non-electrical machinery and transport equipment, exports/sales ratios are much lower in Japanese affiliates than in US affiliates, 35 as against 54 per cent and 11 as against 53 per cent. The gap between US and Japanese affiliates is larger in both developed and developing country locations, especially in transport equipment. US affiliates in developed countries exported 54 per cent of their output and Japanese affiliates only 14 per cent. The shares in developing countries were 43 and 7 per cent.

Both the lack of Japanese affiliate production in non-electrical machinery and the low export ratios of Japanese affiliates in electrical machinery and transport equipment probably reflect the relative immaturity of the Japanese affiliates. Japanese manufacturing MNCs seem to be behind US MNCs in dividing up their output into segments and producing each segment in the most efficient or economical location. The future should see more movement in this direction, especially if home labor market restrictions are loosened. The reallocation of production to affiliates should help the parent firms to adjust to the changing conditions of production in Japan and improvements in host countries, and to hold on to or expand their markets in the face of high home production costs.

Much of the reduction in Japanese banking operations abroad, and its timing, must have reflected cyclical conditions in Japan. But the development may also be, to some extent, a response to expectations of future liberalization at home. Until some time in the 1980s, Japanese banks were awash with cheap funds from Japan's high saving rate and the banks' monopoly position at home. With the future promising probably lower saving by an aging population and more competition for funds from foreign financial firms entering the Japanese market, the Japanese banks may have concluded that their problems were not temporary and that large foreign networks would no longer be profitable.

4. The Role of Inward FDI

Japanese outward FDI takes place in industries of existing Japanese firms' comparative advantage, typically also the comparative advantage of Japan itself, present or possibly past. Inward FDI would be expected to come into industries in which foreign firms have some comparative advantage over Japanese firms. They might be export industries in which Japan already has some comparative advantage as a location or could have with the addition of some foreign firms' technology, or they might be non-tradable industries, or sectors of them, in which Japanese firms are backward in some respects.

Inward FDI may affect host countries both directly and indirectly. Investments by foreign companies will directly influence macro variables like capital formation, employment, tax revenues, and trade. Indirectly, foreign investment may also influence the structure of the host economy, as well as the conduct and performance of locally owned firms. Although the direct effects of foreign direct investment may be important in certain situations and/or countries, it is generally accepted that a significant share of the long-run impact of FDI is likely to occur in the form of indirect effects or "spillover" (see Blomström, 1989). This is because FDI, apart from being a financial capital flow, also involves the capitalization of technology, knowledge, skills, and other resources that represent the MNCs' intangible assets.

Spillovers can occur because MNC affiliates import and demonstrate technologies that are not used in the host country, and because their operations (or mere presence) may increase the level of competition and force local firms to search for more efficient methods of production. Among many possible channels for technology spillovers, the most concrete may be linkages with foreign MNCs and hiring of employees trained in MNCs. Recent studies have confirmed that the nature and significance of spillovers appear to vary between countries and industries, and that the positive effects of FDI are likely to increase with the level of local capability and competition (see e.g. Blomström, Zejan, and Kokko, 2000). This suggests that there is a great potential for FDI spillovers in the Japanese economy in the future.

Historically, inward FDI has played an important role in the economic restructuring process in Japan (Sohn, 1998). Although always small, inward FDI was prominent in key industrial sectors in Japan before the Second World War and had a significant impact in the modernization of its industrial base in the interwar period (see Takeshi and Udagawa, 1990). The Japanese government actively encouraged multinational entry in heavy and chemical industries, most notably in petroleum processing, rubber tires, automobiles, and electrical machinery. The impact was notable in the restructuring of Japan's economy toward high value-added manufacturing. Western investors revolutionized the country's industrial base by introducing technology of advanced production, firm organization, and management. From textile MNCs was gained a sense of quality control, Western standards and design, and marketing strategies. The foreign automotive industry brought techniques of mass production and vertical corporate organization. Modern methods were widely disseminated and blended with Japanese cultural practices (see UNCTAD, 1995).

Inward investment is still very low in Japan, as is well documented in the literature (see e.g. Yoshitomi and Graham, 1996). An often-cited figure is that foreign firms in Japan account for only 1 per cent of Japanese sales. However, a more careful look at the numbers would place sales of foreign affiliates at 5.3 to 5.7 per cent of all sales (Weinstein, 1997). These figures are about half of that of the United States, and are well below international averages. Foreign firms' shares of Japanese production, measured by value added, are also low in an international comparison (see Lipsey, Blomström, and Ramstetter, 1998).

Low foreign involvement in the Japanese economy is due to a combination of factors that have been discussed over the years. Until the early 1970s, Japan's policies toward inward FDI were extremely restrictive. Although these restrictions were largely eliminated in 1980, inward FDI is still relatively small, leading some (e.g. Encarnacion, 1992) to suggest that private barriers to FDI have replaced public barriers. Others, however, have argued that these findings are the result of general entry barriers (e.g. Ramstetter and James, 1993). For instance, the cost of doing business in Japan is exceedingly high due to high rental costs, high taxation of corporate profits, and complicated governmental regulations. Rigidities in the labor market, such as an expectation of "lifetime" employment and high living standards, result in very high implicit wages.

Foreign entry is further limited by the difficulty of acquiring ownership in existing Japanese firms. Cross-ownership of shares within *keiretsu*, vertically related groups of firms, are thought to discourage hostile mergers and acquisitions as a low level of stocks are publicly traded (Dunning, 1996). Furthermore, governmental regulations and subsidies favor small and medium-sized enterprises, while multinational activity tends to arise predominantly in large enterprises (Weinstein, 1997).

4.1. The future

Inward FDI will play more of a role than in the past in the sectors we expect to grow in Japan. These include high-tech sectors in manufacturing and financial services, in which Japanese firms are relatively backward. Foreign firms will also benefit from the ongoing deregulation of the Japanese economy. These reforms will act to create new markets, attract foreign investment, and stimulate competition. We can already see the beginning of this structural change.

Compared with foreign rivals, many Japanese firms are either too small or too dependent on their home market to survive. By paring away jobs and unprofitable businesses, they are restructuring to regain competitiveness (see e.g. Whittaker, 1997). This process—known as *risutora*—is rapidly changing those sectors of the Japanese economy that are open to competition. Mergers and acquisitions, which also involve foreign-owned multinationals, make up a big part of this restructuring. In 1998, over 900 mergers took place in Japan, which is more than twice as many as five years earlier, and the number seems to have increased since then. The foreign acquisitions of Japanese firms grew more than sixfold in value the same year. There is still a long way to go, however, in comparison with the United States, where over 11,000 mergers were announced in 1998. The banking crisis is also eroding the cross-shareholdings within the *keietsu*: the major banks are trying to reduce their risk exposure by reducing their holdings of stocks.

Developments in the auto industry can illustrate these changes as well. The companies that were first to respond to the new challenges, primarily Honda and Toyota, are still at the top of the world league, both technologically and financially. The laggards are now in the midst of the restructuring process. Ford's stake in Mazda, Renault's deal with Nissan, and Daimler-Chrysler's with Mitsubishi, are three examples of the mergers and acquisitions that are reshaping Japan's industry.

One sector in which the liberalization of the Japanese economy is expected to have the greatest impact is that of banking and other finance (see e.g. Weinstein, Chapter 1 this volume). These are not industries for which FDI data are plentiful, especially banking, which is something of an orphan in the US FDI data collection system.

US depository institutions, mainly commercial banks, clearly held a smaller toehold in Japan at the latest FDI census data, 1994, than in most other developed countries. For example, the ratio of assets of US depository institutions to GDP was lower in Japan than in the nine other large developed countries for which we have data and lower also than that in Korea, not a country noted for welcoming inward FDI (US Department of Commerce, 1998). The same was true for sales and employment in these institutions. Japan has apparently not been an easy market for US banks to penetrate, at least via FDI.

The US depositary institutions were not only small in Japan in 1994, but had been decreasing in size relative to Japanese GDP since 1982, whether we measure size by assets, sales, or the direct investment stock, calculated at historical cost (US Department of Commerce, 1985). The assets of US-owned banks in Japan declined even more over these twelve years relative to the assets of Japanese domestically licensed banks (Bank of Japan, 1997). Thus, up to 1994 there was no apparent move into the Japanese market by US banks.

Since 1994, the story is somewhat different. The assets of Japanese branches and subsidiaries of US banks rose from 0.24 per cent of those of domestically licensed Japanese banks in 1994, to 0.40 per cent at the end of 1997. Although this US bank share was tiny in comparison to the assets of the domestically licensed Japanese banks, there is some suggestion of an increase in importance of the US banks, although the large fluctuations make it hard to say we can see a trend. The rise in importance of the US banks owes almost as much to the decline in assets of the local banks, as to growth in the US banks.

Another indicator of changes in the finance sector is the US investment position in Japan in that sector, although it is risky to assume a close relationship between the investment stock and activity. Within the banking sector, there was relatively slow growth in the US investment stock until 1997. In that year, the stock jumped by about 50 per cent, possibly foreshadowing larger future moves in response to a loosening of controls. Further evidence of change in the banking sector is given by Japanese data on the assets of foreign banks in Japan. The absolute size of these assets increased in most years until a peak in 1990, fell thereafter in every year until a low point in 1994, and then began to rise again. The largest increase, by about 50 per cent, as in the data for US banks, took place in 1997. Relative to total Japanese bank assets, the foreign bank asset levels jumped from a low of 3.2 per cent in 1994 to 3.7, 4.6, and, in 1997, 6.6 per cent of Japanese bank assets. Thus, the data covering all banks confirm the impression that some barriers have been lifted and that foreign banks, have begun to increase their role in the Japanese financial sector.

The "Other Finance" category involves far more US investment in Japan than the banking sector, but it is hard to know what the appropriate sector within Japan is for comparison. If we compare the US investment stock with the assets of Japanese insurance companies, a procedure that underestimates the US role, because assets are usually much larger than the investment stock, we find little change in the ratio through the 1980s. US investment grew rapidly from 1982 to 1988, but the Japanese insurance sector also grew rapidly. After 1988, however, the US investment grew faster, and the ratio more than doubled, suggesting that some liberalization may have been affecting this sector. However, the US direct investment data for Finance are so heavily suppressed that it is impossible to use them to identify just what parts of the sector are receiving the US investment.

5. Conclusions

We expect both outward and inward FDI to play an increasingly important role in the restructuring of the Japanese economy in the future. Outward FDI is still not very large relative to the Japanese economy, despite the rapid growth since the mid-1980s, so there is still scope for significant increases before it reaches the levels of other OECD countries. The outsourcing and relocation of production will particularly affect labor-intensive manufacturing operations, not least because of demographic factors. On the domestic scene, this will facilitate the necessary restructuring of the Japanese economy towards more advanced activities with higher value added.

Inward FDI will presumably have an even stronger impact on the restructuring of the Japanese economy. Although the stock of inward foreign direct investment is still very small, there are important changes under way. Deregulation has opened up industries as well as service sectors to foreign multinationals. In combination with the economic crisis, this has begun to weaken the cross-shareholding relationships within the *keiretsu* groups, which facilitates mergers and acquisitions between Japanese and foreign firms. The consequences of increasing foreign participation in the Japanese economy are likely to be highly beneficial. The level of competition and the inflow of foreign technology will increase, with higher productivity growth as a major result.

REFERENCES

Bank of Japan (1986), *Economic Statistics Annual 1986* (Research and Statistics Department, Bank of Japan).

——(1996), *Economic Statistics Annual 1996* (Research and Statistics Department, Bank of Japan).

——(1997), *Economic Statistics Annual 1997* (Research and Statistics Department, Bank of Japan).

Blomström, M. (1989), *Foreign Investment and Spillovers* (London: Routledge).

——and F. Sjöholm (1999), "Technology Transfer and Spillovers: Does Local Participation with Multinationals Matter?" *European Economic Review*, 43: 915–23.

——M. Zejan, and A. Kokko (2000), *Foreign Direct Investment: Firm and Host Country Strategies* (London: Macmillan).

Carlile, L. E. and M. C. Tilton (eds.) (1998), *Is Japan Really Changing its Ways? Regulatory Reform and the Japanese Economy* (Washington: Brookings Institution Press).

Dunning, J. (1996), "Explaining Foreign Investment in Japan: Some Theoretical Insights," in Yoshitomi, M. and E. Graham (eds.), *Foreign Direct Investment in Japan* (Cheltenham: Edward Elgar).

Encarnacion, D. (1992), *Rivals Beyond Trade: America versus Japan in Global Competition* (Ithaca, NY: Cornell University Press).

Ito, T. (1996), "Japan and the Asian Economies: A Miracle in Transition," *Brookings Papers on Economic Activity*, 2: 205–72.

Japan, Institute for International Trade and Investment (ITI) (1999), *Analytical Research based on Data from the Survey of Overseas Business Activities, Survey Research on Harmonizing Globalization Based on the 1997 Survey of Overseas Business Activities* (Tokyo: Institute for International Trade and Investment).

Lawrence, R. Z. and D. Weinstein (1998), "The Role of Trade in East Asian Productivity Growth: The Case of Japan," in Stiglitz, J. (ed.), *Rethinking the East Asian Miracle* (Washington: World Bank).

Lipsey, R. E., M. Blomström, and E. Ramstetter (1998), "Internationalized Production in World Output," in Baldwin, R. E., R. E. Lipsey, and J. D. Richardson (eds.), *Geography and Ownership as Bases for Economic Accounting* (Chicago: University of Chicago Press).

MITI (1998), Data received directly from the Ministry of International Trade and Industry.

Ramstetter, E. (1991), "Regional Patterns of Japanese Multinational Activity in Japan and Asia's Developing Countries," *Empirical Studies in Regional and International Economics* (Kansai University: Institute of Economic and Political Studies).

——(1996), "Estimating Economic Activities by Japanese Transnational Corporations: How to Make Sense of the Data?" *Transnational Corporations* (Aug.) 5/2.

——and W. E. James (1993), "Multinationals, Japan–US Economic Relations, and Economic Policy: The Uncomfortable Reality," *Transnational Corporations*, 2/3: 65–93.

Sohn, Y. (1998), "The Rise and Development of the Japanese Licensing System," in Carlile, L. E. and M. C. Tilton (eds.), *Is Japan Really Changing its Ways? Regulatory Reform and the Japanese Economy* (Washington: Brookings Institution Press).

Takeshi, Y. and M. Udagawa (eds.) (1990), *Foreign Business in Japan Before World War II* (Tokyo: University of Tokyo Press).

UNCTAD (1995), *World Investment Report 1995: Transnational Corporations and Economic Restructuring* (New York: United Nations).

US Department of Commerce (1985), *US Direct Investment Abroad: 1982 Benchmark Survey Data* (Washington: Bureau of Economic Analysis).

——(1998), *US Direct Investment Abroad: 1994 Benchmark Survey, Final Results* (Washington: Bureau of Economic Analysis).

Weinstein, D. (1997), "Foreign Direct Investment and *Keiretsu*: Rethinking US and Japanese Policy," in Feenstra, R. (ed.), *Effects of US Trade and Promotion Policies* (Chicago: Chicago University Press).

Whittaker, D. H. (1997), *Small Firms in the Japanese Economy* (Cambridge: Cambridge University Press).

Yoshitomi, M. and E. M. Graham (eds.) (1996), *Foreign Direct Investment in Japan* (Cheltenham: Edward Elgar).

12 A New Millennium for Japanese–North American Economic Policy Relations?

STEVEN GLOBERMAN AND ARI KOKKO

1. Introduction

The broad purpose of this paper is to identify and discuss potential significant future developments in the economic relationship between North America and Japan, and to assess the implications of these potential developments for the Japanese economy and Japanese economic policies in both the public and private sectors.[1]

As any exercise in "futurology," this paper will ultimately and inevitably drift towards educated guesswork. The reliability of the guesswork is a function of the validity of the assumed dynamics linking causal conditions to outcome consequences, as well as inspiration in putting forward a set of assumed causal conditions. Since economic (and political) relationships tend to change slowly and continuously, rather than abruptly and discreetly, it seems useful to develop assumptions about emerging economic relationships between North America and Japan with reference to recent trade and investment linkages. The second section of the paper will therefore provide a brief overview of recent trade and investment flows between the two regions, as well as a brief assessment of how these linkages are likely to change over the next ten to twenty years.

The third section looks more closely at future economic linkages between Japan and North America, and, in particular, at the likely sources of significant future gains from closer economic integration. The assertion made is that increased US foreign direct investment (FDI) in Japan holds the greatest potential for enhancing the benefits of economic integration between North America and Japan both directly and indirectly. The direct benefits are associated with traditional economic advantages of FDI to the host and home countries. The indirect advantages derive from the fact that the political environment in Japan is more likely to be accepting of inward FDI than large increases in directly imported goods. We argue further that Japan will be an increasingly favored destination for US outward FDI. While such increased US FDI can be expected to stimulate interest group opposition in Japan, it should expand and deepen beneficial linkages between the two countries, thereby

---

[1] The developments we consider are essentially "microeconomic" in nature. In particular, we do not discuss current (at the time of writing) US–Japanese frictions surrounding the continued stagnation of the Japanese economy, and the perceptions of US policymakers (and other governments) that Japanese government policy is failing to engineer a recovery in the domestic economy. However, since an important focus of many critics of Japanese government policy is the perceived foot dragging on the part of Japan to deregulate and reform its financial sector, as well as to promote increased competition in financial services and other important sectors of the economy, it is clear that the microeconomic issues we discuss are not independent of broader macroeconomic sources of conflict.

strengthening the positions of groups promoting closer economic integration between the two countries.

The fourth section of the paper considers some "non-conventional" forms of closer economic integration between North America and Japan that offer potential gains to both parties. The primary focus here is cooperative research on "social policy" issues such as the environment, health care, and defense. The decrease in the US emphasis on defense and defense expenditures weakens a traditional linkage between the technological efforts of Japan and the United States; however, common social problems such as protecting the global environment, developing relatively efficient treatments for diseases associated with aging, and promoting economic and social progress in the developing world provides substantial scope for increased joint research by "public sector" organizations in the two countries.

The fifth section consists of conclusions and policy recommendations for both public and private-sector decision-makers.

2. Economic Linkages Between Japan and North America

In this section, we review recent trends and developments in the economic relationship between Japan and North America. The main focus is on the "real" economic linkages, i.e. trade and foreign direct investment flows, although (for reasons to be discussed) portfolio capital investment linkages are also potentially relevant determinants of economic and political relationships between the two regions. As the United States economy overwhelmingly dominates the Canadian and Mexican economies in overall size, our overview of Japanese–North American linkages will primarily focus on the Japanese–US bilateral relationship. Besides providing a background for the discussion about policy relations between Japan and North America, the summary also aims to provide some insights into how these linkages might change in the future. Future trends in trade and investment linkages, in turn, can be expected to shape the net benefits that the two regions are likely to realize from policies designed to "improve" economic relationships, and determine the issues to be included in the future policy agenda.

2.1. Recent trade patterns: magnitude

Table 12.1 reports recent bilateral (US–Japan) export and import flows from the perspective of the United States. Several points are apparent. First, Japan is an important trading partner for the United States in absolute dollar terms, but the bilateral relationship has become less important in relative terms over the past decade. The value of US exports of goods to Japan has grown from some 37 billion dollars in 1988 to 66 billion dollars in 1996–7, but Japan's share of total US exports has fallen by a couple of percentage points over the same period.[2] The share of US imports coming

---

[2] The reduction in the export value in 1998, to 58 billion dollars, is due to the Japanese recession and is not likely to be permanent.

TABLE 12.1. *US international trade in goods with Japan (billion US$ and percentages)*

Year	Exports to Japan	Share of total US exports (%)	Imports from Japan	Share of total US imports (%)	Bilateral trade balance	Bilateral trade deficit as share of total US deficit (%)
1988	37.2	11.6	89.8	20.1	−52.6	41.4
1990	47.8	12.3	90.4	18.1	−42.6	39.1
1992	46.9	10.6	97.4	18.2	−50.5	52.5
1994	51.8	10.3	119.1	17.8	−67.3	40.5
1995	63.1	11.0	123.5	16.5	−60.4	34.8
1996	66.0	10.8	115.2	14.3	−49.2	25.7
1997	65.7	9.8	121.4	13.9	−55.7	30.7
1998	57.9	8.5	122.0	13.4	−64.1	27.9

Sources: Council of Economic Advisors, US (1998). Data for 1997 and 1998 from US Census Bureau web site, at www.census.gov/foreign-trade/www/.

from Japan has fallen even faster, from around 20 per cent in the late 1980s to less than 14 per cent in the late 1990s. Second, the United States continues to run large trade deficits with Japan. These trade deficits have been a traditional source of bilateral trade friction and continue to stimulate US requests for macroeconomic policy changes in Japan, e.g. tax reductions, as well as microeconomic policy changes, e.g. deregulation of domestic industries and the strengthening of competition policy initiatives. While demands are also made on other countries, it can be argued that they are more difficult to motivate when trade is balanced or when the US records a trade surplus. Third, although the bilateral trade deficits have remained at more or less the same level in dollar terms, they have become less dramatic in relative terms, as the aggregate trade deficit has widened. The deficits with Japan accounted for 40–50 per cent of the total US trade deficit around 1990, but less than 30 per cent in 1998.

Some context to the US–Japan relation is provided by contrasting Canada's relative importance as a trading partner for the United States to that of Japan. In 1988, exports to Canada amounted to around 23.2 per cent of all US exports, while imports from Canada accounted for approximately 18.9 per cent of total US imports. In 1997, comparable percentages were 22.5 per cent for exports and 19.6 per cent for imports. The first point to note is that the trade contacts with Canada have been significantly more important for the US, at least in quantitative terms, than those with Japan. The second point to note is that Canada has become an increasingly important trading partner for the US relative to Japan over the past decade. This is true even though the implementation of the Canada–US Free Trade Agreement (CUSTA) in 1988 and the North American Free Trade Agreement (NAFTA) in 1994 has apparently not led to any increase in the US trade intensity with Canada.[3]

[3] A detailed analysis of North American economic integration in the 1990s is provided in Blomström, Kokko, and Globerman (1998).

TABLE 12.2. *Bilateral merchandise trade as a percentage of trade*

Year	Canada	US
1983	72.8	21.5
1984	74.3	21.8
1985	75.4	20.3
1986	73.6	21.3
1987	72.7	20.6
1988	71.8	20.7
1989	72.0	20.3
1990	72.0	19.9
1991	72.3	19.7
1992	74.3	19.7
1993	76.7	20.5
1994	78.3	21.0
1995	77.4	20.7
1996	77.8	20.7
1997*	78.6	20.9

*First 3 quarters at annual rate.

Note: Trade is defined as imports plus exports.

Sources: Statistics Canada (various issues), *Canada's Balance of International Payments*, Ottawa: Ministry of Industry; Council of Economic Advisors, US (various issues).

Table 12.2 indicates the importance of the US to Canada as a trading partner. Specifically, it reports Canada–US imports plus exports as a share of total imports plus exports for each country over the period 1983–97. What is obvious from the table is the overwhelming trade dependency that Canada has with the US. Virtually 80 per cent of Canada's trade is with the US.

The relative importance of Mexico as a trading partner with the United States increased fairly dramatically in the 1990s. For example, US exports to Mexico accounted for around 6 per cent of total US exports in 1988. By 1995 (prior to the severe depreciation of the peso and the severe contraction of the Mexican economy in 1996), exports to Mexico accounted for approximately 13 per cent of total US exports. Similarly, imports from Mexico as a share of total US imports were around 5 per cent in 1988 and around 10.6 per cent in 1995.

Table 12.3 elaborates upon the importance of the US (primarily) and Canada as trading partners for Mexico. Specifically, it reports total Mexican exports and imports, as well as those to its NAFTA partners and to the rest of the Western Hemisphere. The main point to highlight is that almost 90 per cent of Mexico's exports and 80 per cent of imports involve Mexico's NAFTA partners.

An implication of the closer ties between the Canadian and Mexican economies and the US economy over the past decade is that North American policymakers are likely

TABLE 12.3. *Mexican exports and imports 1986–1995 (million US$; percentage of total exports and imports in parentheses)*

Year	Total exports	US + Canada	Total imports	US + Canada
1986	19,074	13,928 (73.0)	14,749	10,666 (72.3)
1987	20,532	13,577 (66.1)	12,758	8,626 (67.6)
1988	20,409	13,726 (67.3)	19,557	13,401 (68.5)
1989	22,975	16,364 (71.2)	22,789	15,911 (69.8)
1990	26,247	18,711 (71.3)	29,556	20,236 (68.5)
1991	27,101	19,523 (72.0)	38,121	26,825 (70.4)
1992	46,153	38,278 (82.9)	61,914	46,522 (75.1)
1993	51,832	44,474 (85.8)	65,188	49,284 (75.6)
1994	60,459	52,588 (87.0)	79,198	56,371 (71.2)
1995	79,324	68,388 (86.2)	73,938	56,344 (76.2)

Source: UN Trade Tapes.

to put an increasingly higher priority on trade and investment issues within the NAFTA region than on those primarily affecting East–West trade linkages. In particular, the closer economic ties between the US and Mexico may leave the US less inclined, at the margin, to work towards closer economic integration with non-North American APEC members, especially developing country members; however, we shall argue below that Japan's status as the major developed economy in the Pacific region may create (over time) a "special" relationship between the US and Japan within the APEC context.

From the perspective of Canada, while Japan is its single largest market in Asia, Japanese–Canadian trade is relatively small. It is also relatively small from Japan's perspective. For example, throughout the early 1990s, somewhat less than 5 per cent of total Canadian exports went to Japan, while less than 3 per cent of total Japanese exports were destined for Canada. Japan was a somewhat more important source of imports (than exports) for Canada, as the former accounted for slightly more than 7 per cent of total Canadian imports. Canada, in turn, accounted for around 3 per cent of total Japanese imports (Flatters and Harris, 1995). As is true for the United States, Japan has traditionally run a relatively large trade surplus with Canada relative to the overall size of the bilateral trade flows.

With the notable exception of the automotive sector, trade relations with Japan have never been a high-priority issue with Canadian policymakers. As a consequence, while a number of Japanese concerns about US trade policies, especially the unilateral application of countervailing duties and antidumping penalties, are shared by Canada, the latter is unlikely to serve as a strong advocate of a more conciliatory US trade policy stance with Japan. Canadian trade diplomacy with the US tends to be bilateral in focus and tries to ensure that Canada's "special relationship" with the US gains it exemption from retaliation primarily aimed at other countries.

While we do not report details of Japanese–Mexican trade linkages in the interests of brevity, the same inferences might be drawn as for Canada. Namely, while Mexico and Japan share a common interest in the ability of Japanese multinational companies (MNCs) to set up within Mexico to serve the North American market, Mexico is unlikely to dissipate any economic "goodwill" with the US by advocating positions that might be particularly helpful to Japan, such as reductions in the North American content-quota on automobiles.

Japan's perspective on trade linkages with North America is further elaborated by data in Table 12.4. This table shows Japanese exports to and imports from the United States, as well as the relative importance of those export and import flows. As with the data reported in Table 12.1, monetary measures of trade may distort trends in real trade volumes when exchange rates fluctuate. Nevertheless, the main point underscored by Tables 12.1 and 12.4 is unlikely to be compromised by the manner in which trade flows are measured over time. Namely, the United States is relatively more important to Japan as a trading partner than Japan is to the United States. Furthermore, the bilateral surplus from the trade relation with the US remains quite significant, although its share in Japan's aggregate surplus has fallen from the top levels recorded around 1990. Yet, it is notable that the bilateral surplus accounts for about 40 per cent of Japan's total surplus, whereas the bilateral deficit only makes up a little more than a quarter of the total US trade deficit. It should also be noted that Canada and Mexico together only account for about 4 per cent of Japanese exports and imports. The ready implication one might draw is that Japan's economic linkages with North America will remain predominantly conditioned by its economic relationship with the United States barring a substantial (and unexpected) change in traditional Japanese trading patterns with the individual NAFTA members.

TABLE 12.4. *Japan's international trade with the United States (100 million yen and percentages)*

Year	Exports to US	Share of total exports (%)	Imports from US	Share of total imports (%)	Bilateral trade balance	Bilateral trade surplus as share of total surplus (%)
1988	114,874	34.5	53,883	25.5	60,991	50.1
1990	130,566	32.2	75,859	24.2	54,707	59.4
1992	121,210	28.2	66,221	22.4	54,989	34.9
1994	120,358	29.7	64,244	22.9	56,114	38.1
1995	113,330	27.3	70,764	22.4	42,566	34.5
1996	121,771	27.2	86,310	22.7	35,461	39.0
1997	141,689	28.6	91,493	24.6	50,196	40.8

Sources: Ministry of Finance, Japan, *Annual Report of Customs and Tariffs Bureau*, June 30, 1997; and *IMF Country Reports* (various issues).

2.2. Recent trade patterns: composition

The composition of trade flows provides potential insight into the prospects for increased or decreased trade integration between North America and Japan, as well as sources of future trade frictions. For example, Canadian exports to Japan are highly concentrated in crude material and resource-based manufactures. Within this category, a handful of products comprise the bulk of Canadian exports. They include wood products, coal, metal ores, cereals and oil seeds, and pulp. These import categories are declining in importance in Japan, as the economy becomes increasingly focused on producing technology-intensive secondary manufactures and services, and as Japan continues to shift to offshore production in many resource-consuming and resource-processing sectors. Furthermore, major new threats to Canadian producers of raw materials and primary manufactures have arisen in Southeast Asia and South America which should further reduce Japan's relative importance to Canada as a destination for exports (Nakamura and Vertinsky, 1994). Dwindling supplies of fish and domestic restrictions on logging forests further constrain the future growth of Canadian exports to Japan.

The principal categories of Japanese exports to Canada differ markedly from the leading exports from Canada to Japan. Specifically, road vehicles and parts dominate in accounting for over 40 per cent of total Japanese exports to Canada. Other leading Japanese exports to Canada are office machinery and computers, and telecommunications and recording equipment. Exports of final products in the road vehicles segment have been declining in importance relative to exports of parts and semi-finished products, as Japan has increased its foreign direct investment in the North American automobile sector. It is less clear whether the increase in Japanese direct investment in the North American road vehicles and parts sector has increased or decreased (on net balance) Japanese exports to North America in this industry; however, it does appear that outward FDI and exports are complementary in the case of electronics products (Ries and Head, 1994).

The outlook for Japanese exports to Canada therefore depends quite heavily upon the outlook for Canadian domestic demand for transportation and electronic equipment, as well as the competitiveness of Japanese suppliers of these products compared to other potential suppliers. Since these are matters for speculation, little of a conclusive nature can be said; however, it seems clear that Canadian tariffs against imported Japanese vehicles will be maintained for the foreseeable future, and that the continuation of the Canadian 7 per cent tariff against Japanese imports of vehicles, which does not apply to the Canadian units of the Big Three auto-makers, represents a continuing disadvantage for Japanese affiliates in Canada. This means that the US affiliates can bring in vehicles made by their parents outside of Canada (to round out their product offerings in Canada) duty-free, while Japanese affiliates must pay a tariff for the same privilege.[4]

---

[4] Japan continues to complain about this "unfair" treatment which applies because the Canadian units of the Big Three US auto-makers are members of the 1965 Canada–US Auto Pact. See Keenan (1998).

The transportation equipment sector is also a prominent component of the trade linkage between the US and Japan. For example, in the first half of the 1990s, vehicles and auto parts comprised around one-quarter of all US merchandise imports from Japan. The US market has clearly been a major target for Japanese auto companies: the exports of vehicles and parts to the US accounted for over 40 per cent of total Japanese exports of those products (Donnelly, 1996). Electronic goods including computers, consumer electronic appliances, imaging equipment, and the like have also been important Japanese exports to the United States. Taken together, the SITC-7 category (machinery and transport equipment) has accounted for nearly 80 per cent of Japanese exports to the US in recent years.[5] US exports of vehicles and parts to Japan have traditionally been small in both relative and absolute terms, although there has been some increase in recent years owing to the exporting of US-made vehicles to Japan by Japanese affiliates in the United States. However, automobiles only accounted for some 3.5 per cent of Japanese imports from the US in 1996. The share of the machinery and transport equipment category in US exports to Japan has reached around 40 per cent in recent years. Food and beverages have accounted for about 20 per cent of US exports to Japan, with raw materials and fuels adding another 10 per cent. Parenthetically, it is interesting to note that the intra-industry trade in computers and related goods is more balanced than the overall trade relation. For instance, in 1996, Japan's exports of computers and ICs to the US amounted to about 13.7 billion dollars, while imports from the US reached 12 billion dollars (Asahi Shimbun, 1998). One reason is arguably the heavy US pressure on Japan to improve market access for US firms in these sectors, e.g. through the Semiconductor Trade Agreements dating back to the mid-1980s (see further Bergsten and Noland, 1993; and Tyson, 1992).

Since patterns of revealed comparative advantage tend to be relatively stable over time, it seems unlikely that patterns of merchandise trade between the United States and Japan will change markedly over the foreseeable future. In this context, the potential for future growth in Japanese–US trade in manufactures should primarily reflect the future economic growth rates of the two countries, as well as exchange rate patterns. A potentially more significant future structural influence on US–Japanese economic linkages is the anticipated steady growth in the absolute and relative sizes of service sector activities such as health care, telecommunications, financial services and environmental services in both countries, but especially in Japan.[6] These tend to be sectors in which US companies are acknowledged to be world leaders and where exploitation of firm-specific competitive advantages will likely oblige US producers to undertake substantially more FDI in Japan than has been true in the past. We therefore turn to a review of FDI linkages between North America and Japan.

---

[5] For details, see the US Census Bureau web site, at www.census.gov/foreign-trade/sitc1/.

[6] In a recent speech, a MITI official identified several sectors that MITI has highlighted as having especially favorable high-growth potential. They include information services, environment, health care and social services. See Arai (1998).

2.3. Direct investment linkages

As noted above, FDI is another facet of economic integration. To the extent that trade and FDI are complementary ways of serving foreign markets, trends in trade will mirror trends in FDI; however, since trade and FDI are imperfect complements, at best, and substitutes in specific circumstances, focusing on FDI behavior does add a useful additional perspective on the economic linkages between countries. As well, the magnitude and nature of FDI flows create separable (to some extent) policy issues from those surrounding trade flows. For example, inward FDI from Japan has generally been considered more desirable by North American governments than imports from Japan. At the same time, the limited degree of exporting to Japan from North America, at least from the perspective of the US government, has been partly linked to the limited amount of outward FDI from the United States to Japan.

The growth in the absolute and relative importance of Japanese FDI in the United States over the period of the 1970s and 1980s is well known.[7] Thus, by the mid-1990s, Japanese companies accounted for almost one-quarter of the stock of foreign-owned assets in the United States. To be sure, the relative importance of Japanese FDI in the United States is smaller by other measures such as share of total employment in all foreign-owned firms (Graham and Krugman, 1995: 27). Also, European MNCs remain the largest single source of inward FDI into the United States, regardless of whether FDI is measured in stocks or flows. For instance, the stock of European FDI in the US in 1997 was estimated at around 425 billion dollars (on a historical-cost basis), while the stock of Japanese investment stood at 124 billion dollars. The same year, Europe accounted for 60 billion of the 91 billion dollars of FDI entering the US; the flow from Japan was about 9.4 billion dollars.[8]

What is noteworthy (and also well known) is the relatively small role that inward FDI has played in the Japanese economy (see further Blomström, Konan and Lipsey, Chapter 11 this volume). A relatively crude measure of the role of inward FDI in linking Japan to other economies is the ratio of FDI inflows to total imports. In a rough and ready way, this measure "holds constant" the degree to which the Japanese economy is open to foreign competition and focuses specifically upon the mode that foreign suppliers have chosen (as a first-best or second-best method) to serve the Japanese market. Over the period 1993–6, the simple average of this ratio was 1.63 per cent. By way of comparison, the ratio for the United States over the same period was 7.93 per cent.[9]

Table 12.5 suggests the relative importance of linkages to North America through the direct investment process from Japan's perspective. Specifically, it shows the share

---

[7] See, for example, Graham and Krugman (1995).

[8] The data on FDI in the US are taken from the Bureau of Economic Analysis web site, at www.bea.doc.gov/bea/di/longcty.htm (June 30, 1999).

[9] Authors' calculations from data in Ministry of Finance (1997a,b) and Council of Economic Advisors (1998). Another indication of relative FDI "openness" is provided by the following observation: the inward FDI stock in Japan is less than one-tenth the value of Japan's outward FDI stock. The ratio for the US is closer to eight-tenths. Moreover, Japan accounts for only around 6 per cent of the total stock of US outward FDI, while the US accounts for approximately 40 per cent of the total stock of Japan's outward FDI. See Donnelly (1996).

TABLE 12.5. *North America's share of Japanese outward and inward FDI (percentages)*

	1993	1994	1995	1996
Japanese Direct Investment abroad	42.4	43.3	45.2	47.9
Inward Direct Investment	35.2	45.8	48.3	31.7

Source: Ministry of Finance, Japan, International Finance Bureau, *Conditions of Inward and Outward Direct Investment* (1997b).

of total outward Japanese FDI that went to North America, as well as the share of total inward FDI to Japan accounted for by North American MNCs.[10] The latter statistic is fairly volatile, as total flows of inward FDI are relatively small, as noted above. Thus, over the period 1993–6, North America was the destination for between 40 per cent and 50 per cent of total outward Japanese FDI, while North American companies were the source of between 35 per cent and 50 per cent of inward FDI to Japan. An implication of the data in Table 12.5 is that the North American direct investment linkage is relatively important to Japan in the context of Japan's total inward and outward FDI flows.

It is difficult to predict future trends in North American–Japanese direct investment flows. In particular, direct investment flows to and from a region are heavily conditioned by the real economic growth rates of those regions, as well as other factors such as relative costs and expected exchange rate relationships.[11] Government policies can also influence FDI flows directly (e.g. by increasing or decreasing legislative and regulatory barriers to FDI) and indirectly (e.g. by increasing or decreasing barriers to trade in goods and by impacting the overall profitability of capital investment in the regions). Hence, a "bottom-up" forecast of future FDI flows would presumably require forecasts of the relevant determinants, as well as the weights attached to those determinants.

A detailed structural analysis of FDI linkages between North America and Japan is clearly beyond the mandate of this essay.[12] Moreover, the current deep and prolonged recession in Japan, combined with the economic turmoil in the Asia-Pacific region, may be influencing FDI flows in fundamental ways that are not readily captured by traditional structural models of the FDI process. For example, the liquidity crisis confronting many Japanese financial organizations has undoubtedly made those companies much more receptive to equity-sharing partnerships with or takeovers by American companies than they have been in the past. It has also arguably made

[10] Our understanding is that inward FDI from North America does not include FDI from Japanese affiliates based in North America.

[11] For a review of the literature on the determinants of FDI flows from the host country perspective, see Caves (1996).

[12] A more detailed analysis of inward and outward FDI for Japan is provided by Blomström, Konan, and Lipsey's contribution to this volume (Chapter 11).

Japanese (corporate) borrowers and household savers more willing to deal with foreign-owned financial institutions. On the other hand, the uncertainty surrounding long-term exchange rate relationships in the Asia-Pacific region may be delaying or discouraging FDI flows that would otherwise occur.

Our tentative view is that FDI, particularly from the United States to Japan, is likely to be a much more important source of welfare gains from closer economic integration between the two countries than it has been in the past. One reason is that demographic trends in North America and Japan (primarily the absolute and relative growth of older, retired individuals) will accentuate demand for new product offerings, as well as cheaper and better product offerings, in service-sector areas such as finance (e.g. insurance and retirement savings vehicles), health care, tourism, consulting, and so forth. These include sectors in which the United States has a well recognized comparative advantage. Direct trade in these services is problematic, and gains from trade are generally captured through the activities of affiliates located in host countries.

2.4. Summary

The primary economic linkage between North America and Japan takes the form of Japan's trade and investment linkages with the United States. There are no compelling reasons to believe that this situation will change significantly over the foreseeable future. Japan's trade and investment linkages with Canada are likely to become relatively less important over time given the decline in Canada's natural resource-based trade sector. Mexico's relatively low-cost labor force combined with tariff-free access to the US market suggests that it is a potentially attractive site for increased Japanese FDI within North America to serve the US and Canadian markets; however, NAFTA domestic content requirements limit the ability of Japanese MNCs to source inputs for their Mexican affiliates from outside North America.[13]

From the US perspective, Japan is becoming a relatively less important trading partner. Again, there is no obvious reason to expect a significant reversal of this situation in the foreseeable future. This decreasing importance may encourage US policymakers to be less committed to devoting resources and political goodwill to the "Japan brief" and more inclined to implement unilateral policy initiatives, some of which may have adverse economic consequences for Japan. The declining borrowing needs of the US government may also indirectly weaken the latter's commitment to preserving friendly economic relations with Japan (hitherto a large buyer of US government debt) in the face of what is perceived by American policymakers to be a continuation of Japanese mercantilistic policies. Even though Canada and Mexico share some of Japan's concerns about unilateral trade initiatives undertaken by the US, they are unlikely to champion Japanese efforts to blunt such initiatives.

US demands for a more "open" Japanese domestic market remain a prominent feature of US–Japanese relations. The focus of policy attention in recent years has

---

[13] Japanese FDI in Mexico to produce and assemble automobiles and components is the major manifestation, to date, of this phenomenon.

shifted from eliminating tariff barriers to eliminating nontariff barriers to market access, including barriers to inward FDI.[14] With respect to nontariff barriers to market access, the prolonged recession in Japan combined with that country's banking crisis may be having a substantial *de facto* liberalizing impact that will, over time, defuse much of the rancor surrounding current Japanese–US economic relations. In particular, it appears to be increasingly feasible for US MNCs to invest in Japan, either through wholly-owned affiliates or as part of an alliance with local companies. Hence, while US policymakers may have less patience for negotiating with Japan, it may also feel increasingly less provoked by Japanese trade and industrial policies.

3. The Future Potential for Japanese–North American Linkages

Given the large absolute size of merchandise trade flows between the US and Japan, there is little doubt that trade policy issues will remain important, and that substantial gains from trade make it worthwhile for both countries to address those issues. Nevertheless, our main proposition in this section is that substantial new gains to closer economic integration between the two countries are more likely to be realized from increased bilateral FDI, especially from increased FDI in Japan by US MNCs.

3.1. Overview of the "Trade Dimensions"

Without attempting to predict the magnitude of future trade flows between the US and Japan, it seems safe to conclude that traditional policy initiatives to promote trade (such as tariff reductions) have been largely exploited.[15] Less traditional efforts, notably structural initiatives to improve market access for US firms, have had unclear success (Schoppa, 1997). In the latter regard, US policymakers have been putting increased emphasis on competition policy reforms within Japan. For example, the final two areas covered under the Structural Impediments Initiative (SII) talks between the US and Japan dealt with Japan's competition policies. In order to mitigate "exclusionary business practices," the US urged the Japanese to strengthen their enforcement of the Anti-Monopoly Law and (specifically) to aggressively attack price cartels, group boycotts, and related conspiracies to close markets that were normally open to competitive imports. There were also calls for Japan to supplement traditional antitrust enforcement with regulatory reforms designed to foster greater openness and accountability within "*keiretsu* business groups."

The opinion of most observers is that the Japanese response to US calls for competition policy reforms was quite modest (Schoppa, 1997; and Donnelly, 1996). In

[14] Rounds of multilateral trade negotiations have left Japan's average tariff level for industrial and mining products below that of the United States. See Sato (1996). While there is a consensus that Japanese non-tariff barriers to trade and investment are significant, there is less agreement about their precise nature and relative significance. See, for example, Ozawa (1997).

[15] We say this notwithstanding Japan's refusal at the November 1998 APEC meetings to allow more imports of forestry and fish products.

particular, while the Japanese agreed to stiffen penalties under the Anti-Monopoly Law, the Japanese government did not accede to the American demands for restrictions limiting cross-shareholdings among *keiretsu* firms.

At the same time, the deregulation agreement reached by the two countries and announced in June 1997 potentially liberalized several sectors in which FDI flows are a prominent mode of international business. The June 1997 Agreement specifically covered trade in telecommunications, housing, medical devices and pharmaceuticals, financial services, and distribution. In telecommunications, Japan agreed to lower the rates that telecommunications carriers must pay to connect to Japan's local telecommunications network, to introduce measures to facilitate access to land and physical facilities that new companies need to construct their own networks, and to permit a doubling of the number of channel broadcasts that can be provided to Japanese consumers. Each of these measures should make US FDI in this sector more profitable. In the area of medical devices and pharmaceuticals, Japan is committed to cut the approval period for new drugs and to expand the acceptance of foreign clinical data in its approval of new medical devices and pharmaceuticals. The measures being taken for the financial sector include an easing of the registration process for new securities companies and an expansion in the scope of financial products that banks and security firms, including investment trusts, will be allowed to market. The measures included in the "Big Bang" reform package are seen by some US trade officials as significantly enhancing the ability of US mutual fund companies, among others, to establish branches in Japan.[16] Finally, Japan has abolished its Large-Scale Retail Store Law, which is expected to lead to an increased placement of US retail establishments in Japan.

At this stage, it is unclear where future US demands for competition policy reforms are likely to go. It seems unlikely that bilateral negotiations in this area will be completely successful in challenging the complex network of long-term relationships and reliance on relational contracting which are at the heart of the informal barriers to trade that are suggested to thwart US exporters. While US officials continue to express dissatisfaction with continued structural barriers to competition in Japan, they are not suggesting specific new initiatives (Schlesinger, 1998).[17] Nor are multilateral approaches to harmonizing competition policies likely to provide any significant breakthroughs in the foreseeable future.[18]

A policy direction that the US might take in the future is to "negotiate around Japan." From Japan's perspective, the most worrisome potential manifestation of this direction would be significant efforts on the part of the US to deepen its economic integration with the European Union (EU). The 1998 agreement between the US and the EU to begin implementing a "Transatlantic Economic Partnership" action plan,

---

[16] The "Big Bang" package is discussed in more detail by Ito and Melvin in Chapter 7 of this volume. See also Press Briefing of Deputy US Trade Representative Richard Fisher (May 15, 1998).

[17] Deregulation of Japan's energy sector including regulations regarding inspection and testing of equipment, as well as narrow technical standards for equipment is one recently announced US government objective.

[18] An overview of the environment for global competition policies is provided by papers in Graham and Richardson (1997).

aiming to enhance US–EU trade relations, may be a harbinger of this policy direction. Bilateral discussions with the EU will be initially focused on issues that have traditionally been contentious at the multilateral level; namely, agriculture, intellectual property rights, insurance and telecommunications.[19] While a free trade initiative between the US and the EU is an unlikely political event in the foreseeable future, indications that the US is willing to address trade issues with a triad member outside of the usual multilateral forum should be a worrisome development for Japanese policymakers. In addition, continued negotiations to structure a Free Trade Area of the Americas (FTAA) may further encourage US policymakers to limit, if not abandon, good-faith efforts to improve and strengthen trade linkages between the US and Japan.

A potentially more worrisome development is that the US government will ultimately agree with calls for "isolating" the Japanese economy if specific US export targets are not met (Wolff, 1992). Actions in this direction might include the imposition of tariff and nontariff barriers to Japanese imports, as well as restrictions on cooperative agreements between Japanese and American firms in areas such as high-technology. US frustration with Japanese government trade liberalization efforts and reactions thereto may be less temperate than in the past because of the demise of the Soviet Union as a military threat in the Pacific. The role of Japan as a primary ally in the Pacific almost certainly mitigated the calls of "trade hawks" in the US government for economic retaliation against Japan. Moreover, as US concerns about military threats from the Soviet Union have largely disappeared, concerns about economic threats (most notably from Japan) have increased. For example, Japanese organizations such as MITI and JETRO are increasingly seen as potential enemies engaged in subversive activities such as industrial espionage (Holstein, 1997).[20]

More vigorous competition policy and deregulation initiatives by the Japanese government would certainly improve the bilateral negotiating environment; however, it is unclear (as noted above) how much impact they would have on US exports to Japan. Moreover, there is no necessary reason to believe that US suggestions to modify Japan's Anti-Monopoly Law would lead to Japan's antitrust policy becoming an improved instrument of economic efficiency. In this regard, there continues to be substantial disagreement in the academic literature surrounding the economic welfare justifications for attacking contractual restrictions such as exclusive supply and exclusive dealing arrangements, resale price maintenance, territorial restrictions, and so forth.

The one point of fairly widespread agreement among economists is that policymakers should aim to keep markets competitive wherever they are inherently structurally contestable. Inward FDI is acknowledged to be a major source of contestability in host country markets, especially in markets characterized by above-average

---

[19] See "Clinton's Trade Crusade", *Business Week*, June 8, 1998, 34–5.

[20] In the long run, it is also possible that the US may enter into closer partnerships with either Russia or China, which would of course reduce the importance of Japan to the US as a defense ally in the Pacific. However, it is difficult to imagine either of these two countries as a stable and predictable partner for the US in the near future.

barriers to entry. Hence, eliminating government-imposed barriers to inward FDI should be a major focus of Japanese policymakers committed to "boosting industrial competitiveness and the efficiency of Japanese service industries." (Arai, 1998: 7.)

3.2. Overview of the "Investment Dimension"

Increasingly, US policymakers and observers have been linking the low import penetration of the Japanese domestic market to barriers to inward FDI in Japan (Tyson, 1998). The broad evidence from the academic literature supports the view that FDI and trade are complements, on balance: the primary impact of FDI, at least in the manufacturing industries, has been to encourage and facilitate increased geographical specialization of production through increased intra-industry trade (Globerman, 1994).

While structural features and government regulations that discourage imports into Japan also arguably discourage inward FDI, there are reasons to believe that changes in the Japanese business environment related to the ongoing banking and financial crises in Japan are directly enhancing the environment for inward FDI and (indirectly, over time) the environment facing US exporters. In particular, liquidity problems in Japan's financial sector have opened up more opportunities for foreign companies to invest in Japan in activities that were hitherto difficult to enter (Shirouzo, 1998).[21] This interpretation is consistent with evidence that *keiretsu* firms have traditionally been heavily influenced by their banks to produce at levels beyond those warranted by pure profit-maximization, and that these higher levels of output have made entry into markets with strong *keiretsu* presence difficult (Weinstein and Yafeh, 1995). The diminishing influence of Japanese domestic banks related to their limited ability to lend money, and the growing importance of "arms-length" financial intermediaries, including US-owned pension and mutual fund managers, promise to invigorate the profit-maximization motive among private-sector managers in Japan.

The structure of the Japanese economy also suggests a growing potential indirect demand for inward FDI. The aging Japanese population will create an increasing demand for health care-related services. The need for Japanese savers to earn relatively high rates of return on their private savings to create wealth for their retirement is encouraging a growing demand for wealth management services. The relatively low penetration of advanced computer communications among Japanese businesses and households will create a demand for both hardware and software companies supplying the relevant goods and services, as well as consulting companies familiar with new applications of computer communications, such as electronic commerce. It is in precisely these sectors that US companies enjoy well-recognized firm-level advantages that serve as a platform for establishing affiliates in Japan.

---

[21] Deregulation, at least in Japan's financial sector, has also apparently encouraged Japanese banks and other financial institutions to form alliances with foreign banks eager to expand in Japan. See Spindle (1998).

Lawrence (1993) argued that difficulties in acquiring existing Japanese companies help explain the low level of foreign ownership in Japan. He highlighted stock cross-holdings of Japanese corporate groups as one of the main barriers to foreign acquisitions of Japanese firms. Ownership by stable shareholders such as insurance companies, or *keiretsu* members with close ties to the management of "target companies," makes hostile takeovers more difficult, much like "poison pills" in the US or Europe. Lawrence also noted the absence of national treatment for foreign companies contemplating Japanese acquisitions. In particular, notification and allowed completion times were different for foreign-owned acquirers. More recently, the Japanese government agreed to remove the requirement that foreign firms notify the Ministry of Finance thirty days in advance of foreign direct investments. It also narrowed national security restrictions on FDI, relaxed takeover bid rules, and enhanced disclosure requirements, all of which should make acquisitions easier. Nevertheless, some observers still believe that these changes will not have much impact in the absence of a compromise on the cross-shareholding issue (Schoppa, 1997).

As noted above, the ongoing financial crisis in Japan is encouraging a *de facto* weakening of FDI restrictions associated with cross-shareholdings. Nevertheless, there are other margins upon which US policymakers might be expected to push to further liberalize the FDI environment in Japan. They include government R&D subsidies, which advantage Japanese producers in the domestic market, and structural barriers taking a variety of forms including standards, testing and certification procedures, and government procurement and bidding practices (Ozawa, 1997). These latter issues are certainly not unique to the US–Japan relationship and have been featured in both multilateral and regional trade negotiations; however, recent developments provide little cause for optimism that significant progress on these issues will be achieved through international organizations such as the WTO, the OECD, or APEC. The unsuccessful conclusion of OECD-orchestrated talks on a Multilateral Agreement on Investment (MAI), as well as the recent failure of APEC to advance its trade liberalization agenda, underscore the difficulties that US policymakers face in promoting their agenda at the multilateral level.[22]

3.3. The direction of US policy

As suggested in an earlier section, US frustration with Japanese trade and FDI policies may encourage the US to move more aggressively to isolate Japan by promoting trade and investment liberalization with other partners including the EU and South America. This strategy would be even more likely if US officials believed that bilateral or regional bargaining would create a more "fluid" negotiating environment at the WTO level. On the other hand, Asia is too important a market for American policymakers to ignore, and the threat of a Japanese-dominated Asian trading bloc has always been of concern to US officials (Frieden, 1993). Moreover, the US has an

---

[22] With respect to FDI specifically, APEC members have not shown a willingness to go beyond WTO initiatives. See Edwards (1997).

interest in the existence of a strong "anchor" economy in Asia that can provide financial and economic linkages to help stabilize currency movements and promote long-term economic development among emerging economies in that region. As long as Japan is the most likely anchor economy, a truly serious deterioration in US–Japanese economic relations will be unacceptable to American policymakers. However, Japan's most likely future rival, China, has arguably gained stature amongst Western countries by virtue of its superior economic performance during the Asian financial crisis, including its ability to maintain a stable value of the yuan relative to the US dollar for the first years following the crisis. While China is far from open to imports and FDI, US officials may not be as cynical about China's professed motives to liberalize their domestic economy as they are about Japan's professed motives. Hence, in the long run, if the negotiations with Japan do not produce the desired results, it is possible that the US may come to invest more in establishing closer economic integration with China.

In summary, the "constrained" economic conflict between the US and Japan is likely to continue for the foreseeable future. The growth of US FDI in Japan is a force that could restrain the US from escalating economic conflict with Japan through unilateral measures such as the adoption of aggressive reciprocity in allowing inward FDI, or applying trade sanctions against Japan on a more widespread basis. At the same time, the clock may be winding down on the restraint that US officials perceive themselves as exercising towards Japan. Perhaps the most troubling future scenario for Japan in this regard is a vigorous attempt by the US to "fast track" closer economic relations with China.

An implication of the foregoing argument is that Japanese policymakers are confronting potentially much larger economic costs associated with promoting or tolerating domestic trade and FDI restrictions than in the past. While a consideration of the domestic political forces conditioning Japanese domestic economic policies is beyond the scope of this paper, casual analysis suggests that Japan's major MNCs and their employees remain the most likely champions of domestic economic reform. Hence, if our speculations are reasonable, Japanese managers of those companies may need to become much more aggressive champions of domestic trade and investment liberalization than they have been in the past. Moreover, the resistance to import competition within Japan may itself be weakened by increased foreign direct investment in Japan. This is because the economic rents generated by trade protection will increasingly be shared by foreign-owned companies, and these shared rents are unlikely to be as easily tolerated by the rest of Japanese society as rents earned by Japanese-owned companies.

4. Other Areas for Economic Cooperation

In this section, we briefly consider other prominent issues surrounding the US–Japanese economic relationship which offer the potential for closer economic relations between the two countries or the potential for additional conflict.

4.1. Technological cooperation

A long-standing concern on the part of US officials is that the United States has disproportionately financed basic research which, in turn, has provided the basis for the industrial patenting that Japanese and other foreign companies have undertaken in the postwar period.[23] A basic problem in evaluating this claim is the US government's substantial funding of defense-related research and development. This type of R&D has spawned enormous breakthroughs, such as the semiconductor chip and the Internet, that, in turn, have provided enormous industrial opportunities for companies around the world. Given the US role as the leader of the Western Alliance in the postwar period, as well as the weakened state of the Japanese and European economies in the early part of that period, it was inevitable that the US would shoulder the major responsibility for investing in the development of new weapons systems and related technologies. Even at this point in time, it would be unrealistic for American leaders to expect Japan to assume the burden of a large military R&D budget.

Nevertheless, Japanese public funding of R&D has remained relatively low compared to US government funding of R&D in the postwar period. For example, Beason and Weinstein (1996) note that publicly financed R&D is approximately 50 per cent of gross R&D expenditure in the US versus only 20 per cent in Japan. With respect to government funding of industrial R&D, the US government accounted for around 35 per cent as compared to only 2 per cent on the part of the Japanese government. In short, if government funding of R&D creates technological spillovers that are accessible to foreign as well as domestic firms, the US government has arguably been creating a disproportionate share of those technological spillovers.

Whatever the "objective" merits of the US position, it can be argued that it is increasingly in Japan's self-interest to play a greater role in expanding the developed world's stock of basic scientific knowledge. For one thing, Japan is increasingly in a position to benefit from the commercialization of basic science. For example, developing new techniques to deal with chronically sick elderly patients will be an increasingly relevant policy issue for Japan. Basic scientific breakthroughs in the areas of genetic engineering and biophysics will likely underlie any substantial innovations in the practical treatment of the elderly. As another example, environmental protection and remediation continue to gain in prominence as policy issues in both developed and developing countries. Basic scientific knowledge about both the causes and consequences of environmental and biochemical hazards will help promote an efficient set of policies to deal with those hazards. As a large and densely populated industrial country, Japan has a strong self-interest in promoting knowledge gains in this area.

It can also be argued that, barring a significant change in the existing geopolitical situation, the US will continue to scale down significantly its funding of major defense system-related initiatives, at the same time as it begins to emphasize strengthening its

---

[23] A description and evaluation of this criticism is provided in Mowery (1993). See also Maskus and McDaniel (1998).

defense response capabilities to international and domestic terrorism and regional conflicts involving small military powers. Japan has some shared interests in strengthening its own capabilities to deal with domestic terrorism. It will also perforce need to assume greater responsibility for protecting its sea lanes and for contributing to equipping military regional alliances, as the decreasing real US defense budget forces a contraction of the military-related expenditures that the US has made on behalf of its allies in Western Europe and the Pacific.

In sum, it seems increasingly beneficial for the Japanese government to assume more of a responsibility for funding basic research having "public goods" qualities. Doing so through cooperative arrangements with US academic and government research organizations offers a potentially prominent vehicle for bilateral cooperation. To be sure, US critics of Japan also stress the "one-way" nature of knowledge flows related to commercial innovation. Indeed, a fairly common criticism is that Japanese firms have routinely gained access to proprietary technology of US firms without paying a "fair" price for it. There is no serious political momentum in the US to block the transfer of commercial technology from the US to Japan, nor is any likely given the manifest futility of any such effort. Nevertheless, the convergence of Japan's industrial technological capabilities with US capabilities obliges Japanese businesses to do more "innovating" and less "technology borrowing," since there is relatively less foreign technology to borrow, especially for manufacturing companies. Opportunities for a two-way flow of commercial technology will inevitably grow over time. The intrusion of Japanese government agencies such as MITI into this flow would, however, be viewed with suspicion by US officials and would also likely dampen the growth and deepening of commercial alliances between Japanese and American companies.

4.2. Cooperation on global economic policies

A number of major multilateral trade and investment issues are on the negotiation agenda. They include issues ranging from the liberalization of trade in agriculture and services, whether and how to incorporate environmental and labor standards into trade agreements, the protection of intellectual property, international cooperation on competition policy and its enforcement, rights of establishment for and national treatment of foreign investors, and transparency and disclosure rules for financial institutions.

The US and Japan continue to disagree about the appropriate speed and scope of liberalization in sectors such as agriculture and investment, as well as about the harmonization of antitrust enforcement initiatives; however, Japan has a very strong interest in constraining US trade policy initiatives within a multilateral trade framework. The vitality and legitimacy of the WTO are therefore of substantial importance to Japan, since multilateral initiatives to constrain the application of US Anti-dumping and Countervailing Trade laws will be more effective in the long run than bilateral or regionally focused initiatives, such as APEC. In the new millennium, the robustness of the WTO as the major multilateral trade and investment forum will depend upon the continued commitment of the United States to that agency. This commitment would arguably be substantially reinforced if Japan finally took a leading role in proposing trade and investment liberalization initiatives through the WTO's auspices.

In areas such as the application of environmental and labor standards to trade and investment relations, the US and Japan have a shared interest in ensuring that environmental and labor standards are not used as barriers to trade among developed countries, or as inappropriate restrictions on the economic development efforts of developing countries. Collaboration between US and Japanese trade policy officials on these and related issues might also lead to improved harmonization of disputes in areas of trade and investment where the two countries have more diverging positions.

5. Summary and Conclusions

This paper has discussed some issues concerning trade, direct investment and other economic linkages between North America and Japan. Regarding trade, the US is likely to remain Japan's preeminent trading partner and a major contributor to Japan's trade surplus. At the same time, Japan is becoming a relatively less important trade partner for the US, and this trend is also likely to continue. On the other hand, Japan will likely be an absolutely and relatively more important destination for US FDI, and this increase in FDI has the potential to transform US–Japanese economic relations in more substantial ways than bilateral trade negotiations have done in the past. A number of sectors have particularly great potential for future gains from increased bilateral economic integration through the FDI process. They include financial services, health care, tourism, and consulting. Domestic demand for the outputs of these sectors will grow in Japan, partly for demographic reasons and partly because of the relatively high income elasticities characterizing those outputs.

US companies enjoy well-recognized firm-level advantages in a number of the sectors that are likely to enjoy robust growth in Japan (and the US) over the next few decades. The exploitation of those firm-specific advantages is more likely to proceed through outward FDI from the US than from increased US exports given the service-oriented nature of the outputs involved. Indirect economic integration between Japan and the US might also proceed through technical cooperation in areas such as defense, health and environmental protection, where companies and nonprofit institutions in both countries are carrying out research and development activities.

Although future developments in these areas offer potential economic gains, they also contain the potential for conflict. While it would be unfortunate, it seems likely (based upon past experience) that relations with North America will influence the direction of Japanese economic policy primarily through US threats to the bilateral trade relationship rather than through perceived gains to closer economic integration. In the trade area, we foresee continued US pressure on Japan to reduce various nontariff barriers to trade and to continue to reform competition policy. This type of pressure is not new to Japan, but US threats of retaliation may become more credible as Japan's relative importance as a trading partner for the US diminishes. Slow progress in resolving outstanding trade disputes may provoke the US to focus its policy attention elsewhere, including a renewed commitment to implementing a Free Trade Area of the Americas agreement, deeper economic integration with the EU, and closer economic relations with China. The consequences for Japan might be an increasingly isolated position among the developed countries in formulating trade and investment policies, as well as heightened risks of serious disruptions of its trade flows with North America.

In effect, we see the potential for much higher economic costs to Japan associated with its maintaining formal and informal barriers to protect domestic producers. At the same time, economic forces, including the continued severe recession in Japan, are promoting increased US FDI in Japan which, itself, will be a direct and indirect force for integrating the Japanese and US economies. Increased FDI flows offer the potential for mutual economic gains. A continued liberalization of Japanese restrictions on inward FDI—which remain significant in some service sectors—would not only contribute to making the Japanese economy more dynamic, but it could also diffuse some of the frictions that characterize trade relations between the US and Japan. However, in most industries, foreign investors have been kept out by the same barriers that impede the entry of new domestic firms. What is needed to facilitate FDI in these sectors is not only more active investment and competition policy, to keep markets contestable, but also changes in some of the structural characteristics of Japanese industry, such as cross-shareholding, discriminatory treatment of minority shareholders, rigid labor markets, and so forth.

Increased technological cooperation between the US and Japan offers the prospect of mutual gains in the form of increased innovation in "public goods" activities such as defense and environmental protection. It might also diffuse US–Japanese tensions surrounding US policy concerns that it has undertaken a disproportionately large share of basic R&D carried out by developed countries, while Japan has disproportionately exploited the technological spillovers of US-funded basic research for commercial purposes. Bilateral cooperation might involve the Japanese government assuming a heavier funding responsibility for basic research having "public goods" qualities, possibly in collaboration with US academic and government research organizations.

In summary, we have pointed to a number of areas where the bilateral relationship between Japan and North America is likely to result in pressure for reform of the Japanese economy. In some cases, this pressure will likely succeed in bringing about significant changes in the Japanese economy. In particular, US calls for an opening up of the Japanese service sector to increased foreign ownership will coincide with increases in Japanese domestic demand for many services, as a result of demographic and economic factors. It is also possible that a substantially increased presence of US-owned companies in Japan will itself contribute to further Japanese trade and investment liberalization, as well as to further domestic deregulation, as the perception spreads among Japanese interest groups that the rents generated by domestic protection are increasingly being shared by foreign producers.

REFERENCES

Arai, H. (1998), "A Scenario for Dynamic Recovery from the Asian Economic Crisis," address to the Thai–Japanese Association and JETRO Bangkok, Bangkok, Thailand, August 21.

Asahi Shimbun (1998), *Asahi Shimbun Japan Almanac 1998* (Tokyo: Asahi Shimbun).

Beason, R. and D. Weinstein (1996), "Growth, Economies of Scale and Targetting in Japan (1955–1990)," *Review of Economics and Statistics* (May), 286–95.

Bergsten, C. F. and M. Noland (1993), *Reconcilable Differences: United States–Japan Economic Conflict* (Washington: Institute for International Economics).

Blomström, M., A. Kokko, and S. Globerman (1998), "Regional Economic Integration and Foreign Direct Investment: The North American Experience," Working Paper No. 269, Stockholm School of Economics (Oct.).

Caves, R. E. (1996), *Multinational Enterprise and Economic Analysis*, 2nd edn. (Cambridge: Cambridge University Press).

Council of Economic Advisors, US (1998), *Economic Report of the President* (Washington: US Government Printing Office).

Donnelly, M. (1996), "Coping with Interdependence: Japan and the United States," in Dobson, Wendy and Hideo Sato (eds.), *Managing U.S.–Japanese Trade Disputes: Are There Better Ways?* (Ottawa: Centre for Trade Policy and Law), 22–130.

Edwards, L. J. (1997), *APEC's Agenda: 1997 and Beyond* (Washington: The Heritage Foundation).

Feldstein, M. (1990), "National Security Aspects of United States–Japan Economic Relations in the Pacific-Asian Region," in Jones, R. and A. Krueger (eds.), *The Political Economy of International Trade* (Cambridge: Blackwell), 449–57.

Flatters, F. and R. G. Harris (1995), "Trade and Investment: Patterns and Policy Issues in the Asia—Pacific Rim," in Dobson, Wendy and Frank Flatters (eds.), *Pacific Trade and Investment: Options for the 90's* (Kingston, Ont.: John Deutsch Institute), 111–40.

Frieden, J. A. (1993), "Domestic Politics and Regional Cooperation: The U.S., Japan and Pacific Money and Finance," in Frankel, J. A. and M. Kahler (eds.), *Regionalism and Rivalry: Japan and the United States in Pacific Asia* (Chicago: University of Chicago Press), 423–44.

Globerman, S. (1994), "The Public and Private Interests in Outward Direct Investment," in Globerman, S. (ed.), *Canadian-Based Multinationals* (Calgary: University of Calgary Press), 1–34.

Graham, E. M. and P. R. Krugman (1995), *Foreign Direct Investment in the United States* (Washington: Institute for International Economics).

——and J. D. Richardson (eds.) (1997), *Global Competition Policy* (Washington: Institute For International Economics).

Holstein, W. J. (1997), "With Friends Like These," *US News Online*, June 16.

Keenan, G. (1998), "Big Three Fight for the Tariff," *The Globe and Mail*, May 2, B3.

Lawrence, R. Z. (1991), "How Open is Japan?," in Krugman, Paul (ed.), *Trade with Japan: Has the Door Opened Wider?* (Chicago: University of Chicago Press), 9–38.

——(1993), "Japan's Low Level of Inward Investment: The Role of Inhibitions on Acquisitions," in Froot, K. A. (ed.), *Foreign Direct Investment* (Chicago: University of Chicago Press), 85–110.

Maskus, K. E. and C. McDaniel (1998), "Impacts of the Japanese Patent System on Productivity Growth," Discussion Papers in Economics 99-1, Department of Economics, University of Colorado at Boulder (Dec.).

Ministry of Finance, Japan (1997*a*), *Annual Report of Customs and Tariffs Bureau* (Tokyo: Customs and Tariffs Bureau).

——(1997*b*), *Conditions of Inward and Outward Direct Investment* (Tokyo: International Finance Bureau).

Mowery, D. C. (1993), "Japanese Technology and Global Influence," in Unger, D. and P. Blackburn (eds.), *Japan's Emerging Global Role* (Boulder: Lynne Rienner), 171–93.

Nakamura, M. and I. Vertinsky (1994), *Japanese Economic Policies and Growth* (Calgary: University of Alberta Press).

Ozawa, T. (1997), "Japan," in J. H. Dunning (ed.), *Governments, Globalization and International Business* (Oxford: Oxford University Press), 337–406.

Ries, J. C. and K. C. Head (1994), "Causes and Consequences of Japanese Direct Investment Abroad," in Globerman, Steven (ed.), *Canadian-Based Multinationals* (Calgary: University of Calgary Press), 303–39.

Sato, H. (1996), "Overview and Introduction," in Dobson, Wendy and Hideo Sato (eds.), *Managing US–Japanese Trade Disputes: Are There Better Ways?* (Ottawa: The Centre for Trade Policy and Law), 1–34.

Schlesinger, J. M. (1998), "Fault Lines: Behind US Rift with Japan," *Wall Street Journal*, April 13, A8.

Schoppa, L. J. (1997), *Bargaining with Japan: What American Pressure Can and Cannot Do* (New York: Columbia University Press).

Shirouzu, N. (1998), "US's Cargill Acts to Save Toshoku of Japan," *Wall Street Journal*, Oct. 13, A18.

Spindle, Bill (1997), "Outsiders are Set to Jump when 'Big Bang' Opens Finance," *Asian Wall Street Journal*, 19/51 (22 Dec.), 3.

Tyson, L. (1992), *Who's Bashing Whom? Trade Conflict in High-Technology Industries* (Washington: Institute for International Economics).

——(1998), "Don't Worry: China Isn't Following in Japan's Footsteps," *Business Week*, April 20, 26.

Weinstein, D. E. and Y. Yafeh (1995), "Japan's Corporate Groups: Collusive or Competitive? An Empirical Investigation of Kensetsu Behavior," *Journal of Industrial Economics*, 43 (Dec.), 359–76.

Wolff, A. W. (1992), "Improving United States Trade Policy," in Howell, T. R. (ed.), *Conflict Among Nations: Trade Policies in the 1990's* (Boulder: Westview Press), 527–98.

13 Japan as Number Three: Effects of European Integration

ARI KOKKO, BRUCE HENRY LAMBERT, AND FREDRIK SJÖHOLM

1. Introduction

A couple of decades ago, Ezra Vogel's book *Japan as Number One* attracted much attention and reflected the understanding that the US and Japan were the main players in the race for the top position in the world economy. In fact, the Japanese edition of Vogel's book is Japan's all-time, non-fiction bestseller by a Western author. Recently, however, international statistics on trade and market size have established a ranking with *Japan as Number Three*. The emergence of the European Single Market in the early 1990s has made the European Union (EU) the world's largest exporter, the second largest importer, and the world's second largest market (see Table 13.1). The establishment of the European Monetary Union in 1999 and the introduction of the European common currency, the Euro, has strengthened the Single Market and also led to coordination of national economic policies within the EU. It is fair to say that this development has been somewhat of a surprise for Japan, as well as for the EU—in many respects, the relations between Japan and Europe form the weak link in the Japan–US–Europe triad. A likely reason for the relatively underdeveloped ties between Japan and Europe is that Europe was, until recently, fragmented into fifteen more or less separate markets that were all much smaller and less attractive than the US market. The central question in this chapter is whether European integration will motivate a change in Japanese behavior towards Europe.

Hence, this chapter will discuss how European integration has influenced and will continue to influence relations between Japan and Europe. The first part of the chapter describes past Japanese trade and foreign direct investment (FDI) relations with Europe and the US. The second part includes a brief summary of the Single Market Program, the EMU, and the plans for an eastern enlargement of the EU, and discusses how these developments may affect Japanese trade and foreign direct investment. Here, we will find reason to distinguish between effects at the macro and micro levels. At the macro level, it is clear that the establishment of the Single Market and the EMU have made Europe more similar to the US as a potential destination for Japanese exports and as a location for Japanese FDI. This implies significant increases in the trade and investment contacts between Japan and Europe. At the micro level, however, many Japanese companies are facing various obstacles to increased trade and investment in Europe. A history of voluntary export restraints and other anticompetitive practices make it difficult and costly—in some cases perhaps even impossible—to increase market shares in Europe, which suggests that

TABLE 13.1. *Leading exporters and importers in world merchandise trade 1998, excluding intra-EU trade (billion US$ and percentages)*

Exporters	Value	Share of world exports	Importers	Value	Share of world imports
EU-15	813.8	20.3	US	944.6	22.5
US	683.0	17.0	EU-15	801.4	19.1
Japan	388.0	9.7	Japan	280.5	6.7

Source: WTO (www.wto.org/wto/intltrad/009app2.htm), June 28, 1999.

the short- and medium-run response to European integration may turn out to be weaker than what the macro analysis implies.

The third part of the chapter looks at the European view of Japan, in order to identify the main areas of interest and concern from a European perspective. The question here is to what extent, and in which sectors, Europe will try to influence Japanese development. The fourth section summarizes and concludes the chapter.

2. Japanese Trade and Foreign Direct Investment

The past few decades have witnessed the emergence of a new pattern in international production and trade. The production and export of simple manufactured goods have shifted away from the rich economies of Western Europe, North America, and Japan to more labor-abundant countries in Asia and South America. Some newly industrialized economies in East and Southeast Asia have even become significant producers of high-tech goods. Three large blocks of countries have increasingly come to dominate the world economy. A unified trading block has emerged in Europe as a result of the widening and deepening of European integration. The North American area has been united in NAFTA, with the US, Canada, and Mexico as members. The East Asian share of the world economy has increased as China, South Korea, Taiwan, and the ASEAN countries have managed to replicate aspects of the Japanese growth miracle of the 1950s and 1960s.

In light of this dynamic development of international production and trade, it is not surprising that the Japanese pattern of trade has changed significantly over the past decades. Both the commodity structure and the geographic distribution of imports and exports have adjusted to the changes in the world economy, although one measure of trade has stayed remarkably constant. The ratio of trade to GDP has remained at around 18 per cent since the 1950s, which is significantly lower than the corresponding ratio in the US (about 23 per cent) and Europe (where ratio of extra-EU trade to GDP is about 21 per cent, and the trade ratios of individual countries are in the range of 45–60 per cent).

Regarding the commodity structure of Japanese trade, it is clear that the largest changes are found on the export side. The main export goods in the 1950s were labor-intensive commodities such as textiles and light manufactures. The skill and capital intensity of exports has increased gradually since then, with products like TV sets and steel becoming important in the 1960s, and automobiles and capital goods expanding rapidly during the 1970s and 1980s. Since then, Japanese exports have become increasingly concentrated to the machinery sector, which has increased its share of total exports from around 40 per cent in 1970 to 70 per cent in 1995. The commodity structure of imports has also changed over time. The most important trend is an increase in imports of machinery products from less than 10 per cent in the early 1980s to 23 per cent in 1995. This is partly a result of the outsourcing of production by Japanese multinational corporations after the yen appreciation following the Plaza agreement in 1985, but also a sign of the increasing openness of the Japanese market.

The changes in the regional distribution of trade have been smaller than the changes in commodity structure. Table 13.2 shows that Asia has been the most important market for Japanese exports and the most important source of imports for almost every year since 1970. The relative importance of Asia as an export destination has increased somewhat over the period, which is easily explained by the rapid economic development in many of the countries in the region. Asia has also been the main source of Japanese imports, but the Asian share of Japanese imports has varied more than the export share over the period. This is largely a reflection of changes in oil prices, since several oil-producing countries are located in the region. The US share of Japanese exports has also varied significantly, and some of this variation appears to be related to variations in the bilateral dollar–yen exchange rate. The most notable feature of Table 13.2, both for exports and imports, is perhaps the relatively low share of Japanese trade with the EU. Japanese exports to the EU accounted for only 13 per cent of the total in 1970, with an increase to around 17 per cent in 1995. The share of imports from EU has been even lower.

From the figures presented above, it can be concluded that the trade contacts between Japan and the EU were relatively limited until at least the mid-1980s. One

TABLE 13.2. *Regional distribution of Japanese exports and imports (percentage of aggregate imports and exports)*

	Exports to					Imports from				
	1970	1980	1985	1990	1995	1970	1980	1985	1990	1995
Asia	34	38	33	35	39	41	57	52	43	42
US	31	24	38	32	28	29	18	20	23	23
EU	13	16	14	21	17	10	7	8	18	16

Sources: United Nations, *International Trade Statistics.*

reason is arguably the fragmentation of Europe into many different national markets, which made it relatively costly to export to Europe. The preparations for the establishment of the Single Market probably account for some of the increase in the European share of Japanese exports between 1985 and 1990 (as we will discuss in the next section), but the European share fell again during the first half of the 1990s. One reason why the share of Japanese exports to Europe has not increased since the early 1990s could be that Japanese firms have chosen to supply the European market through FDI rather than through exports. It is therefore appropriate to continue with an examination of the FDI flows between Japan and Europe.

Japanese outward FDI grew rapidly during the second half of the 1980s. Two factors are likely to explain much of this growth. First, the appreciation of the yen after the Plaza agreement forced Japanese firms to outsource labor-intensive production to more labor-abundant countries in Southeast Asia to remain competitive. Second, various nontariff barriers to trade in the US and Europe induced many Japanese firms to service their overseas markets through FDI rather than through exports. Hence, Japan's share of the world's outward FDI stock increased from around 4 per cent in 1980 to around 11 per cent in 1995, which makes Japan the world's third largest foreign investor in terms of foreign holdings, after the US and the UK (UNCTAD, 1996a).

Table 13.3 presents some data on the regional distribution of Japanese FDI. The pattern of FDI differs from that of trade in the sense that Asia is not the prime target: the share of Asia in Japan's outward direct investment is only about 17 per cent, in spite of the outsourcing of labor-intensive production since the mid-1980s. Japanese FDI is instead largely concentrated in North America, which accounted for some 44 per cent of Japan's overall FDI stocks in 1995. The concentration to North America has increased substantially since the 1980s, and more than 40 per cent of the FDI flows in the 1990s have been directed to this region. The amount of FDI in the EU

TABLE 13.3. *Regional distribution of Japanese outward FDI 1984–1995 (percentage of aggregate flows or stocks)*

Region	Flows (annual average)	Stocks	
	1991–5	1984	1995
EU–12	18.1	8.6	18.0
Other European OECD	0.7	3.7	1.0
Central and Eastern Europe	0.2	0.3	0.1
North America	43.9	29.8	43.9
South and East Asia	20.1	25.1	17.2
Latin America	8.6	18.1	11.5
Africa	1.1	4.4	1.6

Source: UNCTAD (1996a).

has been relatively modest compared to the investments made in the US, although the European share has increased significantly since the mid-1980s. It is also interesting to note the small Japanese presence in Central and Eastern Europe, despite the radical changes in this region during the past decade. The Japanese pattern differs from that of European, American, and even other Asian investors (such as South Korea) that have shown a larger interest in Central and Eastern Europe. Several explanations for the relatively low Japanese presence can be found: a weakly developed network of trading houses, JETRO offices, and other institutions in the region, as well as preferences to locate outsourcing types of FDI to Southeast Asia.

Whereas Japanese FDI outflows are high, the inflow of FDI to Japan is exceptionally low. Only about 1 per cent of the world's outwards stock of FDI is located in Japan. This figure is obviously much lower than what could be expected, considering that Japan accounts for about a sixth of the world's GDP. Moreover, average annual direct investment flows as a share of GDP amounted only to 0.03 per cent between 1991 and 1994. This can be compared to around 1 per cent in France, 1.4 per cent in the UK, and 0.55 per cent in the US. A host of different explanations for the low foreign presence in Japan have been suggested, ranging from bureaucratic obstacles to problems in recruitment and high production costs (see further e.g. Shinozaki and Endo, 1997; Blomström, Konan, and Lipsey, Chapter 11 this volume; and Globerman and Kokko, Chapter 12 this volume).

The shares of the EU and the US in Japan's inward FDI stocks are shown in Table 13.4. The EU share of foreign direct investment in Japan has increased substantially from around 16 per cent in 1980 to around 34 per cent in 1994. This increase has coincided with a decline in the US share from almost 60 per cent in 1980 to around 28 per cent in 1994.

Summarizing this discussion about Japanese trade and investment, two observations appear particularly important. First, the Japanese economy appears to be relatively closed compared to most other industrialized economies, judging from the low import shares and limited inflows of FDI. Second, the trade and investment contacts with the EU are relatively weak, at least compared with the contacts between Japan and the US, although the advent of the European Single Market has apparently contributed to an increase in the absolute and relative importance of Europe. It is mainly the Japanese exports and outflows of FDI to the EU that remain relatively small, whereas Japanese imports and inflows of FDI from the EU are roughly

TABLE 13.4. *EU and US shares of FDI in Japan (percentages)*

	Flows 1968–79	Stock 1980	Flows 1990–4	Stock 1994
EU	15	16	34	34
US	64	59	32	28

Source: UNCTAD (1996*b*).

comparable to the ones from the US. The next section turns to a discussion of the possible effects of continuing European integration on the relations between Japan and Europe.

3. Effects of European Integration

European integration has advanced significantly since the establishment of the European Coal and Steel Union in the 1950s. With the establishment of the European Economic Community in the late 1950s, integration has gradually become deeper, extending from internal European security policy concerns to internal trade liberalization, a common external trade policy, a common currency, and close cooperation in economic policy and international politics. The Common Commercial Policy was defined already in Article 113 of the Treaty of Rome in 1959. Community-level involvement in negotiating trade treaties began in the 1960s for industrial goods, and most internal tariffs were removed and a Common External Tariff (CET) was introduced in mid-1968. Since 1970, the European Community has been fully responsible for the EU's trade negotiations, not the individual nations. However, the development of European integration has been particularly fast since the mid-1980s. The establishment of the European Single Market, several enlargements of the Union, the introduction of an economic and monetary union, and discussions of admitting some of the former command economies of Eastern and Central Europe into the EU are all changing the continent's economic and political structure as well as its international role and significance. This section summarizes some of the recent developments in European integration—the Single Market, the EMU, and the Eastern enlargement—and discusses the impact they have had and are likely to have on Japan's relations with Europe.

3.1. The Single Market

The Maastricht Treaty, signed in 1987, laid the foundation for the European Single Market, which was established in 1992. The Treaty removed all trade barriers between the twelve members of the EU and created a unified market comparable in size to the US and Japan. The size and significance of the Single Market increased in 1994, when the EFTA countries (with the exception of Switzerland) were included through the European Economic Area agreement, and in 1995, when Austria, Finland, and Sweden joined the EU.

In addition to the removal of all tariffs, the Maastricht Treaty removed most non-tariff barriers (NTBs) between the participating countries. For instance, a principle of mutual recognition was introduced to unify widely differing national technical standards, government procurement regulations were revised to guarantee national treatment to producers from other member countries, and customs procedures were harmonized and simplified. As a result of these changes, the twelve national markets of the EU were essentially unified into one Single Market. A product manufactured

TABLE 13.5. *Key features of EU-11, Japan, and US economies*

	EU-11	Japan	USA
Reserves including gold (Ecu) (bn.)	377	209	119
Reserves excluding gold (Ecu) (bn.)	290	203	50
Net balance on current and capital account for 1997 (bn.)	+109	+81	−147
GDP (Ecu) 1997 (bn.)	5,546	3,712	6,848
Stock market capitalization (Ecu) (bn.)	3,110	4,020	10,578
Population (m.)	291	126	269

Note: Stock market capitalization for Japan includes Tokyo and Osaka exchanges; for USA includes NYSE and Nasdaq.

Source: Eurostat (1998), "EMU: A Powerful Economic Entity," *Statistics in Focus: General Statistics 1998:1* (Luxembourg: Eurostat).

in or imported into one of the EU countries automatically qualifies to be sold in the other member countries as well.

However, the Single Market program is not the acme of European integration. The Economic and Monetary Union established on January 1, 1999 deepens the integration in the EU area, and negotiations for a first Eastern enlargement of the EU have already commenced.

3.2. The EMU

The most prominent feature of the EMU is the introduction of the common currency, the Euro, in 1999 (and the subsequent abolishment of the national currencies of the eleven participating economies by the year 2002).[1] The introduction of the Euro is likely to have a profound impact on the world's financial markets. As shown in Table 13.5, the eleven member countries of the EMU hold international reserves that are larger than those of Japan and the US taken together, and the aggregate current account surplus of the EMU area is larger than that of Japan. This suggests that the Euro may become a relatively strong currency in the long run, and may eventually challenge the US dollar as the leading international reserve currency. At a macroeconomic level, the implications of such a development could be quite significant. Many countries that presently hold US dollars and Japanese yen in their international reserves would probably substitute some of these for Euro. The accumulation of Euro balances by central banks around the world might also allow the EMU group to run a deficit in its aggregate current account. This, in turn, would require a remarkably large restructuring of world trade, considering that the EU-11 has registered substantial current account surpluses in recent years (see Table 13.5).

[1] The EMU initially includes all EU members except for Denmark and the UK, who negotiated an exemption from the commitment to join the EMU, as outlined in the Maastricht Treaty, and Greece and Sweden, who did not fulfil the formal requirements for qualification to the EMU. It is likely that all or several of these four countries will join the Monetary Union during the next few years.

An even more significant aspect of the EMU project is the coordination of the macroeconomic policies of member countries, with price stability as a prime objective. This has already made the EU a more stable investment location as the various national governments have exercised fiscal control to bring their economies in line for inclusion in the EMU (for example, keeping fiscal deficits below 3 per cent of GDP and public debt below 60 per cent of GDP).

3.3. Eastern enlargement

The first formal steps in the Eastern enlargement of the EU were taken during the spring of 1998, with the start of negotiations between the EU and a first group of potential entrants, including Hungary, Poland, the Czech Republic, Slovenia, and Estonia. A second group of candidates includes Romania, Bulgaria, Slovakia, and Cyprus. There is no serious discussion of EU membership with Russia and other former Soviet republics (excluding the Baltic states). An Eastern enlargement of the EU would greatly increase the range of factor price differences within the Union, and radically change the conditions for foreign investment as well as trade. If the Central and Eastern European transition economies were guaranteed free access to the entire EU market, several of the countries in question would become very attractive locations for labor-intensive manufacturing operations. It is likely that this would encourage both exports and vertically integrated FDI.

3.4. Effects on Japan

There is no doubt that the reduction in trade costs from treating the EU as one destination rather than as twelve or fifteen individual markets has made Europe a more attractive market for the rest of the world. The expected growth effects from the Single Market program and the EMU have also contributed to making the EU a more attractive investment location for foreign firms.[2] The combined effect of these changes is probably to make Europe more similar to the US as a destination for Japanese exports and a location for Japanese FDI.

However, the adjustment to a unified Europe is far from completed. How should we expect Japanese trade and investment flows to change in the medium and long run if Japanese firms choose to treat the European Union like the US? The previous section concluded that Europe has hitherto received small amounts of Japanese exports and FDI relative to the US. In a macro perspective, it would therefore be reasonable to expect increases in the amounts of Japanese exports and FDI destined for Europe. This motivates a closer comparison between the US and Europe as destinations for Japanese exports and FDI to identify the sectors where the potential for increased trade and investment are greatest.

---

[2] See Dunning (1998) and the references provided there for evidence on the investment effects of European integration.

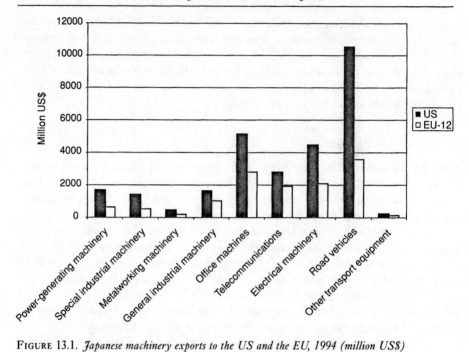

FIGURE 13.1. *Japanese machinery exports to the US and the EU, 1994 (million US$)*
Source: United Nations, *Commodity Trade Statistics*.

Figure 13.1 presents a more detailed breakdown of Japanese machinery exports to the US and the EU in 1994. The machinery industry accounts for roughly 70 per cent of total Japanese exports (see Table 13.2). Asia and the US are the main destination for Japanese machinery exports, and account together for 70 per cent of the sector's total exports. The share of exports destined to the EU is less than 15 per cent. This suggests that there is great potential for increased Japanese machinery exports to Europe. Looking more specifically at some of the two-digit industry groups in Figure 13.1, it can be seen that electrical machinery and road vehicles constitute the bulk (almost 50 per cent) of Japanese machinery exports. The EU is clearly underrepresented in both of these sectors. In road vehicles, the EU share is only about a third of the US share; in electrical machinery, the EU share is less than half of the US share. The EU shares are also remarkably low in some of the industrial machinery categories.

Figure 13.2 shows the distribution of Japanese FDI in the US and the EU across ten selected industries during the 1981–95 period.[3] Overall, Japanese firms invested nearly 2.5 times more in the US than in the EU during this period, although the EU share of investment increased temporarily around 1990. The US had a distinct advan-

---

[3] The investment data are expressed in current prices, for lack of industry-specific and country-specific price indices. However, it should be noted that the impact of inflation in investment good prices—which underestimates the real investment values in earlier periods—is at least partially offset by depreciation.

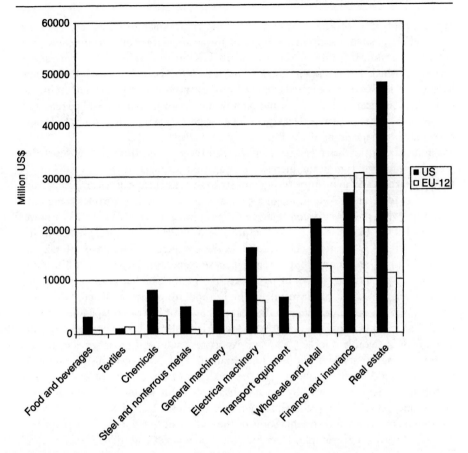

FIGURE 13.2. *Japanese FDI in the US and the EU, 1981–1995, selected industries (million US$, current prices)*
Source: Ministry of Finance, Tokyo, unpublished data.

tage in all sectors except textiles and financial services, which suggests a potential for increased Japanese presence in the EU. In manufacturing, the EU shares are particularly low in chemicals, steel and nonferrous metals, electrical machinery, and transport equipment.

Considering that the EU shares of Japanese exports of several machinery industries were also quite low, it is reasonable to expect that these sectors will be subject to significant changes in the future, if the EU actually becomes an economic giant of the same dimension as the US.

The EU has also received relatively little Japanese investment in the real estate sector, but it is unclear whether this signals a potential for larger investment. Much of the real estate investments in the US were made during the late 1980s, when the rapid appreciation of the yen, large Japanese trade surpluses, and the Japanese asset bubble created exceptional conditions for accumulation of foreign assets. The Japanese investments in the European (mainly UK) finance industry, by contrast, are very large, which complicates predictions about future developments. While the establishment of the EMU is expected to make Europe a more attractive location for investments in finance and banking, it is unclear how much new investment will be required. However, it is likely that a reallocation of investments, from the UK to other EU countries, may be forthcoming if the UK remains outside the EMU.

Summarizing this brief comparison between the EU and the US, it appears that there is scope for significant increases in Japanese exports to and investments in Europe, particularly in manufacturing industries such as chemicals, electrical machinery, and road vehicles. Yet, although a comparison with the US provides some indications of what to expect if continuing European integration makes the EU a power on par with the US, it is of course not possible to make any detailed predictions on the basis of the US pattern. Differences in the competitive advantages of US and European firms will motivate different Japanese responses. Hence, while European integration reduces the number of parameters for production localization, neither the pattern nor the effects of investments in Europe are easily predicted. Moreover, although the macro picture suggests a great potential for increased Japanese presence in the European market, it is easy to point to various obstacles to increased trade and investment at the micro level. Voluntary export restraints and other types of market sharing arrangements have not been uncommon in Europe's recent history, and will, in the short and medium run, temper the prediction from the macro analysis.[4] The picture is further complicated by the industrial policies of various EU member states. For instance, subsidies to potential foreign investors may affect the location as well as the volume of inward investment. Some of the complexities involved are perhaps best illustrated with a few examples from individual companies and industries.

3.5. Toyota in Europe

The European Commission and Japan have maintained a quota system for Japanese motor vehicle exports to the European Union since 1993, in an agreement due to expire at the end of 1999. Production within the EU by Japanese firms is not counted against the quota, which has stimulated Japanese investment in EU-based manufacturing. In 1997, EU car imports from Japan were 1,030,000 units (10.8 per cent of the EU market), well below the quota of 1,114,000 (European Report, 1998*a*). But

---

[4] It should be noted that there are obstacles to increased Japanese exports to Europe also at the macro level. One interesting question in this context is whether Europe is prepared to absorb the increase in imports that would be necessary if the Euro becomes an international reserve currency. The European problem would not be the financing of the current account deficit—as in the US case, an economy that is home to an international reserve currency does not need to worry about raising foreign exchange to pay for imports—but rather the ability to manage the real effects of a large increase in imports. There is a real risk of increasing European protectionism if the aggregate EU current account deficit increases rapidly without a corresponding depreciation of the Euro; this would clearly limit the potential for increased exports from Japan and elsewhere.

the fact that a quota exists sends a signal—if conditions worsen, control mechanisms are in place that can readily be activated.

According to Toyota's *1998 Annual Report*, in 1997 the company sold 471,000 vehicles in Europe (about 10 per cent of the 4,843,563 vehicles sold worldwide, and about 3 per cent of the European market). They produced 104,830 vehicles in the UK in 1997, while a further 6,364 vehicles were manufactured in Portugal. Thus, less than a quarter of Toyota's total European sales were produced in Europe. Meanwhile, Toyota's US sales in 1997 were 1,230,114 vehicles, or some 8 per cent of the overall US market). US local production was 729,117 units, or about 60 per cent of Toyota's American sales. With European integration making Europe a more significant market, perhaps comparable to the US, it appears obvious that Toyota's presence in Europe would have to increase.

In late 1997 Toyota announced plans to build a new 2,000-job production facility in northern France (the town of Onnaing, Nord-Pas-de-Calais region, 20 km from the Belgian border). The decision to invest in France was in preference to expanding an existing facility in Burnaston, central England, which could potentially produce around 400,000 cars per year, and was the result of a long and hotly contested siting search. According to Krause (1998) and Davison-Aitkins (1998), the whole of Western and Eastern Europe were considered in the siting search. Toyota kept the list of candidates secret, but about twenty-five areas were in active competition, with areas shortlisted in Britain, Spain, Poland, and France. The French bid was weakened due to expected difficulties with French language and culture, but France reportedly offered cheaper land than that in the UK, special construction subsidies, and lower cost electricity and transport. In total, the French offered subsidies worth about one-third of the total investment costs (*The Economist*, Nov. 29, 1997: 64). Moreover, France had the added advantage of being one of the founding members of the EMU; the UK, by contrast, has decided to stay outside the common currency area.

Candidate sites not only lobbied via their inward investment agencies, but also made use of various top government officials. After Toyota's announcement that the project would go to France, the British government response was muted, stating that the decision reflected the firm's "wider business strategy." But critics of Britain's Labour government were loud: the Conservative Party industry spokesman claimed that the decision showed that "Labour was bad for business," while a British trade union leader declared that the fault lay with British governmental unwillingness to participate in European Monetary Union (Sylvester, Marston, and Herbert, 1997). Toyota management first confirmed, but soon refuted, that the UK decision to remain outside the EMU was an important determinant of choice of the French location.

Just one month later, Toyota announced plans worth US$242 million to expand production in Britain (Nakamoto, 1998). Toyota had decided that the engines for the output of their French car plant would be British-made, supplied by Toyota Motor Manufacturing (UK) from Deeside, north Wales. Press reports noted that state aid offered for the Deeside expansion was the first that Toyota would receive in Britain (Gribben, 1998). However, this was not the first case where a Japanese auto-investor benefited from European subsidies. For example, in 1996, Nissan Motor Iberica, a Spanish subsidiary of Nissan Motor Corporation, received a regional aid subsidy of 975 million pesetas (US$7.8 million) to keep open their technical center in Barcelona. Similarly, Suzuki Manufacturing received 1.7 billion pesetas (US$14.3 million) to bring in new production and safeguard jobs at their Manzanares plant in Spain.

3.6. Investments by Japanese electronics manufacturers

The European Electronic Component Manufacturer's Association (EECA), with support from the EU Commission, and the Electronics Industries Association of Japan (EIAJ) have agreed about various "voluntary" antidumping and price control measures, similar to those for the car industry. The agreements require manufacturers to report to both associations their home market and export prices, and data on production costs. Strict confidentiality is then supposed to be maintained, with company and product-specific data kept secret. The objective is to ensure an orderly market which "will not be disrupted by price-cutting wars, or interrupted by formal anti-dumping inquiries" (European Report, 1998*b*). Some examples of the kind of interventions taking place are several EU anti-dumping and countervailing duty decisions on the import of DRAMs from Japan, and the Commission's 1990 decision to implement a price undertaking that was intended to lead to a 60 per cent increase in component prices.

According to Tharakan (1997: 17), "there is little doubt that the anti-dumping actions of the EC in general and those related to the electronics sector in particular, triggered a wave of Japanese inward investment." However, the establishment of European affiliates has not always reduced the frictions between European and Japanese producers. In some cases, Japanese investors have clashed directly with the EC Commission. Because of concern that some inward FDI was intended to circumvent trade policy measures, the Commission has tried to regulate the operations of foreign investors in various ways. One example is the revision of the European Community's anti-dumping code in 1987, to permit the imposition of anti-dumping duties on the component imports of foreign affiliates located in Europe. The new antidumping code also led to the establishment of a system to monitor the behavior of foreign affiliates, including Japanese producers of electronic typewriters and photocopiers. Quite predictably, these measures caused serious concern among Japanese companies (Bourke, 1996: 74–5). Hence, in 1988, Japan complained to the GATT about the EC extension of anti-dumping to component parts and was eventually supported by a GATT panel decision forcing the EC to change its rules (Bourke, 1996, ch. 4). In other cases, the clashes have been with European companies and industry organizations. For instance, in 1990 when the Japanese computer firm Fujitsu bought an 80 per cent share in Britain's largest computer company, ICL, there was substantial friction with ICL's continuing participation in European research projects. ICL was dropped from the regular membership of Jessi, the publicly-funded European semiconductor design project, because of its Japanese ties, although it was allowed to continue with some activities as a guest participant. The European IT Industry Round Table, a lobbying organization made up of European manufacturers, also expelled ICL in early 1991. Similarly, the NEC decision to purchase a stake in the French Group Bull met with some resistance.

In general, it can be argued that there has been an element of negative discrimination against the Japanese as foreign investors when compared to US investment in Europe. The reason is arguably that Japanese firms have been seen as less responsive in terms of corporate governance and shareholder relations than Western companies. The lack of transparency concerning both long- and short-term plans has been considered a particular problem. However, the European fears regarding Japanese ownership have diminished in recent years. It is not clear whether this is a reflection of the reduction in Japanese outward investment, or a result of the closer contacts between Japan and Europe.

3.7. Financial services

Japanese securities and investment firms have the most one-sided European profile of all major industries: 92 per cent of Japanese nationals posted to Europe by this industry are based in the UK, almost wholly in London (Toyo Keizai, 1998). The importance of London as a financial center is under some threat, however, with the advent of the European Monetary Union which the UK has not joined. The companies based in London will face a serious challenge to their collective preeminent position, as most of the rest of Europe has been in the Eurozone from the start.

The new Eurozone is also asserting an independence from London by attempting to set its own benchmark interest rate measurement to replace the British-constructed Libor. The Libor (London Interbank Offer Rate), set by sixteen London-based banks of the British Bankers' Association (BBA), has been a major benchmark from which derivatives and major cross-institutional lending rates are determined. The advent of the Euro requires adjusting the measure, and a new form has been introduced by the BBA named the EuroLibor. The European Banking Federation offers an alternative measure, named the Euribor, determined by fifty-seven European and international banks. Some European interests are not keen that one of their major quoted indicators would be in the hands of London financiers outside of the Eurozone: the French Bankers Association has pledged to support the more pan-European Euribor (*Reuters*, Oct. 14, 1998). According to *The Economist* (Oct. 31, 1998) if the Euribor alternative is successful, it might lead sections of the London-centered major finance houses to relocate to the continent: proximity to decision-makers is considered to be important from an information perspective.

However, Japanese financial companies have yet to react strongly to the EMU project. For instance, Nomura International has made considerable efforts to position itself as a leading light in the EMU transition, and particularly as a gateway to the Euro for Japan and Asia, offering a series of high-profile seminars in Tokyo and Singapore to display their preparation and commitment (*Euro Times*, October 1998). Nevertheless, Nomura remains headquartered in London, and has not taken any major steps to relocate their key activities to the EMU countries. This limited response is puzzling if it is assumed that the UK will stay outside the EMU. One reason could be that the uncertainties surrounding the EMU project have been so large that it has been appropriate to adopt a wait-and-see strategy. It is also possible that Nomura and other Japanese finance companies expect that the UK will join the Monetary Union in the future, in which case relocations from their UK bases are not warranted.

3.8. Summary on company and industry cases

The examples of company and industry reactions to European integration discussed above illustrate some of the factors that will temper the general conclusion from the analysis of aggregate statistics on trade and investment flows: that Japanese exports to and direct investments in Europe should be expected to increase and perhaps match those directed to the US. A first point to note is that the amounts of trade and investment may in some cases be restricted by various anticompetitive agreements, such as those in the auto and electronics industries. Second, as illustrated by Fujitsu's investment in ICL and other cases, it is possible that trade-barrier jumping FDI will not eliminate the frictions between Japanese and European firms, which could reduce the investment flows. Third, although the establishment of the EMU is expected to lead to a significant restructuring of European industry—particularly since some EU members have decided to stay outside the EMU—the effects on FDI are still hard to predict. On the one hand, the different EU members are competing for foreign investment, and the various subsidies and concessions offered to foreign investors may well outweigh the effects of integration. On the other hand, there is still considerable uncertainty whether countries like the UK will be able to stay outside the EMU in the long or medium run.

In addition to these factors, it should be noted that the effects of a future Eastern enlargement of the EU are also quite uncertain. Although some Japanese companies have cautiously begun to invest in countries like Hungary, Poland, the Czech Republic, and Russia, it is unclear how large the net increases in Japanese investments in Europe would be if these countries were admitted to the EU. While they would be attractive production locations for many kinds of manufacturing industries, it can be expected that their own national markets will remain small in relation to Western Europe. A significant share of the Japanese investments in these countries would therefore substitute for existing production in Western Europe. For instance, how much of Japanese automobile production would be retained in the UK if low-wage countries like Poland and Hungary entered the EU? Furthermore, low-cost production locations in Eastern Europe would perhaps not only compete with Western European locations. To what extent could investments in Eastern Europe become substitutes for current Japanese investments in East Asia? It should be noted that the answers to these questions will not only depend on differences in physical productivities and factor prices, but also on the international policy environment. For instance, would Japanese products manufactured in Poland and China have equally good access to the US market?

4. Political Relations Between the EU and Japan

So far, the discussion has assumed that the possible changes in Japan's attitudes towards Europe depend only on changes in the European economic environment. However, we have already noted that actions by individual EU member countries have had some impact on the behavior of Japanese investors. Most EU countries have national offices promoting inward investment—according to Toyo Keizai (1998: 1693–7), different EU countries operated sixty-six investment promotion offices in Japan in the mid-1990s—and Japanese investment has often been encouraged with various investment subsidies. These agencies are often in direct competition with each other. EU regional policy allows a measure of state aid or structural aid to promote inward investment, but limits aid intensity (as a percentage of total investment) to avoid excessive competition within the EU. The official subsidy ceilings are up to 60 per cent of the investment costs, differing with location and type of program. However, the investment costs are often difficult to define, and subsidy packages are often agreed before actual investment occurs. Predicted calculations may thus be inexact in spite of the best efforts of all concerned, and subsidies can also be wielded to result in unfair advantage over competitors. Barnard (1997) claims that the "massaging" of tax and other subsidies by inward investment agencies often results in incentive packages that are twice the EU limit.[5]

Similar efforts are seen also when it comes to promoting European exports to Japan. In addition to national trade missions, a large number of subnational regions maintain representative offices in Tokyo. Bourke (1996: 141) identified thirty-eight European Community sub-state regional representations in Japan as of early 1993. The operations of these organizations may have been partly responsible for the Japanese investment response to the Single Market program. Similarly, the rapid increases in European exports to Japan may have been facilitated by active investment promotion by the various European organizations rather than only a Japanese wish to import more European goods.

Abstracting from these national programs, it is also likely that the development of Japan–EU relations will be affected by the EU's common policies towards Japan, in the same way as pressure from the US may have some impact on the development of the Japanese economy. Although the EU's approach to Japan has been less confrontational than that of the US, the European view is that the bilateral relation has generated positive results. Part of the reason may be that many European objectives have coincided with those of the US, so that Europe has been able to free-ride on the more aggressive US policies (see Globerman and Kokko, Chapter 12 this volume). This notwithstanding, it is clear that the contacts between the EU and Japan have become more intensive since the early 1990s, and both sides have also invested more

---

[5] New guidelines for regional aid by the European Commission seek to avoid subsidizing internal EU relocation or projects which distort competition and will require those projects receiving aid to maintain investment and jobs in the region for at least five years (European Union, 1997). While maximum aid for a project can still in extreme cases reach 65 per cent, the format is changing so as to avoid excessive competition between EU members and to better concentrate on the poorest regions.

in the bilateral relations. A complex network of institutions and programs has been established to manage the formal contacts between the European Union and Japan. The remainder of this section will provide a brief overview of these institutions, with emphasis on the European objectives and ambitions, and discuss how these may influence the future relations between the regions. In this context, it is convenient to distinguish between political issues, economic issues, and cooperation in other areas of common interest.

4.1. EU–Japan relations

The framework for the formal political dialogue between the EU and Japan is given by the 1991 Joint EU–Japan Declaration. The Declaration sets out, in general terms, the principles and objectives of the dialogue and cooperation between the EU and Japan, and lays down an institutional schedule for formal consultations through regular meetings. These include an annual summit between the president of the European Council, the president of the Commission and the Japanese prime minister, annual meetings between the Commission and the Japanese government at a ministerial level, as well as twice-yearly meetings between EU foreign ministers and the Japanese foreign minister. In addition, there are annual meetings between high-level officials from both sides, as well as various sectoral meetings at ministerial or high official level.

The political dialogue between the EU and Japan has gradually become more intensive since the 1991 Declaration. In the sphere of international politics, the EU aim is to encourage Japan to assume a political role commensurate with its economic importance. One important field is security policy, where both EU and Japan are adjusting their strategies to a world where the US may play a less dominant role than in the past. An early example of political collaboration is the joint initiative in 1991 to establish a UN register on transfer of conventional arms. Another example is the assistance offered by both the EU and Japan to the former command economies in Central and Eastern Europe as well as Mongolia. Both sides are also participating in the security organizations in each other's region—the EU in the ASEAN Regional Forum (ARF) and Japan as a guest in the Organization for Security and Co-operation in Europe. The EU and Japan are also instrumental in forging the new ASEM partnership between Europe and Asia.[6]

Another important political objective of the EU—with important links to Europe's commercial interest in Japan—is to promote and accelerate structural reforms and deregulation in Japan (La Croix and Mak, Chapter 10 this volume). In this context, the EU places particular emphasis on ensuring the equality of market access in Europe and Japan. The EU view is that Japanese exporters face almost no structural barriers

---

[6] ASEM is an acronym for the Asia–Europe Meeting, which is an institution made up of ten East and Southeast Asian countries and the fifteen EU nations. The aim of ASEM is to strengthen the political, economic, and cultural ties between Asia and Europe. The process includes interactions and activities at various levels, with most attention directed to the biannual summits bringing together the heads of state from the twenty-five member countries.

in the EU, and that they have been some of the major beneficiaries of the Single European Market. At the same time, it is felt that European exporters and investors face serious market access difficulties in Japan, as reflected by the large trade deficit and the imbalances in FDI. A permanent EU–Japan deregulation dialogue was therefore agreed in 1994 between the European Commission and the Japanese prime minister. Since then, the Commission has annually presented a number of detailed lists of deregulation proposals to the Japanese government.

The deregulation dialogue has already resulted in some improvements, although much remains to be done. Areas where regulatory reform in Japan has arguably been affected by EU pressure (and facilitated EU exports to Japan) include financial services, automobiles, telecommunications, construction, transport services, electrical equipment, and cosmetics (but it should be noted that it is impossible to determine the specific weight of EU pressure as compared to US pressure, WTO commitments, and purely domestic determinants). A recent list of around 200 deregulation proposals was presented to Japan in late 1997, including proposals ranging from calls for administrative reform and more stringent enforcement of competition law to efforts to establish a Mutual Recognition Agreement between the EU and Japan. Such an agreement would promote international standards and reduce burdensome testing and regulatory requirements, facilitating the flow of trade in both directions between the two regions. Another notable institution is the Trade Assessment Mechanism (TAM), where EU exports to Japan and individual product performance are compared with those to Australia, New Zealand, Canada, and the US; a similar analysis is applied to Japanese output. The bulk of the deregulation proposals submitted by the EU to Japan originate from the TAM. Two areas that often emerge in the assessments, and where EU pressure for change is likely to remain particularly high, are distribution and transportation. It is often pointed out that value added per employee in the distribution sector, which reaches only 60 per cent of the level in manufacturing, is low in comparison with other industrialized countries. Various entry barriers limiting the access to distribution networks reduce the variety of products available, restrict consumer choice, and raise consumer prices.

In addition to the bilateral agenda, the aim of which is to promote structural change and reform in Japan, the EU also has a broad Export Promotion Program (EXPROM) to help European firms enter the Japanese market. The EXPROM includes activities in several fields. The EU Gateway to Japan Campaign focuses on small- and medium-sized enterprises in several sectors, including medical equipment, packaging machinery, food products, beverages, waste management technologies, and information technologies. The Campaign, which is supported by Japan's MITI/JETRO, organizes trade fairs and trade missions, provides sectoral market studies to the participating companies, and offers customized services in the form of product specific market research. The EXPROM also includes various ad hoc activities to support the Gateway to Japan Campaign in sectors that are not explicitly targeted by these programs.

Apart from the programs that are intended to influence the Japanese political or economic environment, there are also numerous sectoral agreements that strengthen the links between the EU and Japan. This kind of cooperation has been developing progressively in many fields from a relatively low level in the 1980s; it covers competition policy, industrial policy, science and technology, R&D, transport, and financial services. For instance, the EU–Japan Centre for Industrial Cooperation, established in Tokyo in 1987 and in Brussels in 1996, organizes training courses for EU managers in Japan, language and in-company training for Japanese engineering students in Europe, and similar programs for European engineering students in Japan. The Executive Training Program (ETP) directed by the EU provides advanced language and business training for young European managers. The program includes an eighteen-month stay in Japan, with a one-year intensive Japanese language course, company visits, seminars on Japanese business culture, and six months of in-house training in one or more Japanese companies. The cooperation in the industrial area also includes joint research programs, as well as technical working groups in the fields of standardization/certification/quality, biotechnology, and information technologies to encourage dialogue on industrial policy issues and to promote convergence in industrial policies. However, it should be noted that the US still has a large advantage in these areas, particularly when it comes to joint research and academic exchanges.

5. Summary and Conclusions

The establishment of the European Single Market and the European Monetary Union have made the EU the world's largest exporter, the second largest importer, and the world's second largest market. Still, economic relations between Japan and the EU remain relatively underdeveloped, particularly in comparison with the relations between Japan and the US. In this chapter, we have asked whether European integration will motivate a change in Japanese attitudes towards Europe and strengthen the economic ties between the two regions.

At the macro level, we have argued that EU integration can be expected to translate into increased Japanese presence in European markets. Comparing Europe with the US, we have suggested that the largest potential for increased Japanese exports and direct investments should be found in the automobile and electronics industries: in both these industries, Japanese firms hold significantly smaller market shares in Europe than in the US.

However, developments at the micro level are likely to temper these conclusions. Various kinds of trade and investment barriers have restricted Japanese sales and investments in some European markets in recent years and are likely to limit the Japanese responses to European integration in the future as well. Moreover, the industrial policies of various EU governments, e.g. in the form of investment subsidies to foreign as well as domestic investors, may affect the location as well as the volume of inward investment. It is also difficult to predict how the closer contacts between Japan and the EU in political issues, economic policy, and other areas of common interest will affect the extent of trade and investment contacts. Yet, in the longer run, it is very likely that Europe will receive more attention from Japan: how much depends on how European integration progresses. In particular, it is relevant to follow the development of the EMU as well as the plans for the Eastern enlargement of the Union.

REFERENCES

ACCJ (1998), *1998 American Chamber of Commerce in Japan Membership Directory* (Tokyo: American Chamber of Commerce in Japan).

Andersson, Thomas (ed.) (1993), *Japan: A European Perspective* (New York: St. Martin's Press).

——"Fortress Europe Again," *Asian Wall Street Journal*, March 18, 1997, 8.

Barnard, Bruce (1997), "No End to Tax-break Beauty Contest," Nov. 20, *European Voice*.

Bayoumi, Tamin and Gabrielle Lipworth (1997), "Japanese Foreign Direct Investment and Regional Trade," IMF Working Paper WP/97/103 (Washington: International Monetary Fund).

Belderbos, Rene and Leo Sleuwaegen (1996), "Japanese Firms and the Decision to Invest Abroad: Business Groups and Regional Core Networks," *Review of Economics and Statistics*, 78/2: 214–20.

Bourke, Thomas (1996), *Japan and the Globalisation of European Integration* (Aldershot: Dartmouth Publishing Company).

Darby, James and Max Munday (1996), "The Origins and Growth of Japanese Manufacturing in Ireland," in Darby, James (ed.), *Japan and the European Periphery* (London: Macmillan), 86–110.

Davison-Aitkins, Nicole (1998), "How Toyota Parked in Europe," *Corporate Location* (Jan/Feb), 6–7.

Dunning, John H. (1998), "The European Internal Market Programme and Inbound Foreign Direct Investment," *Journal of Common Market Studies*, 35/1: 1–30; 35/2: 189–223.

Economist, The (anon.) (1997), "Toyota Learns French," Nov. 29, 64.

——(1998), "The Battle of the Benchmarks," Oct. 31, 86.

European Automobile Manufacturers Association (1997), "Toyota's Investment in North of France will Add to the Overcapacity of the EU Automobile Sector," European Automobile Manufacturers Association (ACEA), press release, Dec. 9.

European Report (1998a), "Japan's Car Import Quota Raised as EU Demand Rises," Oct. 14.

——(1998b), "Commission Backs Europe–Japan Chipmaker's Pact," Oct. 17.

European Union (1997), "Commission Approves Guidelines on Regional Aid for 2000–2006," European Commission, press release, IP/97/1137, Dec. 17.

Eurostat (1998), "EMU: A Powerful Entity," *Statistics in Focus: General Statistics 1998:1* (Luxembourg: Eurostat).

Gribben, Roland (1998), "Japanese Car Part Makers Eye UK Sites," *Daily Telegraph*, Jan. 10, 30.

JETRO (1993), *Directory of Japanese-Affiliated Companies in the USA and Canada, 1993–94* (Tokyo: Japan External Trade Organization).

Michaels, Daniel (1996), "Asian Producers Lured to East Europe by Low Costs, Location and Tariff Cuts," *Wall Street Journal*, June 18.

Nakamoto, Michiyo (1998), "Japan Carmakers Renew Their European Offensive: But EU Manufacturers Claim They Are Trying to Export Their Way Out of Their Troubles," *Financial Times*, Jan. 15, 4.

Nomura International (1998), *Euro Times: Nomura's Euro Newsletter* (London: Nomura International).

Reuters (1998*a*), "Tribunal Outlaws Panasonic France Factory Closure," *Reuters News Service*, May. 4.

——(1998*b*), "French Bankers Back Euribor over Euro-Libor," *Reuters News Service*, Oct. 14.

——(1998*c*), "EU Takes Eight States to Court over U.S. Air Pacts," *Reuters News Service*, Oct. 30.

Shinozaki, Akihiko and Kazumi Endo (1997), "An Analysis of Foreign Direct Investment and Foreign Affiliates in Japan," JDB Research Report No. 72 (Tokyo: Japan Development Bank).

Sylvester, Rachel, Paul Marston, and Susannah Herbert (1997), "Britain Loses Fight for £360 m Toyota Plant: Toyota Want About Eight per cent of the European Market, which is Twice What They Have Now," *Daily Telegraph*, Dec. 10, 10.

Tharakan, P. K. M. (1997), "The Japan–EC DRAMs Anti-dumping Undertaking: Was It Justified? What Purpose Did It Serve?," *De Economist* (Leiden), 145/1: 1–28.

Toyo Keizai (eds.) (1998), *Japanese Overseas Investments (Classed by Country)* (Tokyo: Toyo Keizai Shinposha) (in Japanese).

Ulgado, Francis M. (1996), "Location Characteristics of Manufacturing Investments in the U.S.: A Comparison of American and Foreign-based Firms," *Management International Review*, 36/1: 7–26.

UNCTAD (1996*a*), *Sharing Asia's Dynamism: Asian Direct Investment in the European Union* (New York: UNCTAD).

——(1996*b*), *Investing in Asia's Dynamism: European Union Direct Investment in Asia* (New York: UNCTAD).

Vogel, Ezra (1979), *Japan as Number One*. (Cambridge, Mass.: Harvard University Press).

Yurimoto, Shigeru and Tadayuki Masui (1995), "Design of a Decision Support System for Overseas Plant Location in the EC," *International Journal of Production Economics*, 41: 411–18.

14 Economic Development in China and Its Implications for Japan

SHIGEYUKI ABE AND CHUNG H. LEE

1. Introduction

Since the Four Modernizations undertaken in the late 1970s, China has emerged as one of Asia's most dynamic newly industrializing economies. In the decade following the reform China's real GNP grew at an annual average rate of 10 per cent, up from an annual rate of 6.5 per cent during the 1970s. Although its economy slowed down in the late 1980s due to the government's anti-inflationary measures, it regained momentum in the early 1990s, achieving a 13.4 per cent rate of growth in 1993. China's economy posted somewhat lower growth rates in subsequent years, but not less than 7.8 per cent even in the Asian crisis year of 1998 (Table 14.1).

One of the key elements of China's economic reform was the opening of its economy, which has transformed it into a major trading country—the tenth largest in the world in 1997—and has had a positive effect on economic growth. The opening also has brought about a rapid expansion in economic interactions between China and Japan. China is now Japan's fifth largest export market and second largest supplier of imports and, in terms of the total value of trade (imports and exports combined), it is Japan's second largest trading partner after the United States, accounting for 8 per cent of Japan's total trade.

China has been a major recipient of foreign direct investment (FDI) with an inflow of 83,437 cases worth US$111 billion (on a contract basis) in 1993. The inflow has decreased since then but still reached US$45 billion in 1997. As of 1997, major investors in China were Hong Kong, Japan, Taiwan, the United States, Singapore, and Korea (in a descending order in terms of the amount invested).

The above discussion makes it clear that China has emerged as one of Japan's major economic partners in trade and investment. How this relationship will evolve as we enter the twenty-first century, especially if China accedes to the World Trade Organization (WTO), is an issue that has serious policy implications for Japan. It is possible that, given its size and growing economy, China may become Japan's major export market, invigorating its manufacturing industries, but it is also possible that, with its ambition to rapidly catch up with the advanced economies of the world, China may soon challenge Japan's supremacy in technology and know-how and become a rival instead of a partner.

The authors wish to thank Magnus Blomström, Michael Delaney, Dieter Ernst, Sumner La Croix, Keun Lee, and the participants in the workshop on "Japan in the twenty-first Century" held at the East–West Center, Honolulu, on 7–8 January, 1999 for their helpful comments on an earlier version of the paper.

TABLE 14.1. *Main economic indicators of China*

	Units	1991	1992	1993	1994	1995	1996	1997	1998
Real GDP growth	Percentages	9.2	14.2	13.5	12.6	10.5	9.6	8.8	7.8
Retail inflation	Percentages	2.9	5.4	13.2	21.7	14.8	6.1	0.8	−2.6
Exports	$100 m.	719.1	849.4	917.4	1,210.1	1,487.7	1,510.5	1,827.0	1,837.
Imports	$100 m.	637.9	805.9	1,039.6	1,156.2	1,320.8	1,388.3	1,423.6	1,401
Trade balance	$100 m.	81.2	43.6	−122.2	53.9	167.0	122.2	403.4	435
Exchange rate	yuan/$	5.3227	5.5149	5.7619	8.6187	8.3509	8.3141	8.2898	8.279
DFI									
Execution basis	$100 m.	43.7	110.1	257.6	337.7	375.2	417.3	452.6	454.
Approval basis	$100 m.	119.8	581.2	1,114.4	826.8	912.8	732.8	510.0	521.

Source: Statistical Bureau of China as cited in JETRO White Paper on International Trade, 1999 (in Japanese).

In attempting to answer some of these questions, we assume that China will continue with its market-oriented reforms and thus maintain the momentum of economic
growth, although at a lower rate than in the past (Naughton, 1997).[1] We then argue
that economic development in China will generally follow the "flying-geese" pattern
that Japan has experienced in catching up with the West and the one that the newly
industrializing economies in Asia have been going through in more recent years.

In this "flying-geese" pattern of industrial development (Akamatsu 1962), a technologically lagging economy such as China first imports crude, labor-intensive consumer products, undertakes their domestic production, and then finally exports them
to the rest of the world. The country repeats this process—the cycle of import, domestic production, and export—as it moves up the ladder of technological sophistication
until it finally catches up with the industrially advanced economies of the world.

Although China will generally follow this pattern, there are certain industries in
China that will be able to "leap-frog" to advanced stages without going through the
cycle. This is possible because China already has the necessary human resources and
technology. When it opened its doors to foreign trade and investment in the late 1970s,
China had already established a number of capital-intensive, albeit state-owned,
industries with relatively advanced technology. China therefore has a ready pool of
human resources that it can tap to develop technology-intensive industries. This is a
situation that neither Japan nor the original Asian newly industrializing economies
(Hong Kong, Singapore, Taiwan, and South Korea) had at the beginning of their
respective industrializations.

Even with such "leap-frogging," China is unlikely to become a fully advanced
economy by the early part of the twenty-first century. What is more likely is that in
coming years China will succeed in developing a number of technologically advanced
industries that will seriously challenge their counterparts in Japan and the West, but

---

[1] According to Singh and Singh (1996), by 2010 China's real GDP and per capita GDP (in 1990 US$)
will reach US$2.3 trillion and US$1,635, respectively, while its nominal merchandise exports and imports
will amount to US$953.2 billion and US$966.4 billion, respectively.

TABLE 14.2. *Foreign direct investment in China (number of cases and value in million US$)*

	1996			1997			1998*		
	Cases	Approval	Execution	Cases	Approval	Execution	Cases	Approval	Execution
Hong Kong, China	10,397	28,002	20,677	8,405	18,222	20,632	5,948	11,232	13,749
Virgin Islands	206	3,121	5,376	415	5,156	1,717	495	4,909	2,507
U.S.A.	2,517	6,916	3,443	2,188	4,937	3,239	1,656	4,476	2,641
Singapore	851	6,314	2,244	734	4,469	2,606	406	2,125	2,127
Japan	1,742	5,131	3,679	1,420	3,401	4,326	872	1,997	2,015
Taiwan	3,184	5,141	3,475	3,014	2,814	3,289	2,123	1,987	2,255
Korea	1,895	4,236	1,358	1,753	2,181	2,142	947	1,065	1,063
U.K.	326	2,542	1,301	304	1,446	1,858	168	1,408	1,048
France	171	1,235	424	144	1,081	475	134	326	412
Canada	431	823	338	399	907	344	—	—	—
Australia	366	522	194	329	614	314	—	—	—
Germany	256	998	518	221	613	993	156	2,048	614
Macao	285	449	580	266	359	395	—	—	—
Thailand	205	428	323	158	317	194	—	—	—
WORLD TOTAL	24,556	73,276	41,726	21,001	51,004	45,257	14,741	35,774	31,355

* From January to September.

Source: Foreign Trade Economic Unit, China, as reported in JETRO White Paper on Investment, 1999.

that a majority of its industrial activities will remain in the unskilled labor-intensive manufacturing sector. The reason, as pointed out by Garnaut and Huang (1995), is obvious: given China's large population and its generally low level of education, it will take several more decades of rapid economic growth and human and physical capital accumulation for it to become an advanced industrial economy.

In the following section, we briefly examine the economic relationship between China and Japan in the early part of the twentieth century, as we believe that certain aspects of this relationship have remained basically the same since then.[2] The first is that China is, in a geographical and cultural sense, a close neighbor of Japan, with a potentially vast market for Japanese products. The second is that for the foreseeable future China will lag behind Japan in technological development. Given these *constants*, an examination of the economic relationship between the two countries in the early twentieth century should shed light on what may lie ahead in the early twenty-first century. Section 3 discusses economic changes in the post-reform China, and Section 4 looks into future economic development in China and their implications for Japan. Section 5 concludes the paper.

2. China and Japan in the Early Twentieth Century

In the early twentieth century Japan became the first Asian country to embark on the road to becoming a modern industrial economy. Even though it still had a large traditional sector, it also had an emerging manufacturing sector that accounted for 17 to 23 per cent of its GDP. The manufacturing industries, which relied on imported machinery and technology, were still backward relative to those in the West, but they were advanced enough in 1900–19 to carry out primary export substitution—the substitution of light manufactured goods for agricultural products as exports (Ohkawa and Kohama, 1989). What facilitated this primary export substitution, in spite of the relative backwardness of these industries, was the availability of Chinese markets for their products.

In terms of value, the United States was the most important destination for Japanese exports during 1913–24, but these were mostly raw silk and silk products, i.e. the products of Japan's traditional sector.[3] Although China (including Hong Kong and the Kwangtung Leased Territory) was second to the United States as a market for Japanese exports, its importance for Japan's industrialization lay in its import composition. Chinese imports from Japan were mostly manufactured goods such as cotton piece goods, matches, paper, and machinery. In fact, China accounted for three-quarters of Japan's total manufacturing exports (Uyehara, 1926: 76–7).

---

[2] The years from 1937 when Japan began its military invasion into China until 1978 when economic reform in China began are not a period during which a "normal" trade and investment relationship between the two independent countries existed. For our purpose that period should be regarded as an interregnum in the economic relationship between the two countries.

[3] Japanese exports to the West (the United States, Europe, and the British dominions) were mainly materials and manufactured goods produced by relatively simple processes in which hand labor was the chief element of cost. Beside raw silk and silk textiles, they included such things as tableware, toys, perilla and rapeseed oil, tea, canned fish, and wood and straw products (Lockwood, 1968: 370).

Prior to the First World War, cotton yarn was Japan's most important export to China, followed by cotton piece goods, refined sugar, copper, coal, matches, marine products, timber, hosiery goods, and paper. In 1923, however, cotton piece goods replaced cotton yarn as Japan's most important export to China, while refined sugar, copper, matches, and hosiery decreased greatly in both value and quantity. Paper, machinery, metal manufactures, and marine products also increased (Uyehara, 1926: 80). This change in Japanese exports to China was a sign of the increasing technological sophistication that Japan was achieving in its manufacturing industries during this period. What made this advance in Japan's technological capability possible?

As Lockwood (1968: 320) observes, international trade was a "highway of learning" for Japan, with the imports of Western products and technology having "catalytic effects" on its economy. Obviously, a catalytic effect is not sufficient for an economy to sustain economic development, and in the case of Japan this development process was facilitated by its "social capability" to learn and develop indigenous industries.[4] It must be added, however, that for indigenous industries to grow and prosper there had to be markets for their products. In the case of Japan, they were provided by the growing demand at home and in China.

In other words, Japan's trade performed a dual function in promoting Japan's industrialization in the early twentieth century. Japan's trade with the West was a conduit for machinery and technology from a more technologically advanced part of the world—a highway of learning—while its trade with China, a country less technologically advanced than Japan, was an outlet for the products of the budding Japanese manufacturing industries. Its trade with China made possible the effective utilization of machinery and technology imported from the West and facilitated learning-by-doing within indigenous industries.

This relationship between the two neighboring countries was interrupted when Japan went to war, first with China in 1937 and then with the United States and its Western allies in 1941. The end of the war in 1945 did not, however, bring back the prewar relationship, as China soon became a socialist economy closed to the West. It is only with the reforms starting in 1978 that China began the process of opening its economy and thus restoring its "natural" economic relationship with Japan— a complementary relationship between an economy with advanced technology and abundant capital and an economy with an abundant supply of labor and potentially immense domestic markets.

3. Economic Changes in the Post-Reform China

One striking achievement of China's reforms is its emergence as a major trading nation. Its international trade grew at the average annual rate of 14.5 per cent during the 1990–7 period (with the exception of 1996), and its trade dependence ratio

---

[4] According to Ohkawa and Kohama (1989: 22), social capability is a concept that cannot be directly quantified by statistical measurements, and improving it is a gradual continuous process based on education, training, and learning-by-doing.

increased from 29.9 per cent in 1990 to 36 per cent in 1997. In 1997, its exports and imports reached US$182.7 billion and US$142.4 billion, respectively.

As China's international trade has grown, economic interdependence between China and Japan has increased *pari passu*. Japan has become one of China's major trading partners, accounting for 17.4 per cent and 21.0 per cent of China's exports and imports, respectively, in 1997. In terms of total trade value, Japan is China's largest trading partner. (In 1997, Hong Kong and the United States accounted for 24 per cent and 17.9 per cent of China's exports, respectively.[5] Taiwan accounted for 11.7 per cent, the United States 11.6 per cent, Korea 9.0 per cent, and Hong Kong 5.6 per cent of China's imports.)

China has also become an important trade partner for Japan, if not a major one yet. In 1997, when Japan's exports and imports amounted to US$422.9 billion and US$340.4 billion, respectively, China accounted for 5.2 per cent and 12.4 per cent of Japan's total exports and imports, respectively. The United States is still the largest trade partner for Japan, accounting for 27.8 per cent of Japan's exports and 22.3 per cent of its imports.

Japan's imports from China include food items (12.0 per cent), raw materials (3.5 per cent), and mineral fuel (5.6 per cent), but its largest imports are labor-intensive manufactured products such as textile and apparel (29.6 per cent), machinery and equipment (20.9 per cent) and metal products (4.5 per cent). The largest of Japan's export items to China is general machinery (23.9 per cent), followed by electronic equipment (22.3 per cent), textiles and apparel (11.7 per cent), and metal products (11.2 per cent).

The inflow of FDI to China has also increased at an astonishing speed since the late 1970s, especially in 1992 and 1993. In 1994 it was four times as large as that for the ASEAN-4 countries (Indonesia, Malaysia, the Philippines, and Thailand). Japan has been an important source of FDI for China, especially during the 1990–4 period. Much of the Japanese investment was attracted to China by the country's abundant supply of cheap labor and its potentially large domestic markets (Seki, 1999). It is thus concentrated in industries such as food, textile, garments, chemical products, metal products, general machinery, electric machinery, home electronics, electronic equipment, and precision machinery. Textile-related industries have also attracted much Japanese investment.

The pattern of Japanese FDI in China and the pattern of China's subsequent export expansion are closely correlated, and this apparent linkage between Japanese FDI and Chinese exports resembles the linkage between Japanese FDI and manufacturing exports from ASEAN. Although long time-series data on detailed categories of FDI are necessary to obtain conclusive evidence on this linkage, there is already enough empirical evidence to support the hypothesis that Japanese FDI has contributed to the growth of China'a exports (Kreinin, Plummer, and Abe, 1999).

---

[5] To the extent that many of Hong Kong's imports from China are exported to the US the latter's share of China's exports is larger than the reported figure.

Along with the expansion in China's overall trade there have been significant changes in its commodity composition, particularly among manufacturing exports. Exports increased rapidly in labor-intensive manufactures such as textiles, apparel, footwear, and toys and sporting goods, their share of China's total exports growing from 29.6 per cent in 1985 to 40.2 per cent in 1990. Equally significant was a surge in exports of electrical equipment—mostly black-and-white televisions, radio receivers, telephone equipment, and domestic electrical equipment—whose share expanded from 2 per cent in 1985 to 11 per cent in 1990.

To demonstrate more clearly the changes in China's trade pattern we have calculated the revealed comparative advantage index (RCA) for forty-seven sectors for China and ASEAN for three different years (Table 14.3).[6]

These calculations show that between 1987 and 1996 China made a significant gain in the number of industries in which it has a comparative advantage. What is more remarkable is that this increase was not limited to labor-intensive industries: China has also become internationally competitive in a number of capital-intensive industries.

A comparison with the ASEAN-4 economies sheds light on the speed at which China's trade structure has been changing. First of all, China's RCA in all labor-intensive industries has been increasing, while the ASEAN-4 RCA in the same industries has been decreasing. China, for instance, increased its RCA in apparel from 4.77 in 1990 to 5.34 in 1996 while ASEAN-4 countries found their RCA decreasing from 2.34 to 1.81 in the same period. Second, China has been increasing its RCA in a larger number of capital-intensive industries than the ASEAN-4. Thus, in 1996, China had RCA greater than one in twenty-five sectors while ASEAN-4 had it in only thirteen sectors. In other words, China now has a more diversified trade structure than ASEAN-4.

China has accomplished this diversification more quickly than did its southern neighbors. Between 1987 and 1996 China increased the number of sectors in which it has RCA greater than one from sixteen to twenty-five, while ASEAN-4 increased the number from five to thirteen between 1980 and 1996. In other words, it took only nine years for China to gain nine more sectors in which it has a comparative advantage, while it took sixteen years for the ASEAN-4 to gain eight more sectors. The relative rapidity with which China has been increasing the number of industries in which it has a comparative advantage may be an indication of the speed with which the Chinese economy is becoming industrialized and is replacing ASEAN-4 in world markets for labor-intensive manufactured products.[7]

[6] A country's RCA in a given commodity is measured as the country's share of the world's export of that commodity divided by the country's share of the total exports of the world. An RCA value for a product greater than one is taken to mean that the country has a comparative advantage in that product. Since it is calculated using the actual trade values that may be "distorted" by tariffs and nontariffs, it may not be a true measure of a country's comparative advantage. However, if we can assume that the level of trade barriers has not changed over the period that we consider, then changes in RCA can be taken to indicate changes in comparative advantage.

[7] There are signs that since the Asian crisis of 1997–8 there is a reversal in this trend, due to the exchange rate realignment resulting from the crisis. We believe that in the longer run it will be fundamental changes in comparative advantage of China and ASEAN-4 that will determine their relative position in the world markets for labor-intensive manufactured products.

TABLE 14.3. *Revealed comparative advantage index (RCA) for ASEAN and China for forty-seve* sectors, 1987, 1990, and 1996

1987		RCA	1990		RCA	1996		RC.
Sector			Sector			Sector		
ASEAN								
2	Wood	6.16	2	Wood	7.74	2	Wood	7.24
47	Nonmanufactures	2.33	26	Radios	3.84	26	Radios	7.00
46	Other manufactures	1.88	13	Apparel	2.34	25	Television receivers	3.29
6	Nonferrous metals	1.80	14	Footwear	2.14	27	Phonographs, recorders	2.80
13	Apparel	1.39	47	Nonmanufactures	2.01	41	Telecommunication equipment	2.27
18	Manufactured articles, n.e.c.	1.27	12	Travel goods	1.96	14	Footwear	2.27
42	Electrical machinery, other than 775	1.15	25	Television receivers	1.85	42	Electrical machinery, other than 775	1.99
26	Radios	1.14	16	Toys	1.71	13	Apparel	1.81
4	Precious stones	0.87	18	Manufactured articles, n.e.c.	1.61	11	Furniture	1.54
36	Other chemicals	0.85	41	Telecommunication equipment	1.57	47	Nonmanufactures	1.44
5	Pig iron	0.75	46	Other manufactures	1.54	16	Toys	1.33
7	Textiles	0.67	33	Antiques and jewelry	1.46	33	Antiques and jewelry	1.27
11	Furniture	0.51	42	Electrical machinery other than 775	1.40	7	Textiles	1.03
38	Fertilizer(chemical)	0.50	4	Precious stones	1.39	12	Travel goods	1.03
33	Antiques and jewelry	0.49	27	Phonographs, recorders	1.23	38	Fertilizer(chemical)	0.96
14	Footwear	0.47	11	Furniture	1.21	31	Watches	0.91
12	Travel goods	0.42	5	Pig iron	1.20	5	Pig iron	0.83
41	Telecommunication equipment	0.40	38	Fertilizer(chemical)	1.03	17	Office supplies	0.78
16	Toys	0.39	7	Textiles	0.96	18	Manufactured articles, n.e.c.	0.71
20	Perfume	0.37	1	Leather	0.95	40	Nonelectrical machineray	0.68
China								
7	Textiles	4.36	26	Radios	6.31	12	Travel goods	8.83
16	Toys	4.25	16	Toys	6.02	16	Toys	7.10
13	Apparel	4.11	13	Apparel	4.77	14	Footwear	6.31
18	Manufactured articles, n.e.c.	3.94	14	Footwear	3.89	13	Apparel	5.34
26	Radios	3.93	31	Watches	3.66	26	Radios	4.67
5	Pig iron	3.55	7	Textiles	3.63	5	Pig iron	4.47
12	Travel goods	3.46	18	Manufactured articles, n.e.c.	3.54	18	Manufactured articles, n.e.c.	4.32

TABLE 14.3. *Revealed comparative advantage index (RCA) for ASEAN and China for forty-seven sectors, 1987, 1990, and 1996*

1987			1990			1996		
Sector		RCA	Sector		RCA	Sector		RCA
46	Other manufactures	2.94	12	Travel goods	3.35	31	Watches	3.57
31	Watches	2.75	5	Pig iron	3.11	30	Railway vehicles	3.56
14	Footwear	1.67	25	Television receivers	1.79	7	Textiles	2.82
47	Nonmanufactures	1.46	41	Telecommunication equipment	1.57	28	Household electrical machinery	2.60
25	Television receivers	1.20	8	Glass and pottery	1.52	10	Sanitary, plumbing, heating and lighting fixtures	2.11
17	Office supplies	1.13	47	Nonmanufactures	1.11	15	Plastic articles	2.00
8	Glass and pottery	1.07	24	Metal manufactures	1.09	17	Office supplies	1.68
33	Antiques and jewelry	1.06	3	Mineral manufactures	1.06	8	Glass and pottery	1.65
41	Telecommunication equipment	1.01	17	Office supplies	0.97	33	Antiques and jewelry	1.54
24	Metal manufactures	0.94	30	Railway vehicles	0.94	41	Telecommunication equipment	1.50
37	Medicine	0.89	19	Paints	0.89	27	Phonographs, recorders	1.49
35	Chemical elements	0.79	35	Chemical elements	0.86	24	Metal manufactures	1.42
36	Other chemicals	0.79	46	Other manufactures	0.86	3	Mineral manufactures	1.33
6	Nonferrous metals	0.76	37	Medicine	0.85	1	Leather	1.31
19	Paints	0.69	28	Household electrical machinery	0.85	11	Furniture	1.23
20	Perfume	0.57	2	Wood	0.81	25	Television receivers	1.16
10	Sanitary, plumbing, heating and lighting fixtures	0.57	20	Perfume	0.75	2	Wood	1.08
11	Furniture	0.55	15	Plastic articles	0.72	9	Ships	0.98

Note: Figures in first column refer to industry classifications in Krause (1987).

Sources: United Nations, *International Trade Statistics*.

The manner in which a group of Asian economies has developed since the end of the Second World War has been described as the "flying-geese" pattern of development with Japan leading the Asian NIEs, which in turn were followed by the ASEAN-4. The whole flock has made economic progress while each member has made successive shifts in comparative advantage by acquiring increasingly sophisticated technology from the more advanced economies of the world including Japan. In the late 1970s, China joined the flock at its tail end and since then has been catching up fast with other members of the group.

What is remarkable about China's RCA changes is that China has become a major exporter of labor-intensive products in general as well as some capital-intensive products. This is consistent with the "flying geese" pattern of industrial development, according to which a developing country first exports crude and consumer goods and then later exports refined and capital goods. What is different about China's experience is that it appears to be gaining a comparative advantage in capital-intensive industries very rapidly and even before it begins to lose comparative advantage in labor-intensive sectors. A plausible explanation is that China is a dualistic economy with both a large pool of low-cost labor and an adequate pool of skilled labor capable of producing capital-intensive products. In other words, although China as a whole is still at an early stage of economic development, it has a number of sectors such as electrical and electronic products that are capable of—and in fact already are—catching up with more advanced economies in the region.

4. Future Economic Development in China and Its Implications for Japan

Although it is difficult to predict what the Chinese economy will be like in the twenty-first century, the prospects are good for the country to continue on a high-growth path, as China appears likely to continue with efforts to introduce a rule-based society characterized by markets, private ownership, and pluralistic political institutions (Jefferson, 1997). China should continue to have relative stability, a high saving rate, a strong record of pragmatic reforms, a disciplined and literate labor force, a supportive Chinese diaspora, and a growing administrative capacity, the strengths that have driven its economic growth for the last two decades of the twentieth century (World Bank, 1997).[8]

If China's saving rate is maintained at 35 per cent (for 1978–95 its saving rate was 37 per cent of GDP, although more conservative estimates place it at 33–4 per cent), and if its total factor productivity growth is maintained at 1.5 per cent per year, its annual GDP growth will average 6.6 per cent over the twenty-five years between 1996 and 2020 (World Bank, 1997).

What effect will such economic growth in China and the increasing diversification of its economic structure have on the Japanese economy? According to the World Bank (1997), there will be high growth in demand for capital- and knowledge-intensive products (growing at 8 per cent per year) accompanied by rapid growth in China's exports of labor-intensive manufactured products. If that happens, Japan, as a major exporter of the first group of products, will see an improvement in its terms of trade. In fact, it is estimated that Japan would gain as much as 6.5 per cent in its cumulative terms of trade by 2020 (4.0 per cent for North America and 1.4 per cent

---

[8] China's economic growth has slowed recently, and the country may be in for an extended period of sluggish growth (*The Economist*, 24 Oct., 1998, 23–6). Such economic slowdown, plus an insolvent banking system and a sharp divide between the relatively wealthy parts of the country and the poor regions, could threaten China's stability. Furthermore, unless it is reformed in a radical manner China's ailing financial system will bring about a decrease in the rate of saving, which in turn will deprive China of the resources necessary to address its long-term environmental and other challenges (Lardy, 1998).

for Western Europe). China's export growth in the second group of products—labor-intensive manufactured products—can possibly have an adverse effect on the jobs and income of unskilled workers in Japan, but this effect will be negligible for Japan since it long ago lost its comparative advantage in these industries and has successfully made the necessary structural changes.

Given its present stage of development and large population, it may be years before China joins the ranks of fully developed economies. According to the World Bank study cited above, for the foreseeable future the Chinese people will on average remain less well educated than Indonesians or South Koreans. The World Bank projects that by 2020 the average number of years of secondary education for a Chinese resident will be 5.9 years, and the average number of years in tertiary education will be only 0.4 years. These figures do not compare favorably with 6.2 years and 1.6 years, respectively, for Indonesia, and 6.4 and 6.8 years, respectively, for South Korea.

Given its large, and at present relatively poorly educated, population and given the huge human resource requirement for developing its own scientific and technological foundation, China will remain for the foreseeable future a country with a comparative advantage mainly in the production of unskilled labor-intensive manufactured goods. But, that does not mean that China will be unable to develop in select areas a sufficiently large pool of well-trained people to exploit scale and agglomeration economies in research and development, and thereby develop technologically more sophisticated industries capable of international competition. In fact, China is already a country with "no shortage" of well-trained scientists, engineers, mathematicians, or other technical experts, and as its older researchers retire and are replaced by younger, Western-educated researchers China's ability to absorb, assimilate, and innovate new technologies will grow (Yoshitomi, 1996; Bureau of Export Promotion, 1999).

To improve its technological capabilities, China has also used industrial policies aimed at developing "pillar industries" such as automobiles, electronics, machinery, construction materials, and petrochemicals (Morrrison and Hardt, 1996). These policies include numerous provisions and mandates that require foreign investors to transfer technology as a condition for investment in China. Many high-tech foreign firms have complied with the requirement by establishing a training or R&D center, institute, or lab with China's premier universities or research institutes (Bureau of Export Promotion, 1999).

There is another reason why China may soon succeed in moving up the specialization ladder, albeit in a limited number of areas. This is what some call "Greater China," which includes individuals from the People's Republic of China, Taiwan, Hong Kong, Singapore, and the overseas Chinese in Southeast Asia and throughout the world (Lilley and Hart, 1996). In fact, China has already benefited from being a part of Greater China, as overseas Chinese are the foreign investors largely responsible for its present economic success. It is quite conceivable that with the right incentives they can be induced to invest in the development of high-tech industries in China.

Nelson and Wright (1994) point out that in the period since the 1950s the economic and technological gaps among the major industrial powers have closed dramatically, largely ending the leadership position held by the US for nearly a century. They offer basically two reasons for this convergence: globalization of markets and the advent of science-based technologies. First, because of the decrease in transportation costs and drop in trade barriers the advantages of having large national markets and access to cheap raw materials have been eroded. Consequently, even those firms located in a small, resource-poor economy can exploit economies of scale and acquire raw materials at globally competitive prices.

Second, the advent of science-based technologies has significantly increased the extent to which generic technological understanding is possessed by scientists and engineers. Many technologies are codified and thus more easily transferable across national boundaries and more generally accessible to those, wherever they may be located, with the requisite skills and who are willing to make the required investments.

Given these changes in market conditions and the nature of technology, a country which is willing and able to train at least a portion of its labor force and devote a sufficient proportion of its GNP to research and development will be able to import and utilize technologies from abroad as well as create new technologies. As a case in point, Nelson and Wright cite the rapid speed with which the Japanese, the Koreans, and the Taiwanese learned to command American-made technologies during the 1970s and 1980s. Given what they have done, we see no reason why China will not be able to replicate, if not surpass, the record achieved by the newly industrializing economies in East Asia.

In fact, the World Bank (1997) study projects that by 2020 China will gain 8 per cent of the world's market in transport equipment and other machinery and 4 per cent in highly capital-intensive heavy manufactured goods (chemicals, rubber, plastics, paper, iron and steel, nonferrous metal), while gaining 10 per cent market share in light manufactured goods (leather, fabricated metal products, and miscellaneous manufactured products). If this projection is correct, China's technological advance will present serious challenges to the Asian NIEs and ASEAN-4, the second- and third-tier countries in terms of technological development.

The growing technological capability of China and its abundant supply of cheap labor will make China an attractive host country for Japanese overseas direct investment. An empirical study of Japanese FDI shows that the decline in the rate of return on capital as labor costs increase at home is a driving force for Japanese overseas investment in textile, chemicals, basic metal, machinery, electrical machinery, and transport equipment industries (Ogawa and Lee, 1996). This was also confirmed in the study by Blomström, Konan, and Lipsey, Chapter 11 in this volume. In other words, Japanese FDI is a channel through which its industries extend the economic life of vintage capital that becomes obsolete as new technology and products are developed in Japan. Provided that China becomes a genuinely open economy, it is clear that it will be an attractive location for Japanese investors who are seeking well-trained, low-cost labor. A detailed study of Japanese electronics investment in China also shows that although initially China attracted Japanese investment with its potentially huge domestic market, it now has become a production platform for the export of low-end assembly and simple components manufactures, competing for Japanese investment with Indonesia, India, Malaysia, South Korea, Thailand, and Vietnam (Ernst, 1997).

5. Concluding Remarks

Even though China has achieved spectacular economic development since the beginning of its modernization in the late 1970s, it is not likely to become a fully developed economy by the year 2020. Japan will still lead China and other Asian countries in technology and in capital goods, but with its sheer size and potential for further economic growth China will play an increasingly important role in the region's economic prosperity. It is likely that in place of the Japan-led "flying-geese" pattern of development of the second half of the twentieth century there will emerge a new multipolar East Asia with Japan and China as its major players.

China's emergence as a major economy in East Asia will certainly have many positive effects on the region's economic prosperity, but it will also create problems of structural adjustment in neighboring economies that are currently ahead of China in economic and technological development. While it is highly unlikely that China will overtake Japan as the leading economy in East Asia in the next few decades, some of its leading industries may be able compete with their Japanese counterparts in global markets. For the Asian NIEs and ASEAN-4, however, catching up by China in the areas in which they now have a comparative advantage is a strong possibility, and these economies will be faced with the serious and painful problems of adjustment and structural change. Obviously, structural adjustment will be easier and less costly if China opens up its economy, creating demand for exports from these economies. This is one very important reason why China should become a genuinely open economy and become an engine of economic growth and integration for the region.

Another reason for China to open up its economy is that Asia needs China as well as Japan to be the region's engines of growth. Japan is a country with a rapidly aging population with the possibility of becoming the most aged society in the world by 2020. This increase in the dependency ratio is expected to have a serious negative effect on the country's saving rate. In fact, some studies on Japanese saving predict that by 2010 Japan's net private saving will become negative (Mason and Ogawa, Chapter 2 this volume). In comparison, China will be a young country demographically and can thus play a more dynamic role in the region. Perhaps Japan may be surpassed by China as the leading economy in East Asia at some point in the distant future; in the meantime an open and growing Chinese economy may revitalize Japan with its expanding markets for Japan's sophisticated capital equipment and technologies.

China's accession to the WTO, which is only a matter of time, is likely to accelerate the opening of the Chinese economy. This will be beneficial to Japan, as it will create more opportunities for further trade and investment between the two countries. It will not, however, open a floodgate for trade and investment flows from Japan or the rest of the world. Holton and Lin (1998) point out that many of the practices of China that are now of concern to the WTO are deeply imbedded in her age-old institutional conditions and do not lend themselves to rapid change. These include a weak foundation of the rule of law, ambiguity in the legal culture, and a lack of transparency. This cultural baggage from the past will be a major hindrance to the effective enforcement of new laws and regulations that will accompany China's accession to the WTO. In other words, even if China accedes to the WTO, its move toward an economy based on WTO rules will be a slow one.

Nevertheless, China will still develop into an engine of growth in the twenty-first century and join Japan in this role. Obviously, for two engines to be better than one they will have to work together harmoniously, and this will require coordination at least in trade and investment as well as macroeconomic policies. China's fast growth will surely force structural changes in Japan. Such structural change may lead either to a trade conflict or a complementary relationship between the two, depending on the policies they undertake. If policies can be coordinated, the relationship that will emerge between the two will be likely to be more complementary than competitive. But, for such policy coordination even to be initiated, there will have to be a harmonious political relationship between the two nations.

Up until 1992, Japan's China policy was to support China's modernization programs, its economic development, and its domestic stability. Since then, however, a series of developments have led to changes in Japan's perception of China. Many in Japan now see China as overbearing toward the region and, worse, as having territorial ambitions beyond the confines accepted during the Cold War (Soeya, 1998). If this perception persists in Japan, and if China begins to believe that its economic success should restore it to its rightful place as Asia's Middle Kingdom, the two engines of growth will be at loggerheads instead of working together (Pryzstup, 1996). Therefore what the twenty-first century will bring to the region will depend very much on how the region's two major powers relate to each other politically. If, as argued by Alagappa (1998), a hierarchical order with a single center of power and authority is no longer tenable in East Asia, then China and Japan will have to come to terms with each other and learn to coexist as great powers in the region, historically unprecedented as that may be. Only then can we hope that with two locomotives leading the region, the twenty-first century will turn out to be an age of prosperity for East Asia.

REFERENCES

Akamatsu, Kaname (1962), "A Historical Pattern of Economic Growth in Developing Countries," *The Developing Economies*, 1 (March–Aug.).
Alagappa, Muthiah (1998), "International Politics in Asia: The Historical Context," in Alagappa, M. (ed.), *Asian Security Practice* (Stanford: Stanford University Press).
Bureau of Export Promotion, US Department of Commerce (1999), *US Commercial Technology Transfer to the People's Republic of China* (Washington: Office of Strategic Industries and Economic Security).
Ernst, Dieter (1997), "Partners for the China Circle? The East Asian Production Networks of Japanese Electronics Firms," in Naughton, B. (ed.), *The China Circle* (Washington: Brookings Institution Press).

Funabashi, Yoichi, Oksenberg, Michel, and Weiss, Heinrich (1994), *An Emerging China in a World of Interdependence, Report to the Trilateral Commission*, no. 45 (New York: The Trilateral Commission).

Garnaut, Ross and Huang, Yiping (1995), "China and the Future International Trading System," in *China and East Asia Trade Policy*, Pacific Economic Papers, no. 250, Australia–Japan Research Centre, Australian National University, Canberra, Australia.

Holton, Richard H. and Lin, Xia Yuan (1998), "China and the World Trade Organization: Can the Assimilation Problems be Overcome?," *Asian Survey* (Aug.), 38/8: 745–61.

Jefferson, Gary H. (1997), "China's Economic Future: A Discussion Paper," *Journal of Asian Economics*, 8/4 (Winter), 581–95.

Kosai, Yutaka and Tho, Tran Van (1994), "Japan and Industrialization in Asia," *Journal of Asian Economics*, 5/2 (Summer), 155–76.

Krause, Lawrence (1987), "The Structure of Trade in Manufactured Goods in the East and Southeast Asian Region," in Bradford, C. I. and W. H. Branson (eds.), *Trade and Structural Change in Pacific Asia* (Chicago: University of Chicago Press).

Kreinin, Mordchai, Plummer, Michael G., and Abe, Shigeyuki (1999), "Export and Direct Foreign Investment Links: A Three Country Comparison," in Kreinin, M., S. Abe, and M. G. Plummer (eds.), *International Economic Links and Policy Formulation* (New York: Elsevier).

Lardy, Nicholas R. (1994), *China in the World Economy* (Washington: Institute for International Economics).

——(1998) *China's Unfinished Economic Revolution* (Washington: Brookings Institution Press).

Lilley, James R. and Hart, Sophia C. (1996), "Greater China: Economic Dynamism of the Overseas Chinese," in Joint Economic Committee, US Congress, *China's Economic Future: Challenges to US Policy* (Washington: US Government Printing Office).

Lockwood, William W. (1968), *The Economic Development of Japan: Growth and Structural Change*, expanded edn. (Princeton: Princeton University Press).

Minami, Ryoshin (1994), *The Economic Development of China: A Comparison with the Japanese Experience* (New York: St. Martin's Press).

MITI (1996), *White Paper on International Trade and Industry 1996* (Tokyo: MITI).

Morrison, Wayne M. and Hardt, John P. (1996), "Major Issues in U.S.–China Commercial Relations," in Joint Economic Committee, US Congress, *China's Economic Future: Challenges to US Policy*.

Naughton, Barry (1997), "The Future of the China Circle," in Naughton, B. (ed.), *The China Circle* (Washington: Brookings Institution Press).

Nelson, Richard R. and Wright, Gavin (1994), "The Erosion of U.S. Technological Leadership as a Factor in Postwar Economic Convergence," in Baumol, W. J., R. R. Nelson, and E. N. Wolff (eds.), *Convergence of Productivity: Cross-National Studies and Historical Evidence* (New York: Oxford University Press).

Ogawa, Kazuo and Lee, Chung H. (1996), "Changing Comparative Advantage and Direct Foreign Investment: The Case of Six Japanese Industries," in Hooley, Richard, Anwar Nasution, Mari Pangestu, and M. Dutta (eds.), *Research in Asian Economic Studies*, vii. (Greenwich, Conn.: JAI Press).

Ohkawa, Kazushi and Kohama, Hirohisa (1989), *Lectures on Developing Economies* (Tokyo: University of Tokyo Press).

Pryzystup, James J. (1996), "Thinking about China," in Joint Economic Committee, US Congress, *China's Economic Future: Challenges to US Policy*.

Seki, Mitsuhiro (1999), *Japanese Firms in the Age of New Asia Era*, Chuo Koron Shinsha (in Japanese).

Singh, Virendra and Singh, Narendra, "China's Economic Prospects to 2010," in Joint Economic Committee, US Congress, *China's Economic Future: Challenges to US Policy*.

Söderberg, Marie (ed.), (1996), *The Business of Japanese Foreign Aid*, (London: Routledge).

Soeya, Yoshihide (1998), "Japan: Normative Constraints Versus Structural Imperatives," in Alaggapa, M. (ed.), *Asian Security Practice* (Stanford: Stanford University Press).

Taylor, Robert (1996), *Greater China and Japan: Prospects for an Economic Partnership in East Asia* (London and New York: Routledge).

Uyehara, S. (1926), *The Industry and Trade of Japan* (London: P. S. King).

World Bank (1997), *China 2020: China Engaged* (Washington: World Bank).

Yoshitomi, Masaru (1996), "The Comparative Advantage of China's Manufacturing in the Twenty-first Century," in *China in the 21ˢᵗ Century: Long-Term Global Implications* (Paris: OECD).

Zhao, Suisheng (1997), *Power Competition in East Asia: From the Old Chinese World Order to Post-Cold War Regional Mutipolarity* (New York: St. Martin's Press).

INDEX